HARLEY QUINN

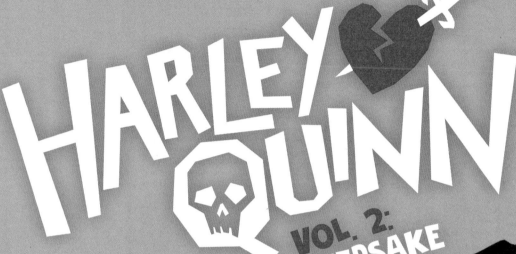

VOL. 2: KEEPSAKE

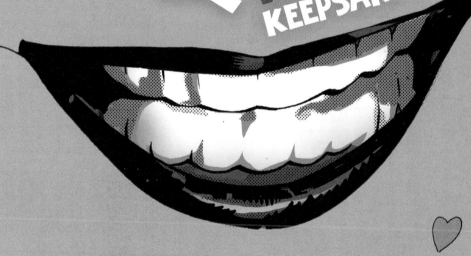

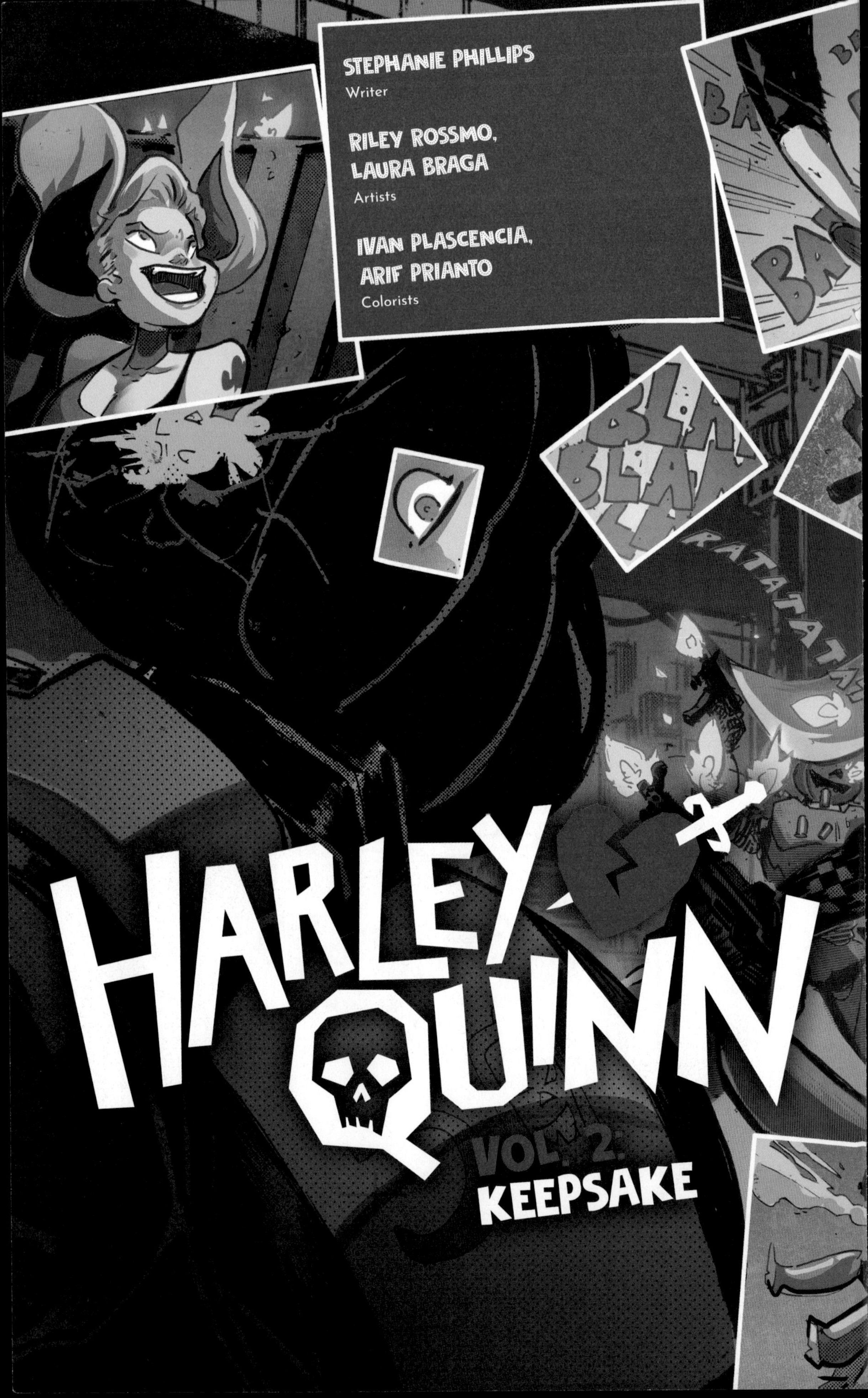

STEPHANIE PHILLIPS
Writer

RILEY ROSSMO, LAURA BRAGA
Artists

IVAN PLASCENCIA, ARIF PRIANTO
Colorists

HARLEY QUINN

VOL. 2: KEEPSAKE

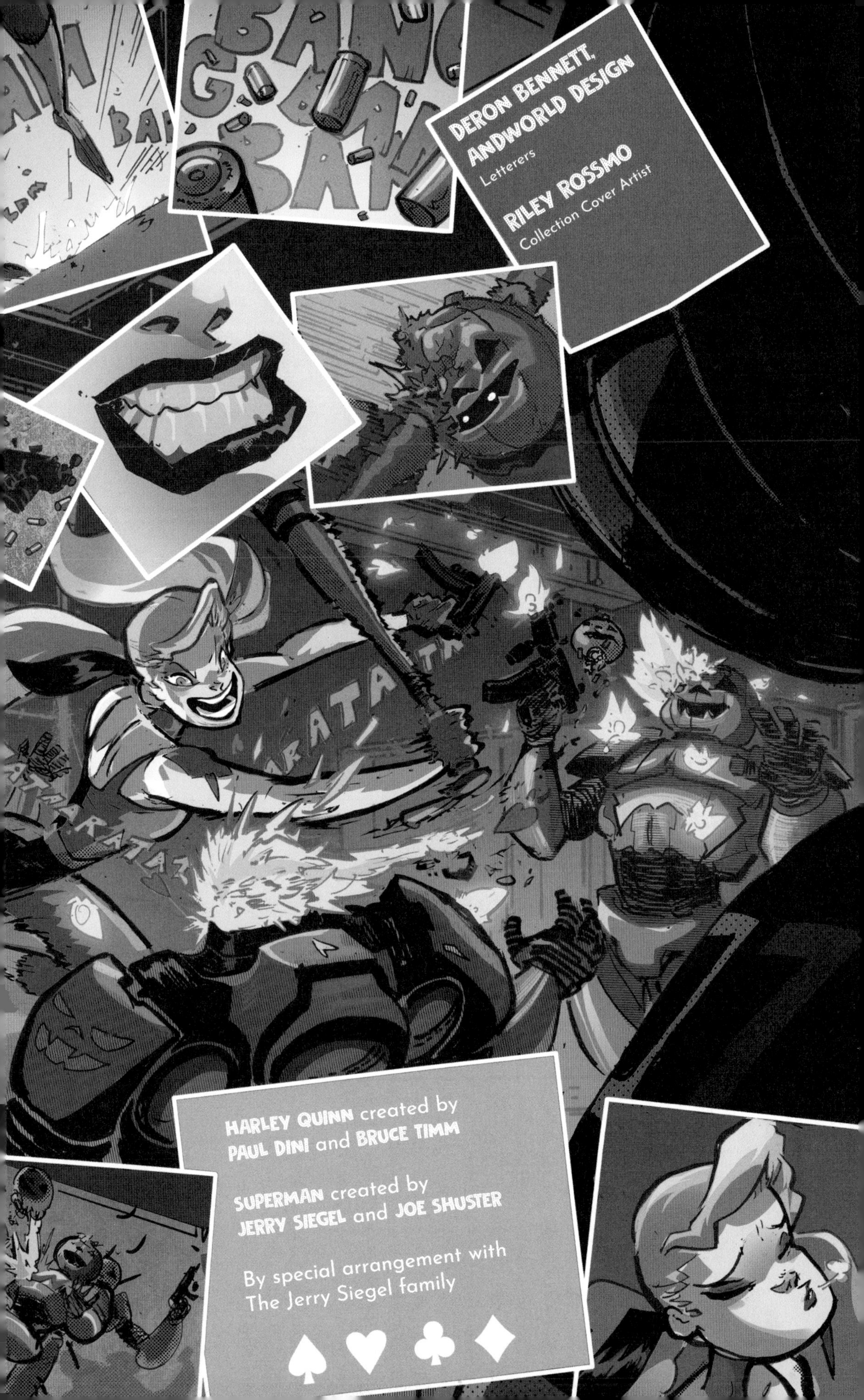

DERON BENNETT, ANDWORLD DESIGN
Letterers

RILEY ROSSMO
Collection Cover Artist

HARLEY QUINN created by **PAUL DINI** and **BRUCE TIMM**

SUPERMAN created by **JERRY SIEGEL** and **JOE SHUSTER**

By special arrangement with The Jerry Siegel family

♠ ♥ ♣ ♦

BEN ABERNATHY
Editor - Original Series & Collected Edition
STEVE COOK
Design Director - Books
MEGEN BELLERSEN
Publication Design
ERIN VANOVER
Publication Production
RYANE LYNN HILL
Production Editor

MARIE JAVINS
VP - Editor-in-Chief

JIM LEE
President, Publisher & Chief Creative Officer
ANNE DePIES
Senior VP & General Manager
LARRY BERRY
VP - Brand Design & Creative Services
DON FALLETTI
VP - Manufacturing & Production
LAWRENCE GANEM
VP - Editorial Programming & Talent Strategy
ALISON GILL
Senior VP - Manufacturing & Operations
NICK J. NAPOLITANO
VP - Publishing & Business Operations
NANCY SPEARS
VP - Sales & Marketing

HARLEY QUINN VOL. 2: KEEPSAKE

DC Comics,
4000 Warner Blvd., Bldg. 700, 2nd Floor,
Burbank, CA 91522

Printed by Transcontinental Printing Interweb Montreal, a division of Transcontinental Printing Inc., Boucherville, QC, Canada. 8/25/23. First Printing.
ISBN: 978-1-77951-663-3

Library of Congress Cataloging-in-Publication Data is available.

PEFC Certified
This product is from sustainably managed forests and controlled sources
PEFC/01-31-106   www.pefc.org

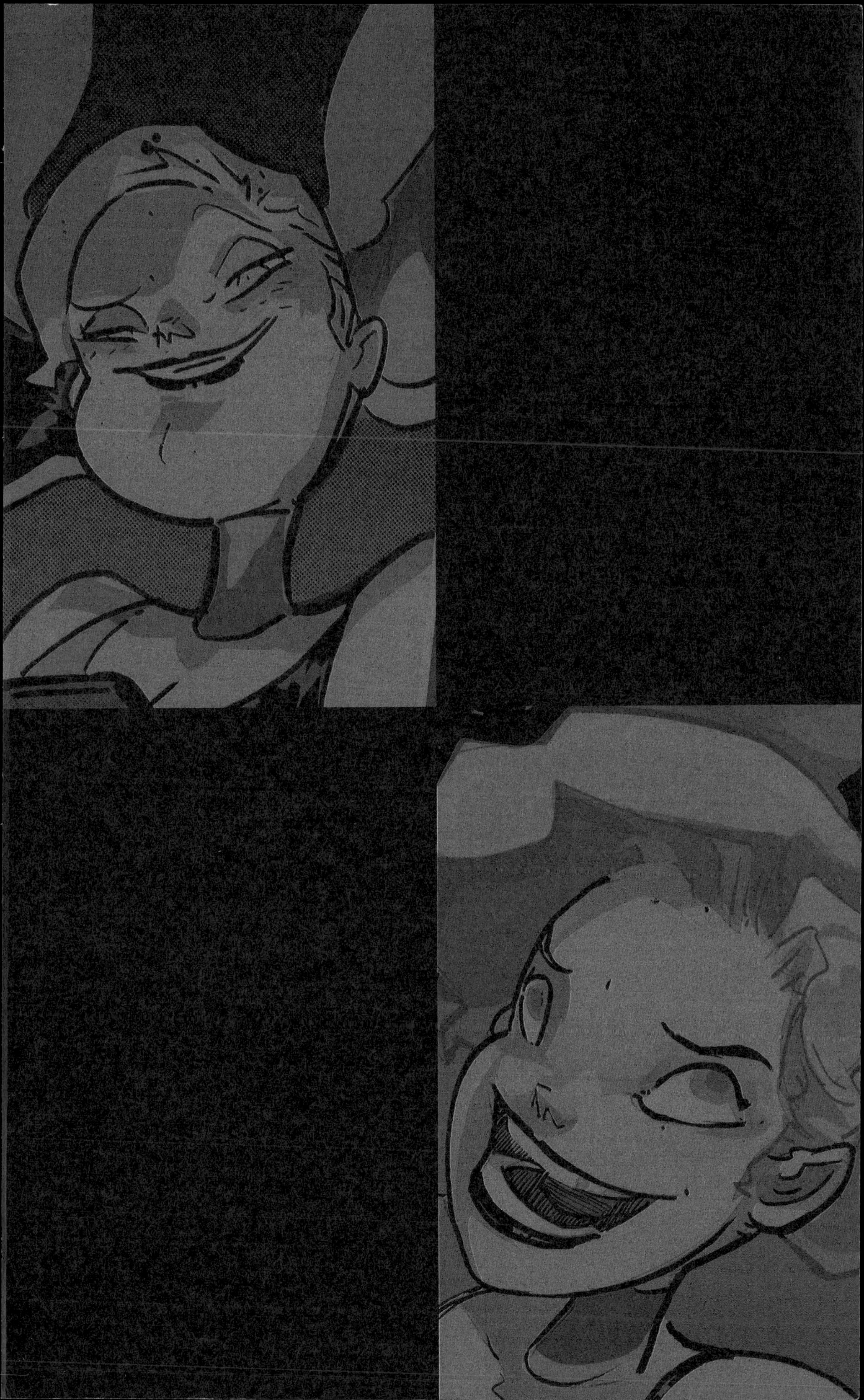

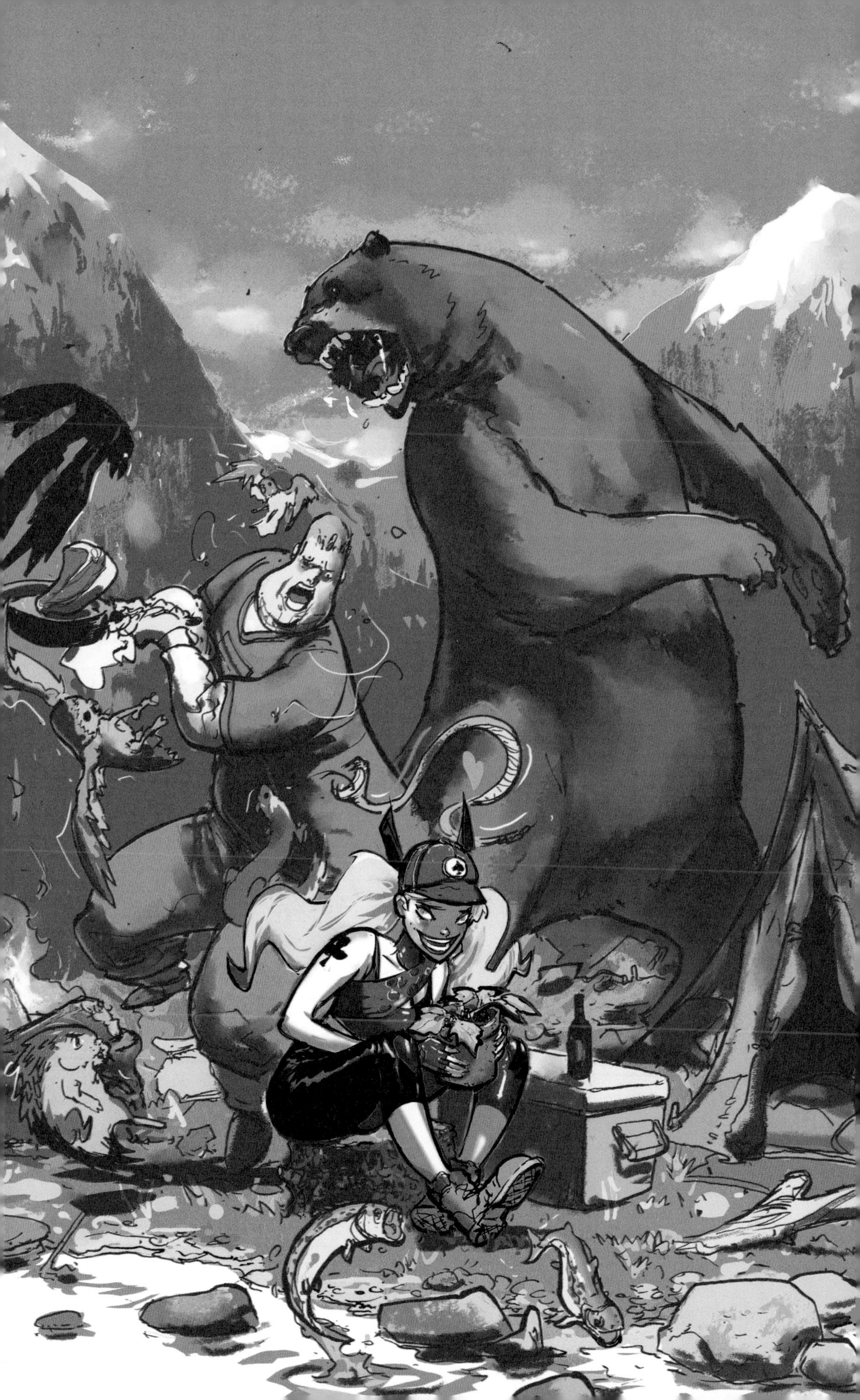

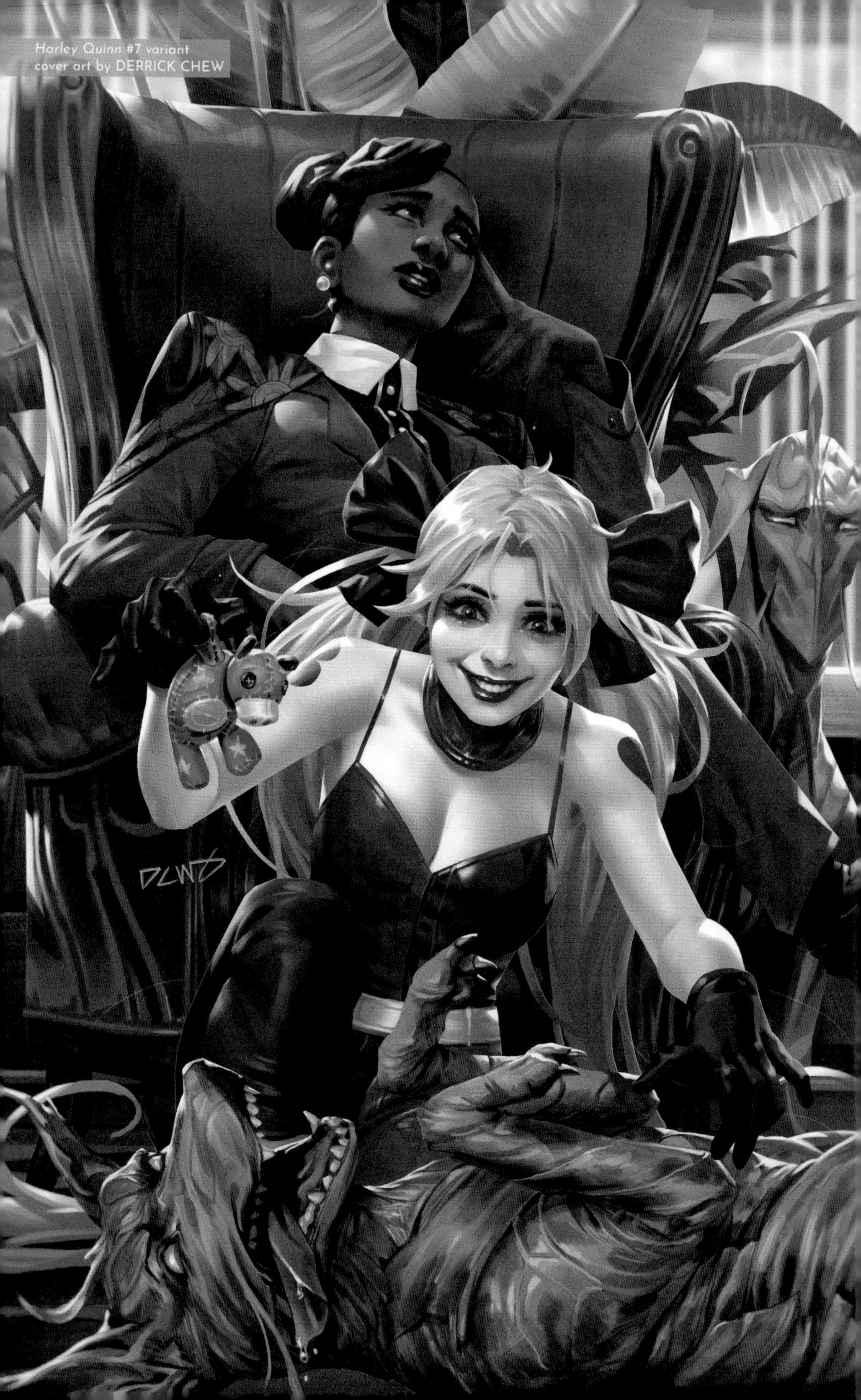

Harley Quinn #7 variant
cover art by DERRICK CHEW

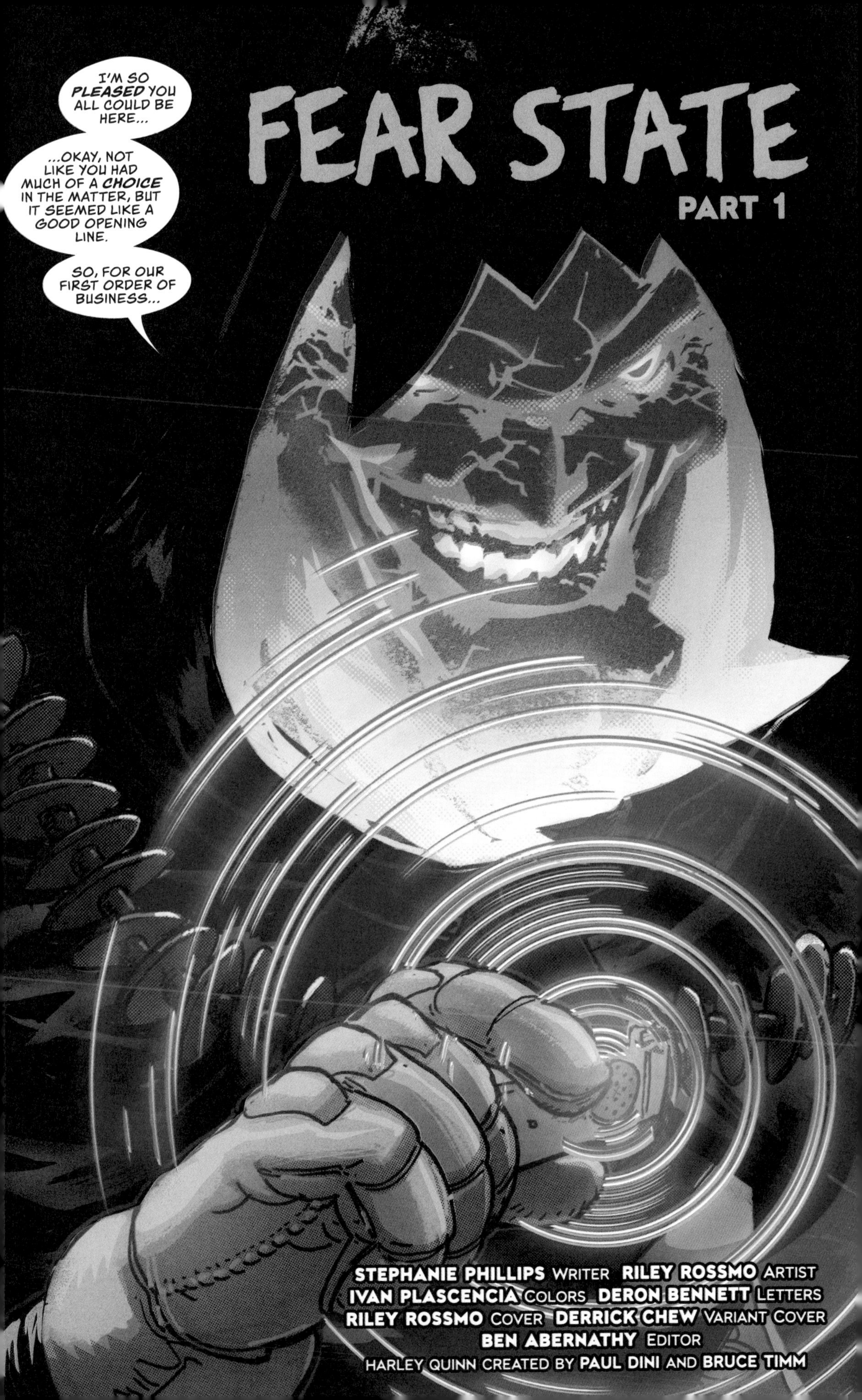

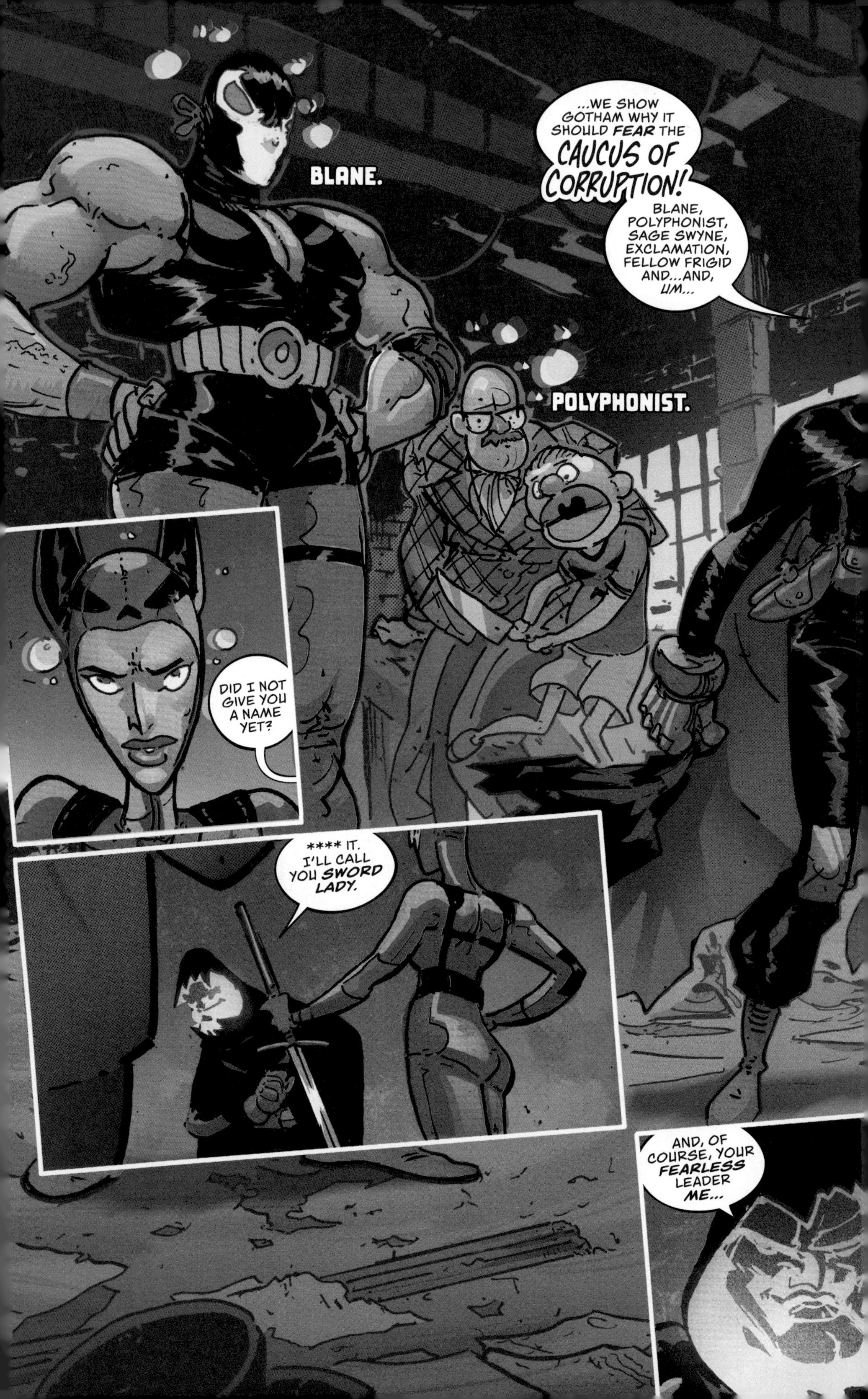
...WE SHOW GOTHAM WHY IT SHOULD FEAR THE CAUCUS OF CORRUPTION!
BLANE.
BLANE, POLYPHONIST, SAGE SWYNE, EXCLAMATION, FELLOW FRIGID AND...AND, UM...
POLYPHONIST.
DID I NOT GIVE YOU A NAME YET?
**** IT. I'LL CALL YOU SWORD LADY.
AND, OF COURSE, YOUR FEARLESS LEADER ME...

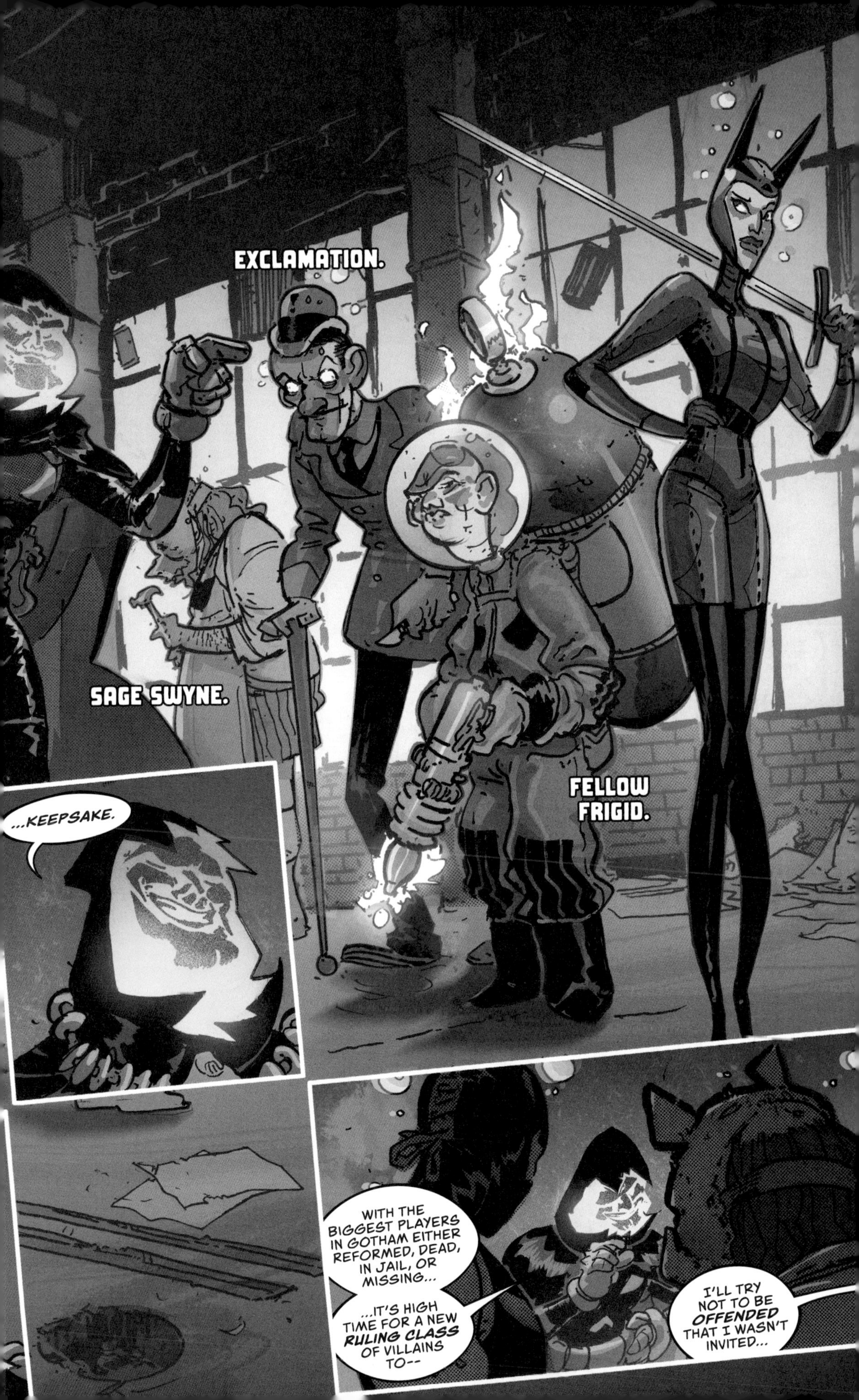
EXCLAMATION.
SAGE SWYNE.
FELLOW FRIGID.
...KEEPSAKE.
WITH THE BIGGEST PLAYERS IN GOTHAM EITHER REFORMED, DEAD, IN JAIL, OR MISSING...
...IT'S HIGH TIME FOR A NEW RULING CLASS OF VILLAINS TO--
I'LL TRY NOT TO BE OFFENDED THAT I WASN'T INVITED...

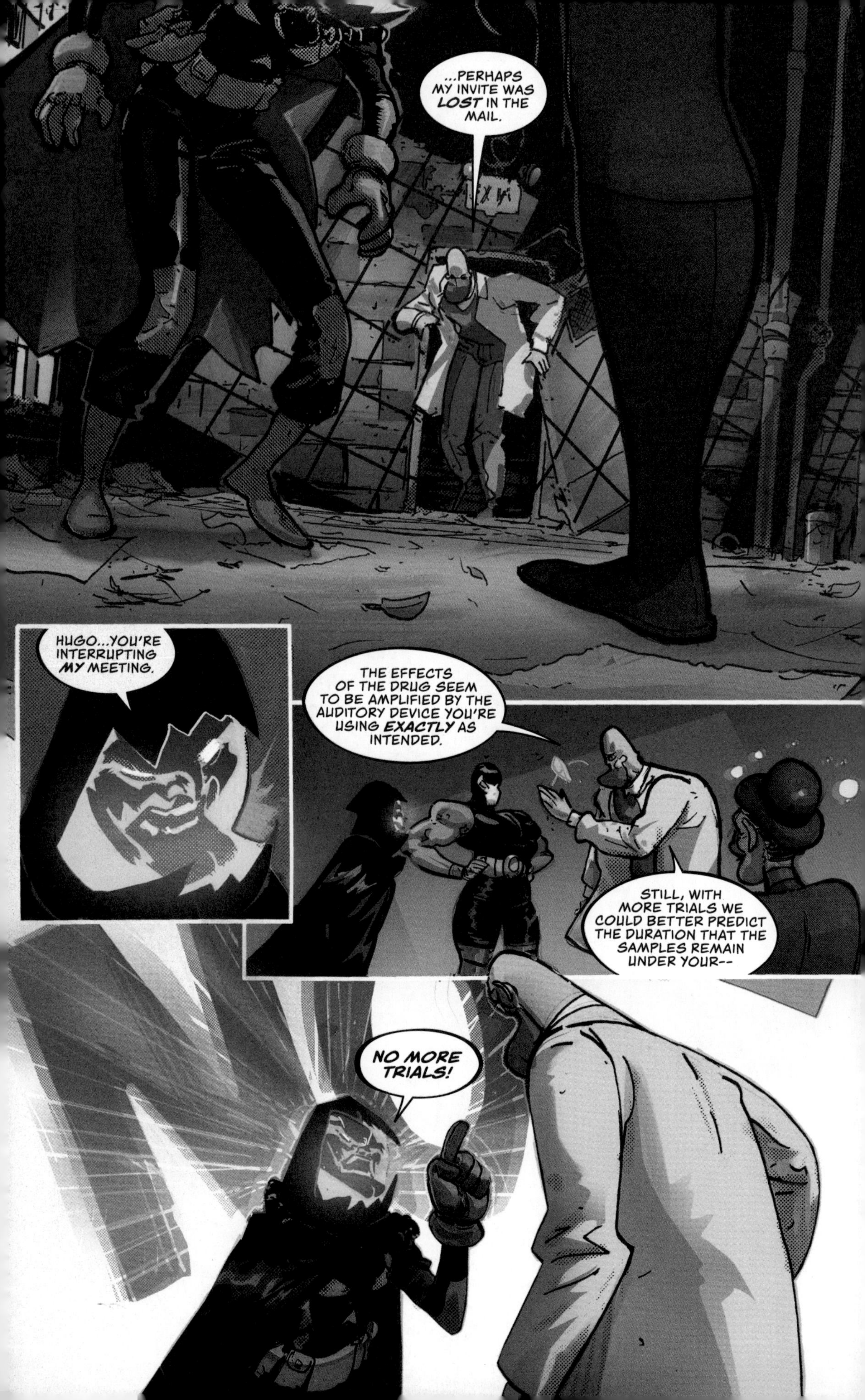
...PERHAPS MY INVITE WAS LOST IN THE MAIL.
HUGO...YOU'RE INTERRUPTING MY MEETING.
THE EFFECTS OF THE DRUG SEEM TO BE AMPLIFIED BY THE AUDITORY DEVICE YOU'RE USING EXACTLY AS INTENDED.
STILL, WITH MORE TRIALS WE COULD BETTER PREDICT THE DURATION THAT THE SAMPLES REMAIN UNDER YOUR--
NO MORE TRIALS!

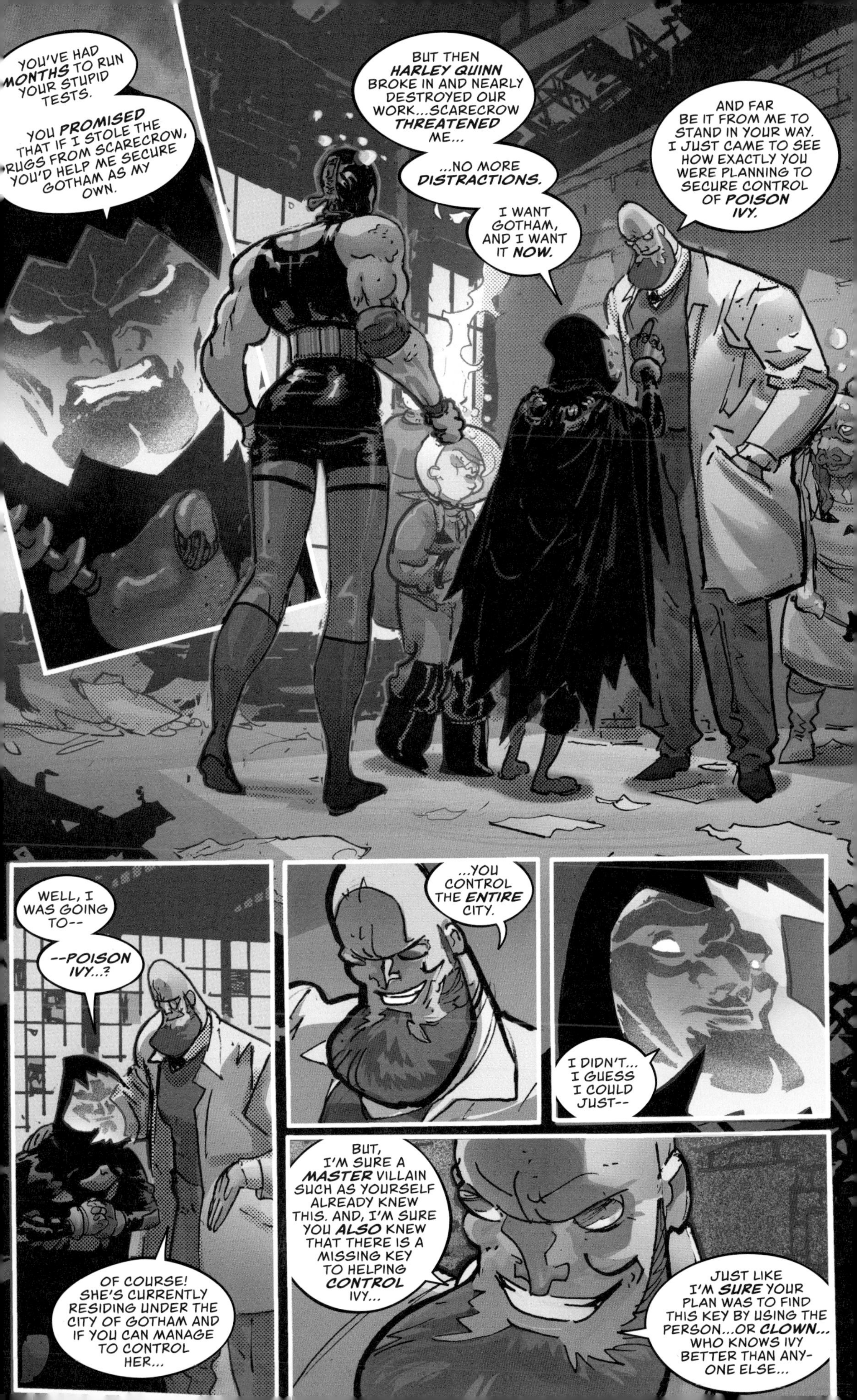
YOU'VE HAD MONTHS TO RUN YOUR STUPID TESTS.
YOU PROMISED THAT IF I STOLE THE RUGS FROM SCARECROW, YOU'D HELP ME SECURE GOTHAM AS MY OWN.
BUT THEN HARLEY QUINN BROKE IN AND NEARLY DESTROYED OUR WORK...SCARECROW THREATENED ME...
...NO MORE DISTRACTIONS.
I WANT GOTHAM, AND I WANT IT NOW.
AND FAR BE IT FROM ME TO STAND IN YOUR WAY. I JUST CAME TO SEE HOW EXACTLY YOU WERE PLANNING TO SECURE CONTROL OF POISON IVY.
WELL, I WAS GOING TO--
--POISON IVY...?
OF COURSE! SHE'S CURRENTLY RESIDING UNDER THE CITY OF GOTHAM AND IF YOU CAN MANAGE TO CONTROL HER...
...YOU CONTROL THE ENTIRE CITY.
I DIDN'T... I GUESS I COULD JUST--
BUT, I'M SURE A MASTER VILLAIN SUCH AS YOURSELF ALREADY KNEW THIS. AND, I'M SURE YOU ALSO KNEW THAT THERE IS A MISSING KEY TO HELPING CONTROL IVY...
JUST LIKE I'M SURE YOUR PLAN WAS TO FIND THIS KEY BY USING THE PERSON...OR CLOWN... WHO KNOWS IVY BETTER THAN ANY-ONE ELSE...

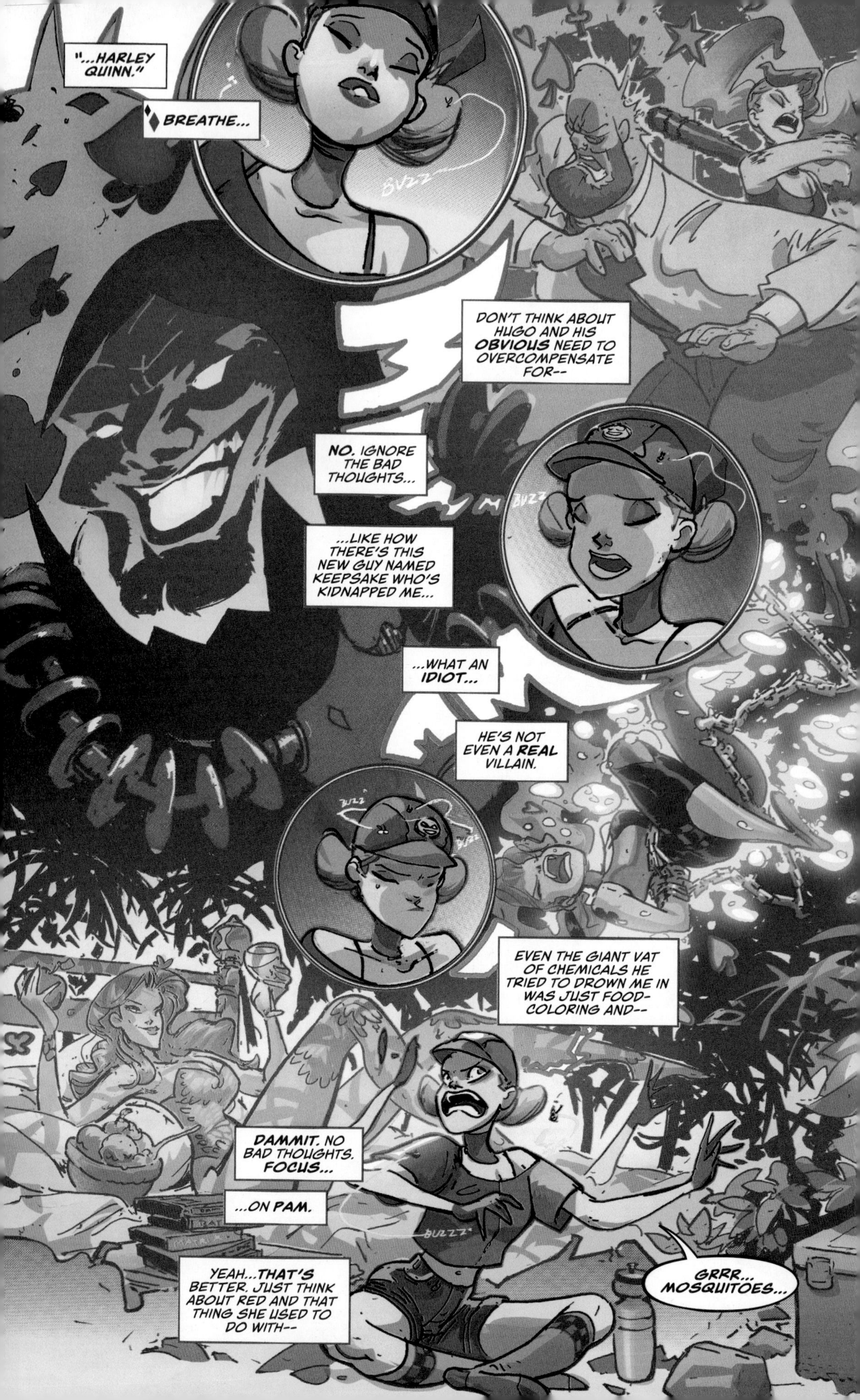
"...HARLEY QUINN."
BREATHE...
BUZZ
DON'T THINK ABOUT HUGO AND HIS OBVIOUS NEED TO OVERCOMPENSATE FOR--
NO. IGNORE THE BAD THOUGHTS...
BUZZ
...LIKE HOW THERE'S THIS NEW GUY NAMED KEEPSAKE WHO'S KIDNAPPED ME...
...WHAT AN IDIOT...
HE'S NOT EVEN A REAL VILLAIN.
EVEN THE GIANT VAT OF CHEMICALS HE TRIED TO DROWN ME IN WAS JUST FOOD-COLORING AND--
DAMMIT. NO BAD THOUGHTS. FOCUS...
...ON PAM.
BUZZZ
YEAH...THAT'S BETTER. JUST THINK ABOUT RED AND THAT THING SHE USED TO DO WITH--
GRRR... MOSQUITOES...

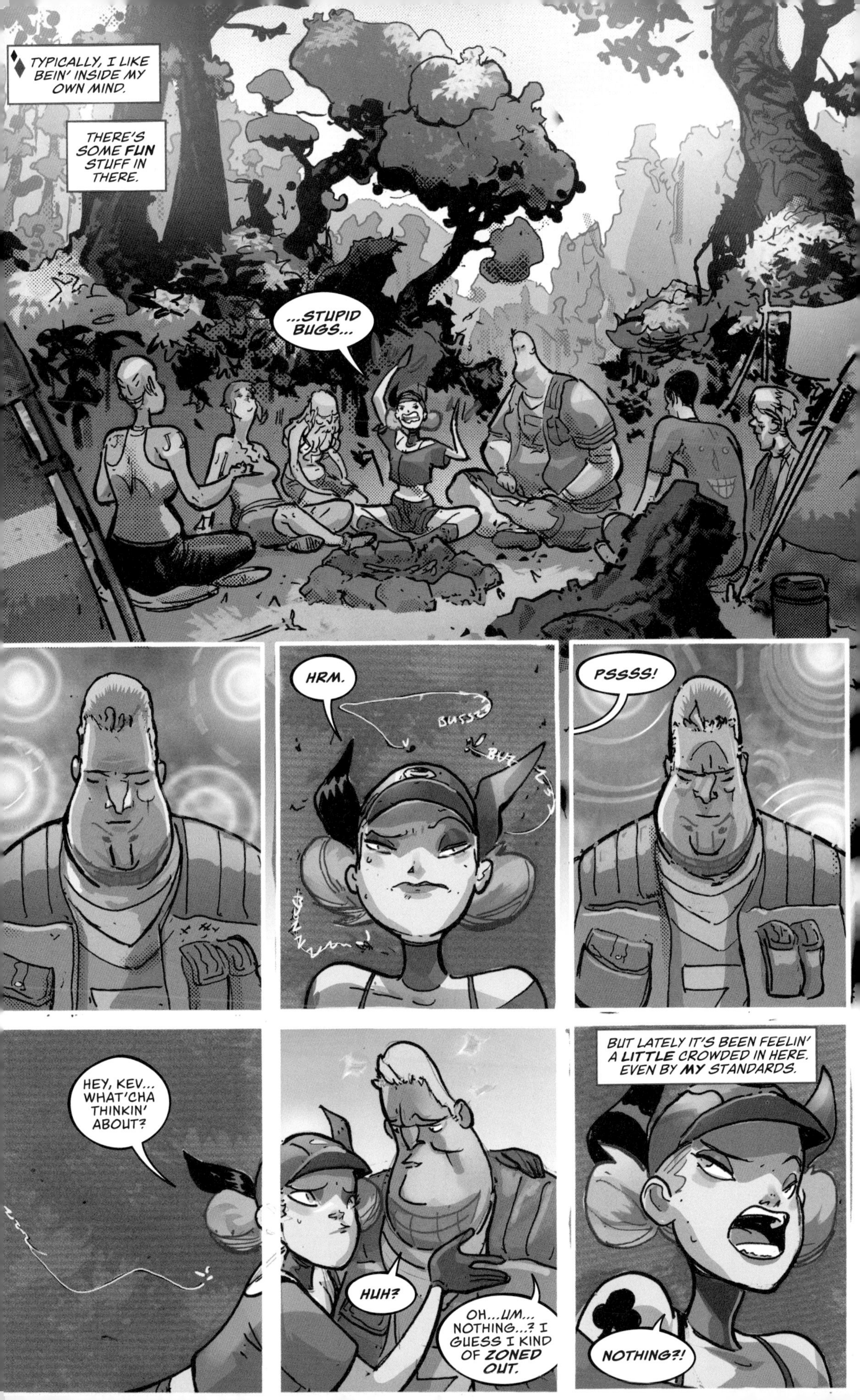
TYPICALLY, I LIKE BEIN' INSIDE MY OWN MIND.
THERE'S SOME FUN STUFF IN THERE.
...STUPID BUGS...
HRM.
PSSSS!
HEY, KEV... WHAT'CHA THINKIN' ABOUT?
HUH?
OH...UM... NOTHING...? I GUESS I KIND OF ZONED OUT.
BUT LATELY IT'S BEEN FEELIN' A LITTLE CROWDED IN HERE. EVEN BY MY STANDARDS.
NOTHING?!

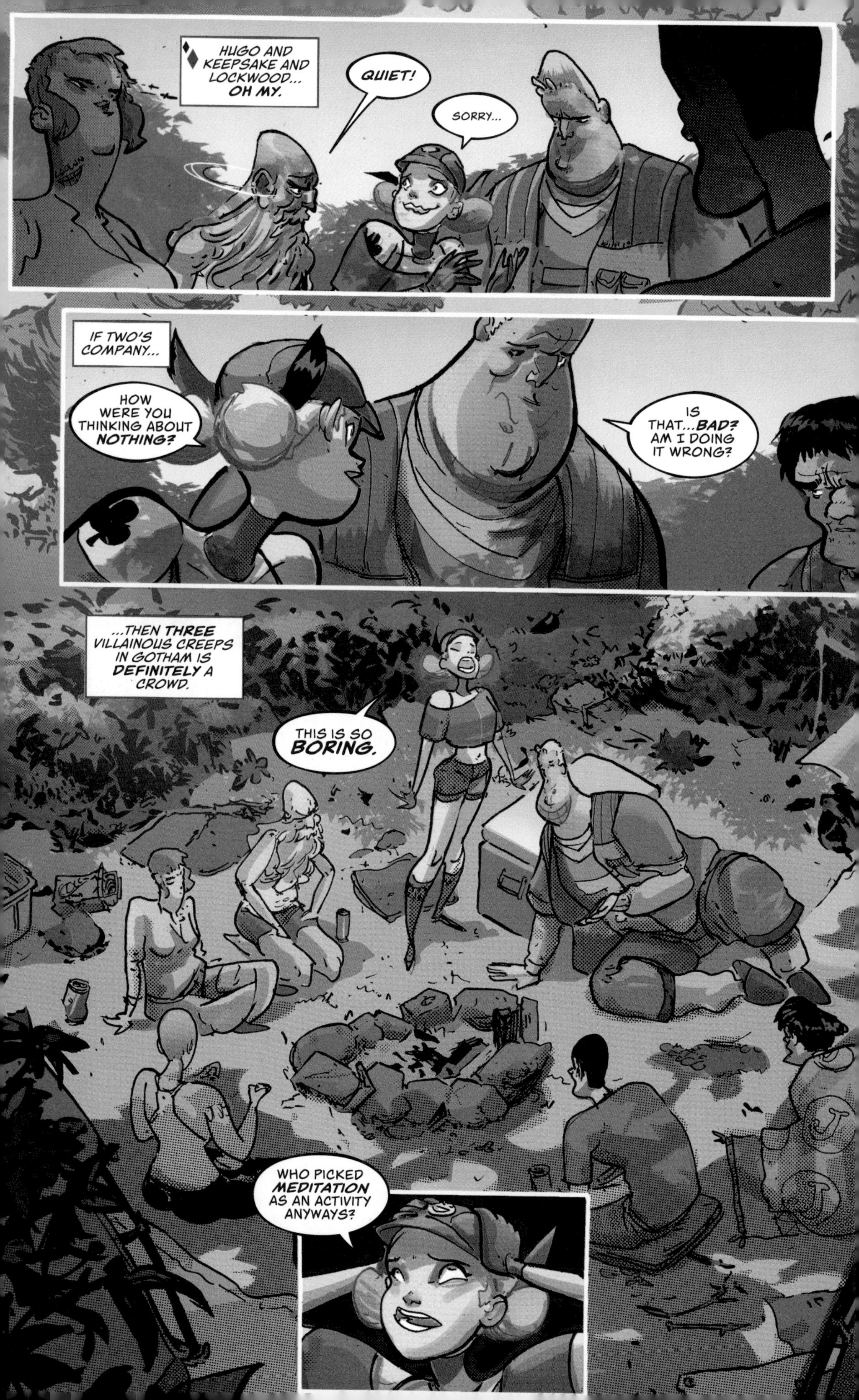
HUGO AND KEEPSAKE AND LOCKWOOD... OH MY.
QUIET!
SORRY...
IF TWO'S COMPANY...
HOW WERE YOU THINKING ABOUT NOTHING?
IS THAT...BAD? AM I DOING IT WRONG?
...THEN THREE VILLAINOUS CREEPS IN GOTHAM IS DEFINITELY A CROWD.
THIS IS SO BORING.
WHO PICKED MEDITATION AS AN ACTIVITY ANYWAYS?

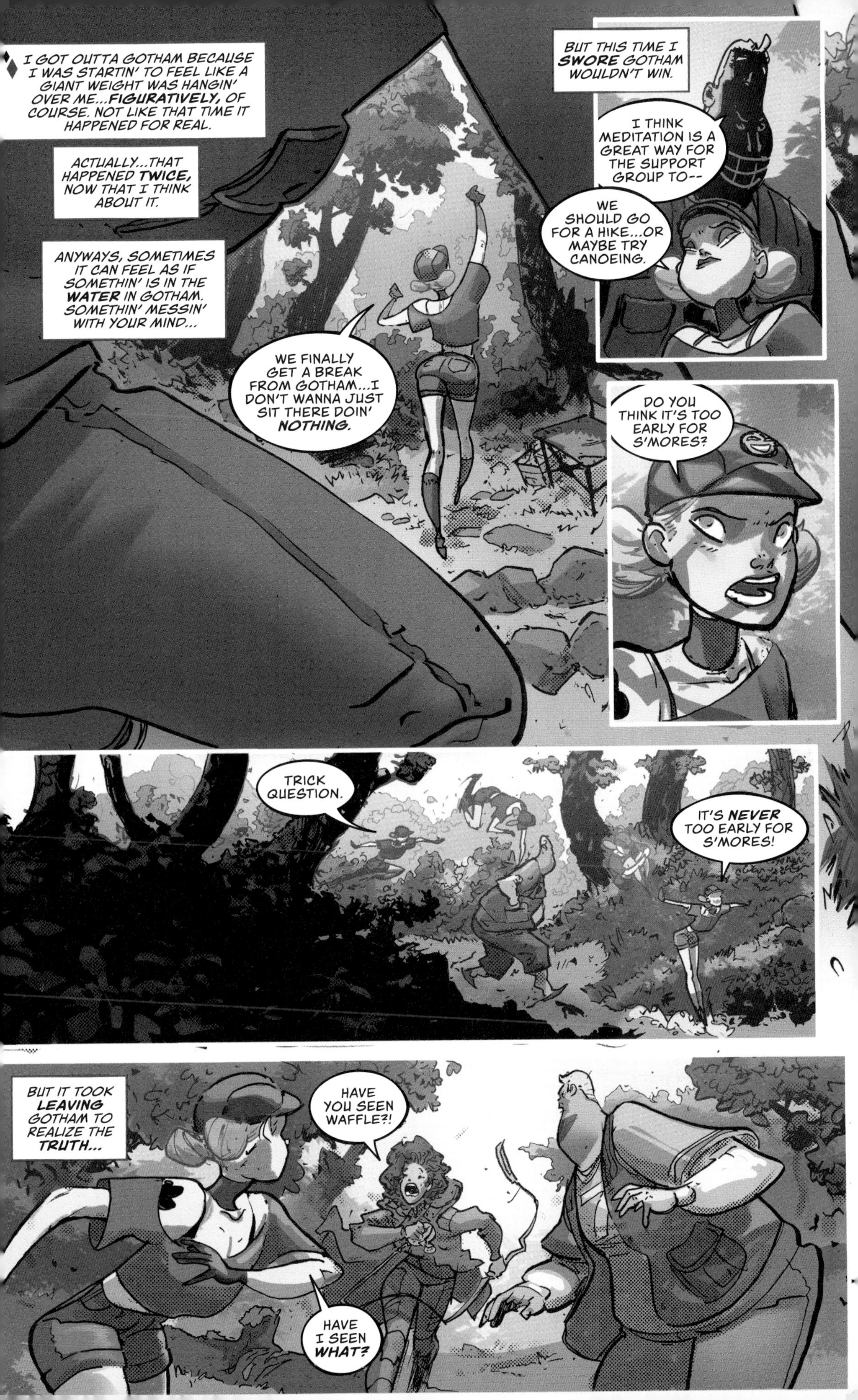
I GOT OUTTA GOTHAM BECAUSE I WAS STARTIN' TO FEEL LIKE A GIANT WEIGHT WAS HANGIN' OVER ME...FIGURATIVELY, OF COURSE. NOT LIKE THAT TIME IT HAPPENED FOR REAL.
ACTUALLY...THAT HAPPENED TWICE, NOW THAT I THINK ABOUT IT.
ANYWAYS, SOMETIMES IT CAN FEEL AS IF SOMETHIN' IS IN THE WATER IN GOTHAM. SOMETHIN' MESSIN' WITH YOUR MIND...
WE FINALLY GET A BREAK FROM GOTHAM...I DON'T WANNA JUST SIT THERE DOIN' NOTHING.
BUT THIS TIME I SWORE GOTHAM WOULDN'T WIN.
I THINK MEDITATION IS A GREAT WAY FOR THE SUPPORT GROUP TO--
WE SHOULD GO FOR A HIKE...OR MAYBE TRY CANOEING.
DO YOU THINK IT'S TOO EARLY FOR S'MORES?
TRICK QUESTION.
IT'S NEVER TOO EARLY FOR S'MORES!
BUT IT TOOK LEAVING GOTHAM TO REALIZE THE TRUTH...
HAVE YOU SEEN WAFFLE?!
HAVE I SEEN WHAT?

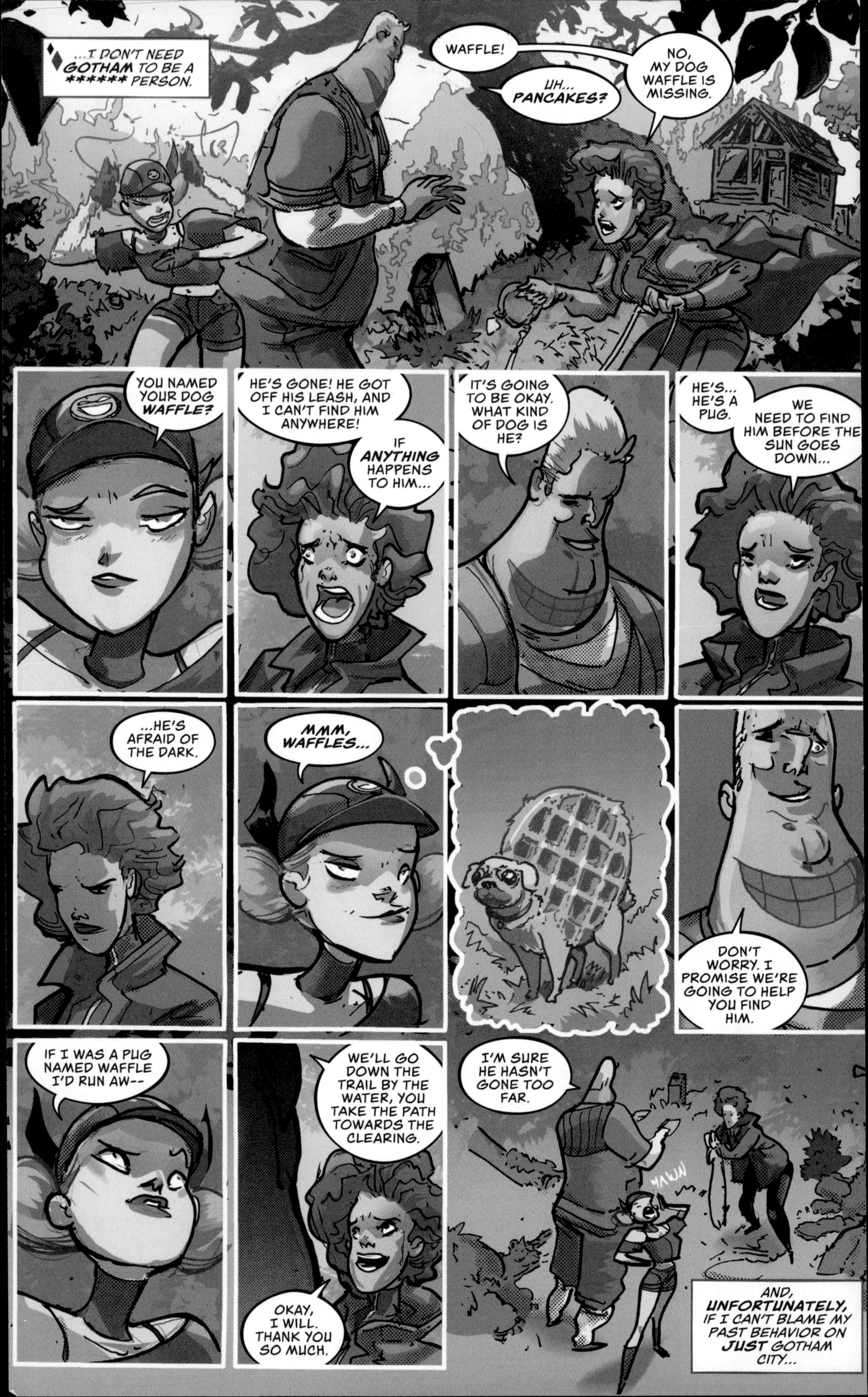
...I DON'T NEED GOTHAM TO BE A ****** PERSON.
WAFFLE!
UH... PANCAKES?
NO, MY DOG WAFFLE IS MISSING.
YOU NAMED YOUR DOG WAFFLE?
HE'S GONE! HE GOT OFF HIS LEASH, AND I CAN'T FIND HIM ANYWHERE!
IF ANYTHING HAPPENS TO HIM...
IT'S GOING TO BE OKAY. WHAT KIND OF DOG IS HE?
HE'S... HE'S A PUG.
WE NEED TO FIND HIM BEFORE THE SUN GOES DOWN...
...HE'S AFRAID OF THE DARK.
MMM, WAFFLES...
DON'T WORRY. I PROMISE WE'RE GOING TO HELP YOU FIND HIM.
IF I WAS A PUG NAMED WAFFLE I'D RUN AW--
WE'LL GO DOWN THE TRAIL BY THE WATER, YOU TAKE THE PATH TOWARDS THE CLEARING.
OKAY, I WILL. THANK YOU SO MUCH.
I'M SURE HE HASN'T GONE TOO FAR.
YAWN
AND, UNFORTUNATELY, IF I CAN'T BLAME MY PAST BEHAVIOR ON JUST GOTHAM CITY...

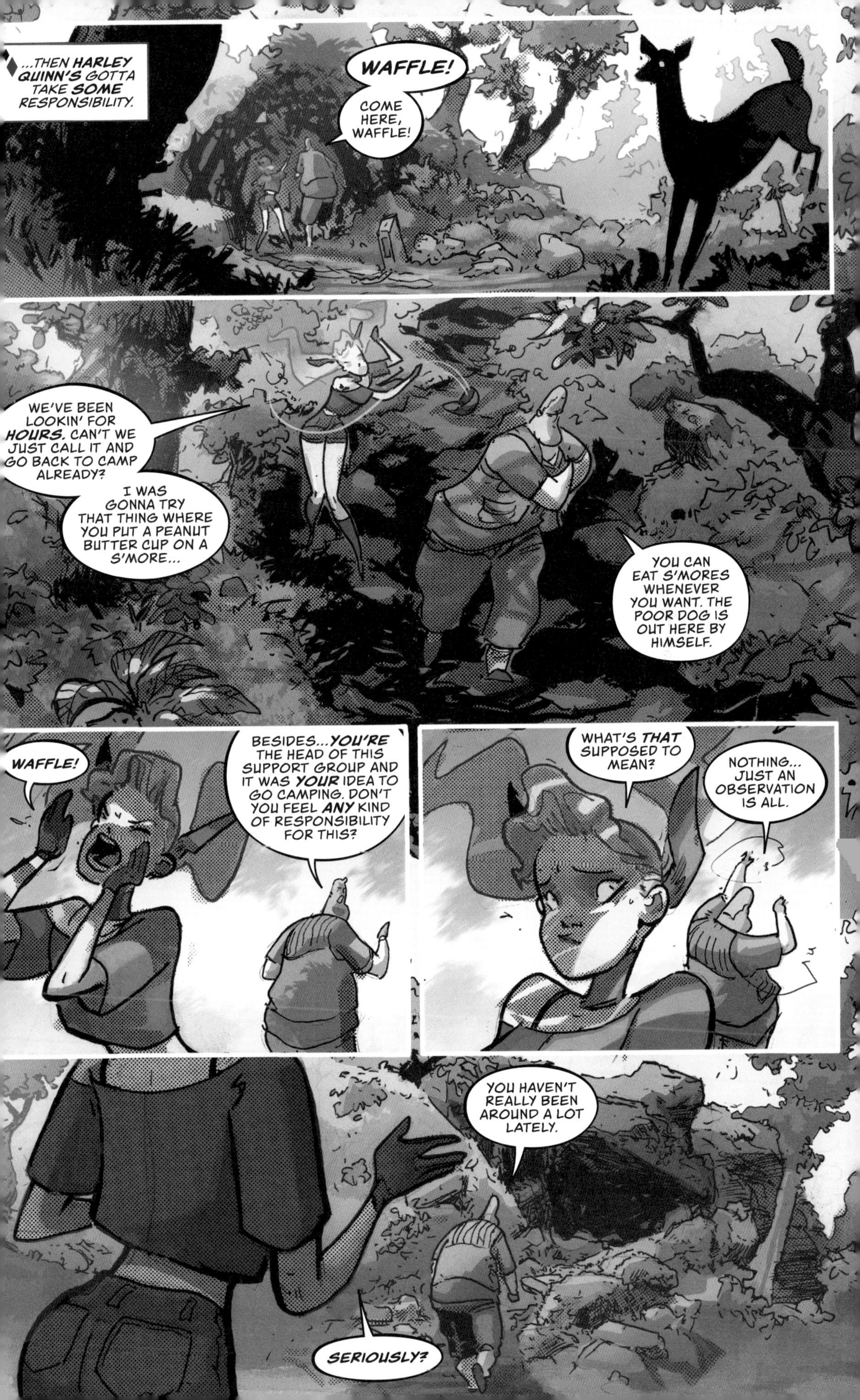

...THEN HARLEY QUINN'S GOTTA TAKE SOME RESPONSIBILITY.
WAFFLE!
COME HERE, WAFFLE!
WE'VE BEEN LOOKIN' FOR HOURS. CAN'T WE JUST CALL IT AND GO BACK TO CAMP ALREADY?
I WAS GONNA TRY THAT THING WHERE YOU PUT A PEANUT BUTTER CUP ON A S'MORE...
YOU CAN EAT S'MORES WHENEVER YOU WANT. THE POOR DOG IS OUT HERE BY HIMSELF.
WAFFLE!
BESIDES... YOU'RE THE HEAD OF THIS SUPPORT GROUP AND IT WAS YOUR IDEA TO GO CAMPING. DON'T YOU FEEL ANY KIND OF RESPONSIBILITY FOR THIS?
WHAT'S THAT SUPPOSED TO MEAN?
NOTHING... JUST AN OBSERVATION IS ALL.
YOU HAVEN'T REALLY BEEN AROUND A LOT LATELY.
SERIOUSLY?

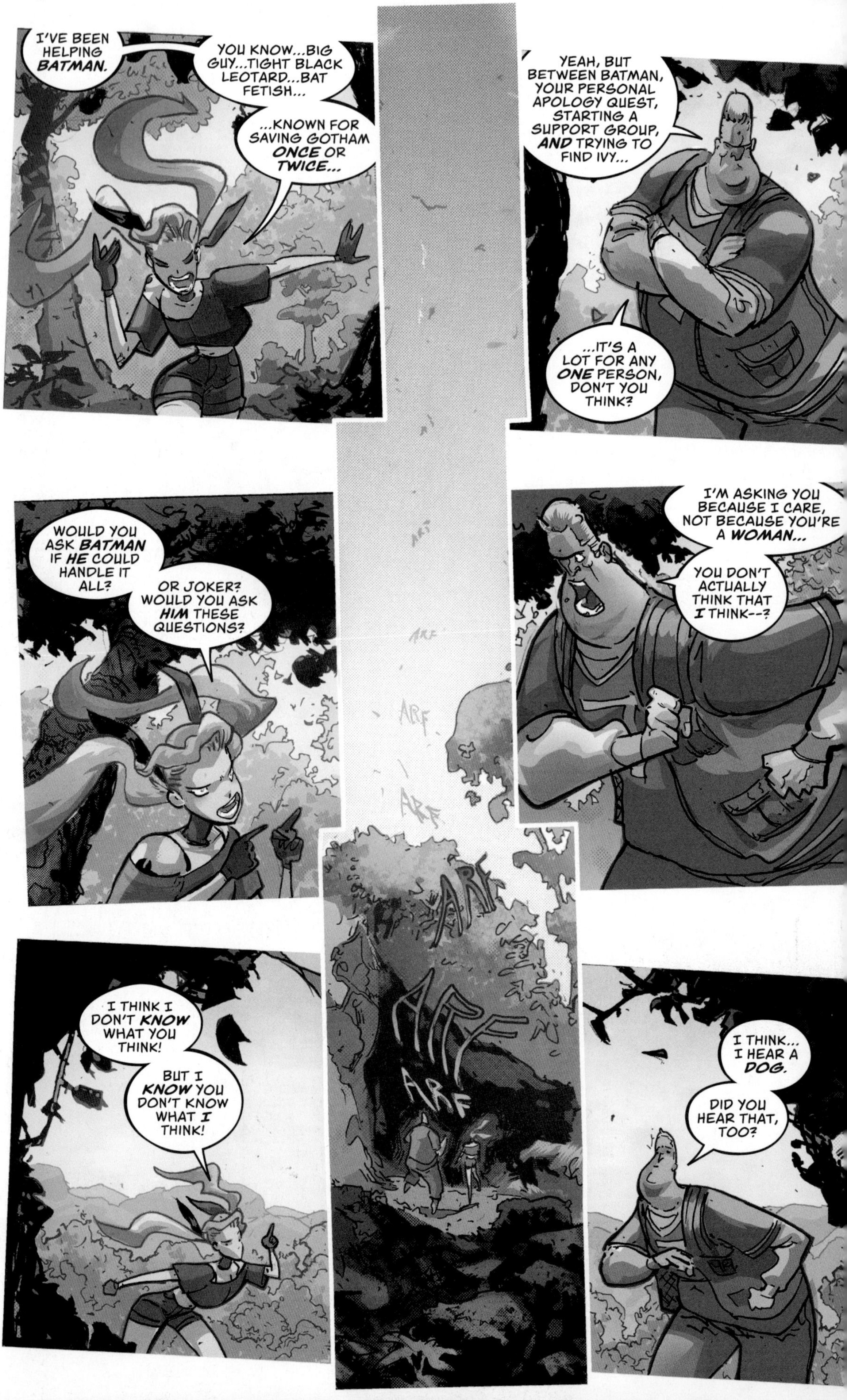
I'VE BEEN HELPING BATMAN.
YOU KNOW...BIG GUY...TIGHT BLACK LEOTARD...BAT FETISH...
...KNOWN FOR SAVING GOTHAM ONCE OR TWICE...
YEAH, BUT BETWEEN BATMAN, YOUR PERSONAL APOLOGY QUEST, STARTING A SUPPORT GROUP, AND TRYING TO FIND IVY...
...IT'S A LOT FOR ANY ONE PERSON, DON'T YOU THINK?
WOULD YOU ASK BATMAN IF HE COULD HANDLE IT ALL?
OR JOKER? WOULD YOU ASK HIM THESE QUESTIONS?
I'M ASKING YOU BECAUSE I CARE, NOT BECAUSE YOU'RE A WOMAN...
YOU DON'T ACTUALLY THINK THAT I THINK--?
ARF
ARF
ARF
ARF
ARF
ARF
I THINK I DON'T KNOW WHAT YOU THINK!
BUT I KNOW YOU DON'T KNOW WHAT I THINK!
I THINK... I HEAR A DOG.
DID YOU HEAR THAT, TOO?

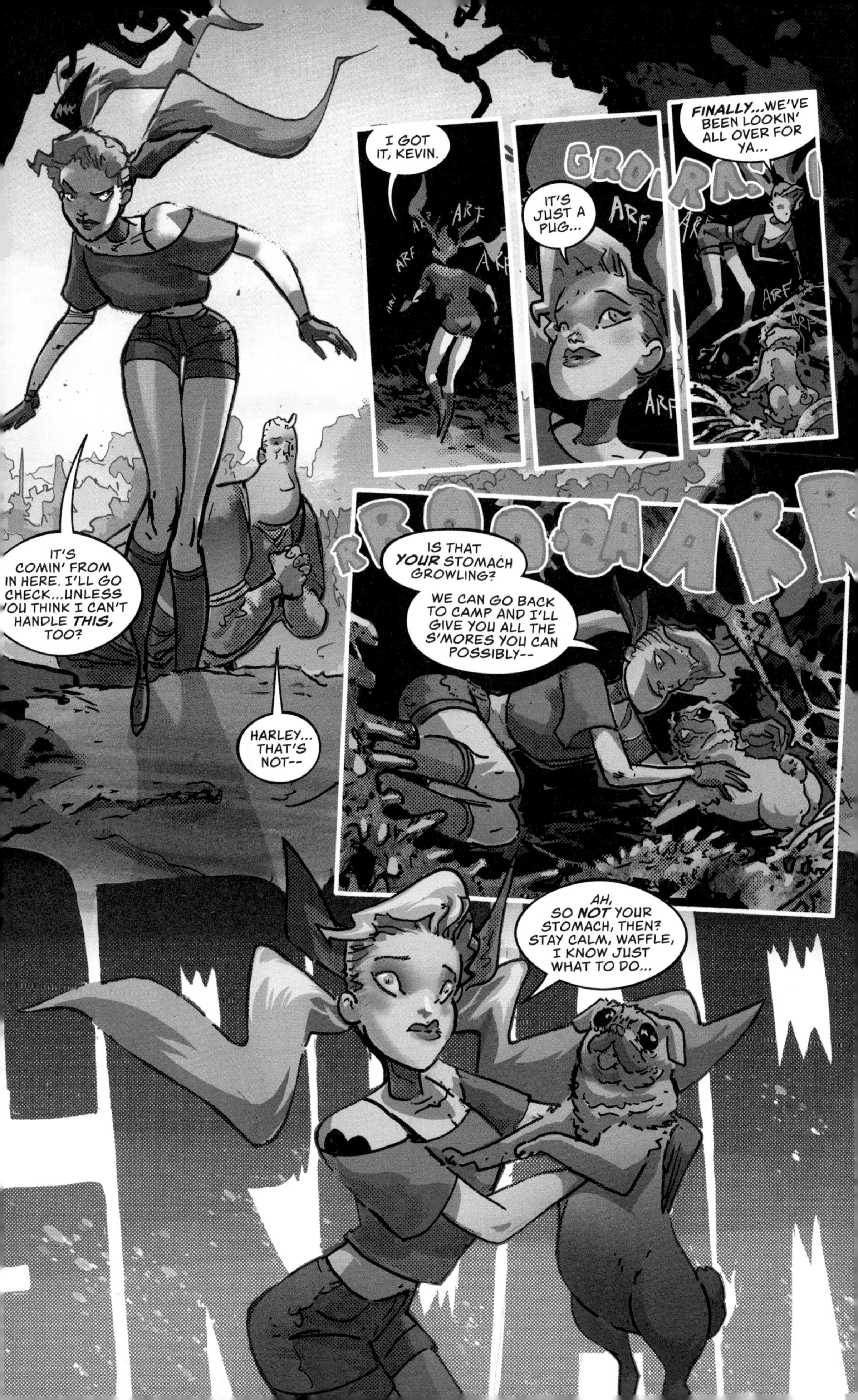

I GOT IT, KEVIN.
ARF
ARF
ARF
ARF
GROWRR
IT'S JUST A PUG...
ARF
ARF
FINALLY...WE'VE BEEN LOOKIN' ALL OVER FOR YA...
ARF
ARF
IT'S COMIN' FROM IN HERE. I'LL GO CHECK...UNLESS YOU THINK I CAN'T HANDLE THIS, TOO?
HARLEY... THAT'S NOT--
IS THAT YOUR STOMACH GROWLING?
WE CAN GO BACK TO CAMP AND I'LL GIVE YOU ALL THE S'MORES YOU CAN POSSIBLY--
AH, SO NOT YOUR STOMACH, THEN? STAY CALM, WAFFLE, I KNOW JUST WHAT TO DO...

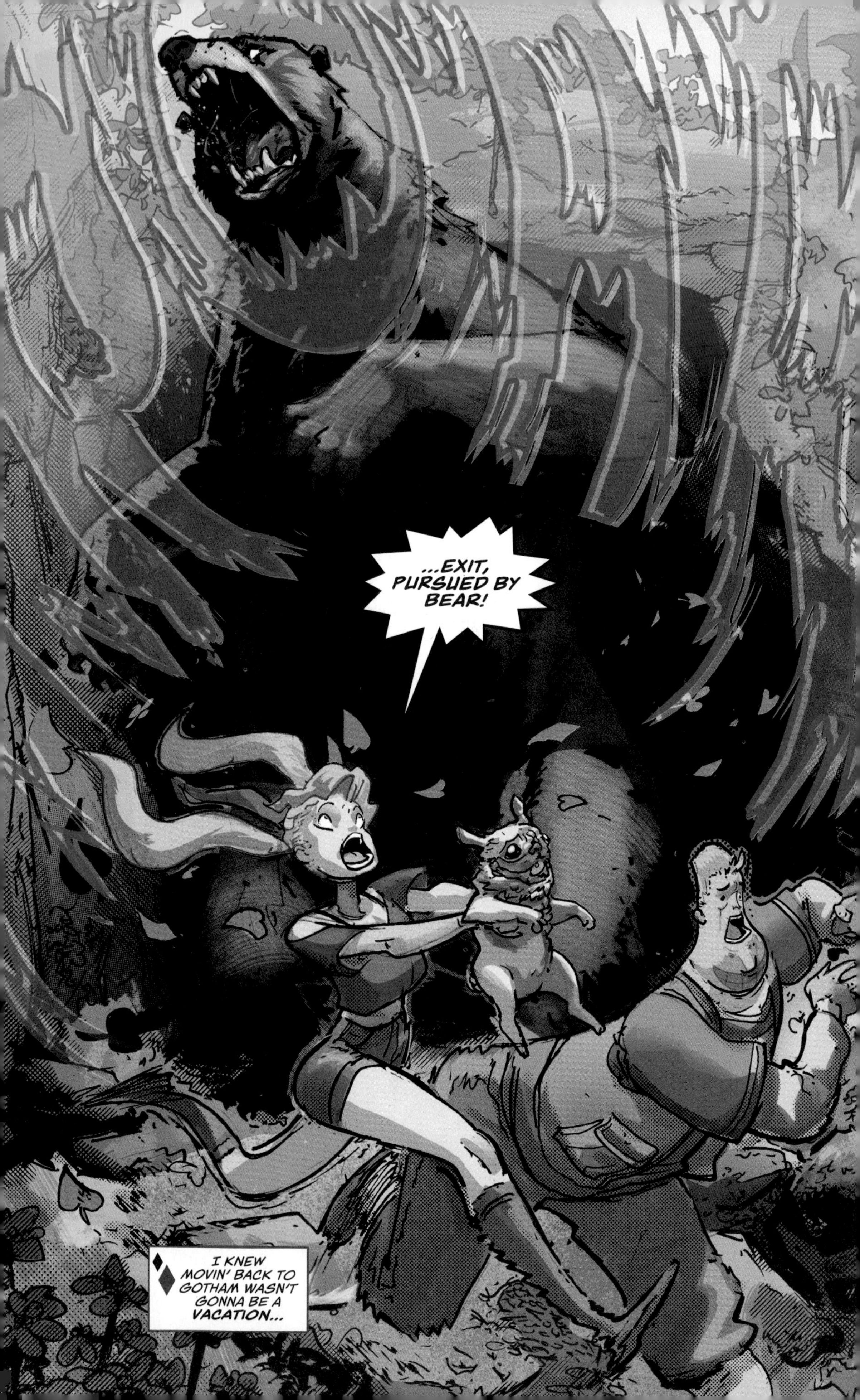
...EXIT, PURSUED BY BEAR!
I KNEW MOVIN' BACK TO GOTHAM WASN'T GONNA BE A VACATION...

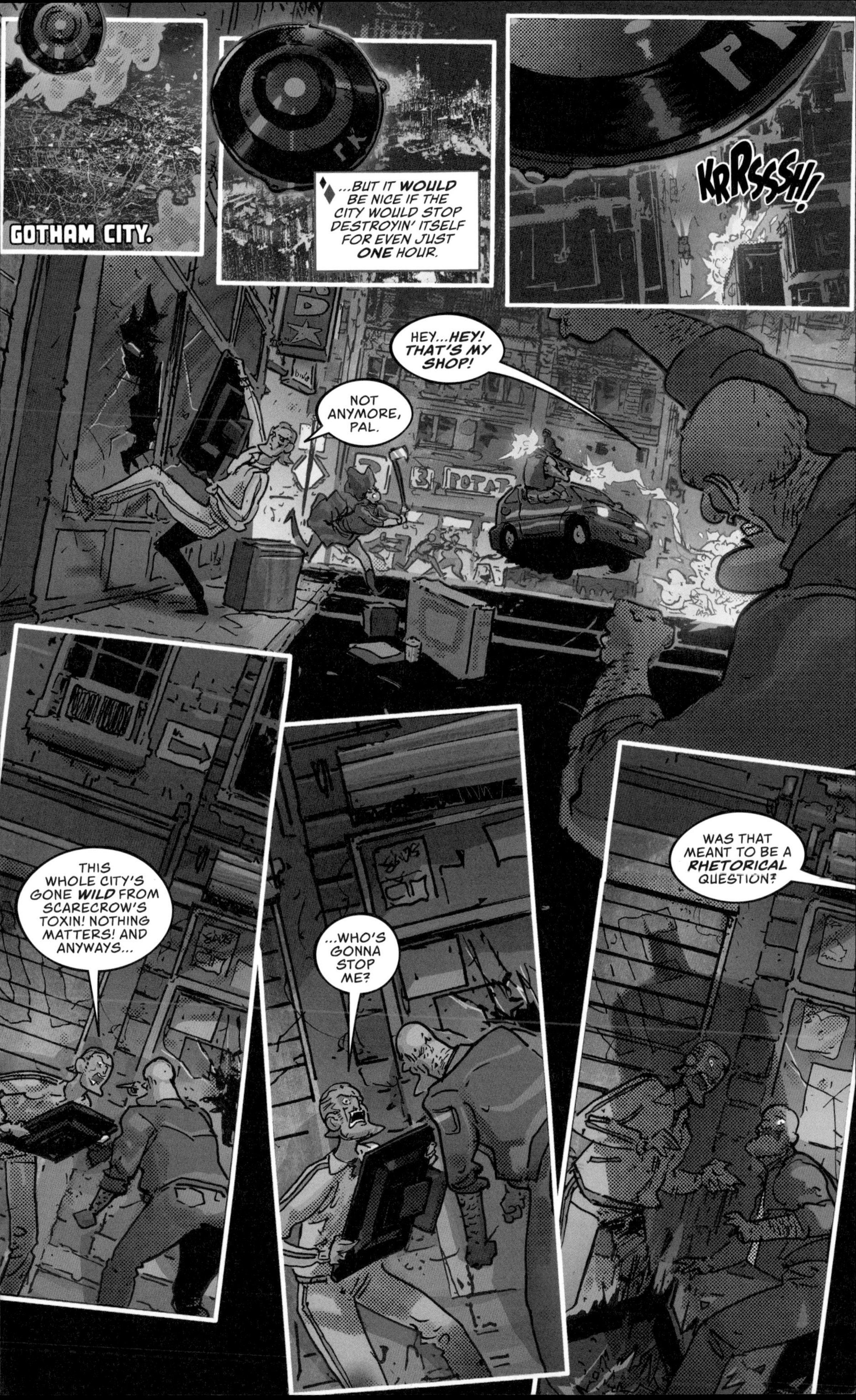
GOTHAM CITY.
...BUT IT WOULD BE NICE IF THE CITY WOULD STOP DESTROYIN' ITSELF FOR EVEN JUST ONE HOUR.
KRRSSSH!
HEY...HEY! THAT'S MY SHOP!
NOT ANYMORE, PAL.
THIS WHOLE CITY'S GONE WILD FROM SCARECROW'S TOXIN! NOTHING MATTERS! AND ANYWAYS...
...WHO'S GONNA STOP ME?
WAS THAT MEANT TO BE A RHETORICAL QUESTION?

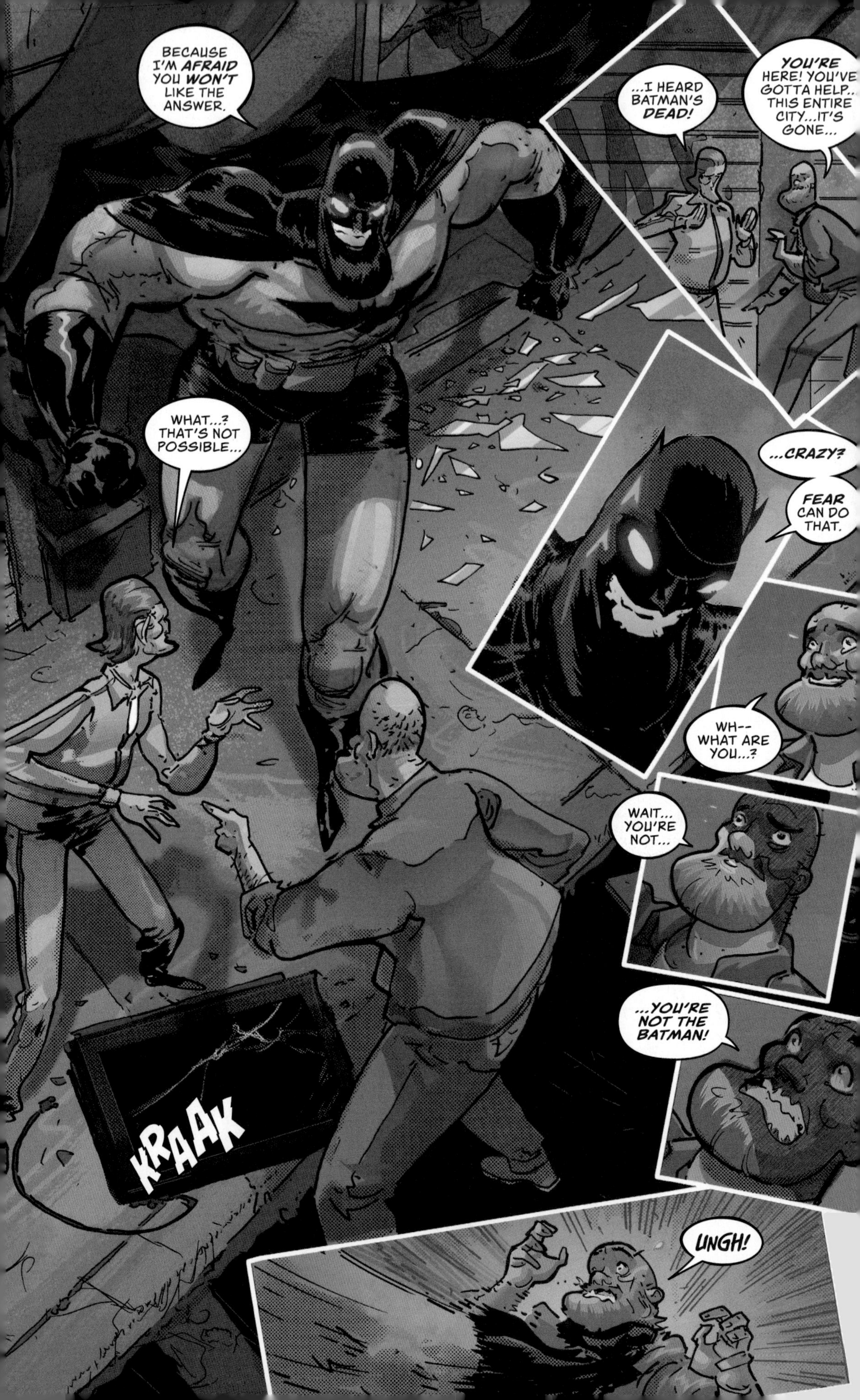
BECAUSE I'M AFRAID YOU WON'T LIKE THE ANSWER.
...I HEARD BATMAN'S DEAD!
YOU'RE HERE! YOU'VE GOTTA HELP.. THIS ENTIRE CITY...IT'S GONE...
WHAT...? THAT'S NOT POSSIBLE...
...CRAZY?
FEAR CAN DO THAT.
WH-- WHAT ARE YOU...?
WAIT... YOU'RE NOT...
...YOU'RE NOT THE BATMAN!
KRAAK
UNGH!

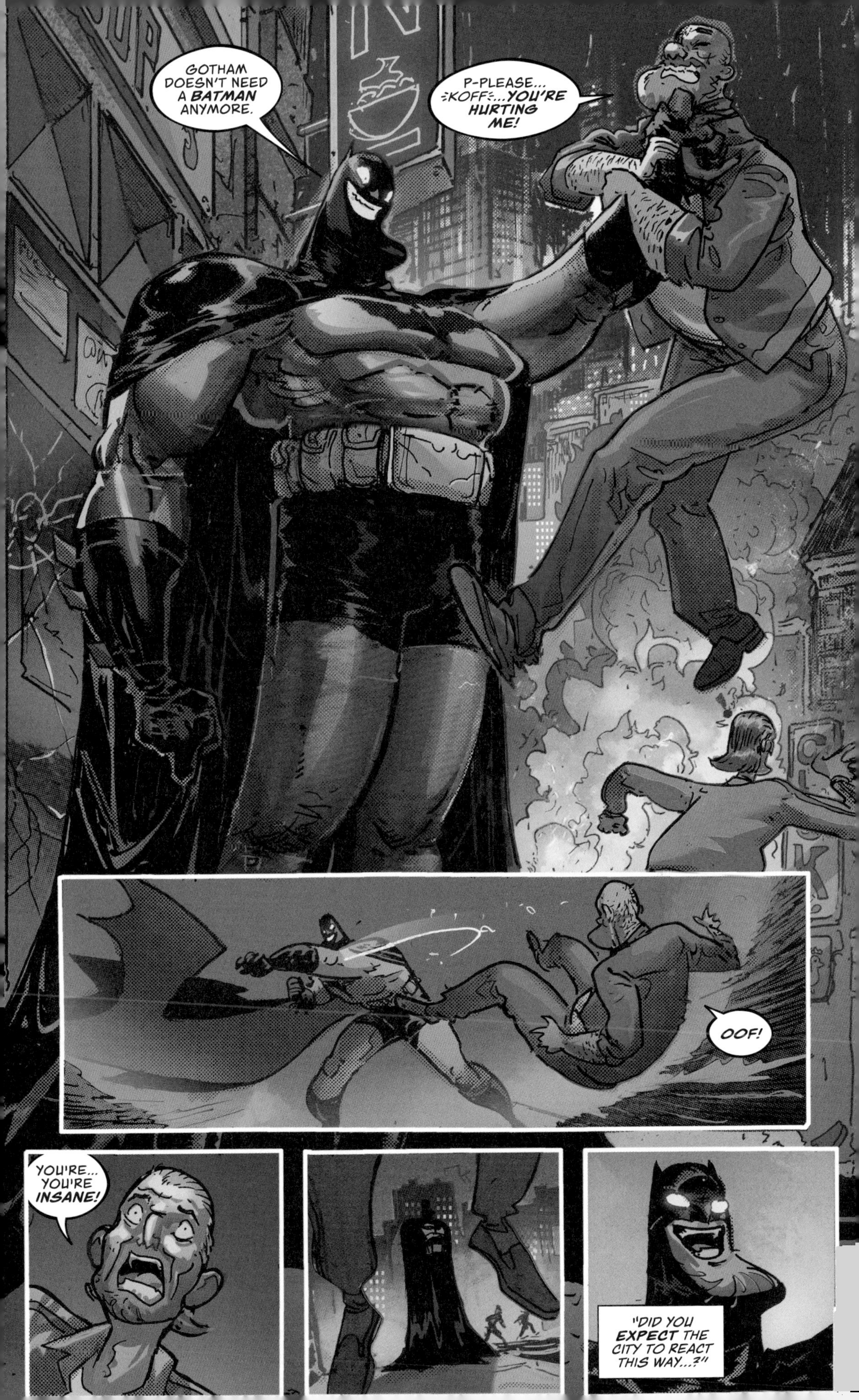
GOTHAM DOESN'T NEED A BATMAN ANYMORE.
P-PLEASE... KOFF ...YOU'RE HURTING ME!
OOF!
YOU'RE... YOU'RE INSANE!
"DID YOU EXPECT THE CITY TO REACT THIS WAY...?"

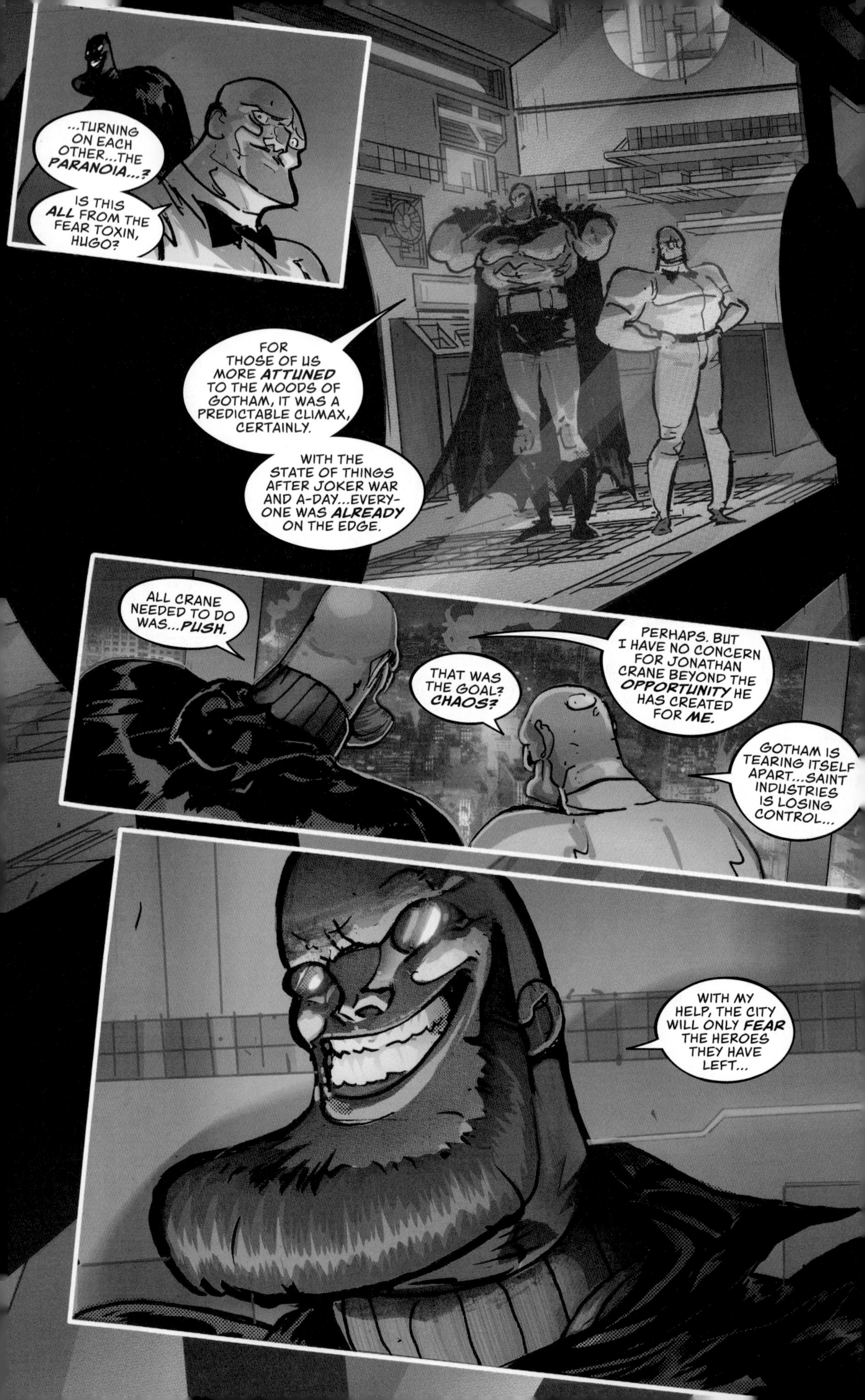
...TURNING ON EACH OTHER...THE PARANOIA...?
IS THIS ALL FROM THE FEAR TOXIN, HUGO?
FOR THOSE OF US MORE ATTUNED TO THE MOODS OF GOTHAM, IT WAS A PREDICTABLE CLIMAX, CERTAINLY.
WITH THE STATE OF THINGS AFTER JOKER WAR AND A-DAY...EVERY-ONE WAS ALREADY ON THE EDGE.
ALL CRANE NEEDED TO DO WAS...PUSH.
THAT WAS THE GOAL? CHAOS?
PERHAPS. BUT I HAVE NO CONCERN FOR JONATHAN CRANE BEYOND THE OPPORTUNITY HE HAS CREATED FOR ME.
GOTHAM IS TEARING ITSELF APART...SAINT INDUSTRIES IS LOSING CONTROL...
WITH MY HELP, THE CITY WILL ONLY FEAR THE HEROES THEY HAVE LEFT...

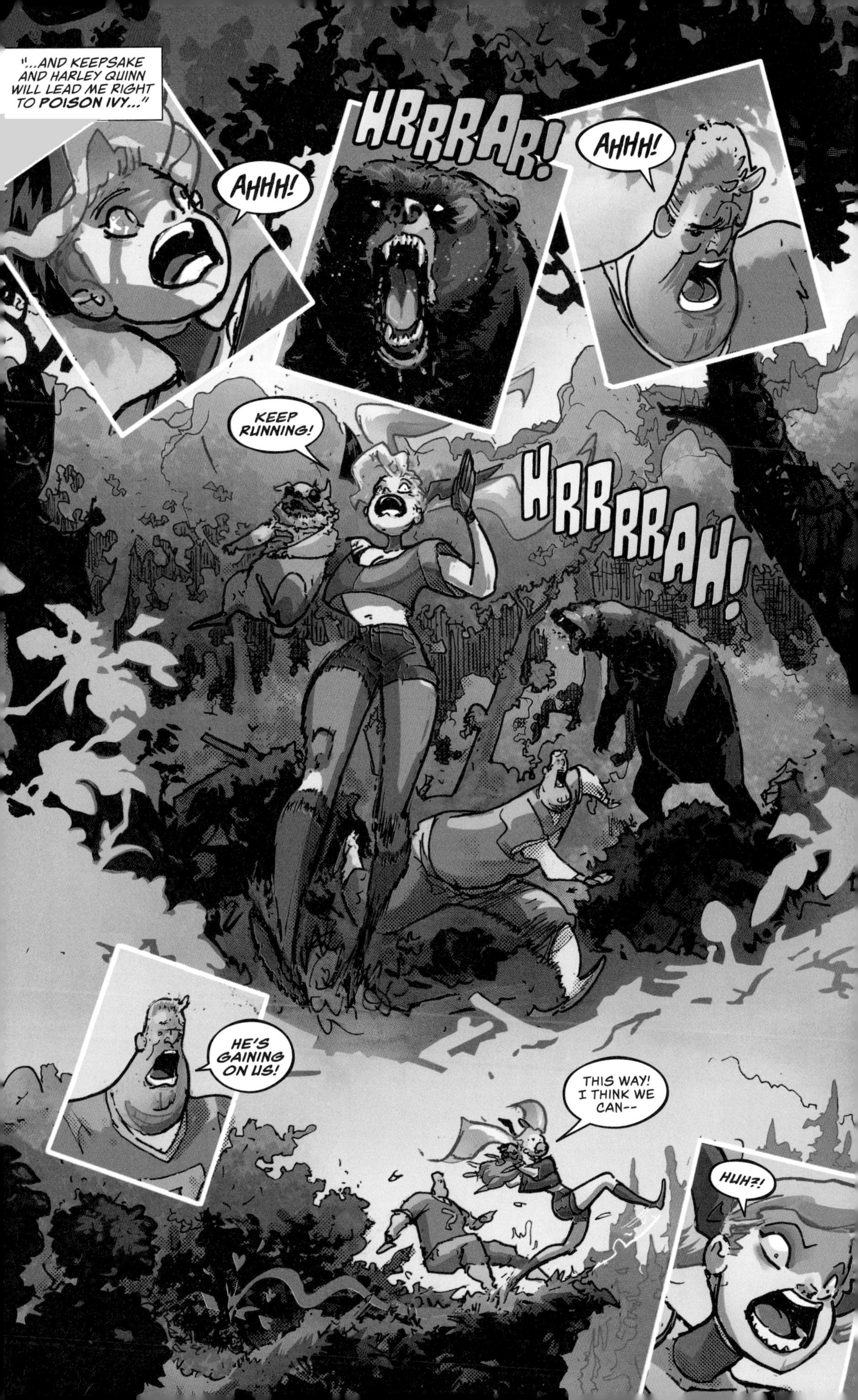
"...AND KEEPSAKE AND HARLEY QUINN WILL LEAD ME RIGHT TO POISON IVY..."
AHHH!
HRRRAR!
AHHH!
KEEP RUNNING!
HRRRRAH!
HE'S GAINING ON US!
THIS WAY! I THINK WE CAN--
HUH?!

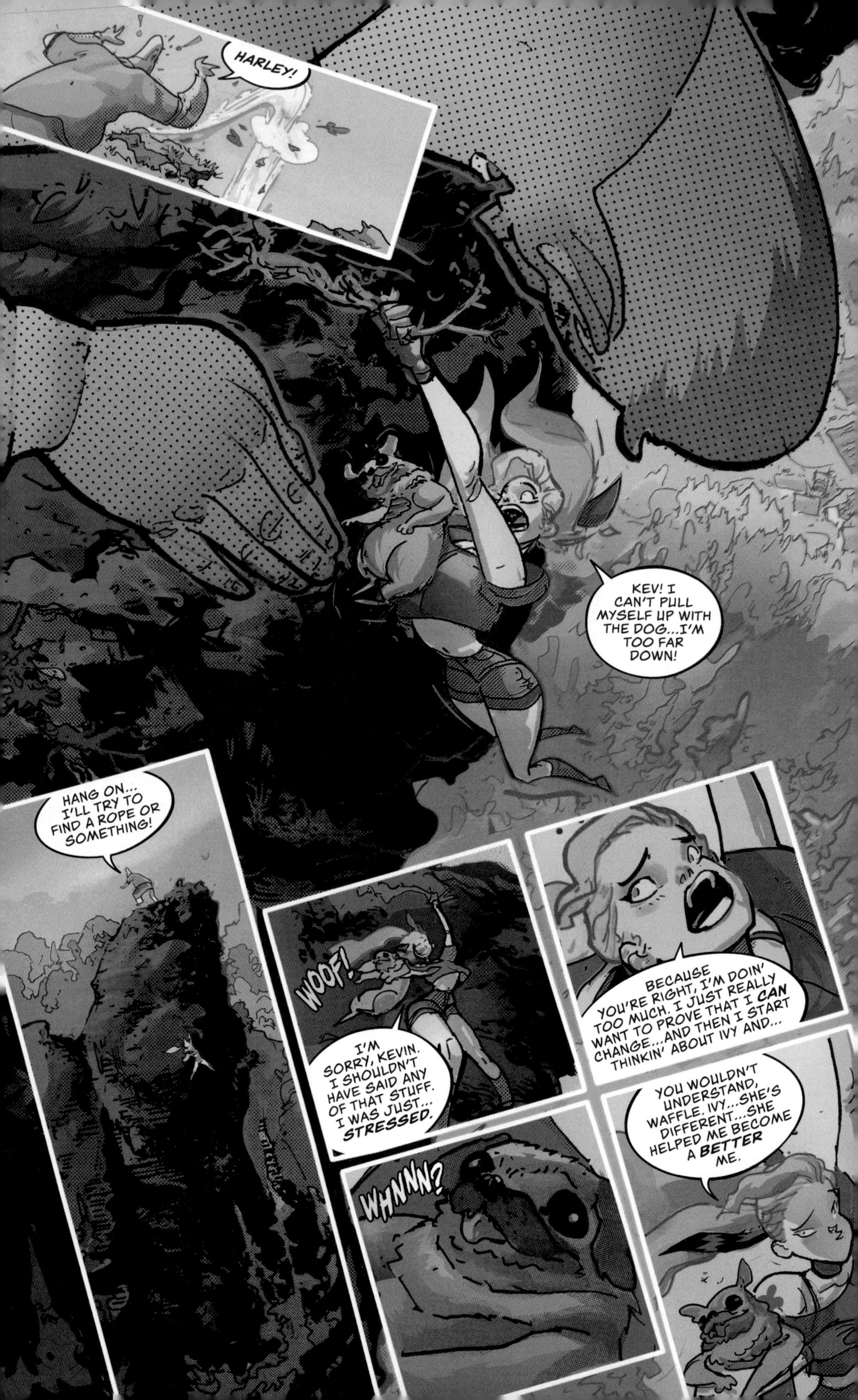
HARLEY!
KEV! I CAN'T PULL MYSELF UP WITH THE DOG...I'M TOO FAR DOWN!
HANG ON... I'LL TRY TO FIND A ROPE OR SOMETHING!
WOOF!
I'M SORRY, KEVIN. I SHOULDN'T HAVE SAID ANY OF THAT STUFF. I WAS JUST... STRESSED.
BECAUSE YOU'RE RIGHT, I'M DOIN' TOO MUCH. I JUST REALLY WANT TO PROVE THAT I CAN CHANGE...AND THEN I START THINKIN' ABOUT IVY AND...
WHNNN?
YOU WOULDN'T UNDERSTAND, WAFFLE. IVY...SHE'S DIFFERENT...SHE HELPED ME BECOME A BETTER ME.

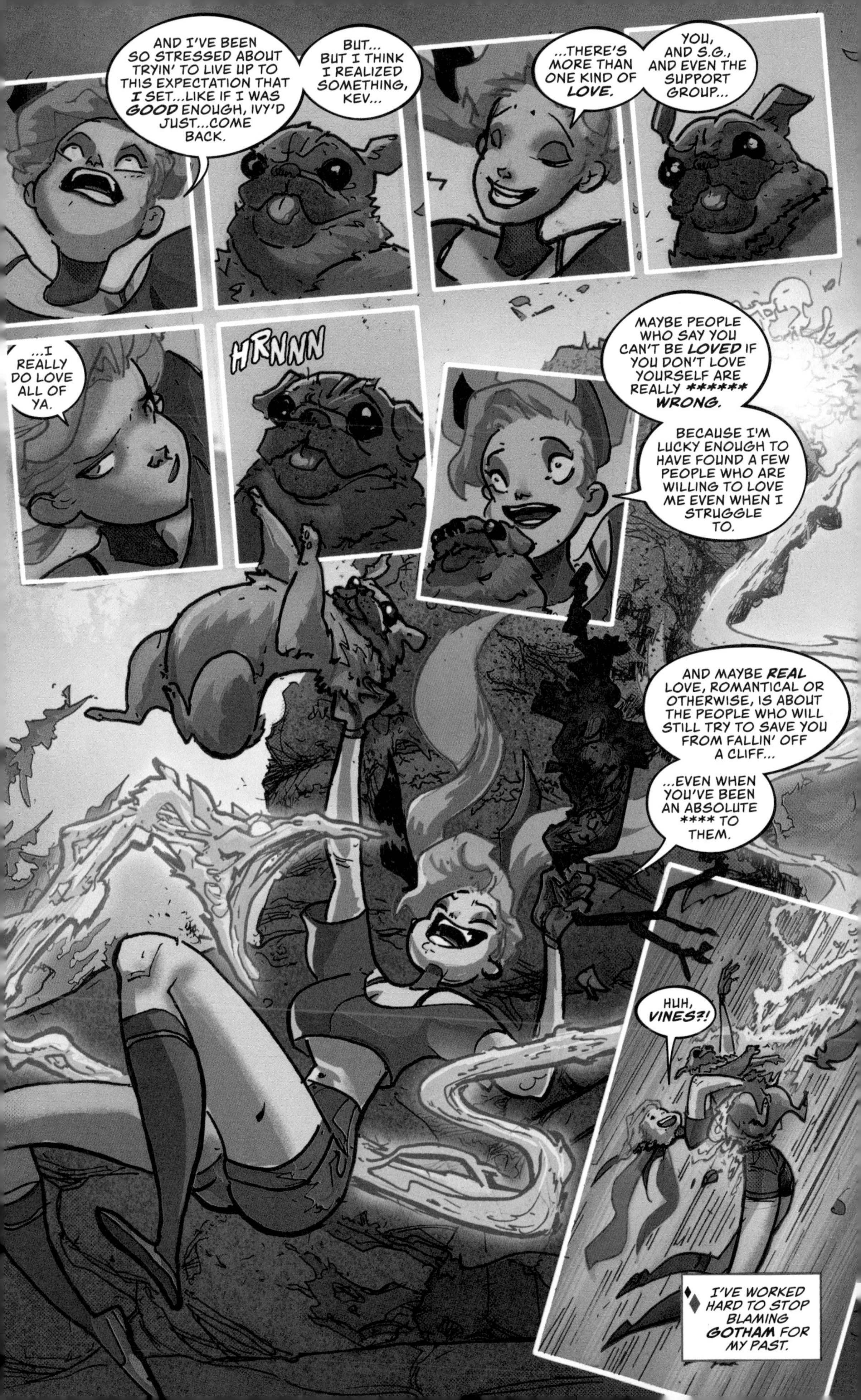
AND I'VE BEEN SO STRESSED ABOUT TRYIN' TO LIVE UP TO THIS EXPECTATION THAT I SET...LIKE IF I WAS GOOD ENOUGH, IVY'D JUST...COME BACK.
BUT... BUT I THINK I REALIZED SOMETHING, KEV...
...THERE'S MORE THAN ONE KIND OF LOVE.
YOU, AND S.G., AND EVEN THE SUPPORT GROUP...
...I REALLY DO LOVE ALL OF YA.
HRNNN
MAYBE PEOPLE WHO SAY YOU CAN'T BE LOVED IF YOU DON'T LOVE YOURSELF ARE REALLY ****** WRONG.
BECAUSE I'M LUCKY ENOUGH TO HAVE FOUND A FEW PEOPLE WHO ARE WILLING TO LOVE ME EVEN WHEN I STRUGGLE TO.
AND MAYBE REAL LOVE, ROMANTICAL OR OTHERWISE, IS ABOUT THE PEOPLE WHO WILL STILL TRY TO SAVE YOU FROM FALLIN' OFF A CLIFF...
...EVEN WHEN YOU'VE BEEN AN ABSOLUTE **** TO THEM.
HUH, VINES?!
I'VE WORKED HARD TO STOP BLAMING GOTHAM FOR MY PAST.

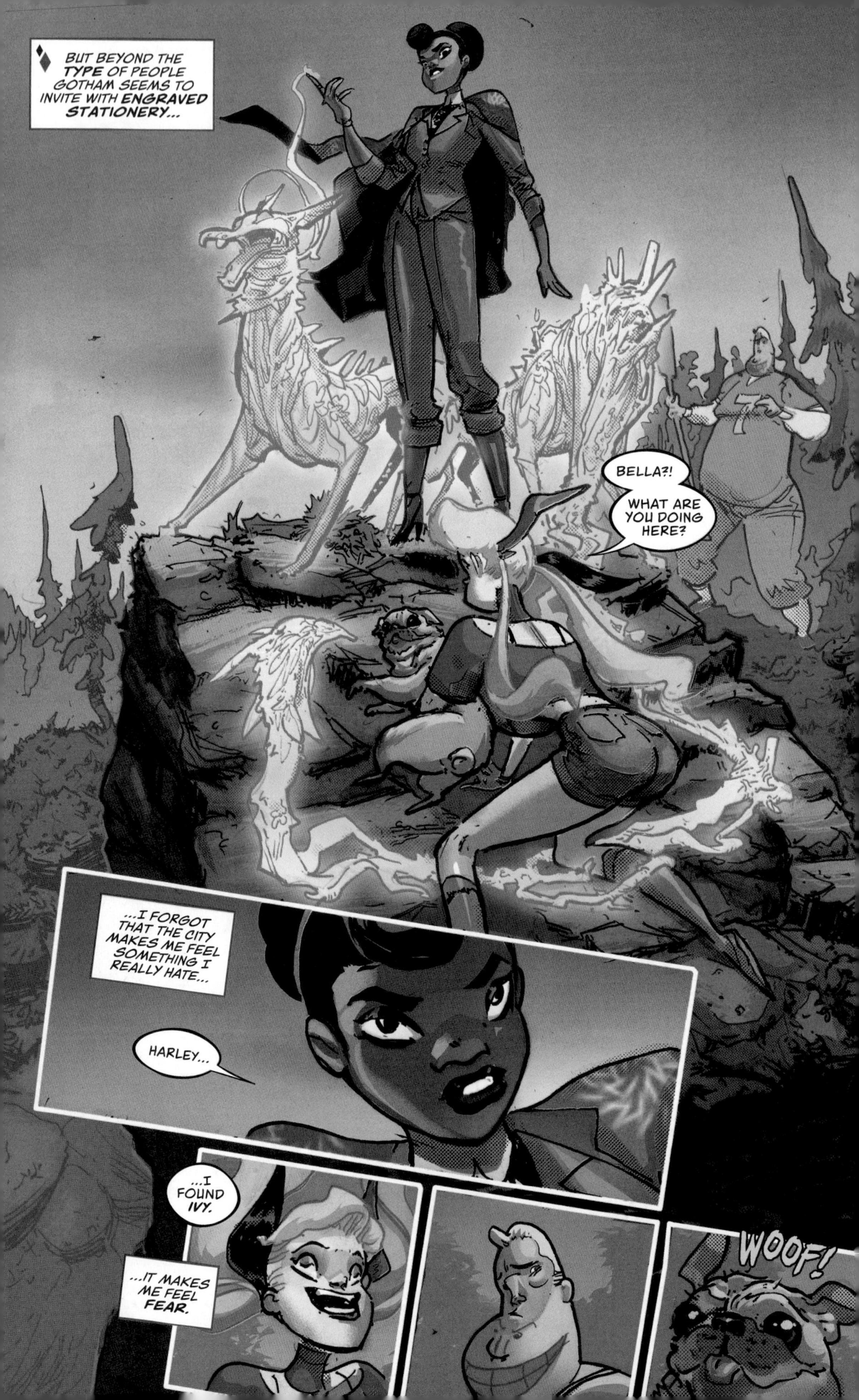

BUT BEYOND THE TYPE OF PEOPLE GOTHAM SEEMS TO INVITE WITH ENGRAVED STATIONERY...
BELLA?!
WHAT ARE YOU DOING HERE?
...I FORGOT THAT THE CITY MAKES ME FEEL SOMETHING I REALLY HATE...
HARLEY...
...I FOUND IVY.
...IT MAKES ME FEEL FEAR.
WOOF!

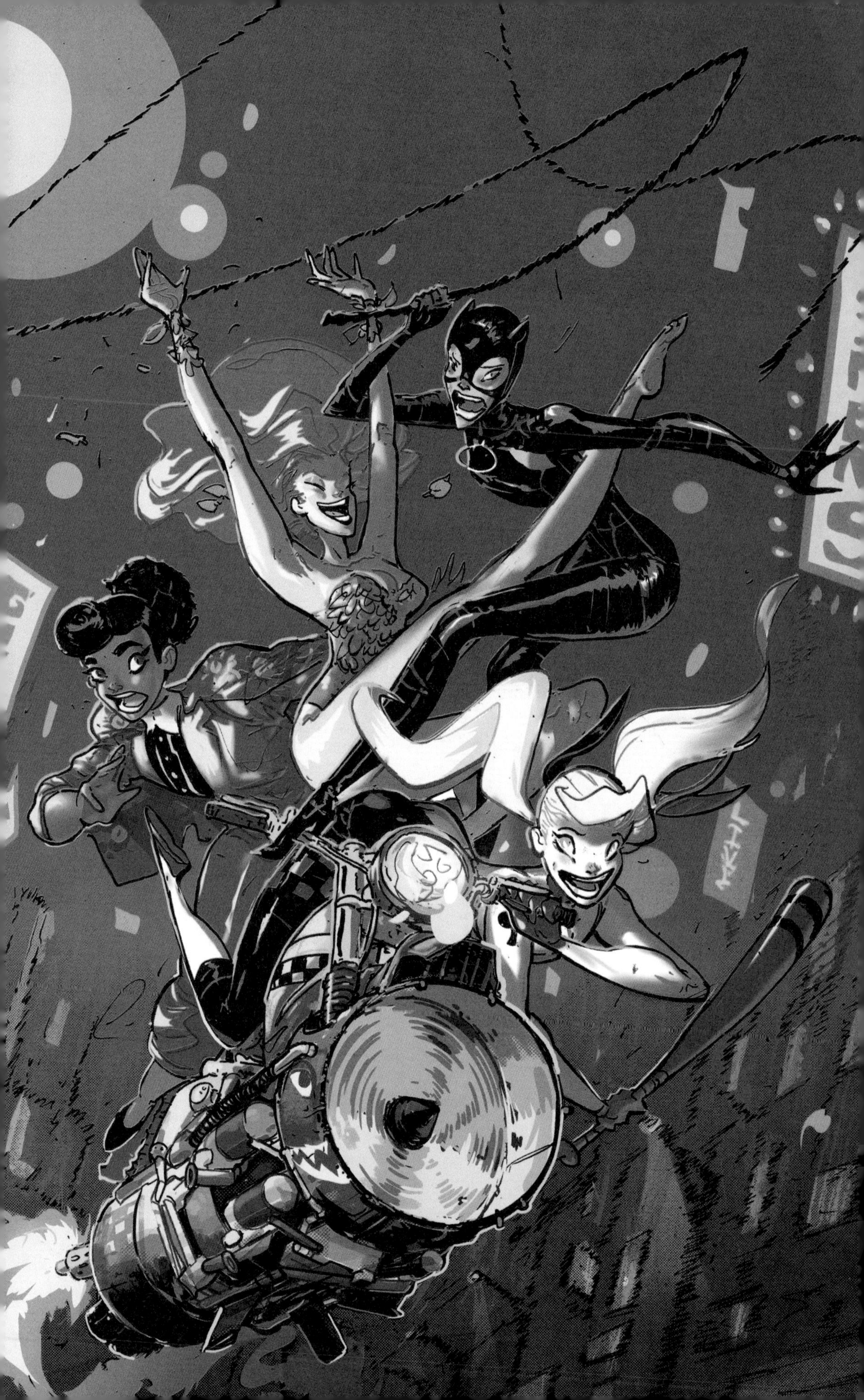

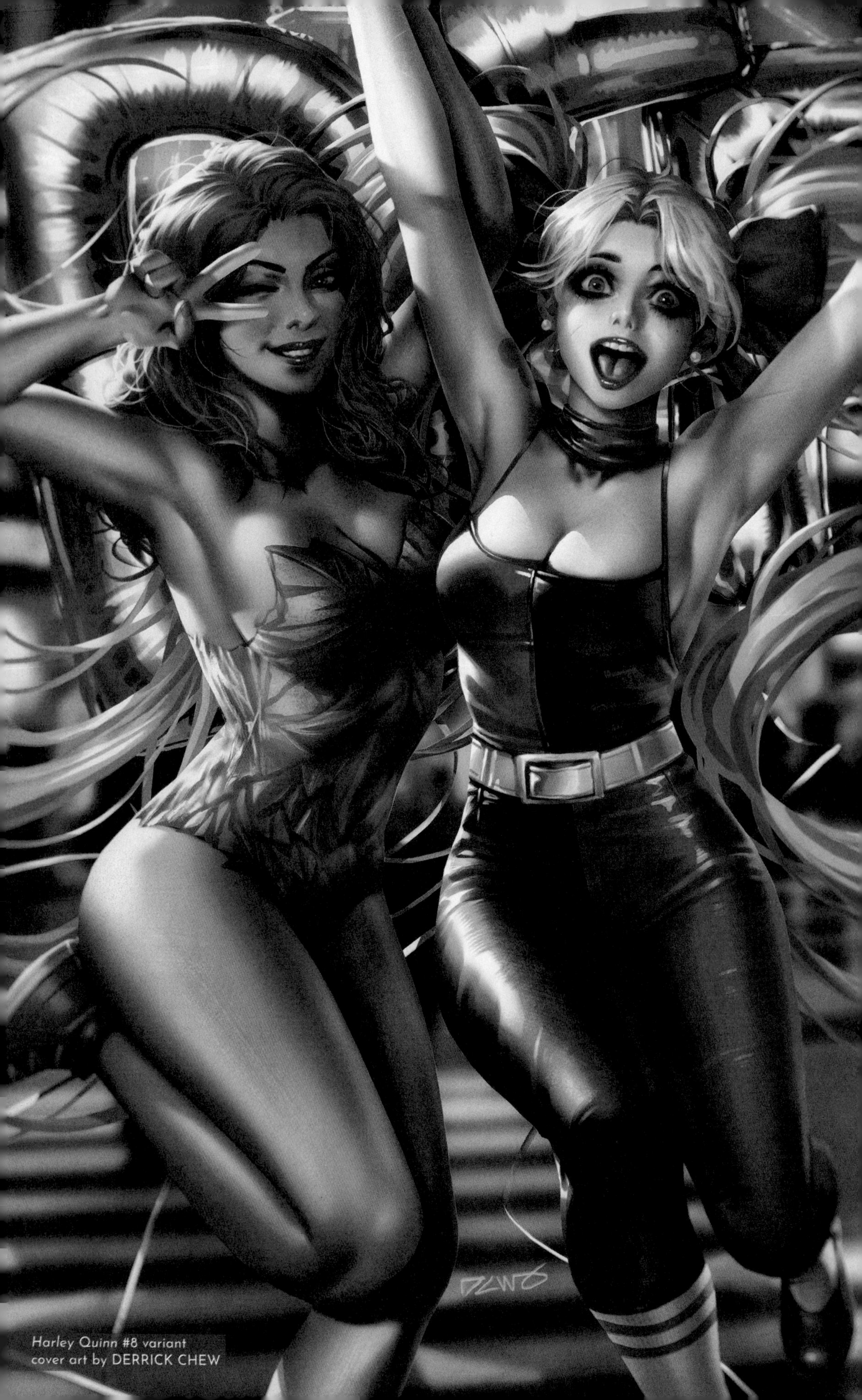

Harley Quinn #8 variant
cover art by DERRICK CHEW

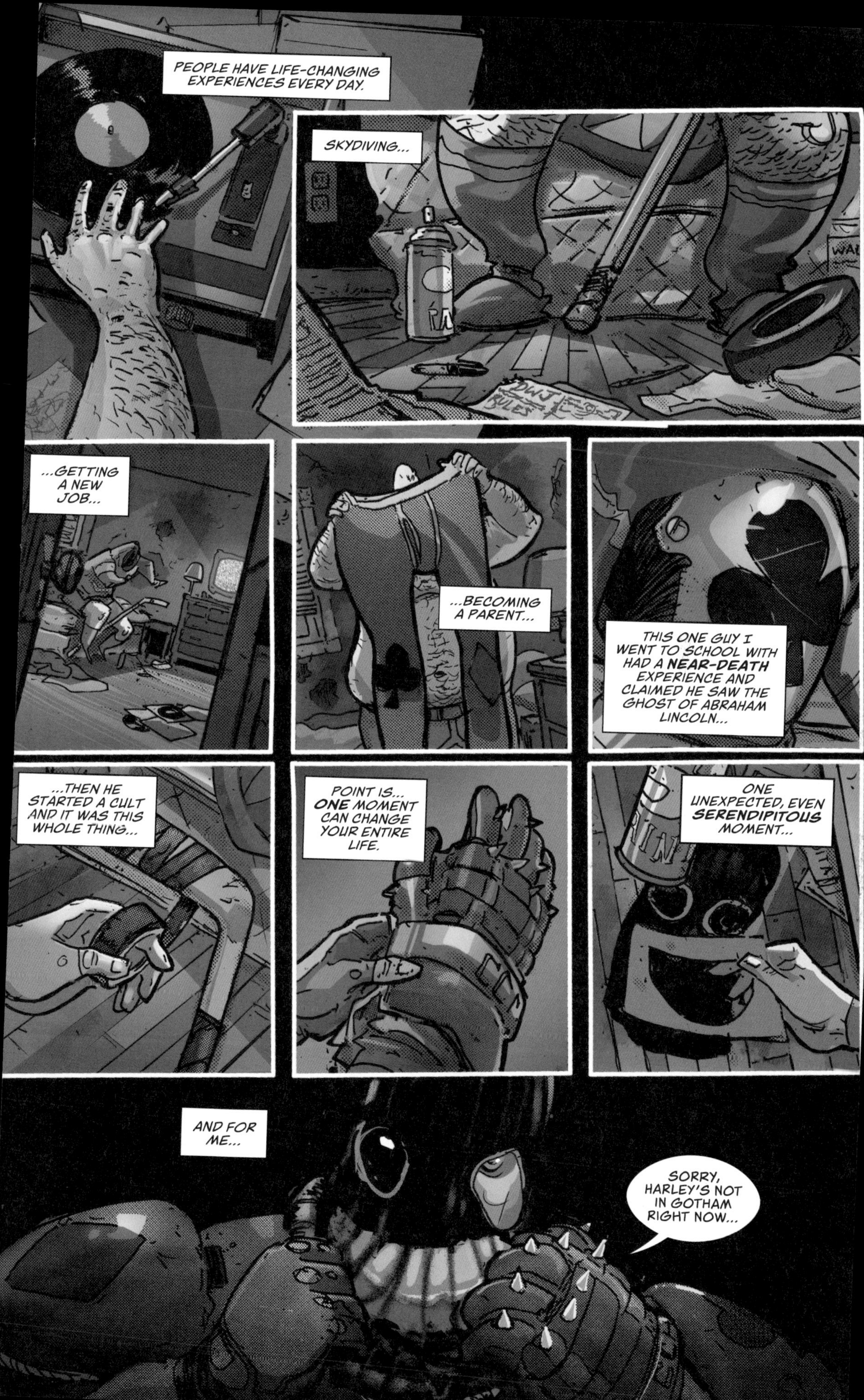
PEOPLE HAVE LIFE-CHANGING EXPERIENCES EVERY DAY.
SKYDIVING...
DWJ RULES
...GETTING A NEW JOB...
...BECOMING A PARENT...
THIS ONE GUY I WENT TO SCHOOL WITH HAD A NEAR-DEATH EXPERIENCE AND CLAIMED HE SAW THE GHOST OF ABRAHAM LINCOLN...
...THEN HE STARTED A CULT AND IT WAS THIS WHOLE THING...
POINT IS... ONE MOMENT CAN CHANGE YOUR ENTIRE LIFE.
ONE UNEXPECTED, EVEN SERENDIPITOUS MOMENT...
AND FOR ME...
SORRY, HARLEY'S NOT IN GOTHAM RIGHT NOW...

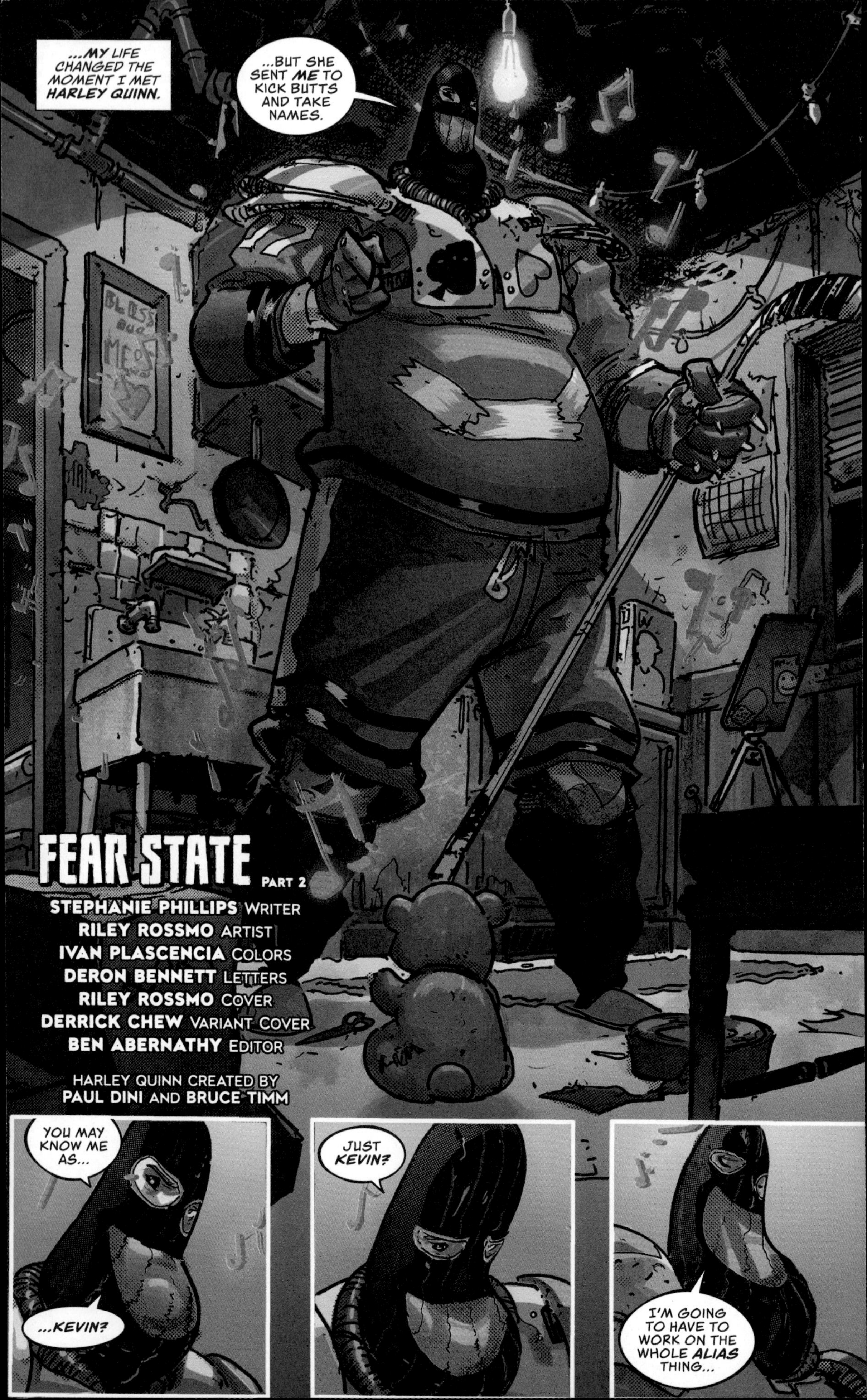
...MY LIFE CHANGED THE MOMENT I MET HARLEY QUINN.
...BUT SHE SENT ME TO KICK BUTTS AND TAKE NAMES.
FEAR STATE PART 2
STEPHANIE PHILLIPS WRITER
RILEY ROSSMO ARTIST
IVAN PLASCENCIA COLORS
DERON BENNETT LETTERS
RILEY ROSSMO COVER
DERRICK CHEW VARIANT COVER
BEN ABERNATHY EDITOR
HARLEY QUINN CREATED BY
PAUL DINI AND BRUCE TIMM
YOU MAY KNOW ME AS...
...KEVIN?
JUST KEVIN?
I'M GOING TO HAVE TO WORK ON THE WHOLE ALIAS THING...

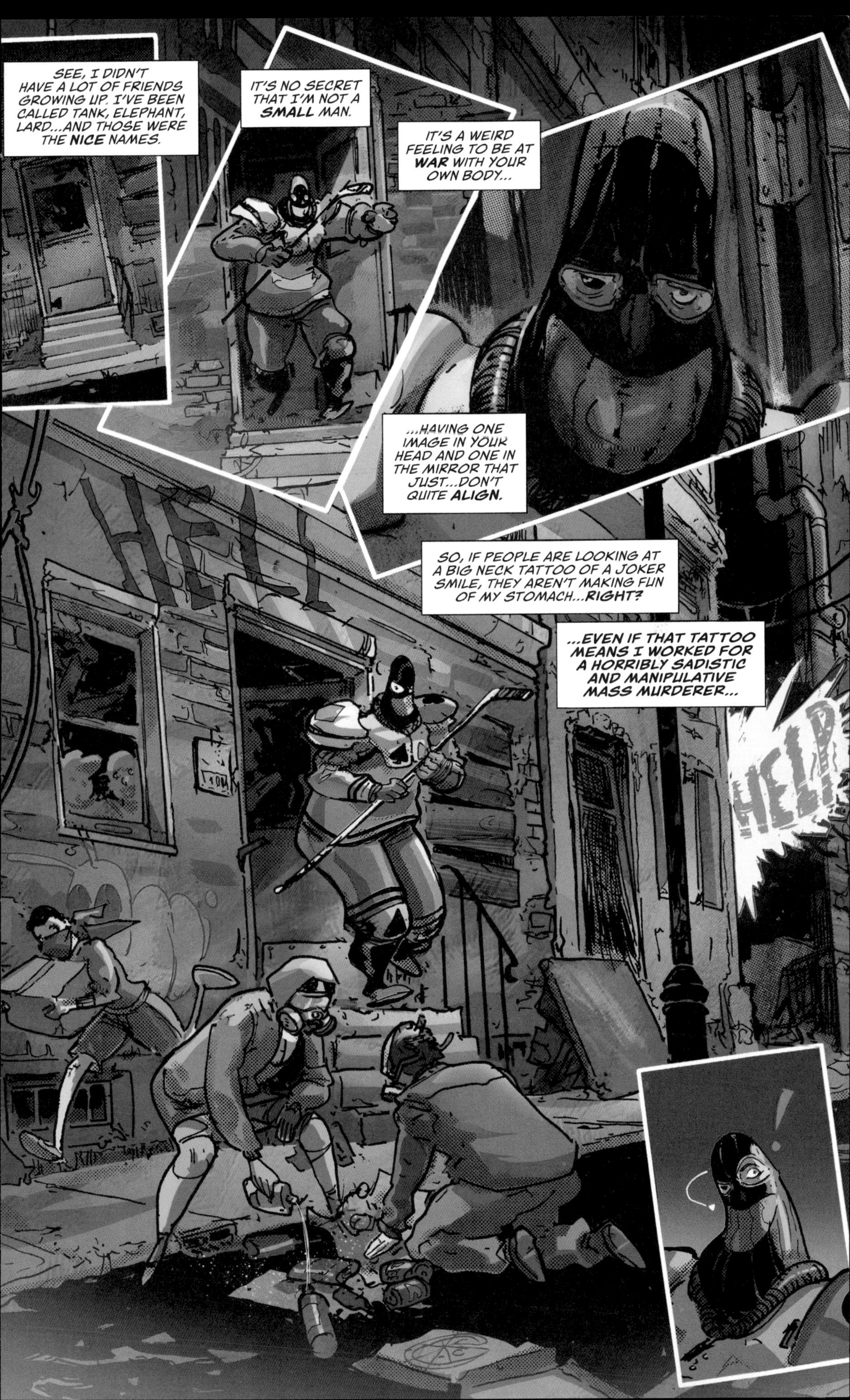
SEE, I DIDN'T HAVE A LOT OF FRIENDS GROWING UP. I'VE BEEN CALLED TANK, ELEPHANT, LARD...AND THOSE WERE THE NICE NAMES.
IT'S NO SECRET THAT I'M NOT A SMALL MAN.
IT'S A WEIRD FEELING TO BE AT WAR WITH YOUR OWN BODY...
...HAVING ONE IMAGE IN YOUR HEAD AND ONE IN THE MIRROR THAT JUST...DON'T QUITE ALIGN.
SO, IF PEOPLE ARE LOOKING AT A BIG NECK TATTOO OF A JOKER SMILE, THEY AREN'T MAKING FUN OF MY STOMACH...RIGHT?
...EVEN IF THAT TATTOO MEANS I WORKED FOR A HORRIBLY SADISTIC AND MANIPULATIVE MASS MURDERER...
HELP!
!

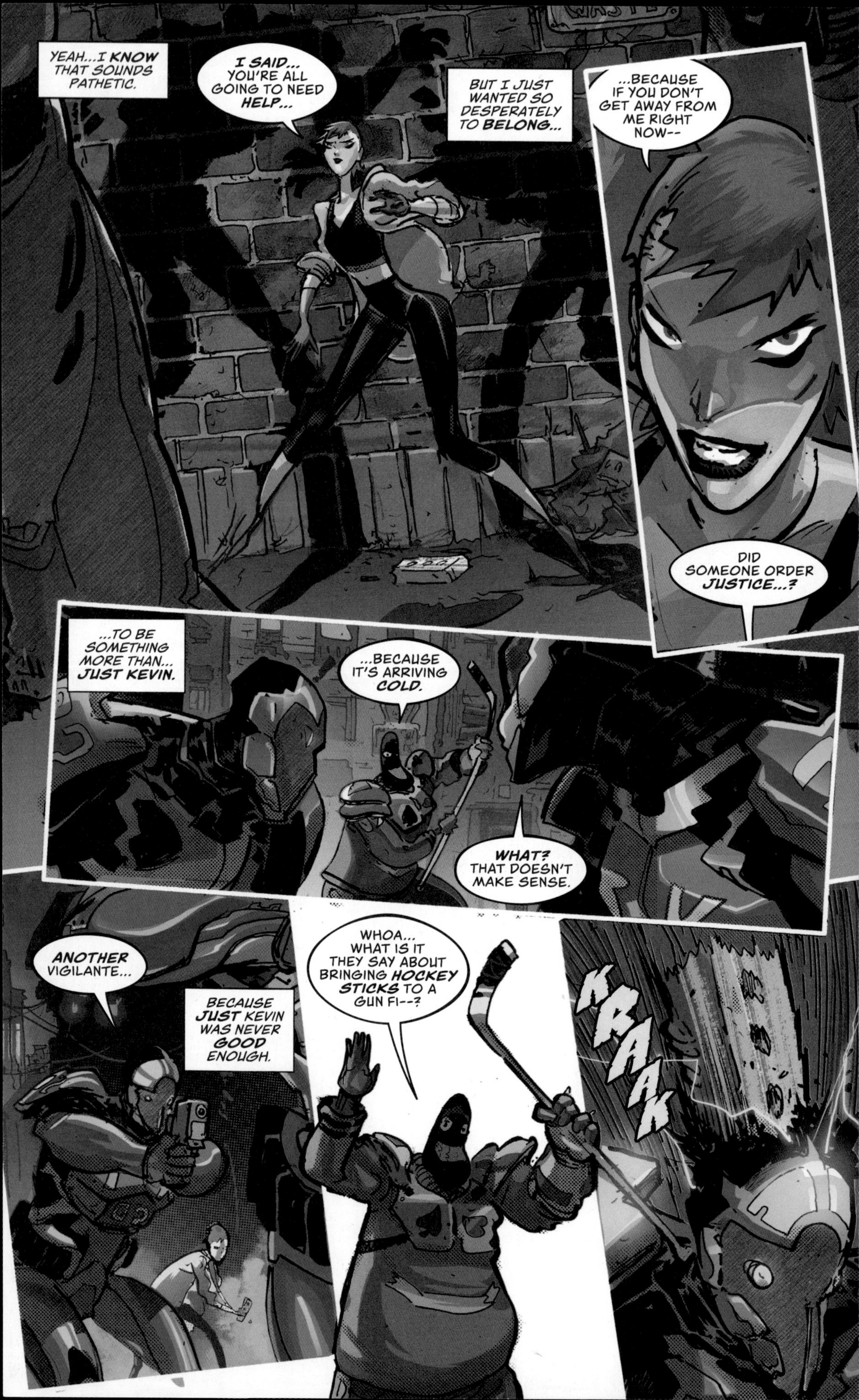
YEAH...I KNOW THAT SOUNDS PATHETIC.
I SAID... YOU'RE ALL GOING TO NEED HELP...
BUT I JUST WANTED SO DESPERATELY TO BELONG...
...BECAUSE IF YOU DON'T GET AWAY FROM ME RIGHT NOW--
DID SOMEONE ORDER JUSTICE...?
...TO BE SOMETHING MORE THAN... JUST KEVIN.
...BECAUSE IT'S ARRIVING COLD.
WHAT? THAT DOESN'T MAKE SENSE.
ANOTHER VIGILANTE...
BECAUSE JUST KEVIN WAS NEVER GOOD ENOUGH.
WHOA... WHAT IS IT THEY SAY ABOUT BRINGING HOCKEY STICKS TO A GUN FI--?
KRAAK

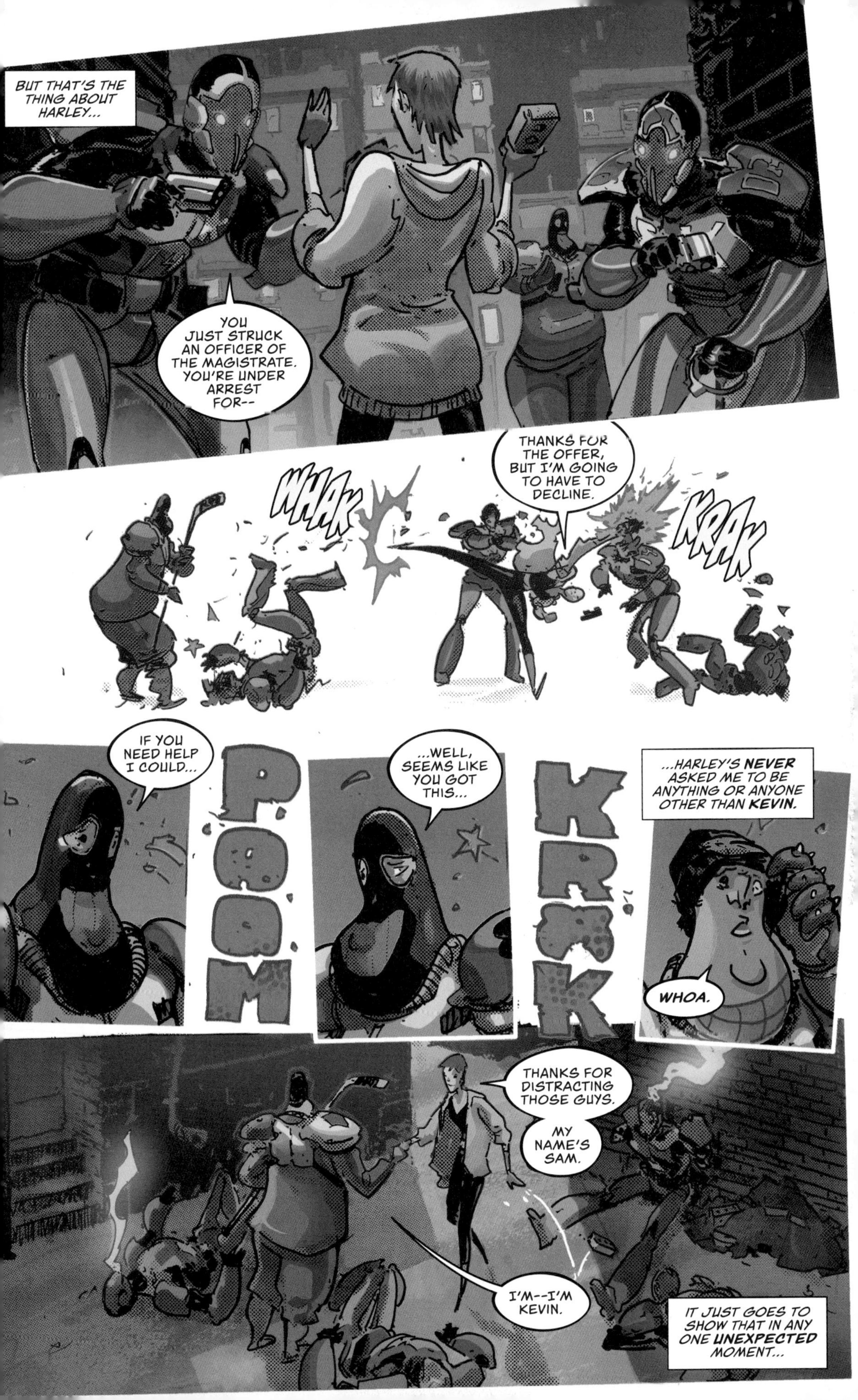
BUT THAT'S THE THING ABOUT HARLEY...
YOU JUST STRUCK AN OFFICER OF THE MAGISTRATE. YOU'RE UNDER ARREST FOR--
WHAK
THANKS FOR THE OFFER, BUT I'M GOING TO HAVE TO DECLINE.
KRAK
IF YOU NEED HELP I COULD...
POOM
...WELL, SEEMS LIKE YOU GOT THIS...
KRRK
...HARLEY'S NEVER ASKED ME TO BE ANYTHING OR ANYONE OTHER THAN KEVIN.
WHOA.
THANKS FOR DISTRACTING THOSE GUYS.
MY NAME'S SAM.
I'M--I'M KEVIN.
IT JUST GOES TO SHOW THAT IN ANY ONE UNEXPECTED MOMENT...

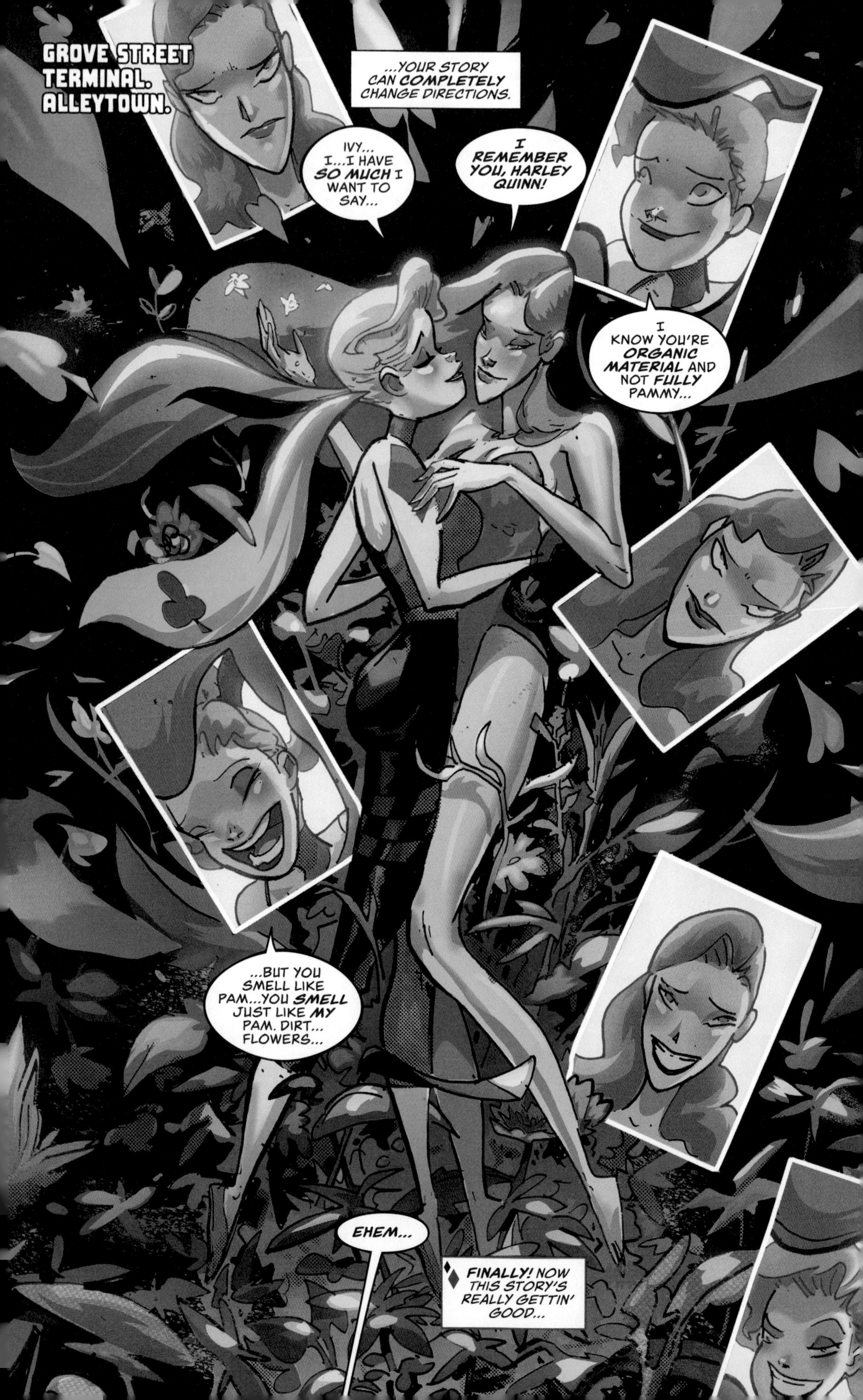
GROVE STREET TERMINAL. ALLEYTOWN.
...YOUR STORY CAN COMPLETELY CHANGE DIRECTIONS.
IVY... I...I HAVE SO MUCH I WANT TO SAY...
I REMEMBER YOU, HARLEY QUINN!
I KNOW YOU'RE ORGANIC MATERIAL AND NOT FULLY PAMMY...
...BUT YOU SMELL LIKE PAM...YOU SMELL JUST LIKE MY PAM. DIRT... FLOWERS...
EHEM...
FINALLY! NOW THIS STORY'S REALLY GETTIN' GOOD...

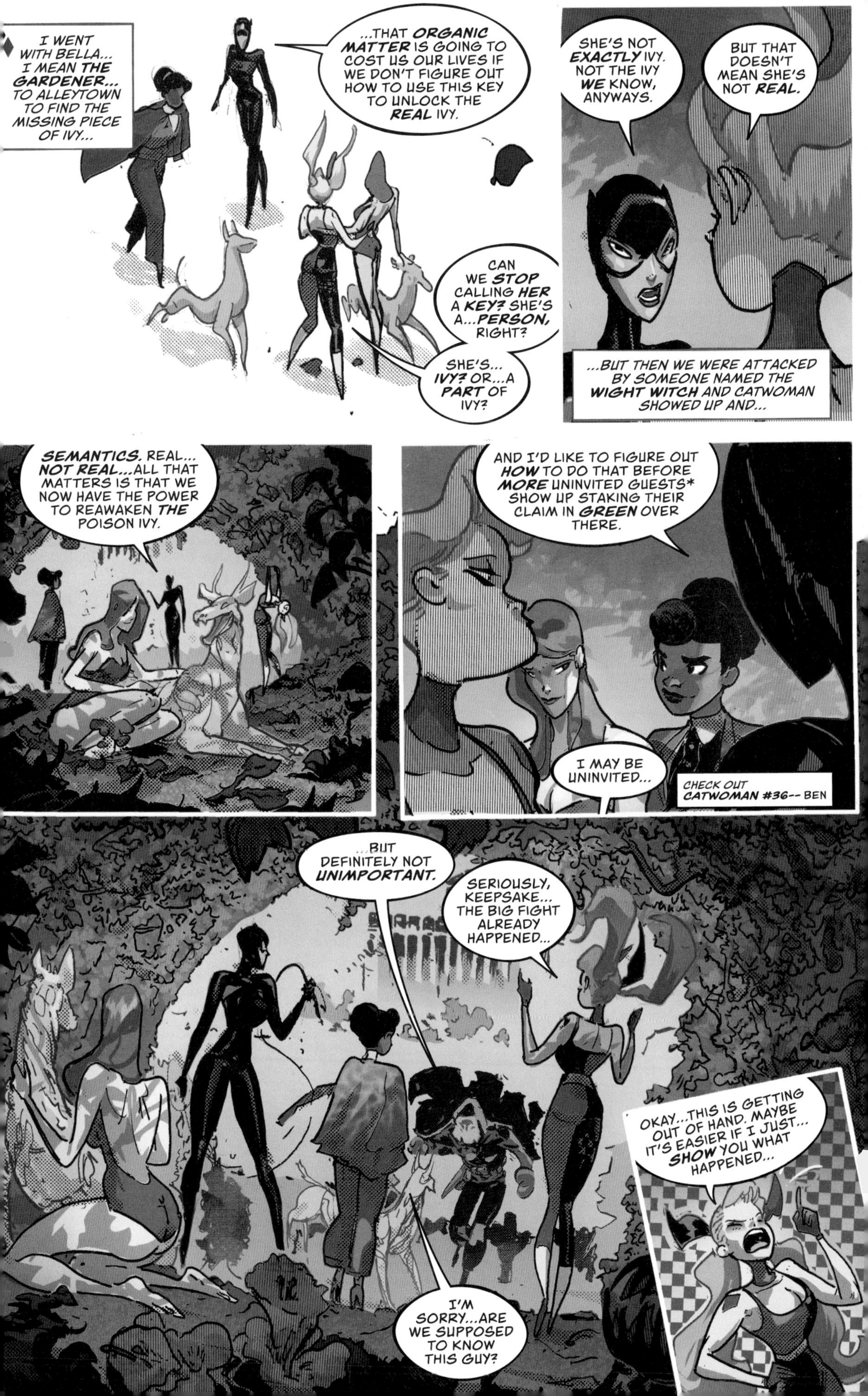
I WENT WITH BELLA... I MEAN THE GARDENER... TO ALLEYTOWN TO FIND THE MISSING PIECE OF IVY...
...THAT ORGANIC MATTER IS GOING TO COST US OUR LIVES IF WE DON'T FIGURE OUT HOW TO USE THIS KEY TO UNLOCK THE REAL IVY.
CAN WE STOP CALLING HER A KEY? SHE'S A...PERSON, RIGHT?
SHE'S... IVY? OR...A PART OF IVY?
SHE'S NOT EXACTLY IVY. NOT THE IVY WE KNOW, ANYWAYS.
BUT THAT DOESN'T MEAN SHE'S NOT REAL.
...BUT THEN WE WERE ATTACKED BY SOMEONE NAMED THE WIGHT WITCH AND CATWOMAN SHOWED UP AND...
SEMANTICS. REAL... NOT REAL...ALL THAT MATTERS IS THAT WE NOW HAVE THE POWER TO REAWAKEN THE POISON IVY.
AND I'D LIKE TO FIGURE OUT HOW TO DO THAT BEFORE MORE UNINVITED GUESTS* SHOW UP STAKING THEIR CLAIM IN GREEN OVER THERE.
I MAY BE UNINVITED...
CHECK OUT CATWOMAN #36-- BEN
...BUT DEFINITELY NOT UNIMPORTANT.
SERIOUSLY, KEEPSAKE... THE BIG FIGHT ALREADY HAPPENED...
I'M SORRY...ARE WE SUPPOSED TO KNOW THIS GUY?
OKAY...THIS IS GETTING OUT OF HAND. MAYBE IT'S EASIER IF I JUST... SHOW YOU WHAT HAPPENED...

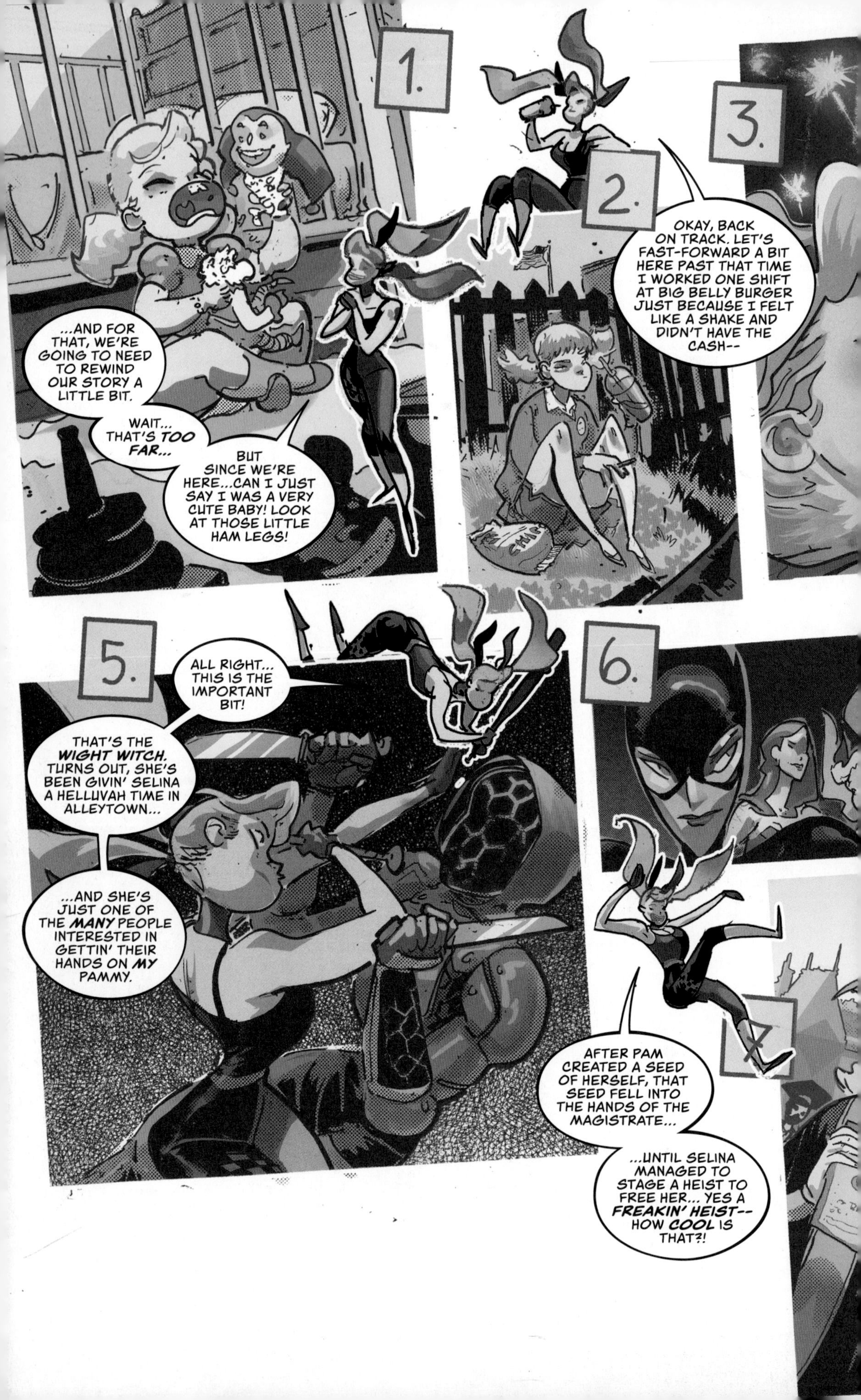
1.
...AND FOR THAT, WE'RE GOING TO NEED TO REWIND OUR STORY A LITTLE BIT.
WAIT... THAT'S TOO FAR...
BUT SINCE WE'RE HERE...CAN I JUST SAY I WAS A VERY CUTE BABY! LOOK AT THOSE LITTLE HAM LEGS!
2.
OKAY, BACK ON TRACK. LET'S FAST-FORWARD A BIT HERE PAST THAT TIME I WORKED ONE SHIFT AT BIG BELLY BURGER JUST BECAUSE I FELT LIKE A SHAKE AND DIDN'T HAVE THE CASH--
3.
5.
ALL RIGHT... THIS IS THE IMPORTANT BIT!
THAT'S THE WIGHT WITCH. TURNS OUT, SHE'S BEEN GIVIN' SELINA A HELLUVAH TIME IN ALLEYTOWN...
...AND SHE'S JUST ONE OF THE MANY PEOPLE INTERESTED IN GETTIN' THEIR HANDS ON MY PAMMY.
6.
AFTER PAM CREATED A SEED OF HERSELF, THAT SEED FELL INTO THE HANDS OF THE MAGISTRATE...
...UNTIL SELINA MANAGED TO STAGE A HEIST TO FREE HER... YES A FREAKIN' HEIST-- HOW COOL IS THAT?!

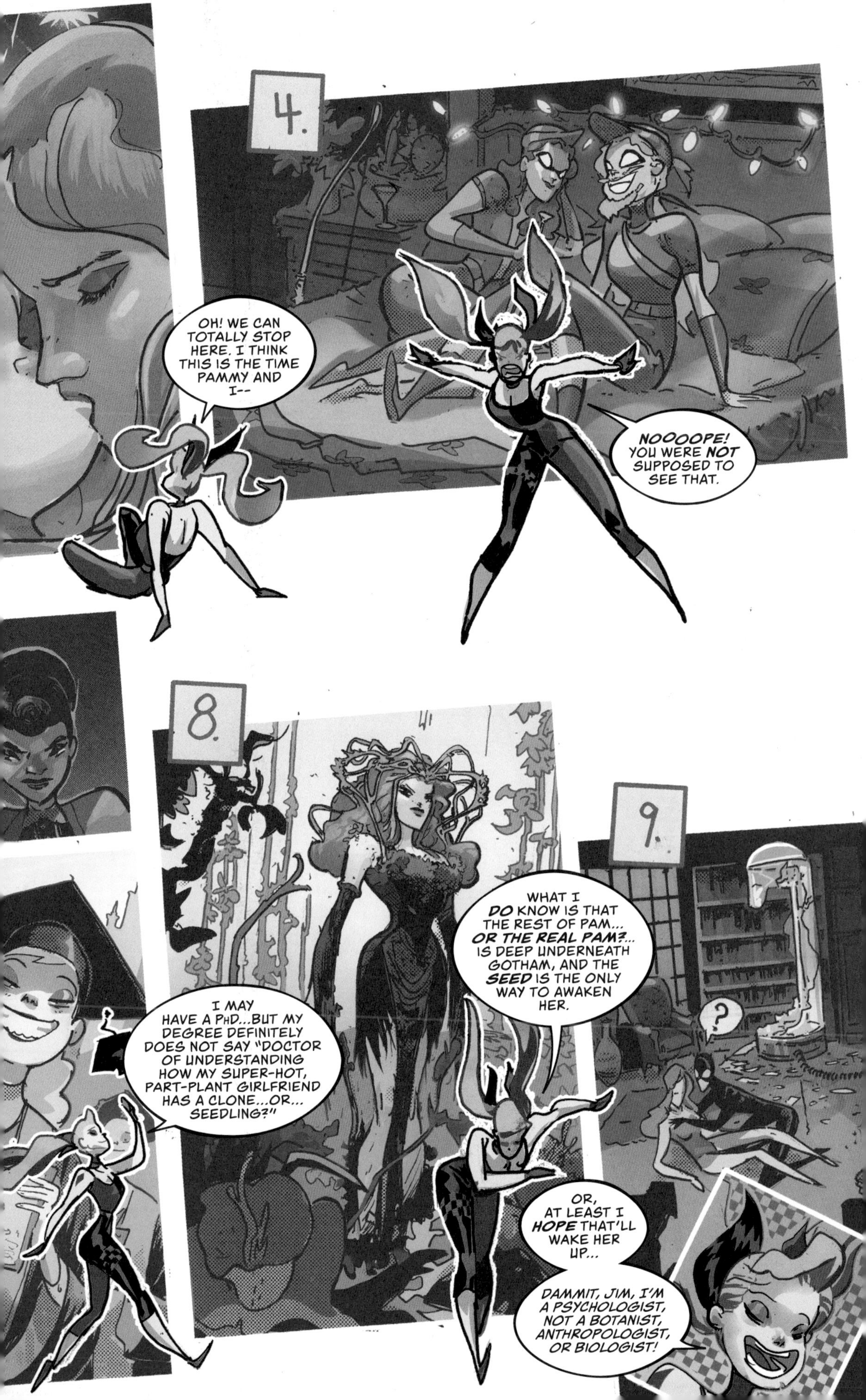
4.
OH! WE CAN TOTALLY STOP HERE. I THINK THIS IS THE TIME PAMMY AND I--
NOOOOPE! YOU WERE NOT SUPPOSED TO SEE THAT.
8.
9.
I MAY HAVE A PHD...BUT MY DEGREE DEFINITELY DOES NOT SAY "DOCTOR OF UNDERSTANDING HOW MY SUPER-HOT, PART-PLANT GIRLFRIEND HAS A CLONE...OR... SEEDLING?"
WHAT I DO KNOW IS THAT THE REST OF PAM... OR THE REAL PAM?... IS DEEP UNDERNEATH GOTHAM, AND THE SEED IS THE ONLY WAY TO AWAKEN HER.
?
OR, AT LEAST I HOPE THAT'LL WAKE HER UP...
DAMMIT, JIM, I'M A PSYCHOLOGIST, NOT A BOTANIST, ANTHROPOLOGIST, OR BIOLOGIST!

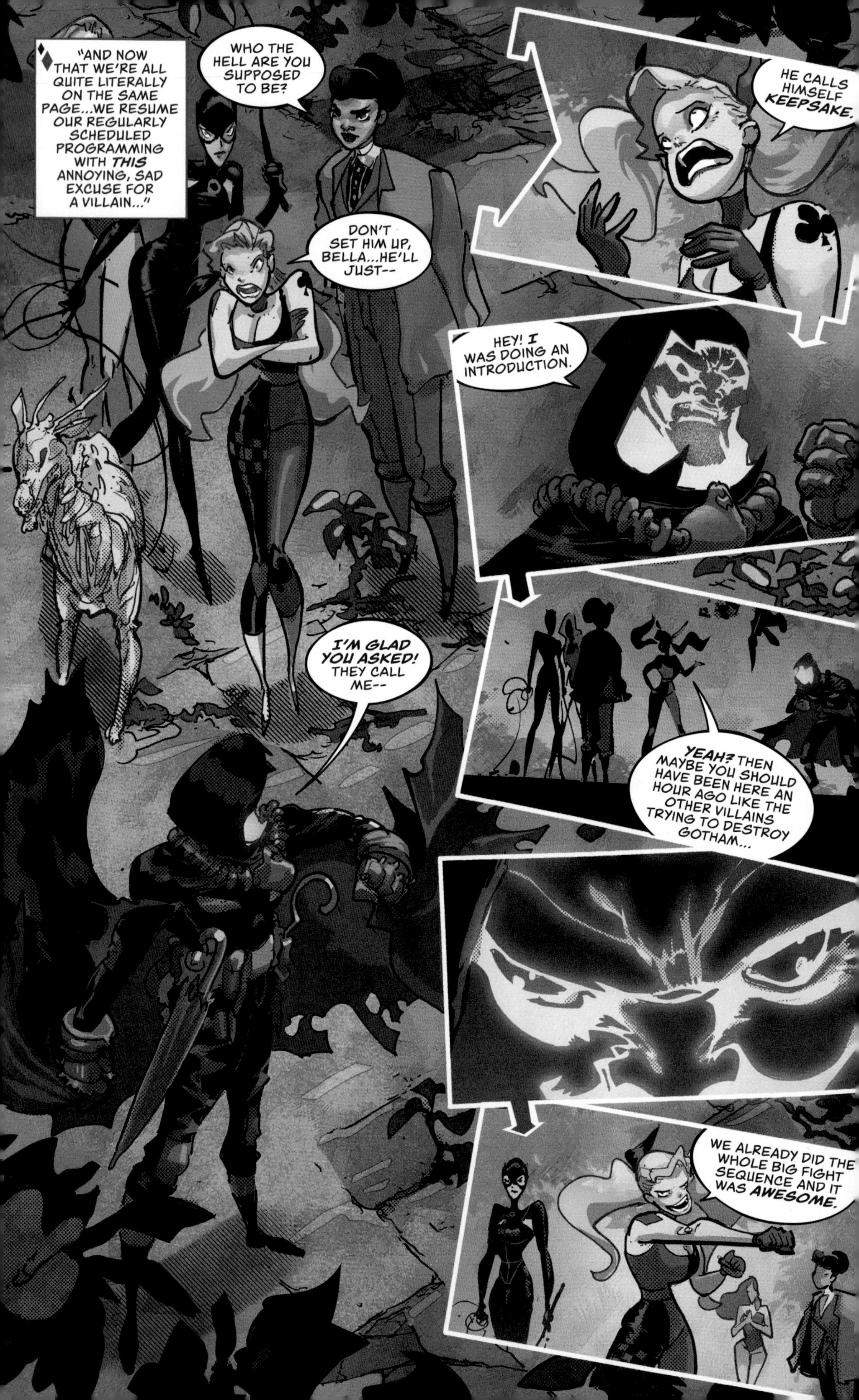
"AND NOW THAT WE'RE ALL QUITE LITERALLY ON THE SAME PAGE...WE RESUME OUR REGULARLY SCHEDULED PROGRAMMING WITH THIS ANNOYING, SAD EXCUSE FOR A VILLAIN..."
WHO THE HELL ARE YOU SUPPOSED TO BE?
DON'T SET HIM UP, BELLA...HE'LL JUST--
I'M GLAD YOU ASKED! THEY CALL ME--
HE CALLS HIMSELF KEEPSAKE.
HEY! I WAS DOING AN INTRODUCTION.
YEAH? THEN MAYBE YOU SHOULD HAVE BEEN HERE AN HOUR AGO LIKE THE OTHER VILLAINS TRYING TO DESTROY GOTHAM...
WE ALREADY DID THE WHOLE BIG FIGHT SEQUENCE AND IT WAS AWESOME.

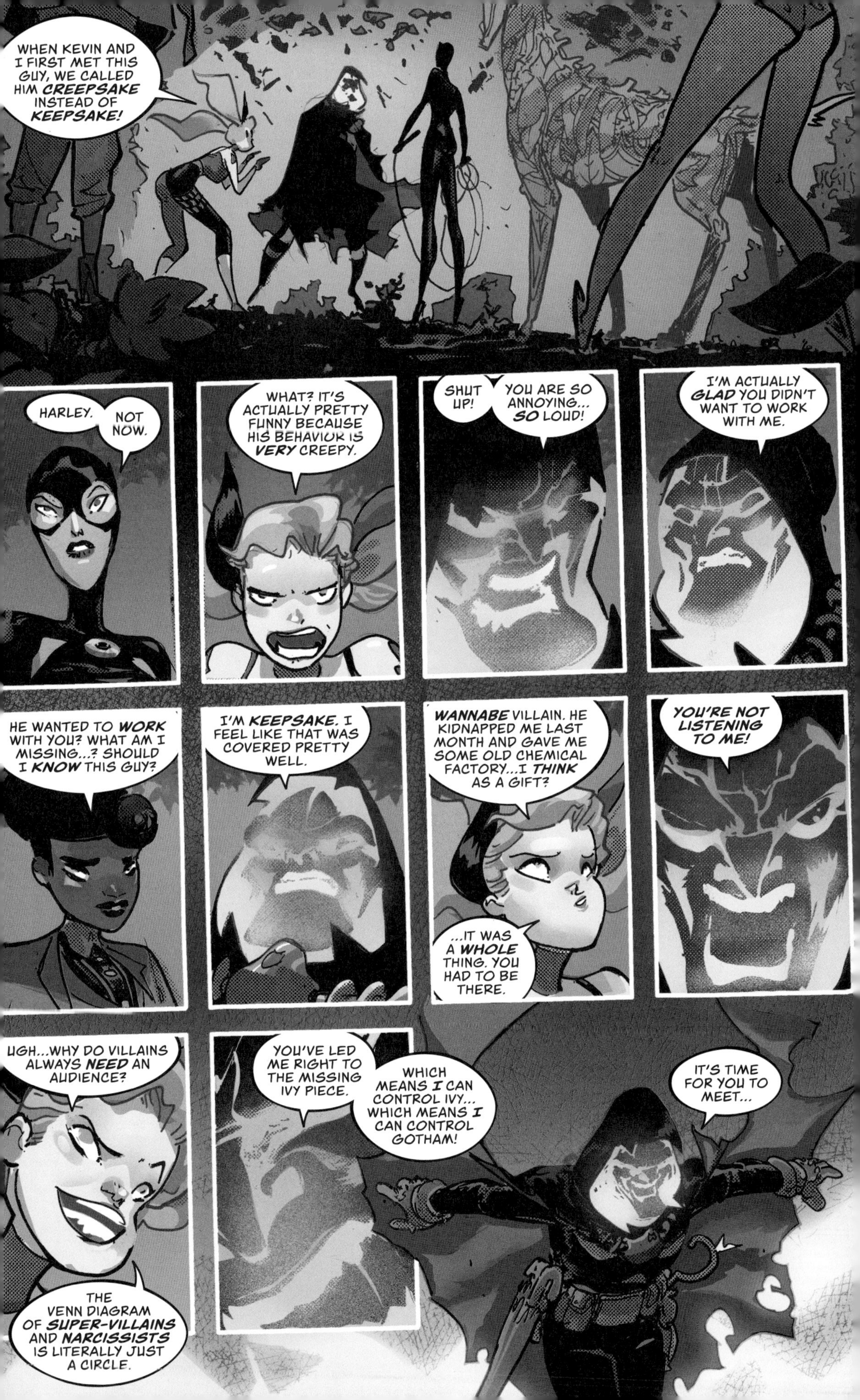
WHEN KEVIN AND I FIRST MET THIS GUY, WE CALLED HIM CREEPSAKE INSTEAD OF KEEPSAKE!
HARLEY.
NOT NOW.
WHAT? IT'S ACTUALLY PRETTY FUNNY BECAUSE HIS BEHAVIOR IS VERY CREEPY.
SHUT UP!
YOU ARE SO ANNOYING... SO LOUD!
I'M ACTUALLY GLAD YOU DIDN'T WANT TO WORK WITH ME.
HE WANTED TO WORK WITH YOU? WHAT AM I MISSING...? SHOULD I KNOW THIS GUY?
I'M KEEPSAKE. I FEEL LIKE THAT WAS COVERED PRETTY WELL.
WANNABE VILLAIN. HE KIDNAPPED ME LAST MONTH AND GAVE ME SOME OLD CHEMICAL FACTORY...I THINK AS A GIFT?
...IT WAS A WHOLE THING. YOU HAD TO BE THERE.
YOU'RE NOT LISTENING TO ME!
UGH...WHY DO VILLAINS ALWAYS NEED AN AUDIENCE?
THE VENN DIAGRAM OF SUPER-VILLAINS AND NARCISSISTS IS LITERALLY JUST A CIRCLE.
YOU'VE LED ME RIGHT TO THE MISSING IVY PIECE.
WHICH MEANS I CAN CONTROL IVY... WHICH MEANS I CAN CONTROL GOTHAM!
IT'S TIME FOR YOU TO MEET...

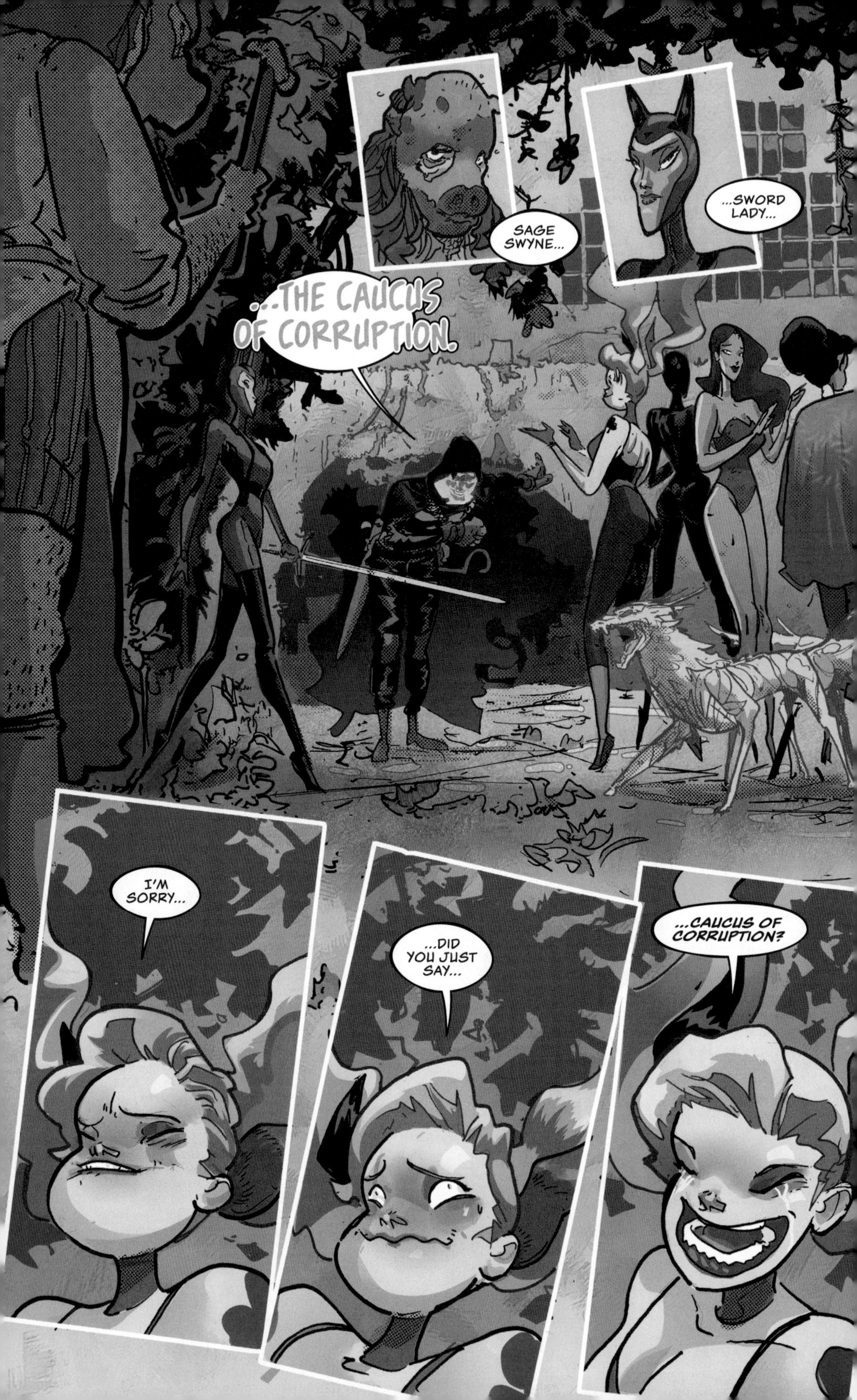

SAGE SWYNE...
...SWORD LADY...
...THE CAUCUS OF CORRUPTION.
I'M SORRY...
...DID YOU JUST SAY...
...CAUCUS OF CORRUPTION?

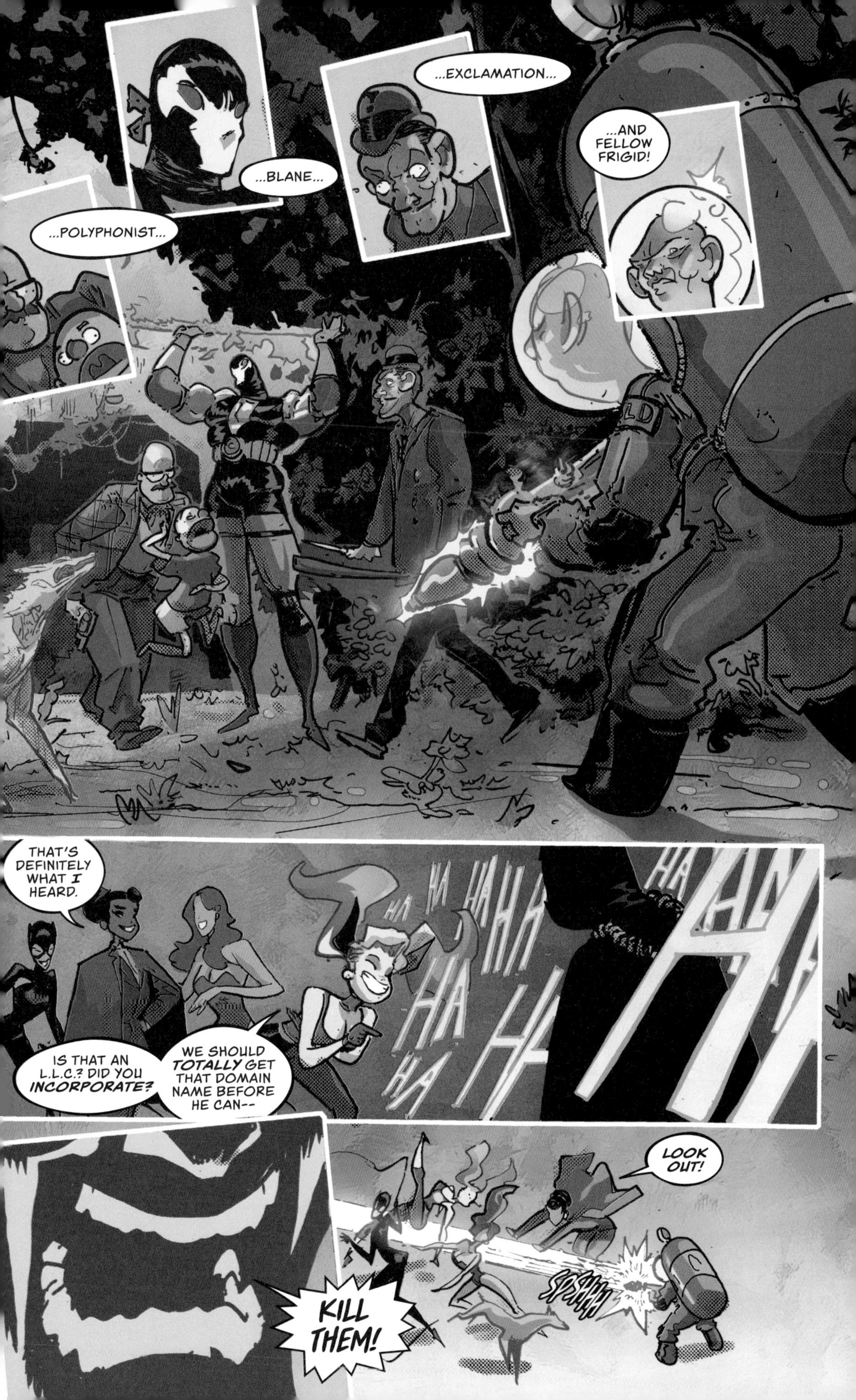
...POLYPHONIST...
...BLANE...
...EXCLAMATION...
...AND FELLOW FRIGID!
THAT'S DEFINITELY WHAT I HEARD.
IS THAT AN L.L.C.? DID YOU INCORPORATE?
WE SHOULD TOTALLY GET THAT DOMAIN NAME BEFORE HE CAN--
HA HA HA HA HA HA HA HA HA HA HA
LOOK OUT!
SPSHHH
KILL THEM!

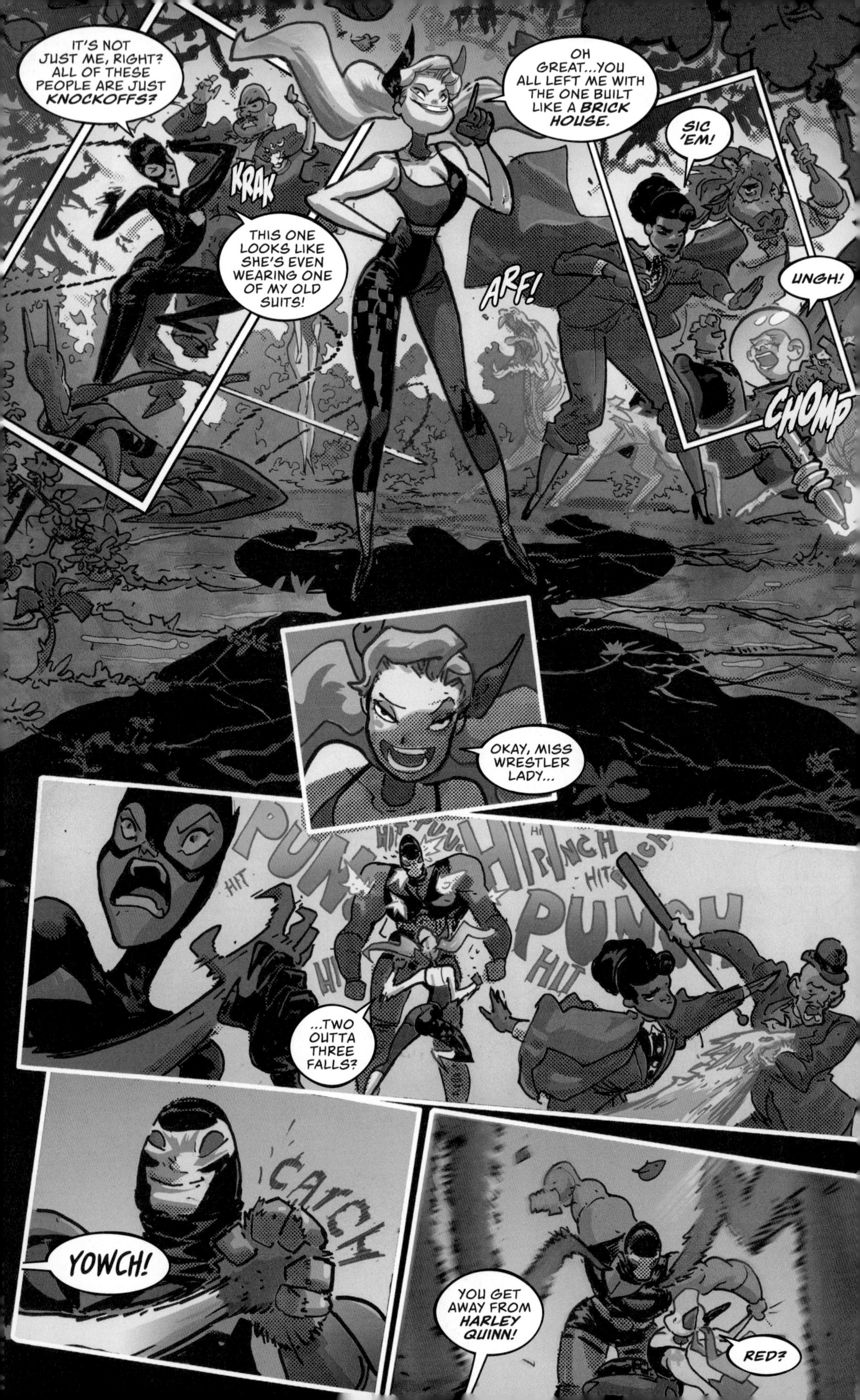
IT'S NOT JUST ME, RIGHT? ALL OF THESE PEOPLE ARE JUST KNOCKOFFS?
KRAK
THIS ONE LOOKS LIKE SHE'S EVEN WEARING ONE OF MY OLD SUITS!
OH GREAT...YOU ALL LEFT ME WITH THE ONE BUILT LIKE A BRICK HOUSE.
ARF!
SIC 'EM!
UNGH!
CHOMP
OKAY, MISS WRESTLER LADY...
PUNCH
HIT
...TWO OUTTA THREE FALLS?
YOWCH!
CATCH
YOU GET AWAY FROM HARLEY QUINN!
RED?

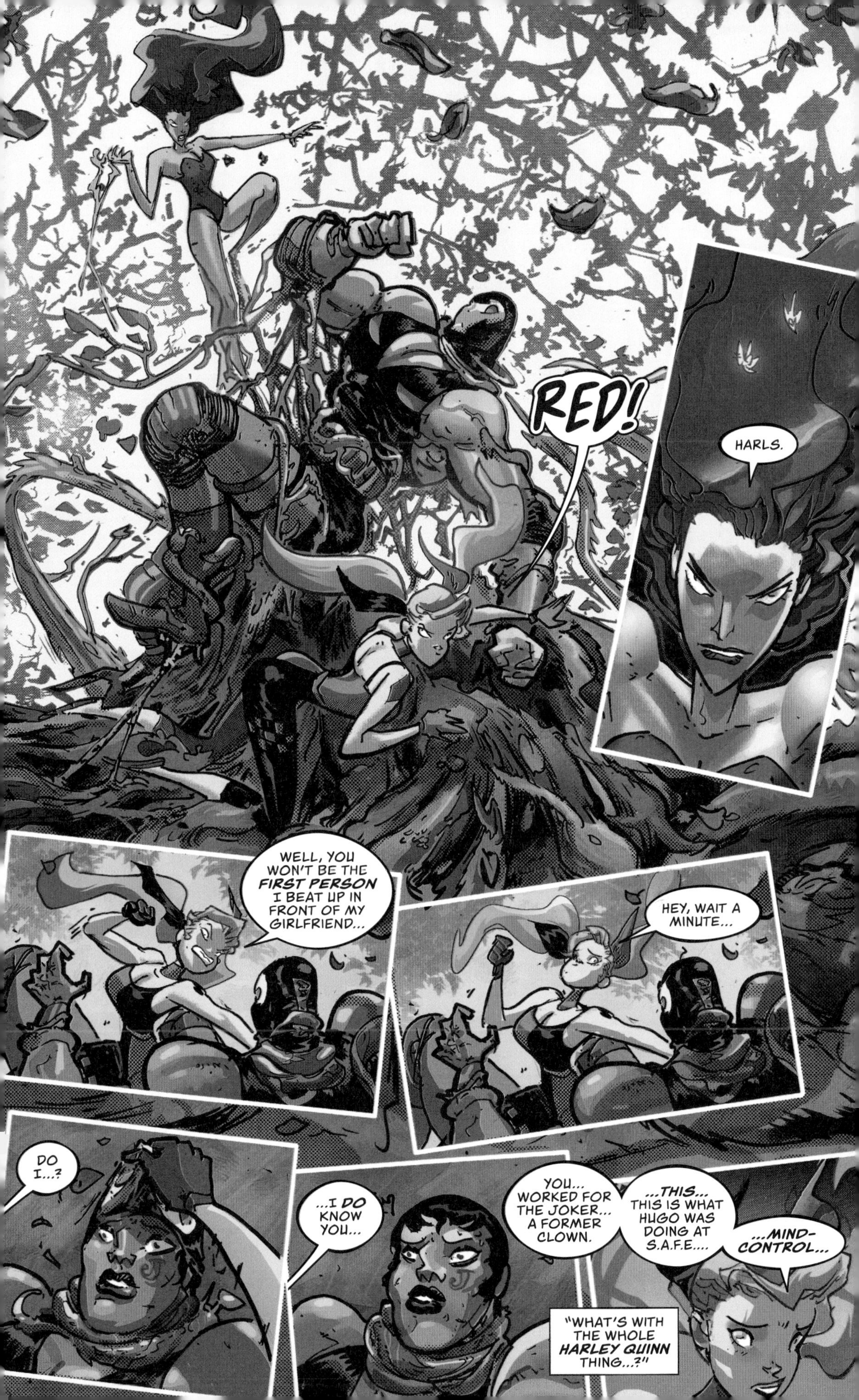
RED!
HARLS.
WELL, YOU WON'T BE THE **FIRST PERSON** I BEAT UP IN FRONT OF MY GIRLFRIEND...
HEY, WAIT A MINUTE...
DO I...?
...I **DO** KNOW YOU...
YOU... WORKED FOR THE JOKER... A FORMER CLOWN.
...THIS... THIS IS WHAT HUGO WAS DOING AT S.A.F.E....
...MIND-CONTROL...
"WHAT'S WITH THE WHOLE **HARLEY QUINN** THING...?"

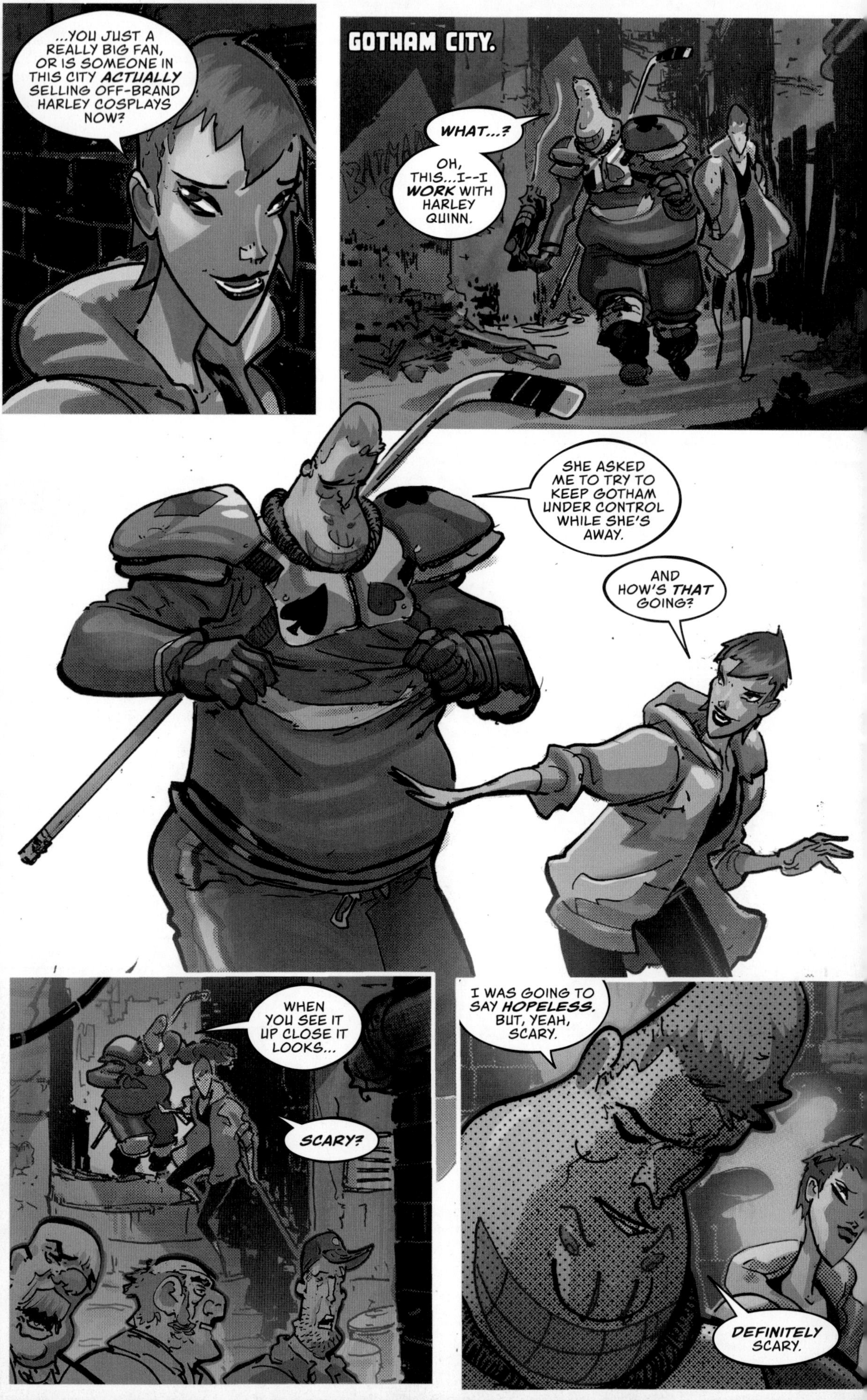
...YOU JUST A REALLY BIG FAN, OR IS SOMEONE IN THIS CITY ACTUALLY SELLING OFF-BRAND HARLEY COSPLAYS NOW?
GOTHAM CITY.
WHAT...?
OH, THIS...I--I WORK WITH HARLEY QUINN.
SHE ASKED ME TO TRY TO KEEP GOTHAM UNDER CONTROL WHILE SHE'S AWAY.
AND HOW'S THAT GOING?
WHEN YOU SEE IT UP CLOSE IT LOOKS...
SCARY?
I WAS GOING TO SAY HOPELESS. BUT, YEAH, SCARY.
DEFINITELY SCARY.

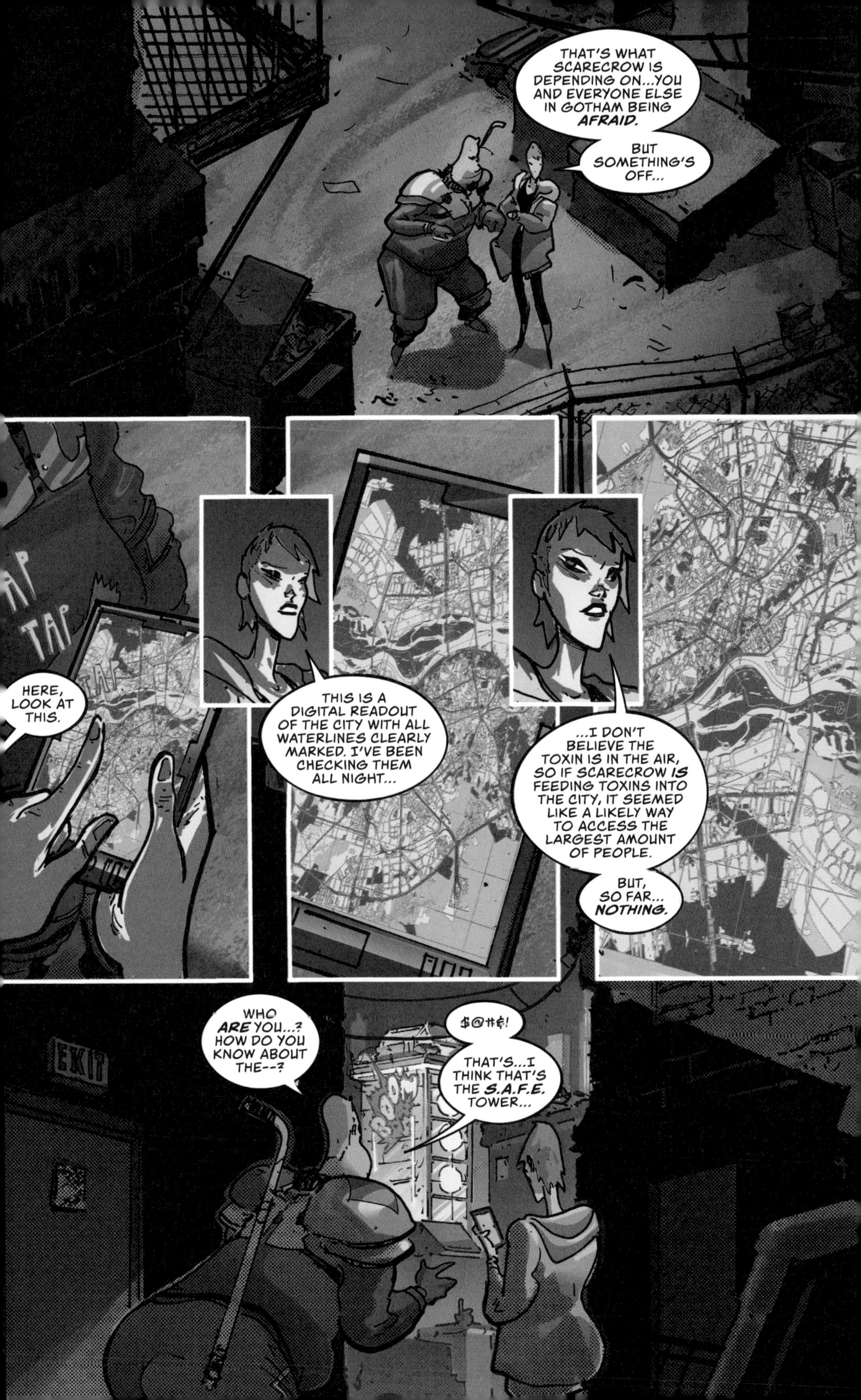
THAT'S WHAT SCARECROW IS DEPENDING ON...YOU AND EVERYONE ELSE IN GOTHAM BEING **AFRAID.**
BUT SOMETHING'S OFF...
TAP
HERE, LOOK AT THIS.
THIS IS A DIGITAL READOUT OF THE CITY WITH ALL WATERLINES CLEARLY MARKED. I'VE BEEN CHECKING THEM ALL NIGHT...
...I DON'T BELIEVE THE TOXIN IS IN THE AIR, SO IF SCARECROW ***IS*** FEEDING TOXINS INTO THE CITY, IT SEEMED LIKE A LIKELY WAY TO ACCESS THE LARGEST AMOUNT OF PEOPLE.
BUT, SO FAR... ***NOTHING.***
EXIT
WHO ***ARE*** YOU...? HOW DO YOU KNOW ABOUT THE--?
$@#¢!
THAT'S...I THINK THAT'S THE ***S.A.F.E.*** TOWER...

S.A.F.E. HEADQUARTERS.

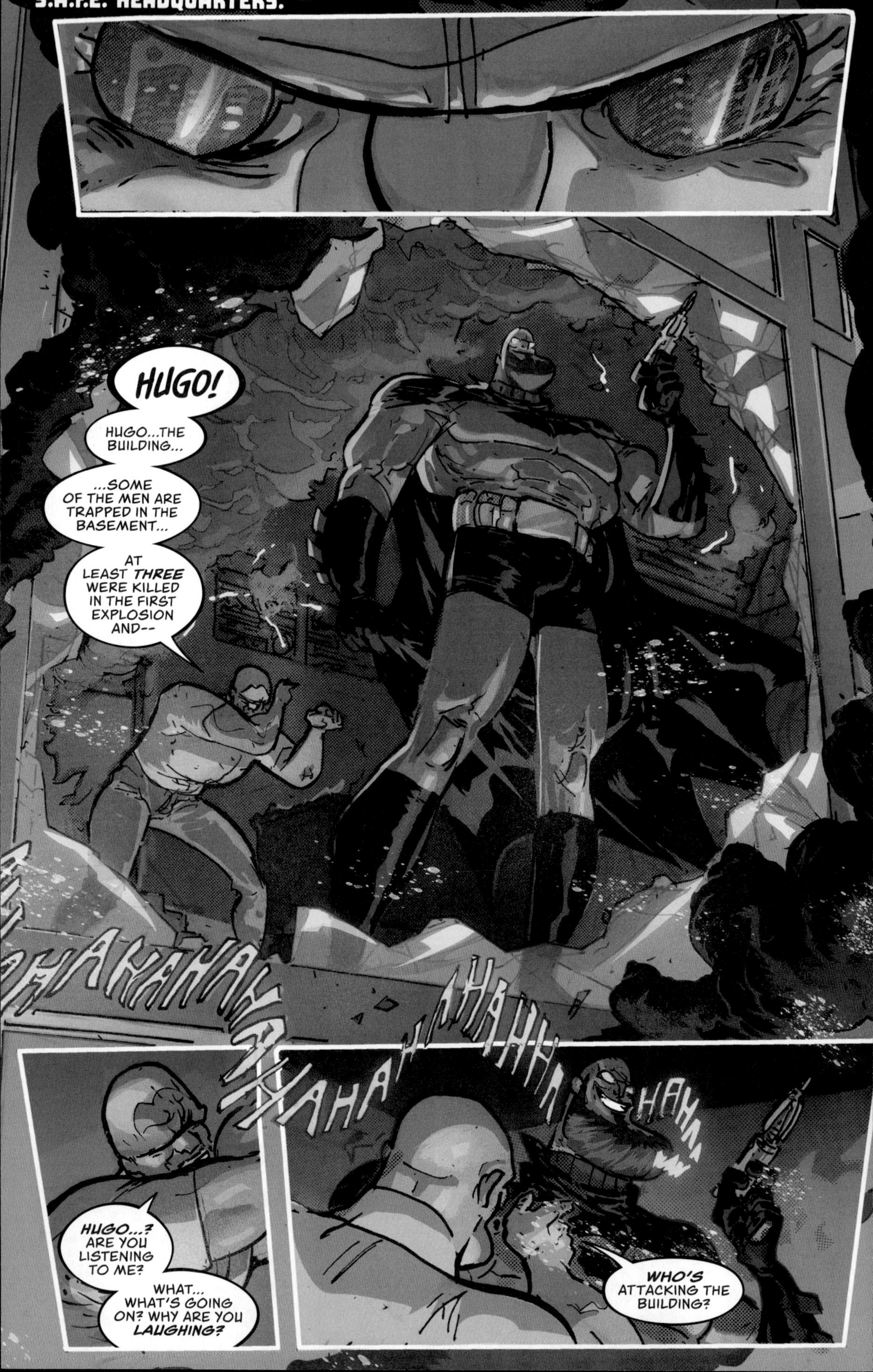
HUGO!
HUGO...THE BUILDING...
...SOME OF THE MEN ARE TRAPPED IN THE BASEMENT...
AT LEAST *THREE* WERE KILLED IN THE FIRST EXPLOSION AND--
HAHAHAHAHAHAHAHAHAHAHAHAHAHA
HUGO...? ARE YOU LISTENING TO ME?
WHAT... WHAT'S GOING ON? WHY ARE YOU *LAUGHING?*
HAHAHA
WHO'S ATTACKING THE BUILDING?

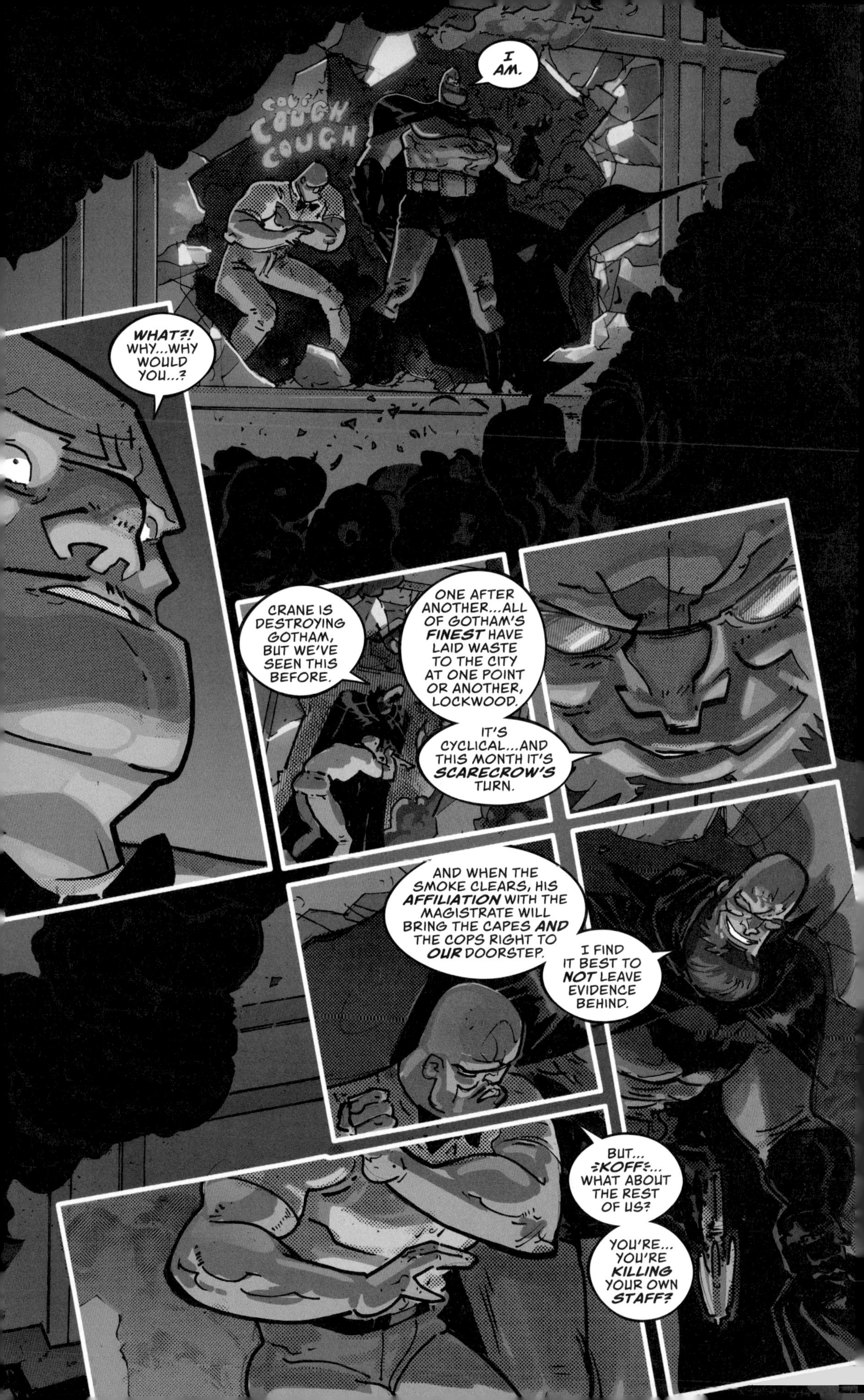
COUGH
COUGH
COUGH
I AM.
WHAT?! WHY...WHY WOULD YOU...?
CRANE IS DESTROYING GOTHAM, BUT WE'VE SEEN THIS BEFORE.
ONE AFTER ANOTHER...ALL OF GOTHAM'S FINEST HAVE LAID WASTE TO THE CITY AT ONE POINT OR ANOTHER, LOCKWOOD.
IT'S CYCLICAL...AND THIS MONTH IT'S SCARECROW'S TURN.
AND WHEN THE SMOKE CLEARS, HIS AFFILIATION WITH THE MAGISTRATE WILL BRING THE CAPES AND THE COPS RIGHT TO OUR DOORSTEP.
I FIND IT BEST TO NOT LEAVE EVIDENCE BEHIND.
BUT... KOFF... WHAT ABOUT THE REST OF US?
YOU'RE... YOU'RE KILLING YOUR OWN STAFF?

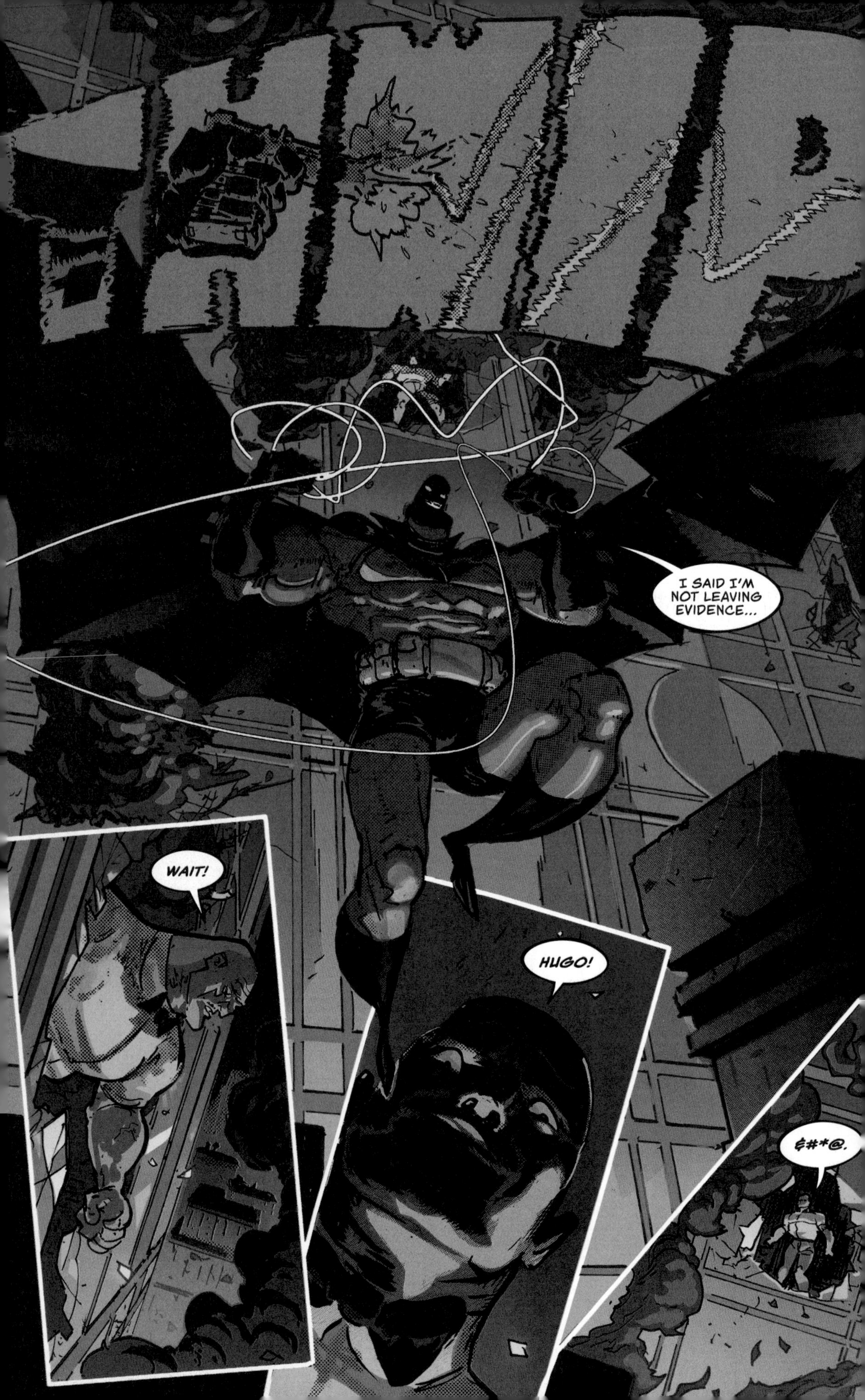
I SAID I'M NOT LEAVING EVIDENCE...
WAIT!
HUGO!
&#*@.

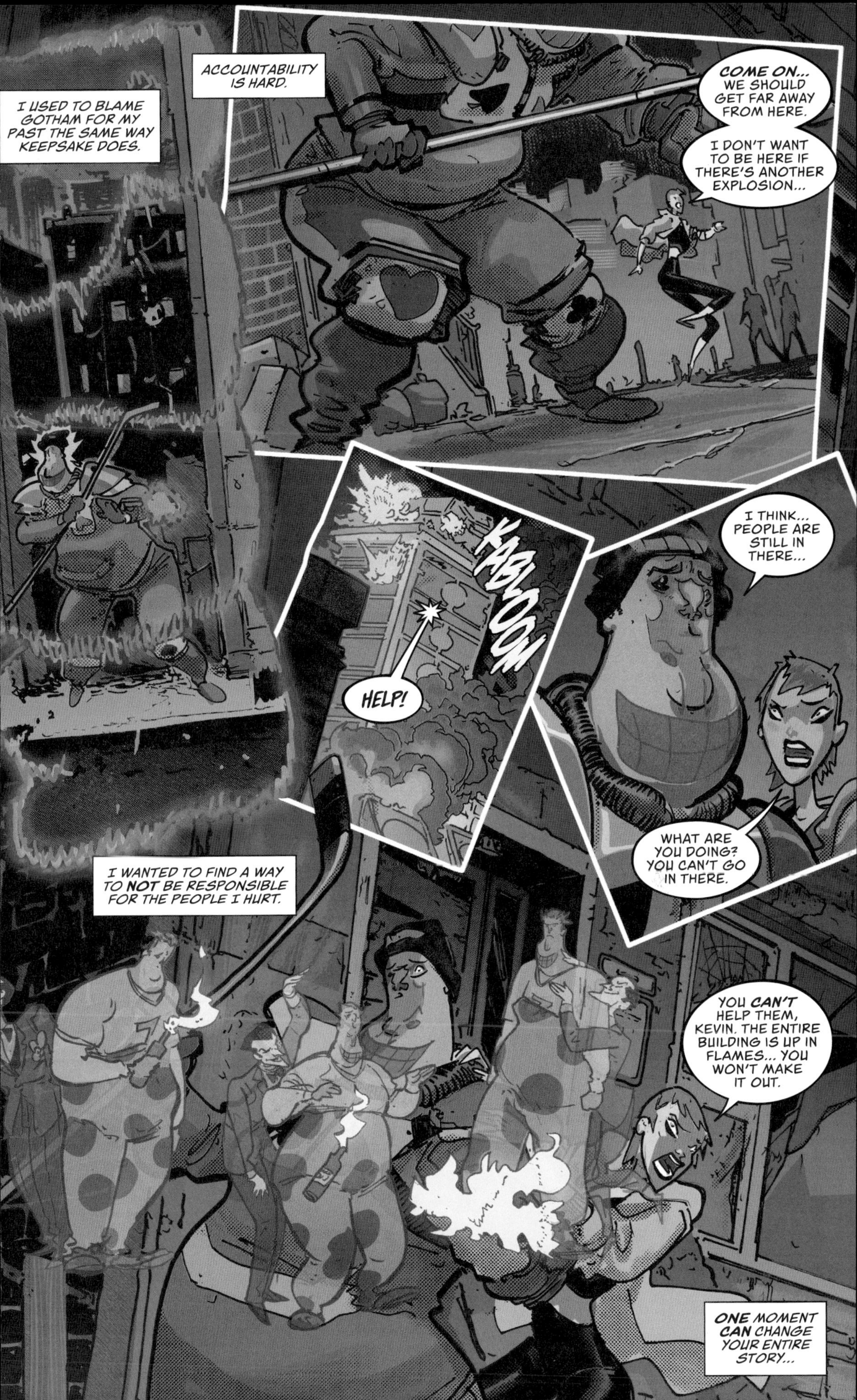
I USED TO BLAME GOTHAM FOR MY PAST THE SAME WAY KEEPSAKE DOES.
ACCOUNTABILITY IS HARD.
COME ON... WE SHOULD GET FAR AWAY FROM HERE.
I DON'T WANT TO BE HERE IF THERE'S ANOTHER EXPLOSION...
KABLOOOM
HELP!
I THINK... PEOPLE ARE STILL IN THERE...
WHAT ARE YOU DOING? YOU CAN'T GO IN THERE.
I WANTED TO FIND A WAY TO NOT BE RESPONSIBLE FOR THE PEOPLE I HURT.
YOU CAN'T HELP THEM, KEVIN. THE ENTIRE BUILDING IS UP IN FLAMES... YOU WON'T MAKE IT OUT.
ONE MOMENT CAN CHANGE YOUR ENTIRE STORY...

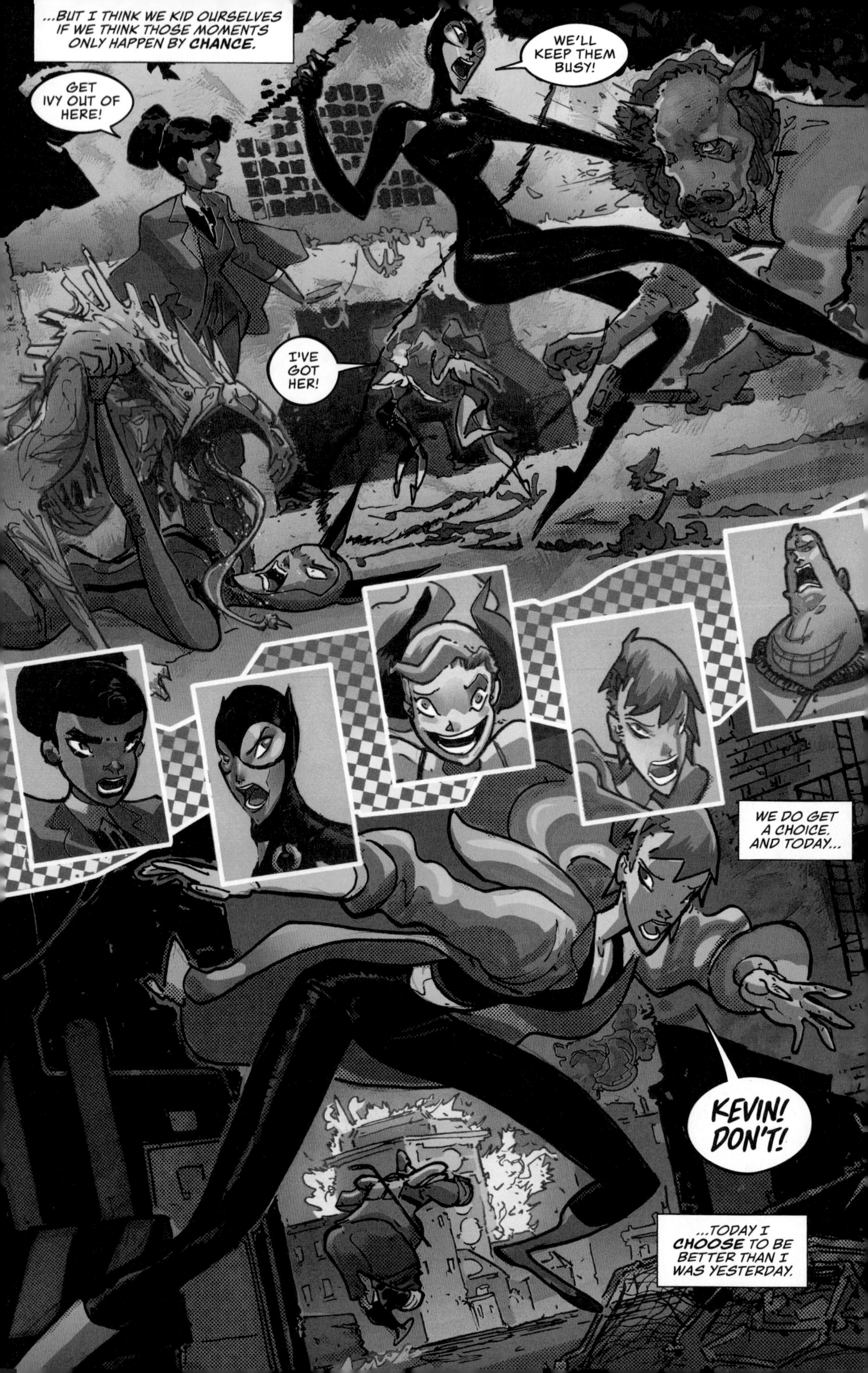
...BUT I THINK WE KID OURSELVES IF WE THINK THOSE MOMENTS ONLY HAPPEN BY CHANCE.
WE'LL KEEP THEM BUSY!
GET IVY OUT OF HERE!
I'VE GOT HER!
WE DO GET A CHOICE. AND TODAY...
KEVIN! DON'T!
...TODAY I CHOOSE TO BE BETTER THAN I WAS YESTERDAY.

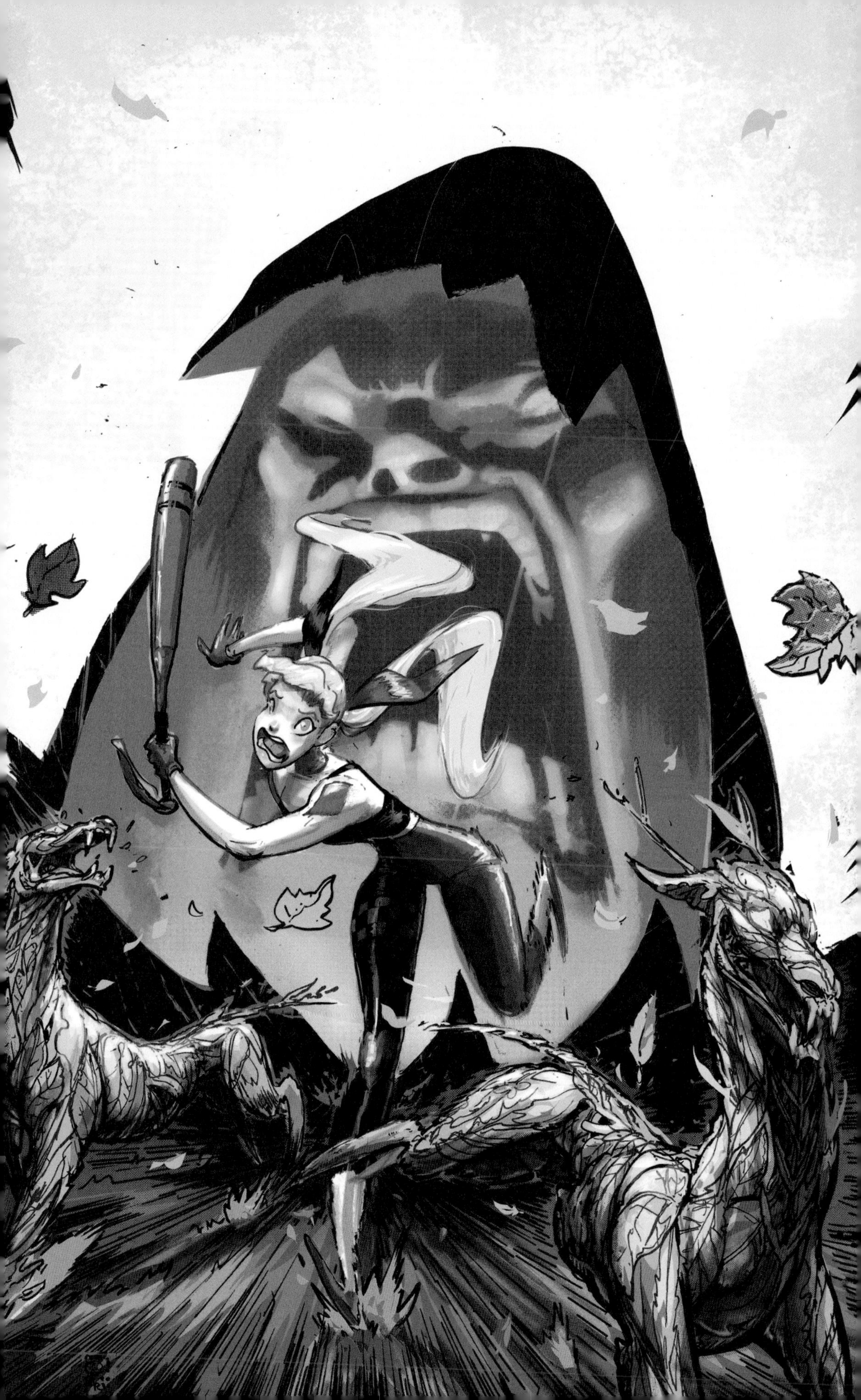

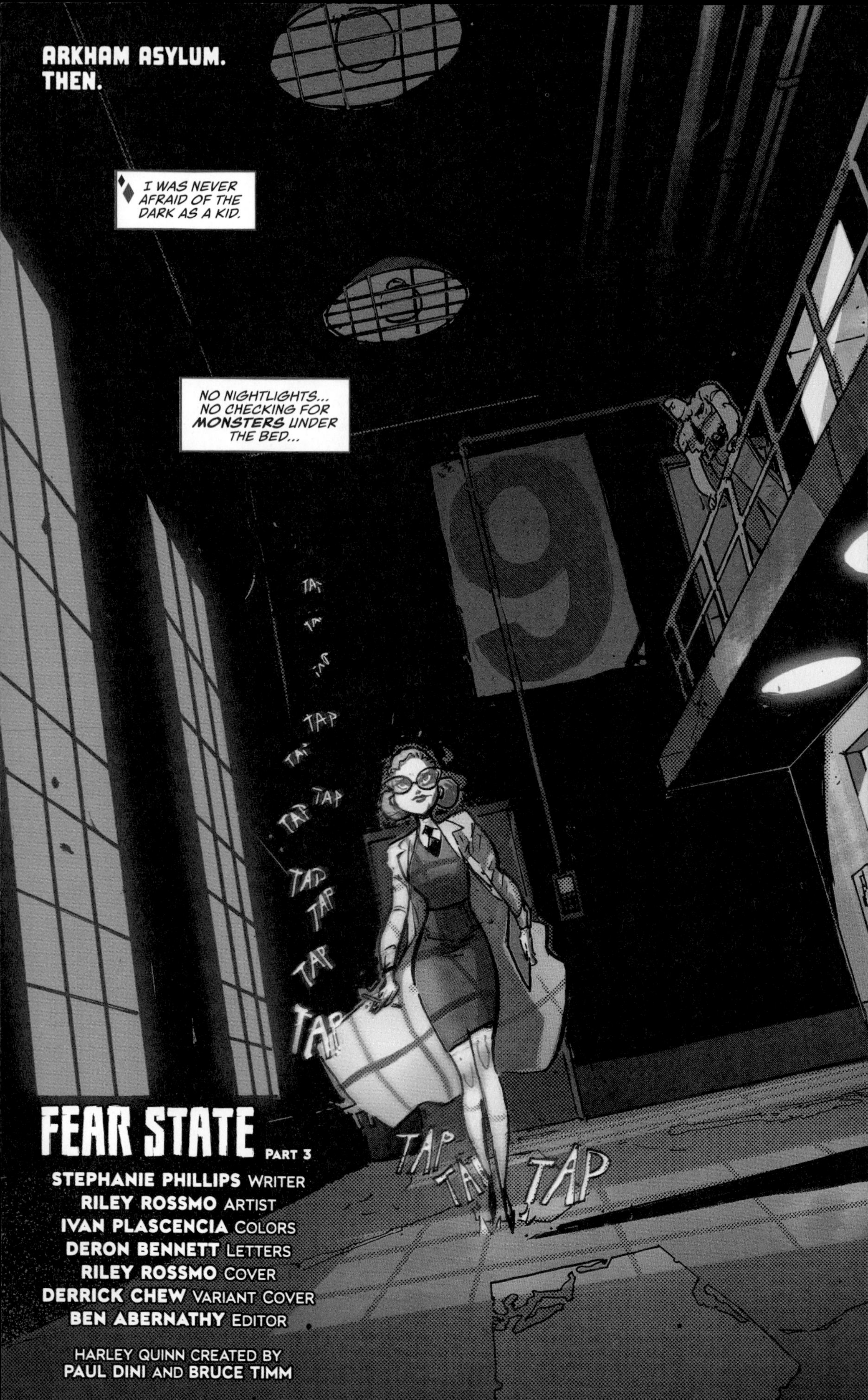
ARKHAM ASYLUM. THEN.
I WAS NEVER AFRAID OF THE DARK AS A KID.
NO NIGHTLIGHTS... NO CHECKING FOR MONSTERS UNDER THE BED...
9
TAP
TAP
TAP
TAP
TAP
TAP
TAP
TAP
TAP
FEAR STATE PART 3
STEPHANIE PHILLIPS WRITER
RILEY ROSSMO ARTIST
IVAN PLASCENCIA COLORS
DERON BENNETT LETTERS
RILEY ROSSMO COVER
DERRICK CHEW VARIANT COVER
BEN ABERNATHY EDITOR
HARLEY QUINN CREATED BY PAUL DINI AND BRUCE TIMM

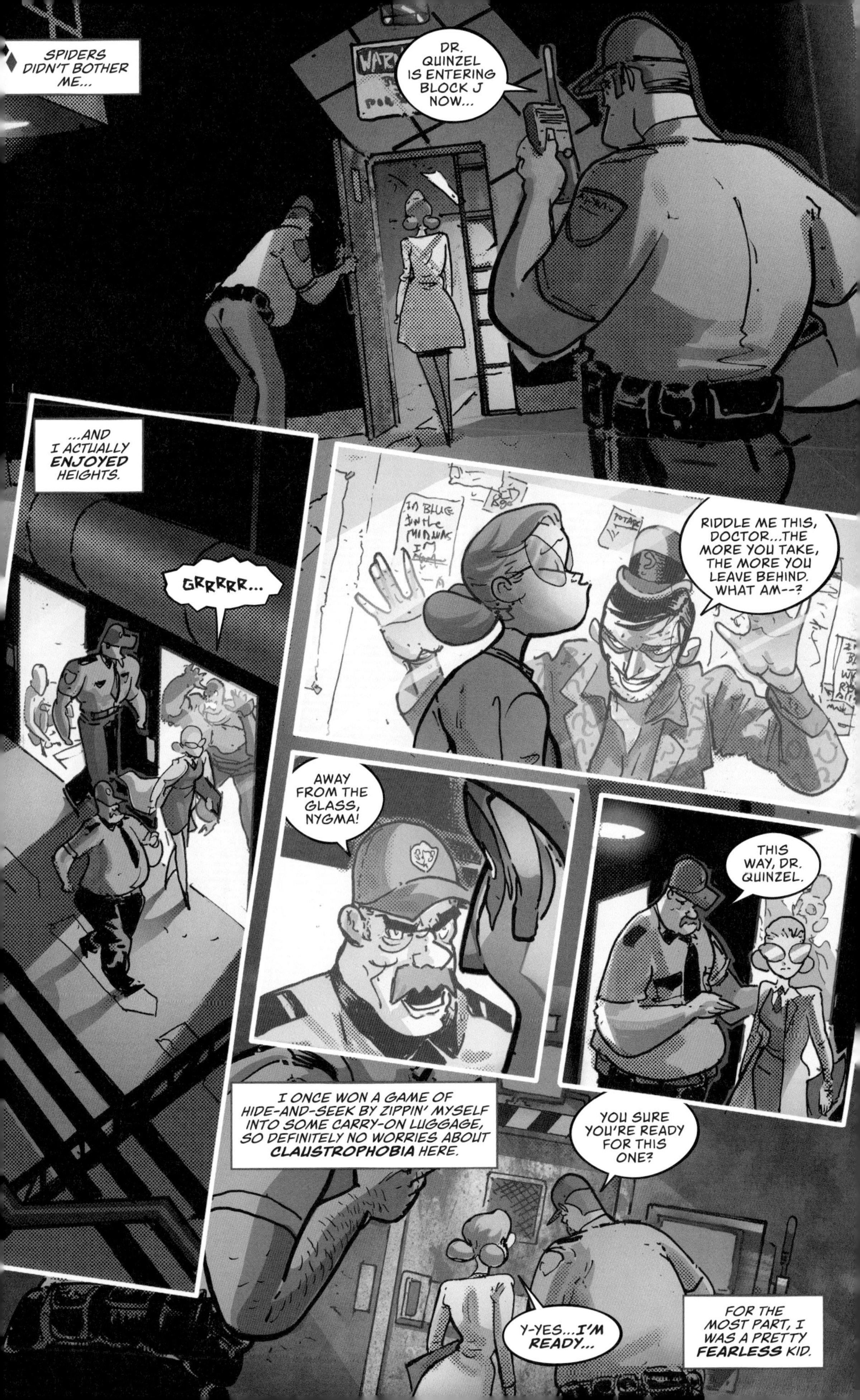
SPIDERS DIDN'T BOTHER ME...
DR. QUINZEL IS ENTERING BLOCK J NOW...
...AND I ACTUALLY ENJOYED HEIGHTS.
GRRRRR...
RIDDLE ME THIS, DOCTOR...THE MORE YOU TAKE, THE MORE YOU LEAVE BEHIND. WHAT AM--?
AWAY FROM THE GLASS, NYGMA!
THIS WAY, DR. QUINZEL.
I ONCE WON A GAME OF HIDE-AND-SEEK BY ZIPPIN' MYSELF INTO SOME CARRY-ON LUGGAGE, SO DEFINITELY NO WORRIES ABOUT CLAUSTROPHOBIA HERE.
YOU SURE YOU'RE READY FOR THIS ONE?
Y-YES...I'M READY...
FOR THE MOST PART, I WAS A PRETTY FEARLESS KID.

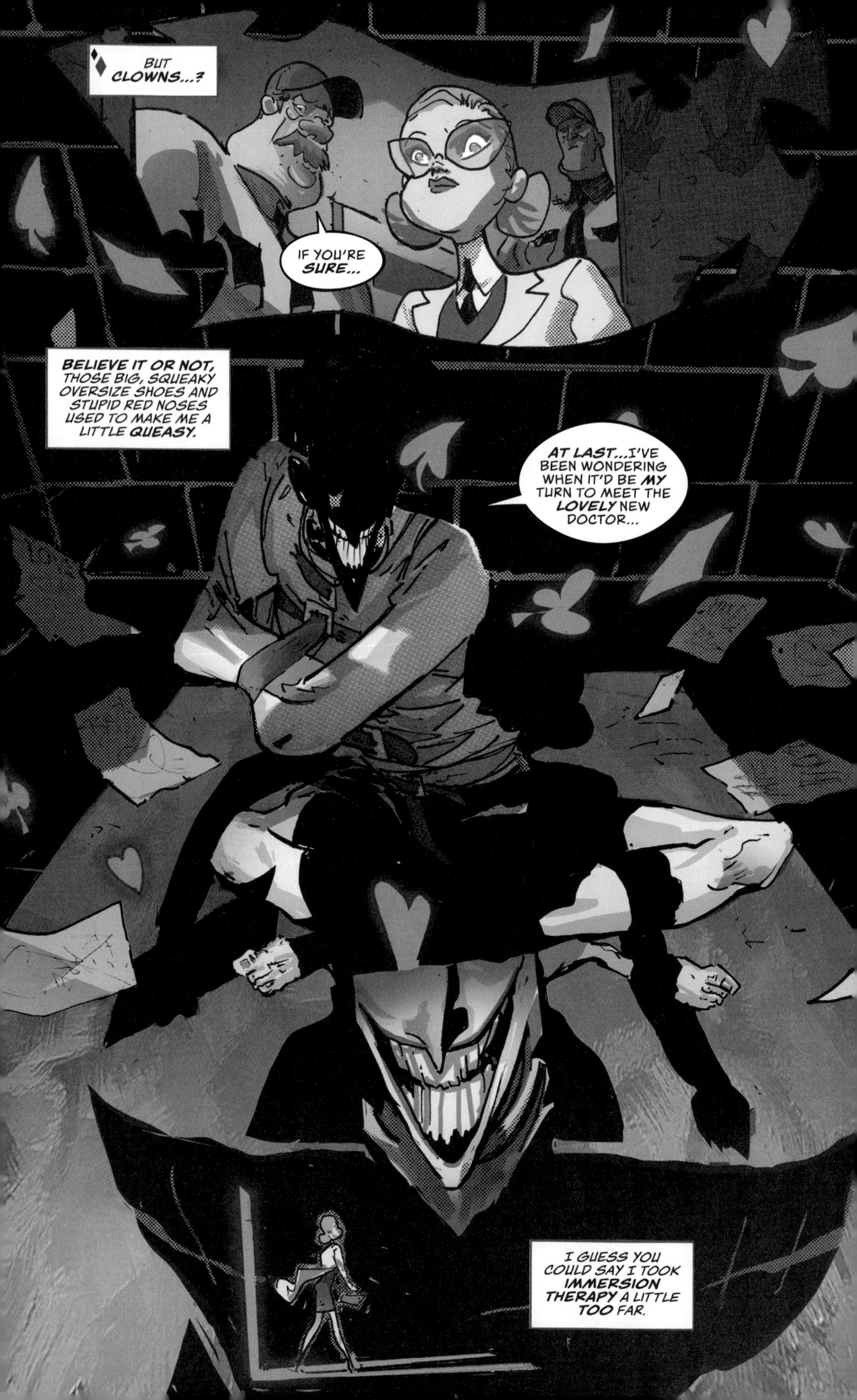
BUT CLOWNS...?
IF YOU'RE SURE...
BELIEVE IT OR NOT, THOSE BIG, SQUEAKY OVERSIZE SHOES AND STUPID RED NOSES USED TO MAKE ME A LITTLE QUEASY.
AT LAST...I'VE BEEN WONDERING WHEN IT'D BE MY TURN TO MEET THE LOVELY NEW DOCTOR...
I GUESS YOU COULD SAY I TOOK IMMERSION THERAPY A LITTLE TOO FAR.

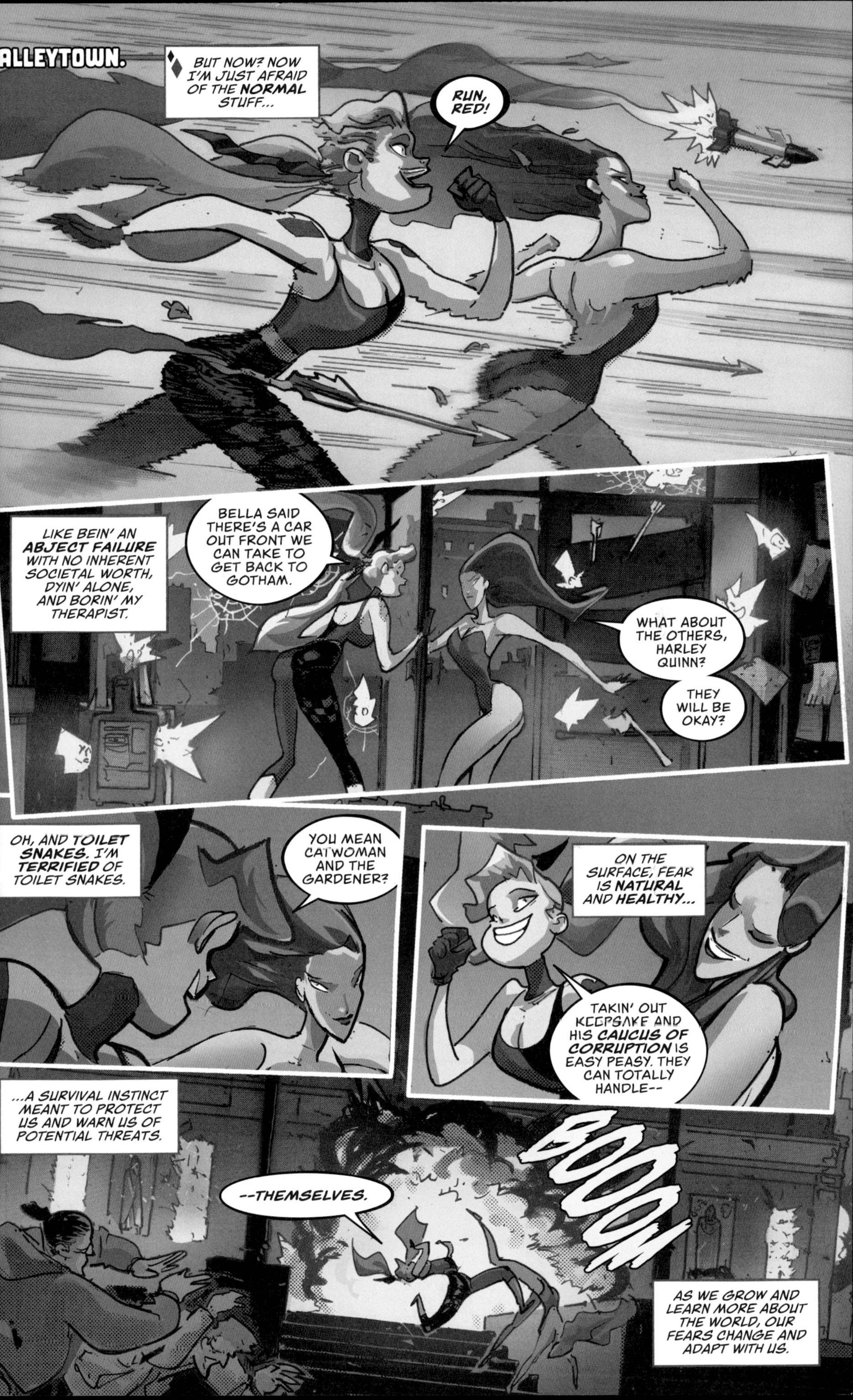
ALLEYTOWN.
BUT NOW? NOW I'M JUST AFRAID OF THE NORMAL STUFF...
RUN, RED!
LIKE BEIN' AN ABJECT FAILURE WITH NO INHERENT SOCIETAL WORTH, DYIN' ALONE, AND BORIN' MY THERAPIST.
BELLA SAID THERE'S A CAR OUT FRONT WE CAN TAKE TO GET BACK TO GOTHAM.
WHAT ABOUT THE OTHERS, HARLEY QUINN?
THEY WILL BE OKAY?
OH, AND TOILET SNAKES. I'M TERRIFIED OF TOILET SNAKES.
YOU MEAN CATWOMAN AND THE GARDENER?
ON THE SURFACE, FEAR IS NATURAL AND HEALTHY...
TAKIN' OUT KEEPSAKE AND HIS CAUCUS OF CORRUPTION IS EASY PEASY. THEY CAN TOTALLY HANDLE--
...A SURVIVAL INSTINCT MEANT TO PROTECT US AND WARN US OF POTENTIAL THREATS.
BOOOOM
--THEMSELVES.
AS WE GROW AND LEARN MORE ABOUT THE WORLD, OUR FEARS CHANGE AND ADAPT WITH US.

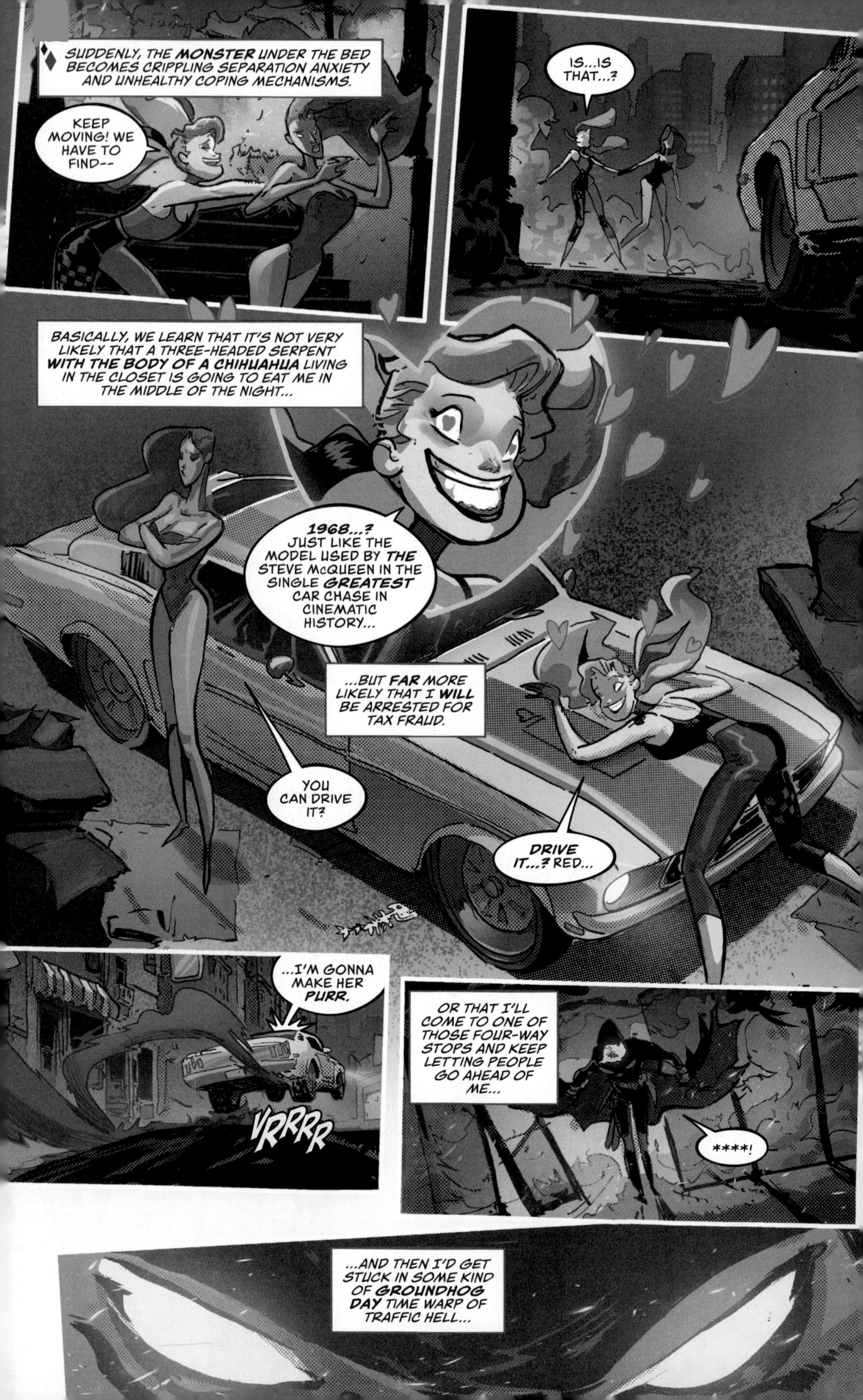
SUDDENLY, THE MONSTER UNDER THE BED BECOMES CRIPPLING SEPARATION ANXIETY AND UNHEALTHY COPING MECHANISMS.
KEEP MOVING! WE HAVE TO FIND--
IS...IS THAT...?
BASICALLY, WE LEARN THAT IT'S NOT VERY LIKELY THAT A THREE-HEADED SERPENT WITH THE BODY OF A CHIHUAHUA LIVING IN THE CLOSET IS GOING TO EAT ME IN THE MIDDLE OF THE NIGHT...
1968...? JUST LIKE THE MODEL USED BY THE STEVE McQUEEN IN THE SINGLE GREATEST CAR CHASE IN CINEMATIC HISTORY...
...BUT FAR MORE LIKELY THAT I WILL BE ARRESTED FOR TAX FRAUD.
YOU CAN DRIVE IT?
DRIVE IT...? RED...
...I'M GONNA MAKE HER PURR.
VRRRR
OR THAT I'LL COME TO ONE OF THOSE FOUR-WAY STOPS AND KEEP LETTING PEOPLE GO AHEAD OF ME...
****!
...AND THEN I'D GET STUCK IN SOME KIND OF GROUNDHOG DAY TIME WARP OF TRAFFIC HELL...

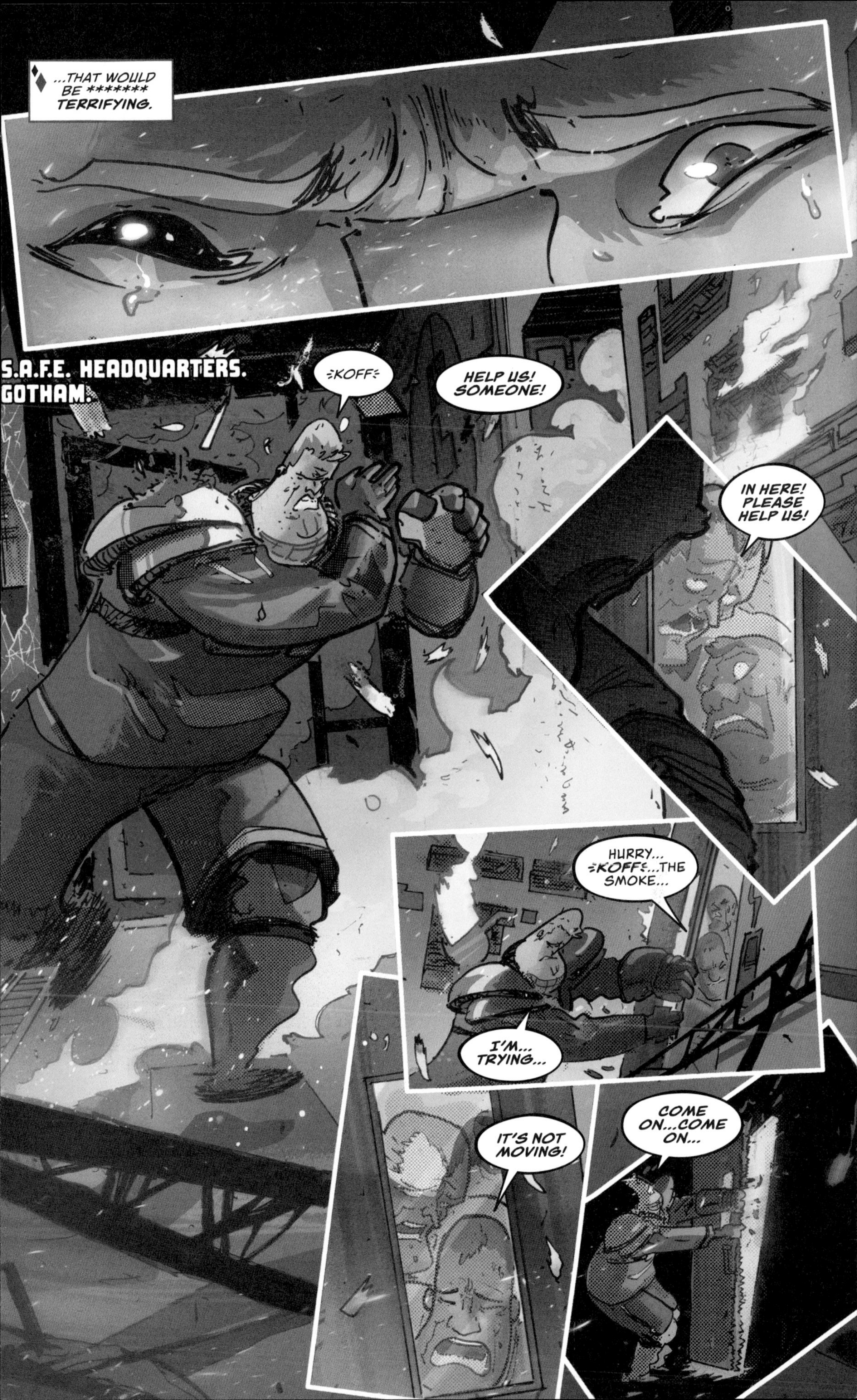
...THAT WOULD BE ******* TERRIFYING.
S.A.F.E. HEADQUARTERS. GOTHAM.
=KOFF=
HELP US! SOMEONE!
IN HERE! PLEASE HELP US!
HURRY... =KOFF=...THE SMOKE...
I'M... TRYING...
IT'S NOT MOVING!
COME ON...COME ON...

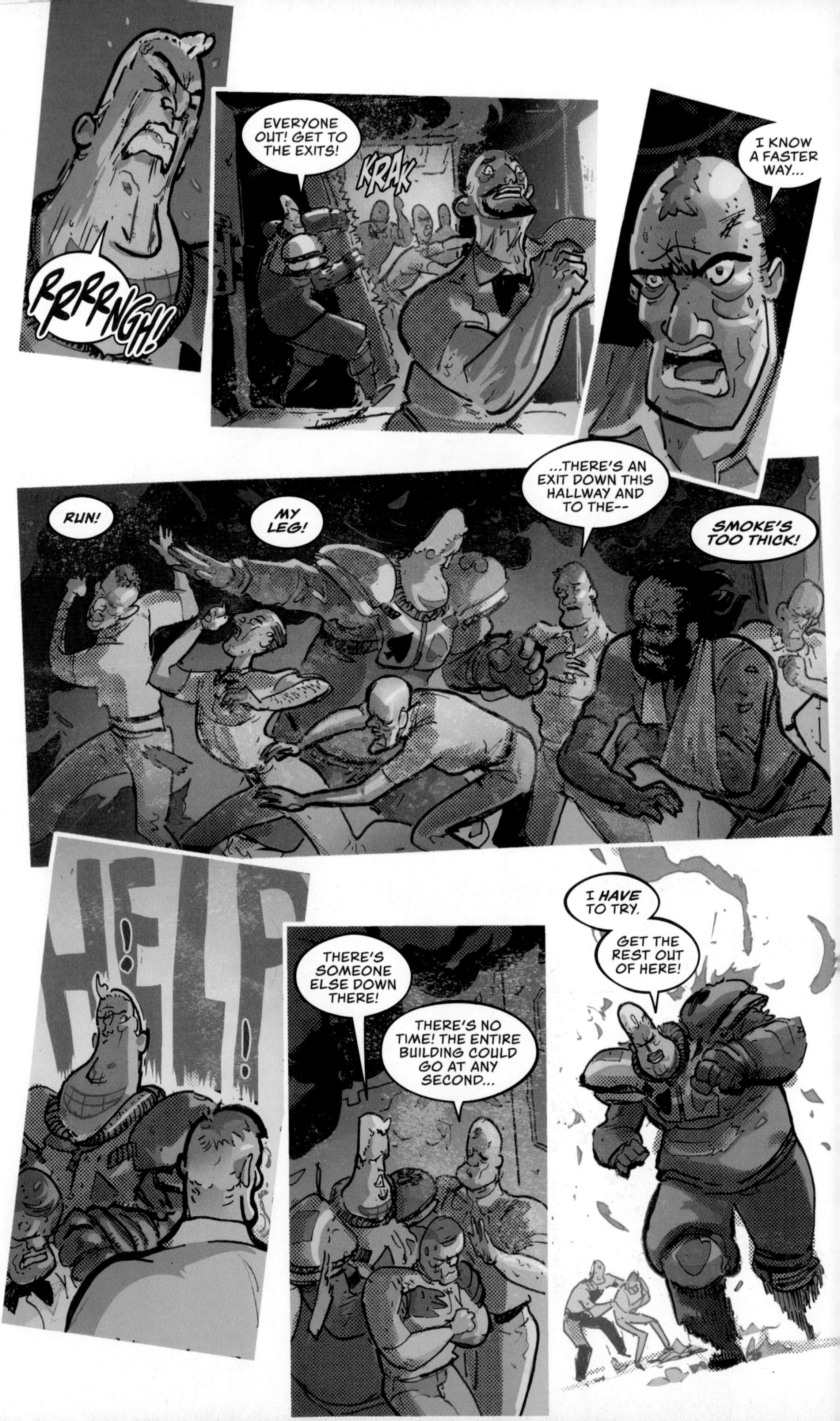
RRRRNGH!
EVERYONE OUT! GET TO THE EXITS!
KRAK
I KNOW A FASTER WAY...
...THERE'S AN EXIT DOWN THIS HALLWAY AND TO THE--
RUN!
MY LEG!
SMOKE'S TOO THICK!
HELP
!
!
THERE'S SOMEONE ELSE DOWN THERE!
THERE'S NO TIME! THE ENTIRE BUILDING COULD GO AT ANY SECOND...
I HAVE TO TRY.
GET THE REST OUT OF HERE!

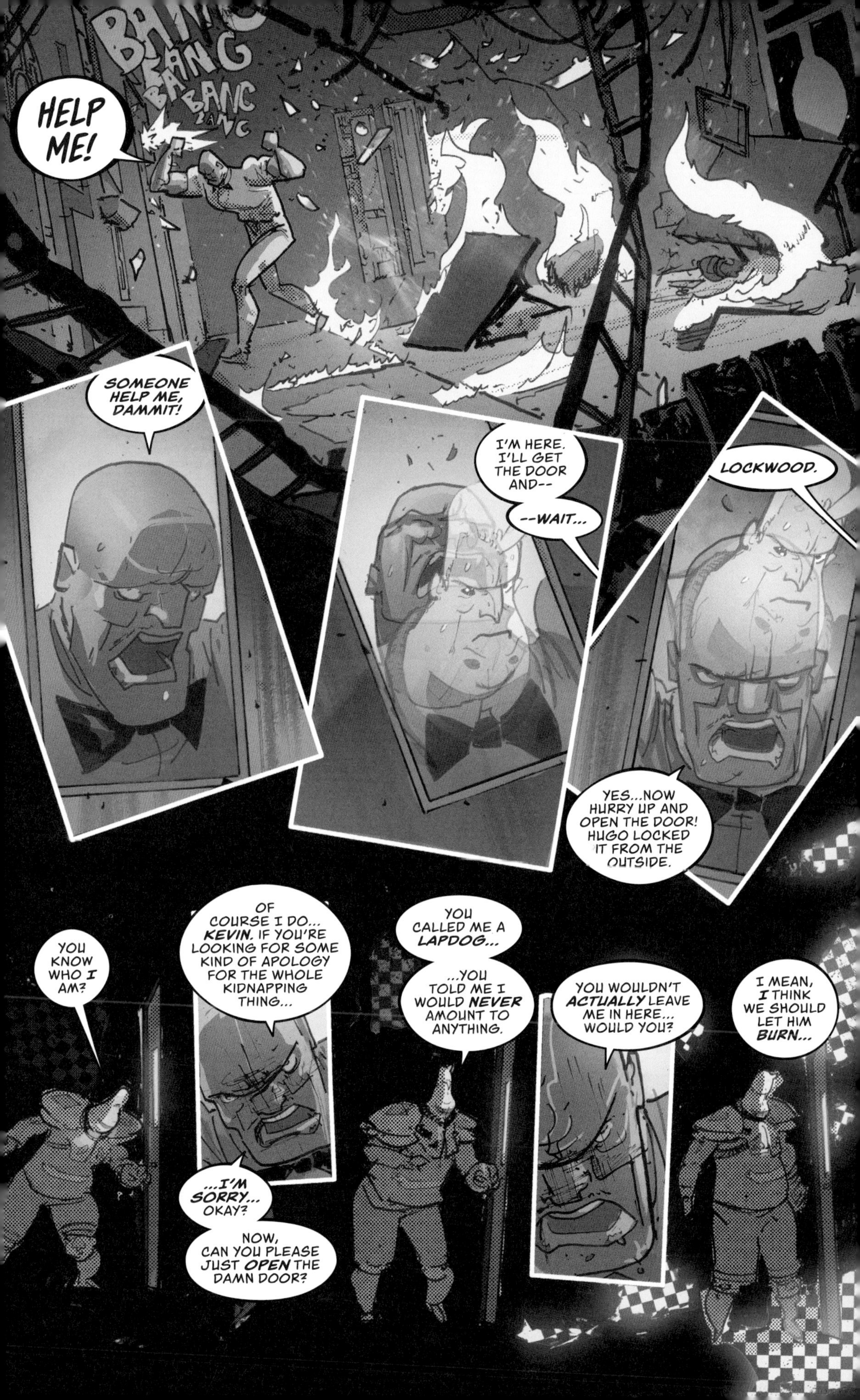
BANG BANG BANG BANG
HELP ME!
SOMEONE HELP ME, DAMMIT!
I'M HERE. I'LL GET THE DOOR AND--
--WAIT...
LOCKWOOD.
YES...NOW HURRY UP AND OPEN THE DOOR! HUGO LOCKED IT FROM THE OUTSIDE.
YOU KNOW WHO I AM?
OF COURSE I DO... KEVIN. IF YOU'RE LOOKING FOR SOME KIND OF APOLOGY FOR THE WHOLE KIDNAPPING THING...
...I'M SORRY... OKAY?
NOW, CAN YOU PLEASE JUST OPEN THE DAMN DOOR?
YOU CALLED ME A LAPDOG...
...YOU TOLD ME I WOULD NEVER AMOUNT TO ANYTHING.
YOU WOULDN'T ACTUALLY LEAVE ME IN HERE... WOULD YOU?
I MEAN, I THINK WE SHOULD LET HIM BURN...

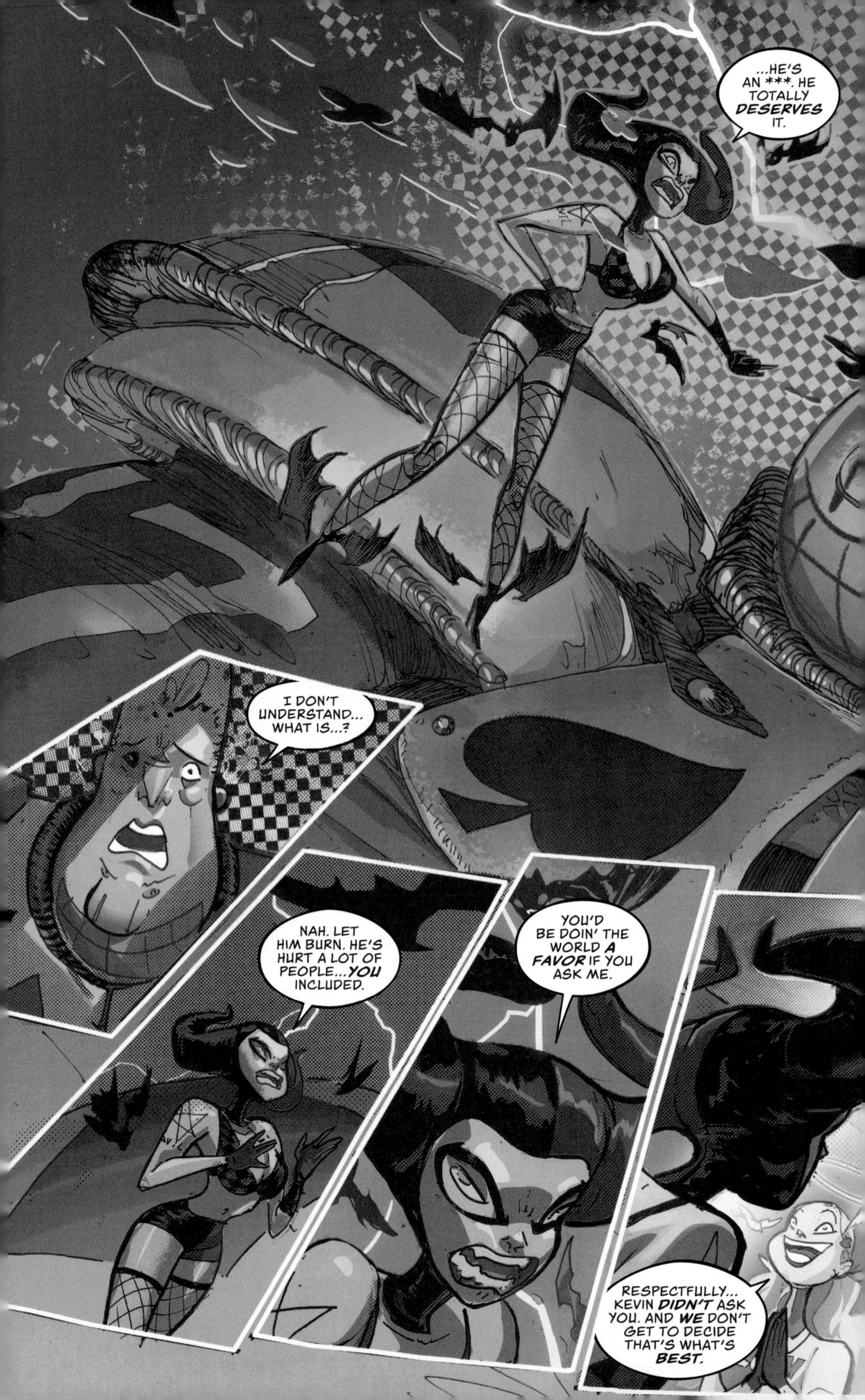
...HE'S AN ***. HE TOTALLY DESERVES IT.
I DON'T UNDERSTAND... WHAT IS...?
NAH. LET HIM BURN. HE'S HURT A LOT OF PEOPLE...YOU INCLUDED.
YOU'D BE DOIN' THE WORLD A FAVOR IF YOU ASK ME.
RESPECTFULLY... KEVIN DIDN'T ASK YOU. AND WE DON'T GET TO DECIDE THAT'S WHAT'S BEST.

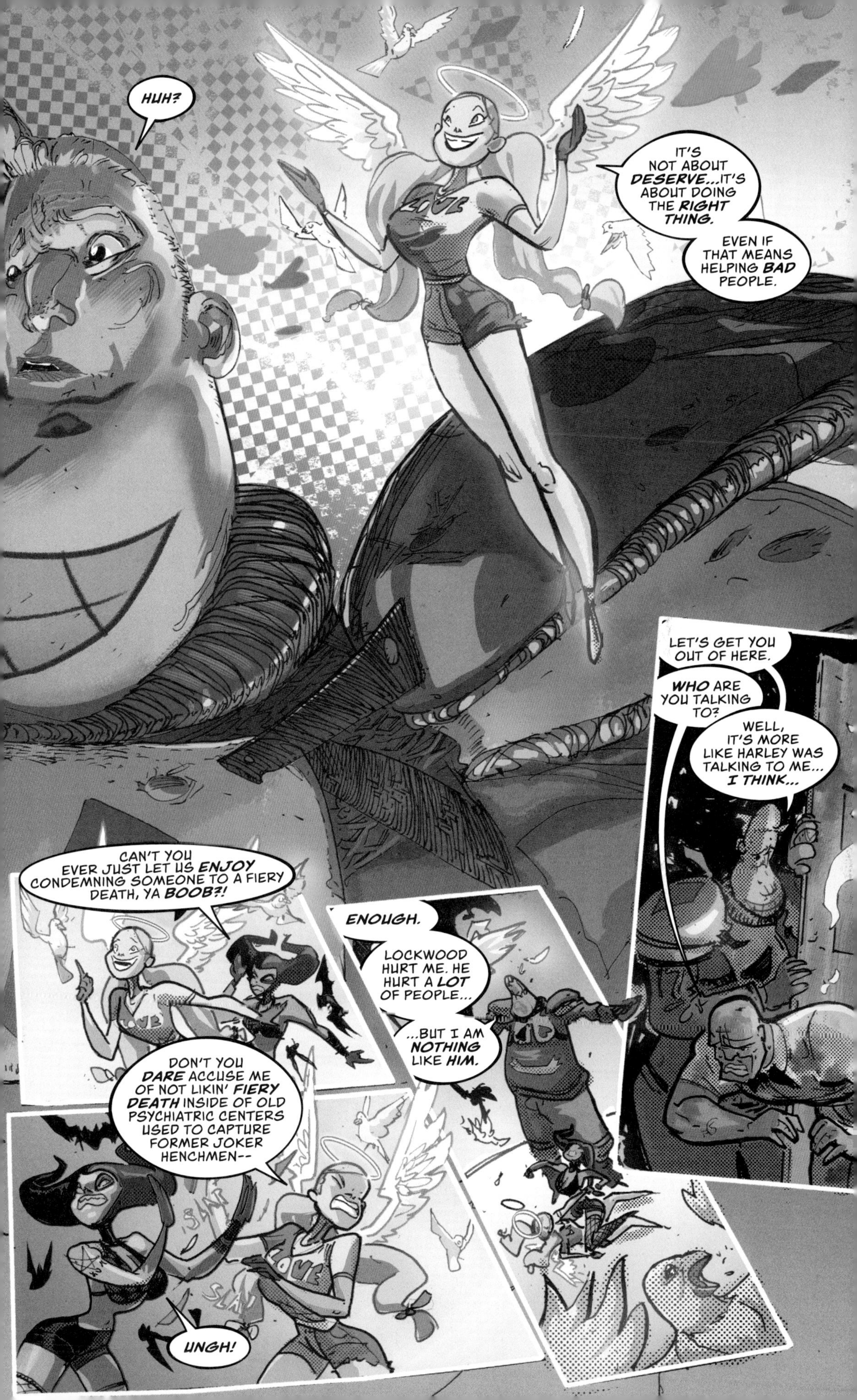
HUH?
IT'S NOT ABOUT DESERVE... IT'S ABOUT DOING THE RIGHT THING.
EVEN IF THAT MEANS HELPING BAD PEOPLE.
CAN'T YOU EVER JUST LET US ENJOY CONDEMNING SOMEONE TO A FIERY DEATH, YA BOOB?!
DON'T YOU DARE ACCUSE ME OF NOT LIKIN' FIERY DEATH INSIDE OF OLD PSYCHIATRIC CENTERS USED TO CAPTURE FORMER JOKER HENCHMEN--
UNGH!
ENOUGH.
LOCKWOOD HURT ME. HE HURT A LOT OF PEOPLE...
...BUT I AM NOTHING LIKE HIM.
LET'S GET YOU OUT OF HERE.
WHO ARE YOU TALKING TO?
WELL, IT'S MORE LIKE HARLEY WAS TALKING TO ME... I THINK...

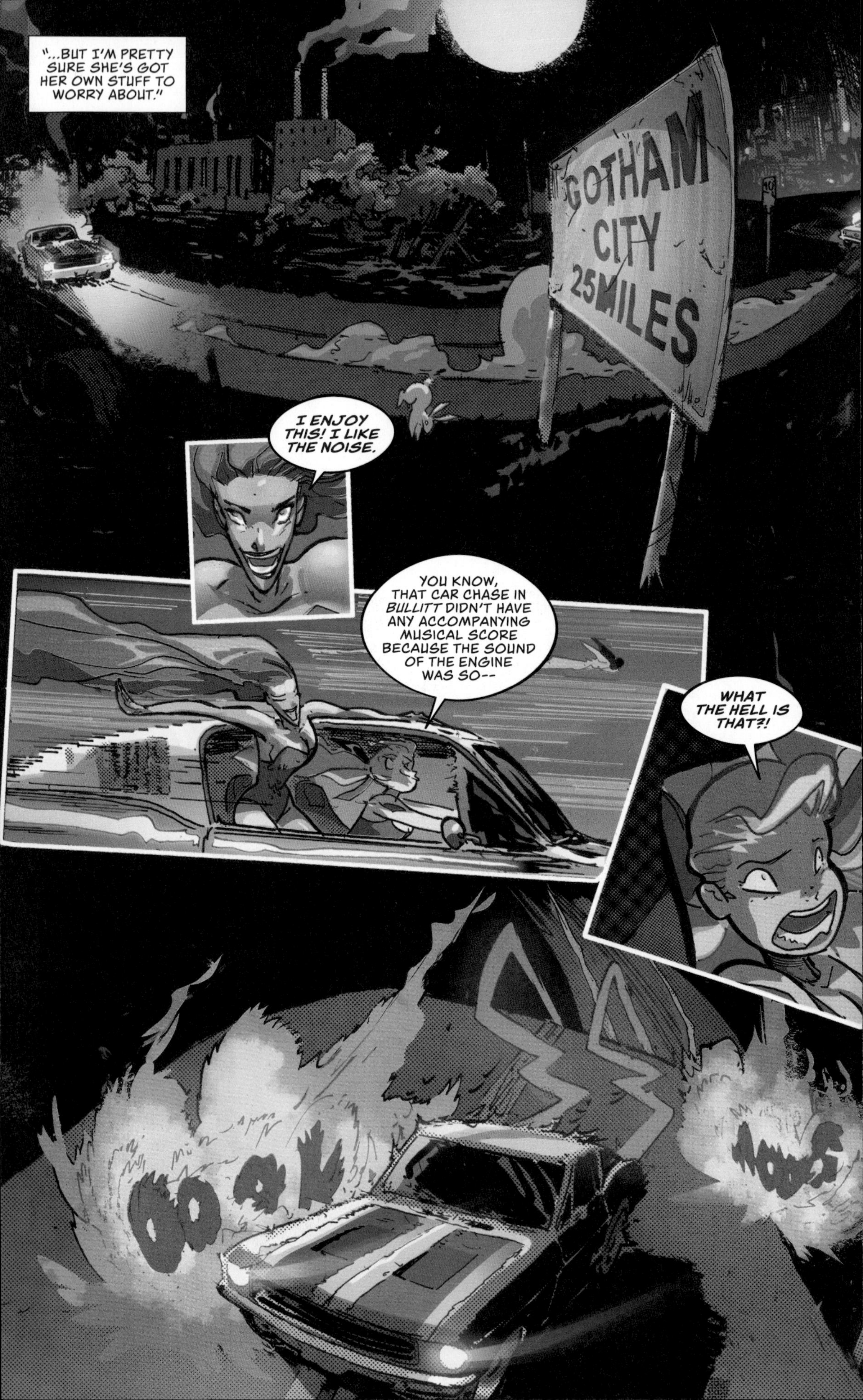
"...BUT I'M PRETTY SURE SHE'S GOT HER OWN STUFF TO WORRY ABOUT."
GOTHAM CITY 25 MILES
I ENJOY THIS! I LIKE THE NOISE.
YOU KNOW, THAT CAR CHASE IN *BULLITT* DIDN'T HAVE ANY ACCOMPANYING MUSICAL SCORE BECAUSE THE SOUND OF THE ENGINE WAS SO--
WHAT THE HELL IS THAT?!

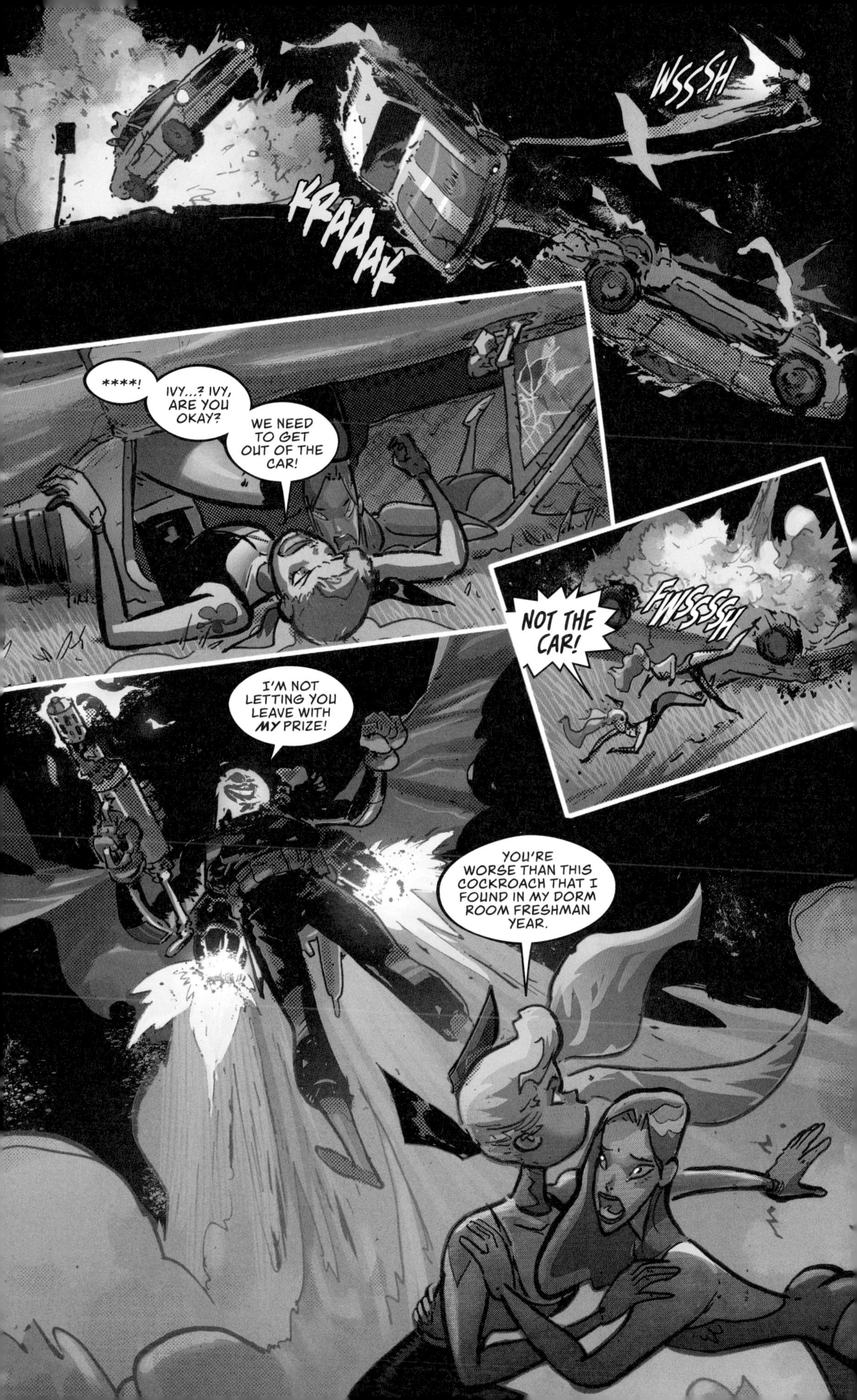
WSSSH
KRAAAK
****!
IVY...? IVY, ARE YOU OKAY?
WE NEED TO GET OUT OF THE CAR!
NOT THE CAR!
FWSSSH
I'M NOT LETTING YOU LEAVE WITH MY PRIZE!
YOU'RE WORSE THAN THIS COCKROACH THAT I FOUND IN MY DORM ROOM FRESHMAN YEAR.

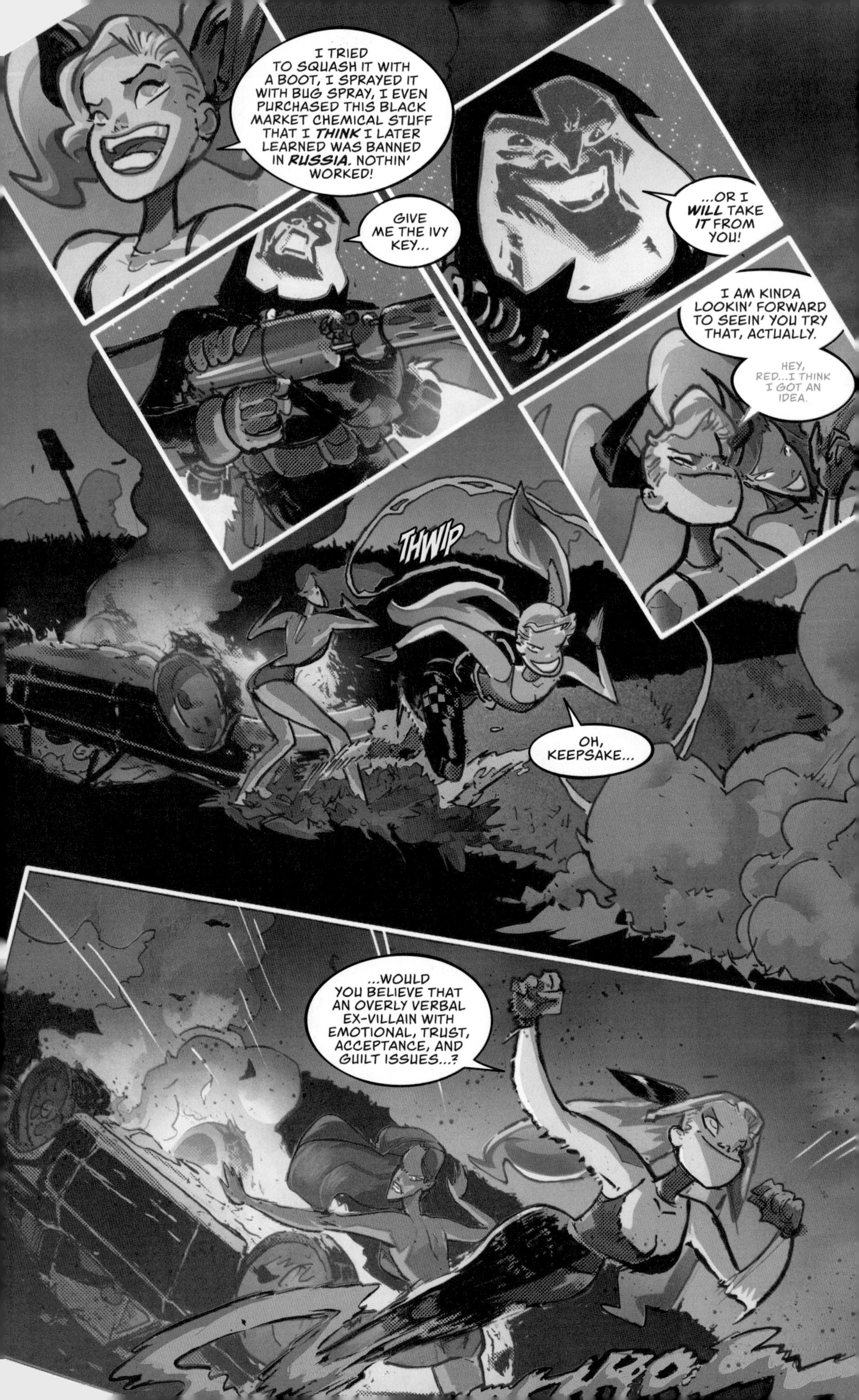
I TRIED TO SQUASH IT WITH A BOOT, I SPRAYED IT WITH BUG SPRAY, I EVEN PURCHASED THIS BLACK MARKET CHEMICAL STUFF THAT I *THINK* I LATER LEARNED WAS BANNED IN *RUSSIA.* NOTHIN' WORKED!
GIVE ME THE IVY KEY...
...OR I *WILL* TAKE *IT* FROM YOU!
I AM KINDA LOOKIN' FORWARD TO SEEIN' YOU TRY THAT, ACTUALLY.
HEY, RED...I THINK I GOT AN IDEA.
THWIP
OH, KEEPSAKE...
...WOULD YOU BELIEVE THAT AN OVERLY VERBAL EX-VILLAIN WITH EMOTIONAL, TRUST, ACCEPTANCE, AND GUILT ISSUES...?

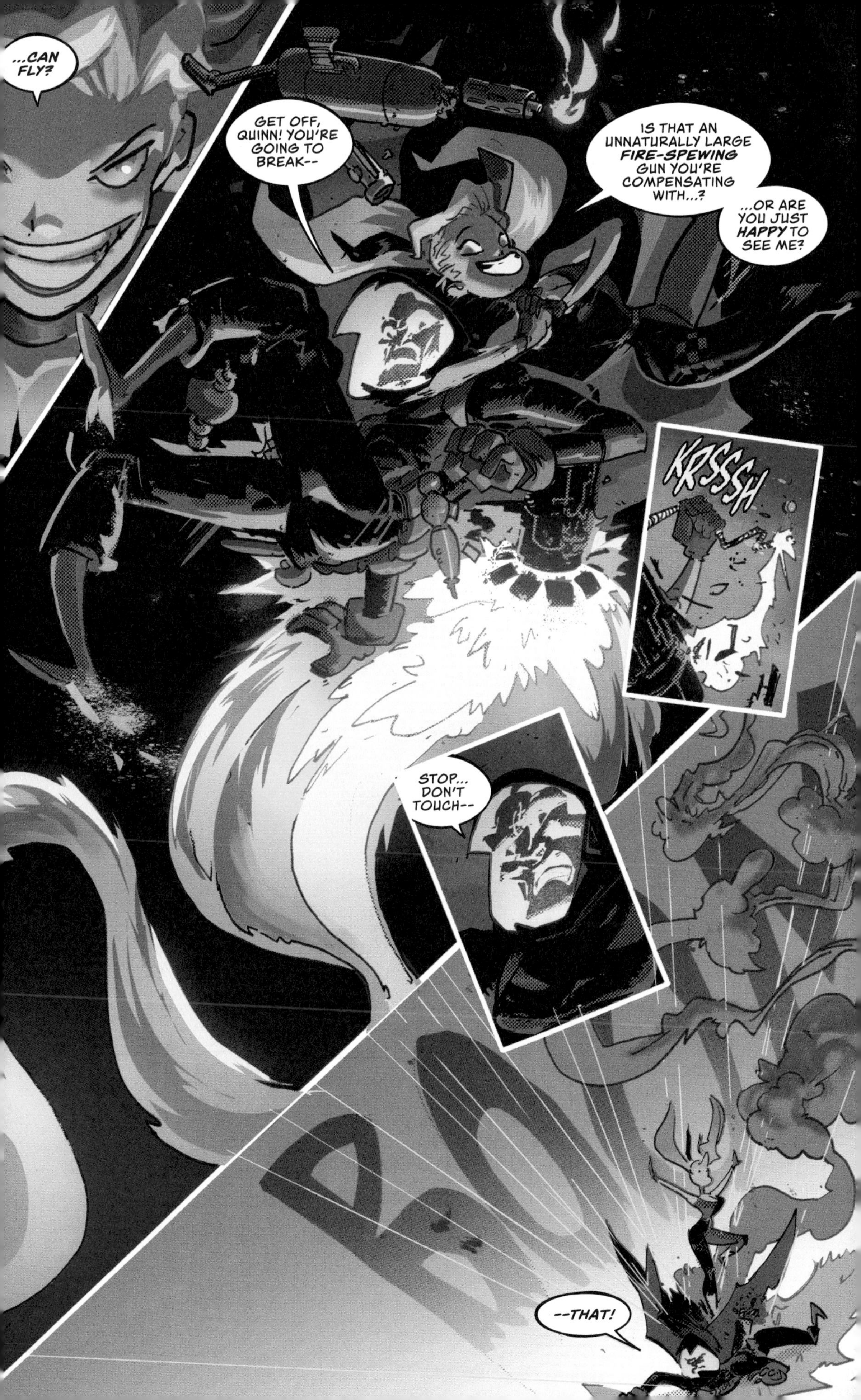
...CAN FLY?
GET OFF, QUINN! YOU'RE GOING TO BREAK--
IS THAT AN UNNATURALLY LARGE **FIRE-SPEWING** GUN YOU'RE COMPENSATING WITH...?
...OR ARE YOU JUST **HAPPY** TO SEE ME?
KRSSSH
STOP... DON'T TOUCH--
--THAT!

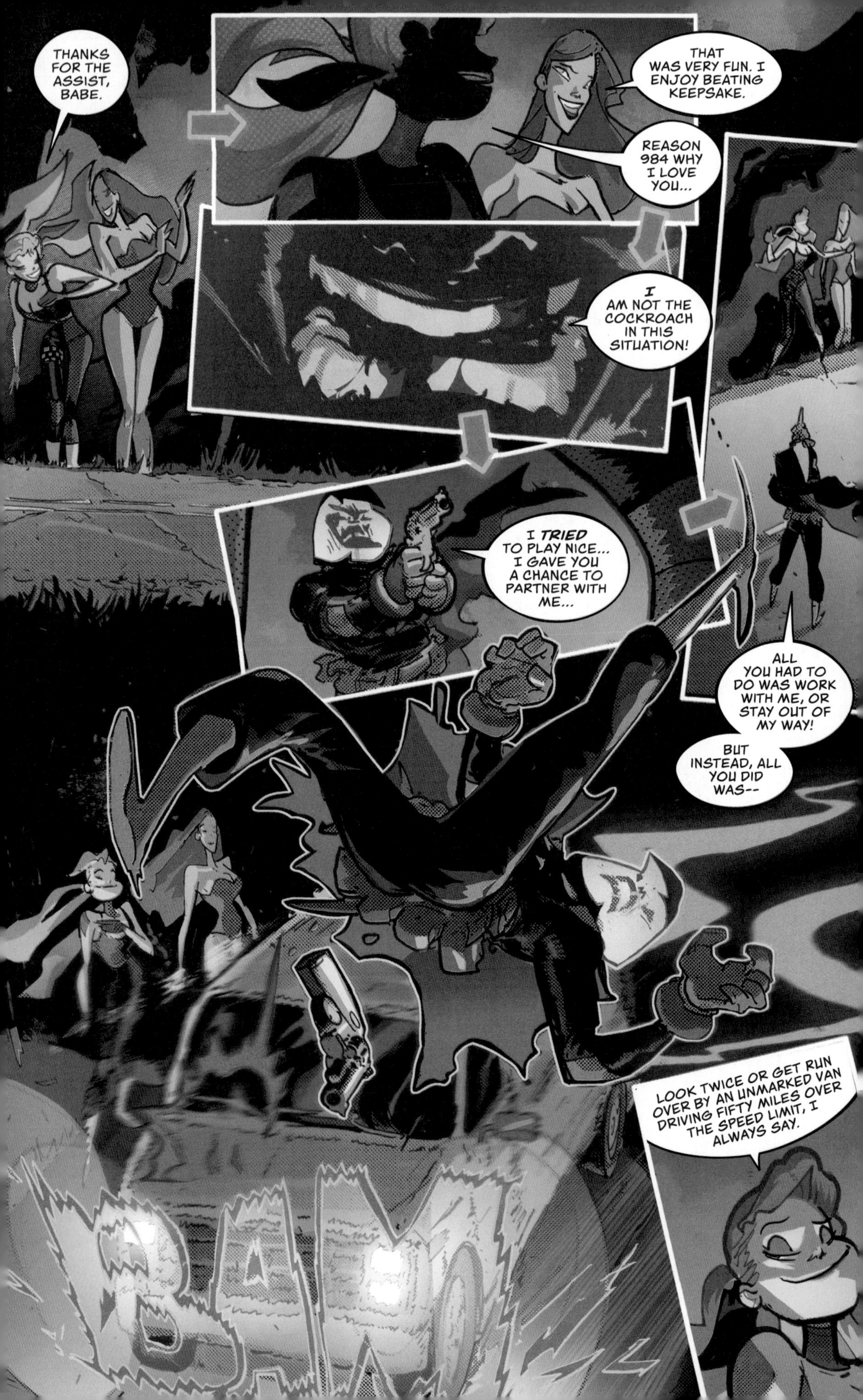
THANKS FOR THE ASSIST, BABE.
THAT WAS VERY FUN. I ENJOY BEATING KEEPSAKE.
REASON 984 WHY I LOVE YOU...
I AM NOT THE COCKROACH IN THIS SITUATION!
I TRIED TO PLAY NICE... I GAVE YOU A CHANCE TO PARTNER WITH ME...
ALL YOU HAD TO DO WAS WORK WITH ME, OR STAY OUT OF MY WAY!
BUT INSTEAD, ALL YOU DID WAS--
BAM!
LOOK TWICE OR GET RUN OVER BY AN UNMARKED VAN DRIVING FIFTY MILES OVER THE SPEED LIMIT, I ALWAYS SAY.

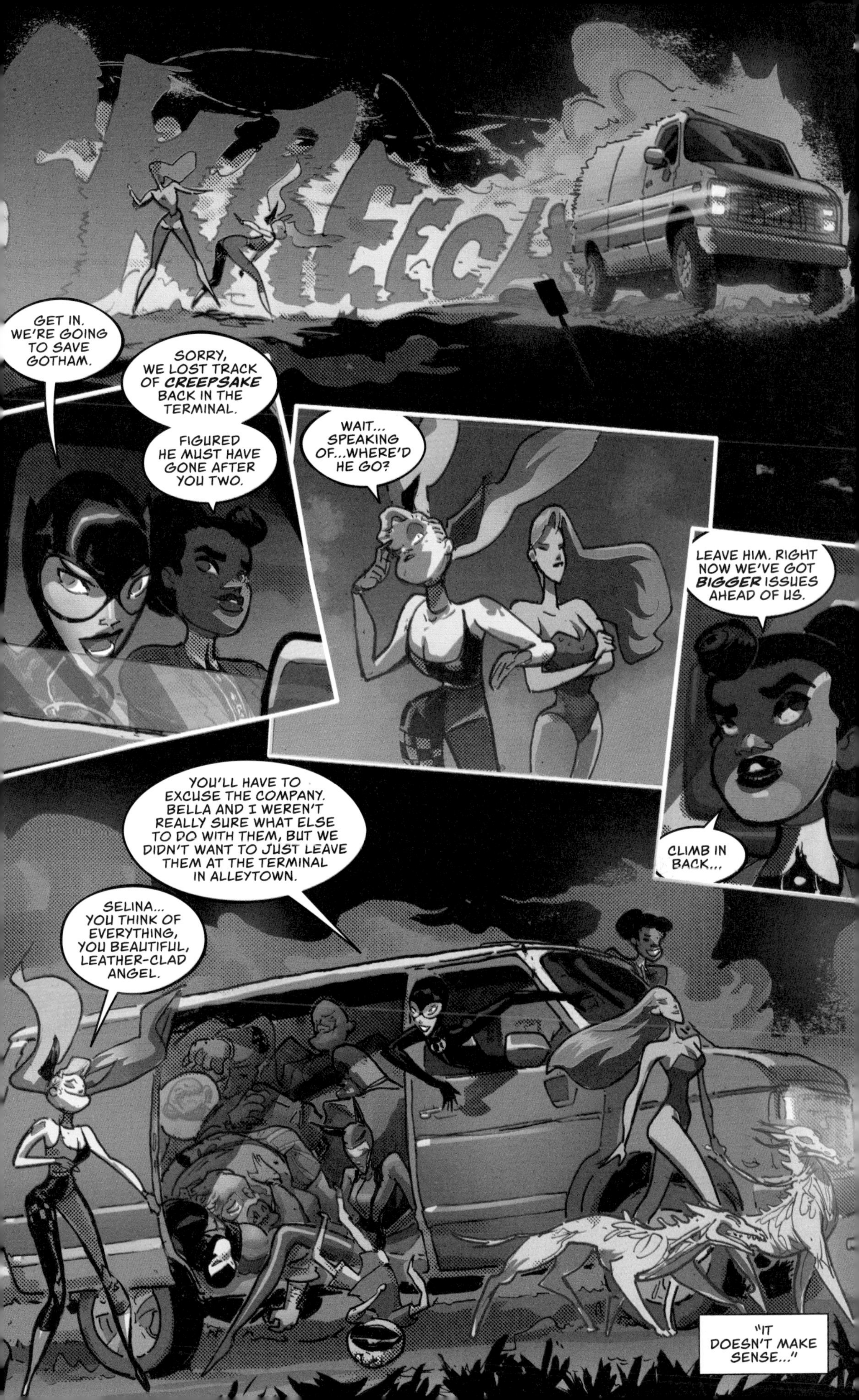
WRECK
GET IN. WE'RE GOING TO SAVE GOTHAM.
SORRY, WE LOST TRACK OF CREEPSAKE BACK IN THE TERMINAL.
FIGURED HE MUST HAVE GONE AFTER YOU TWO.
WAIT... SPEAKING OF...WHERE'D HE GO?
LEAVE HIM. RIGHT NOW WE'VE GOT BIGGER ISSUES AHEAD OF US.
CLIMB IN BACK...
YOU'LL HAVE TO EXCUSE THE COMPANY. BELLA AND I WEREN'T REALLY SURE WHAT ELSE TO DO WITH THEM, BUT WE DIDN'T WANT TO JUST LEAVE THEM AT THE TERMINAL IN ALLEYTOWN.
SELINA... YOU THINK OF EVERYTHING, YOU BEAUTIFUL, LEATHER-CLAD ANGEL.
"IT DOESN'T MAKE SENSE..."

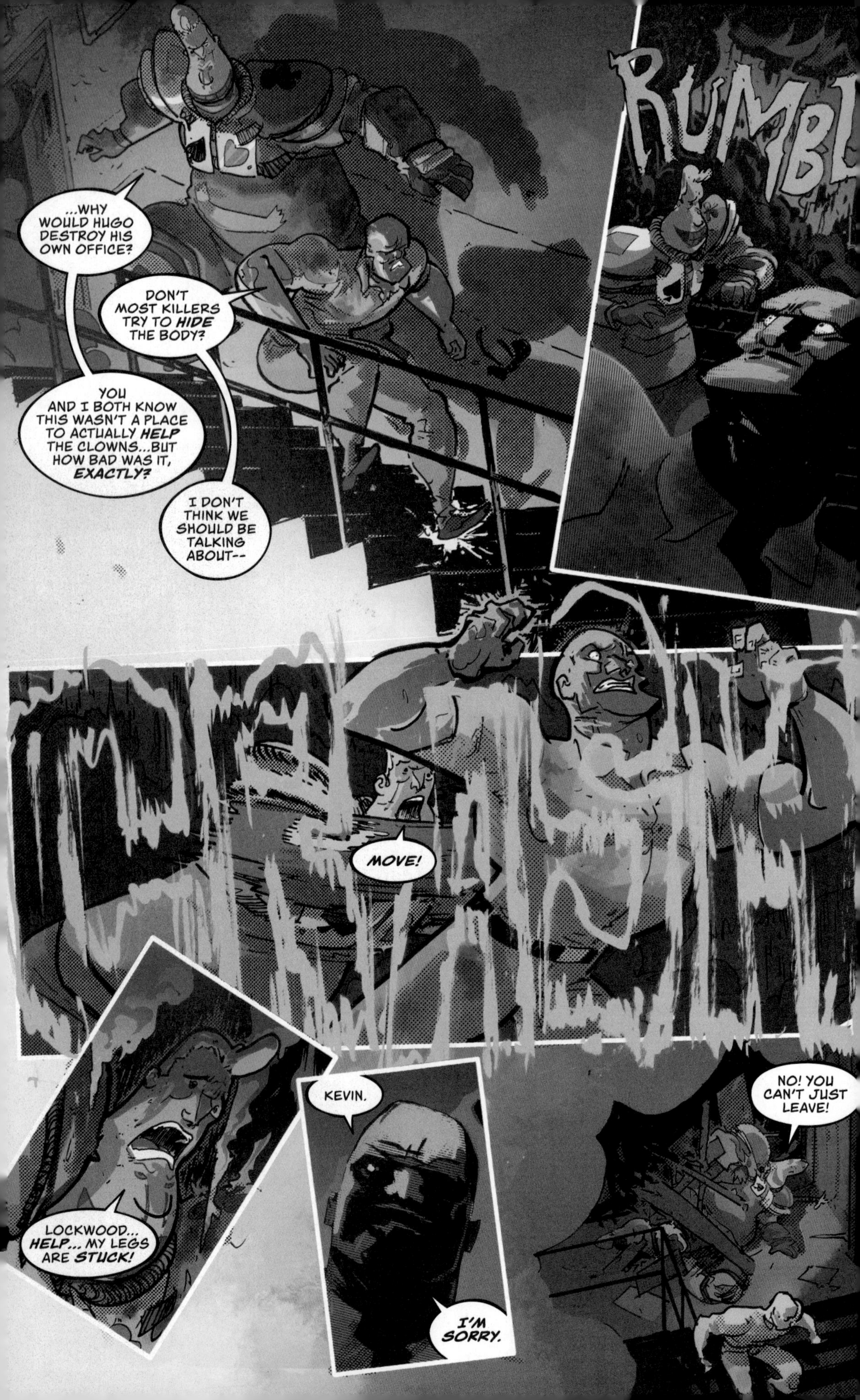
...WHY WOULD HUGO DESTROY HIS OWN OFFICE?
DON'T MOST KILLERS TRY TO *HIDE* THE BODY?
YOU AND I BOTH KNOW THIS WASN'T A PLACE TO ACTUALLY *HELP* THE CLOWNS...BUT HOW BAD WAS IT, *EXACTLY?*
I DON'T THINK WE SHOULD BE TALKING ABOUT--
RUMBL
MOVE!
LOCKWOOD... *HELP*... MY LEGS ARE *STUCK!*
KEVIN.
I'M SORRY.
NO! YOU CAN'T JUST LEAVE!

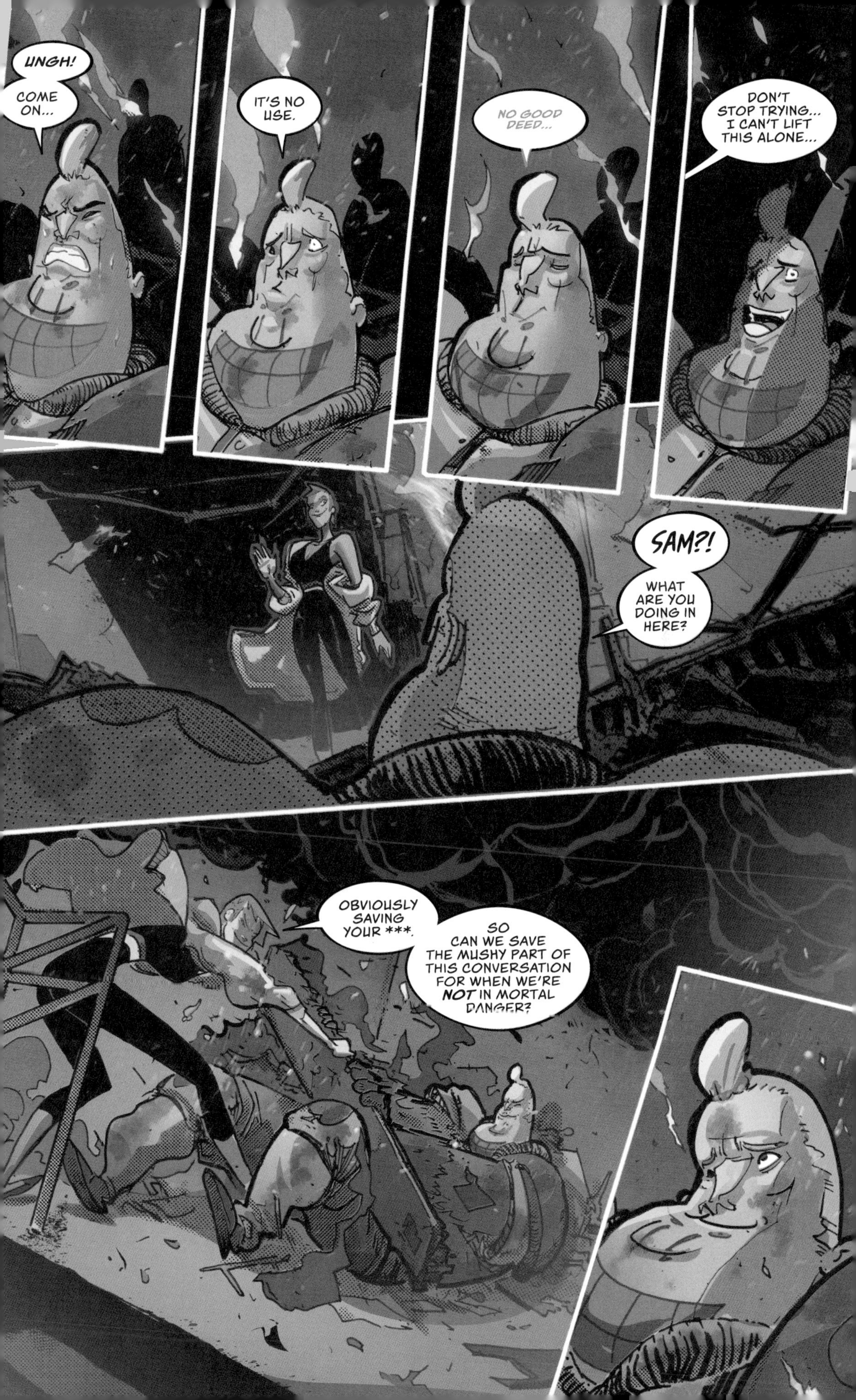
UNGH!
COME ON...
IT'S NO USE.
NO GOOD DEED...
DON'T STOP TRYING... I CAN'T LIFT THIS ALONE...
SAM?!
WHAT ARE YOU DOING IN HERE?
OBVIOUSLY SAVING YOUR ***.
SO CAN WE SAVE THE MUSHY PART OF THIS CONVERSATION FOR WHEN WE'RE NOT IN MORTAL DANGER?

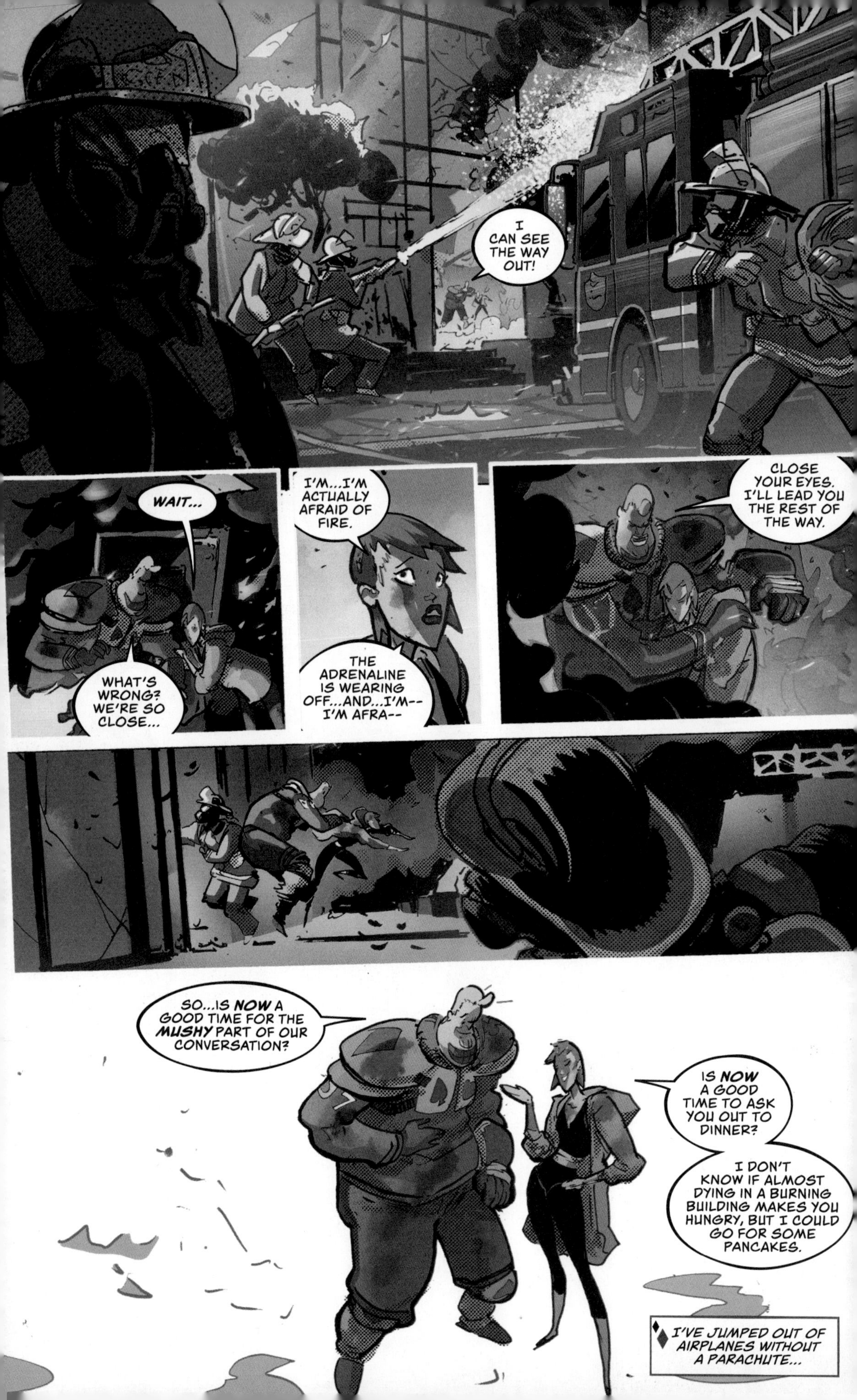
I CAN SEE THE WAY OUT!
WAIT...
WHAT'S WRONG? WE'RE SO CLOSE...
I'M...I'M ACTUALLY AFRAID OF FIRE.
THE ADRENALINE IS WEARING OFF...AND...I'M-- I'M AFRA--
CLOSE YOUR EYES. I'LL LEAD YOU THE REST OF THE WAY.
SO...IS NOW A GOOD TIME FOR THE MUSHY PART OF OUR CONVERSATION?
IS NOW A GOOD TIME TO ASK YOU OUT TO DINNER?
I DON'T KNOW IF ALMOST DYING IN A BURNING BUILDING MAKES YOU HUNGRY, BUT I COULD GO FOR SOME PANCAKES.
I'VE JUMPED OUT OF AIRPLANES WITHOUT A PARACHUTE...

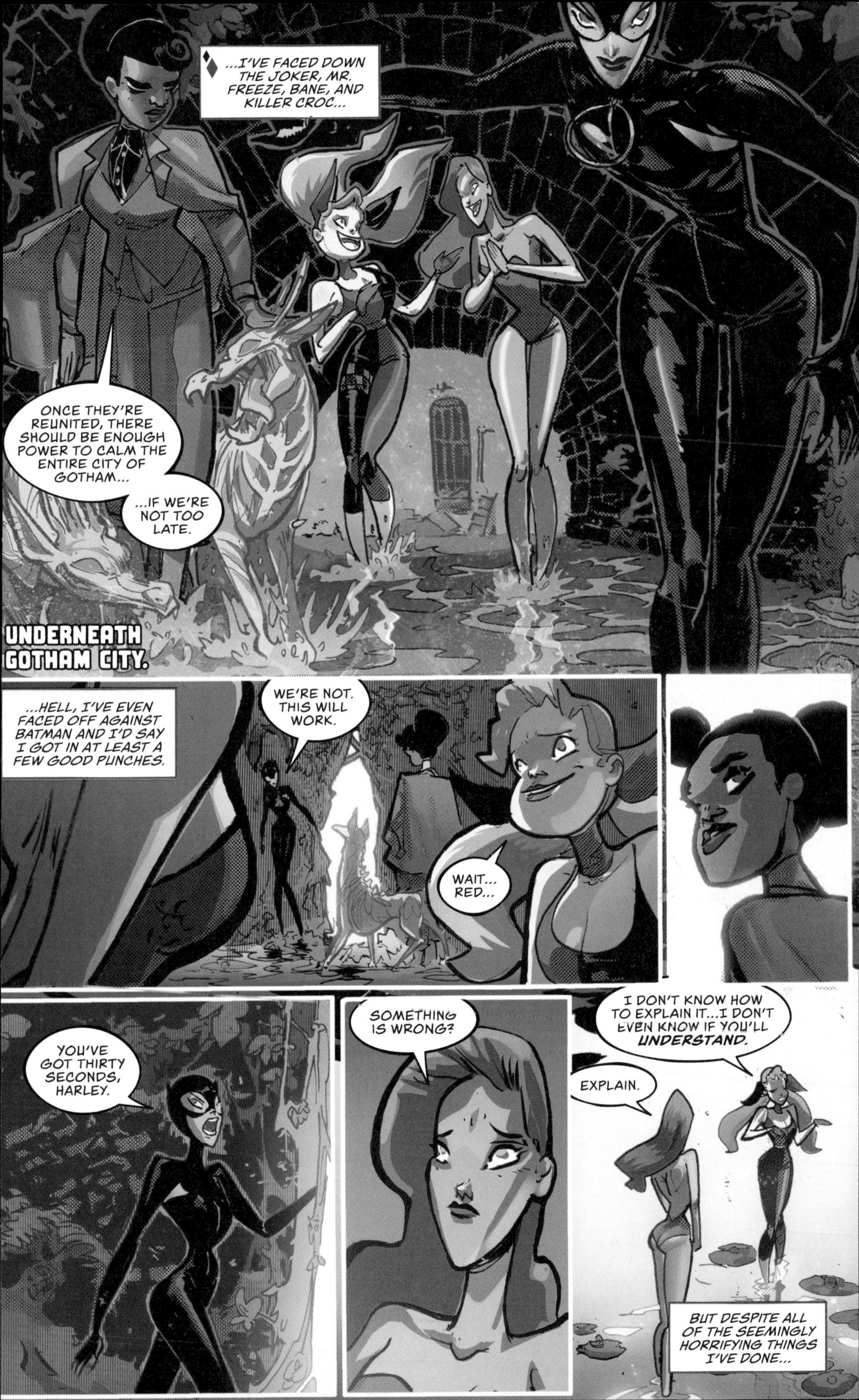
...I'VE FACED DOWN THE JOKER, MR. FREEZE, BANE, AND KILLER CROC...
ONCE THEY'RE REUNITED, THERE SHOULD BE ENOUGH POWER TO CALM THE ENTIRE CITY OF GOTHAM...
...IF WE'RE NOT TOO LATE.
UNDERNEATH GOTHAM CITY.
...HELL, I'VE EVEN FACED OFF AGAINST BATMAN AND I'D SAY I GOT IN AT LEAST A FEW GOOD PUNCHES.
WE'RE NOT. THIS WILL WORK.
WAIT... RED...
YOU'VE GOT THIRTY SECONDS, HARLEY.
SOMETHING IS WRONG?
I DON'T KNOW HOW TO EXPLAIN IT...I DON'T EVEN KNOW IF YOU'LL UNDERSTAND.
EXPLAIN.
BUT DESPITE ALL OF THE SEEMINGLY HORRIFYING THINGS I'VE DONE...

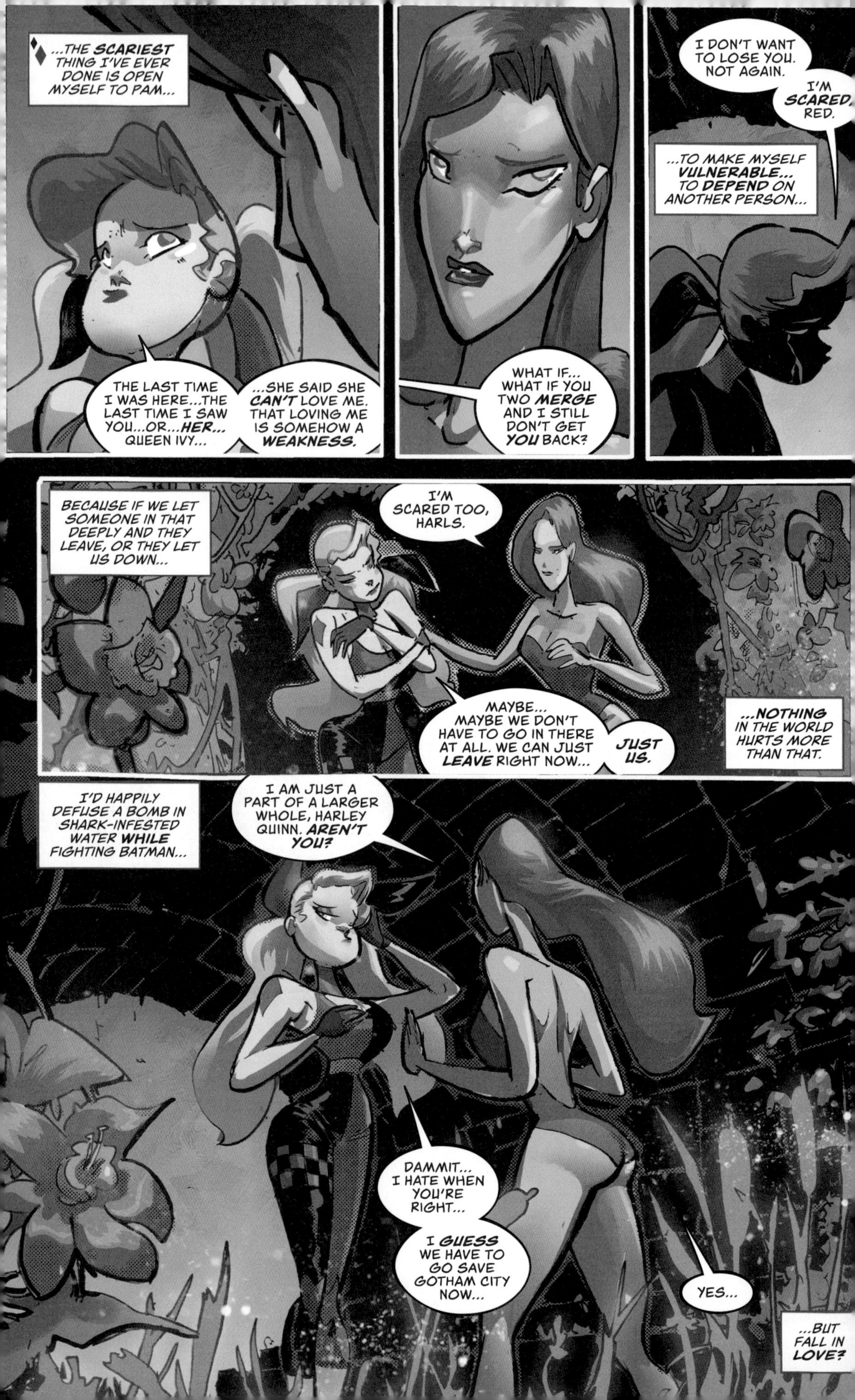

...THE SCARIEST THING I'VE EVER DONE IS OPEN MYSELF TO PAM...
THE LAST TIME I WAS HERE...THE LAST TIME I SAW YOU...OR...HER... QUEEN IVY...
...SHE SAID SHE CAN'T LOVE ME. THAT LOVING ME IS SOMEHOW A WEAKNESS.
WHAT IF... WHAT IF YOU TWO MERGE AND I STILL DON'T GET YOU BACK?
I DON'T WANT TO LOSE YOU. NOT AGAIN.
I'M SCARED, RED.
...TO MAKE MYSELF VULNERABLE... TO DEPEND ON ANOTHER PERSON...
BECAUSE IF WE LET SOMEONE IN THAT DEEPLY AND THEY LEAVE, OR THEY LET US DOWN...
I'M SCARED TOO, HARLS.
MAYBE... MAYBE WE DON'T HAVE TO GO IN THERE AT ALL. WE CAN JUST LEAVE RIGHT NOW...
JUST US.
...NOTHING IN THE WORLD HURTS MORE THAN THAT.
I'D HAPPILY DEFUSE A BOMB IN SHARK-INFESTED WATER WHILE FIGHTING BATMAN...
I AM JUST A PART OF A LARGER WHOLE, HARLEY QUINN. AREN'T YOU?
DAMMIT... I HATE WHEN YOU'RE RIGHT...
I GUESS WE HAVE TO GO SAVE GOTHAM CITY NOW...
YES...
...BUT FALL IN LOVE?

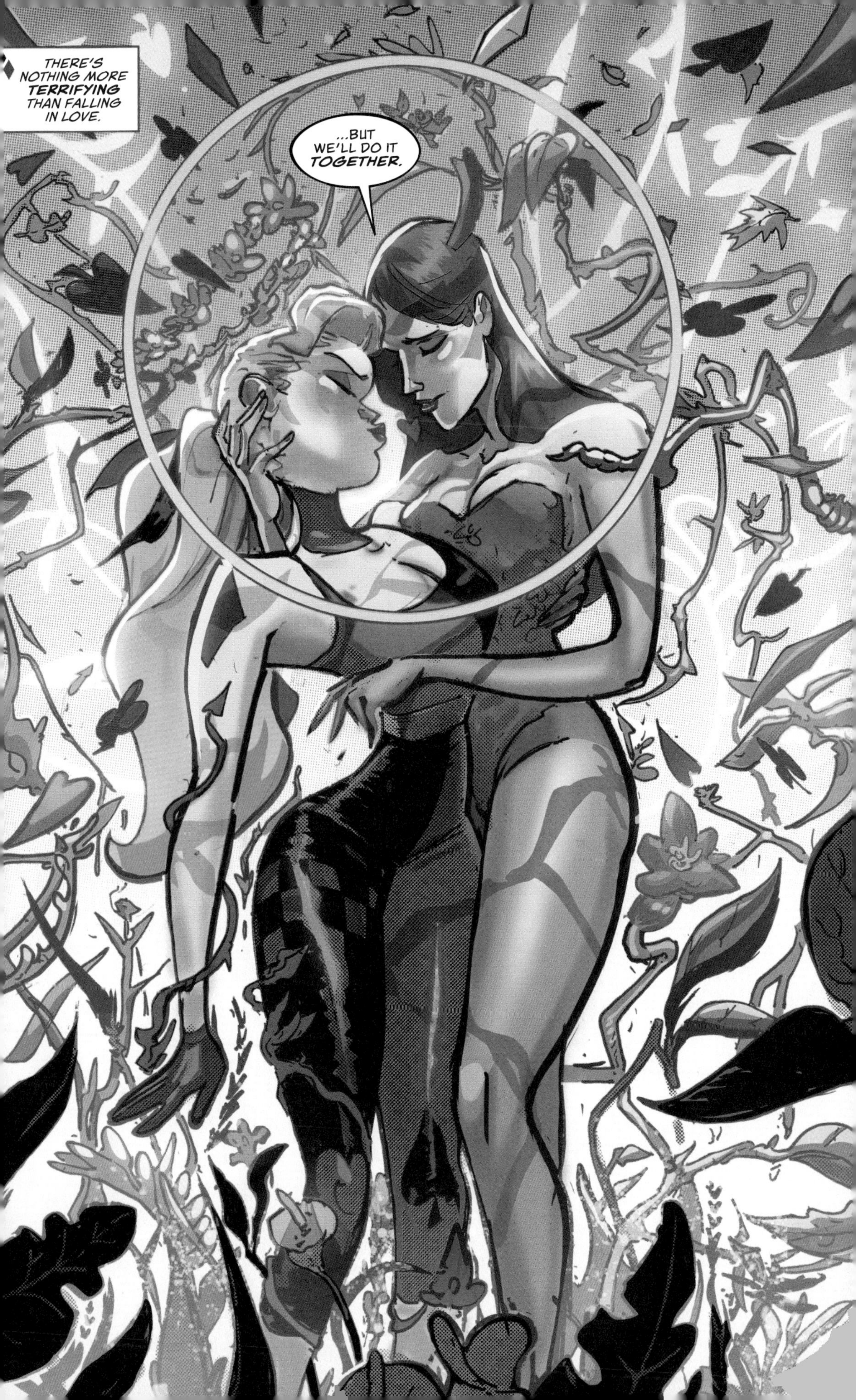
THERE'S NOTHING MORE **TERRIFYING** THAN FALLING IN LOVE.
...BUT WE'LL DO IT **TOGETHER.**

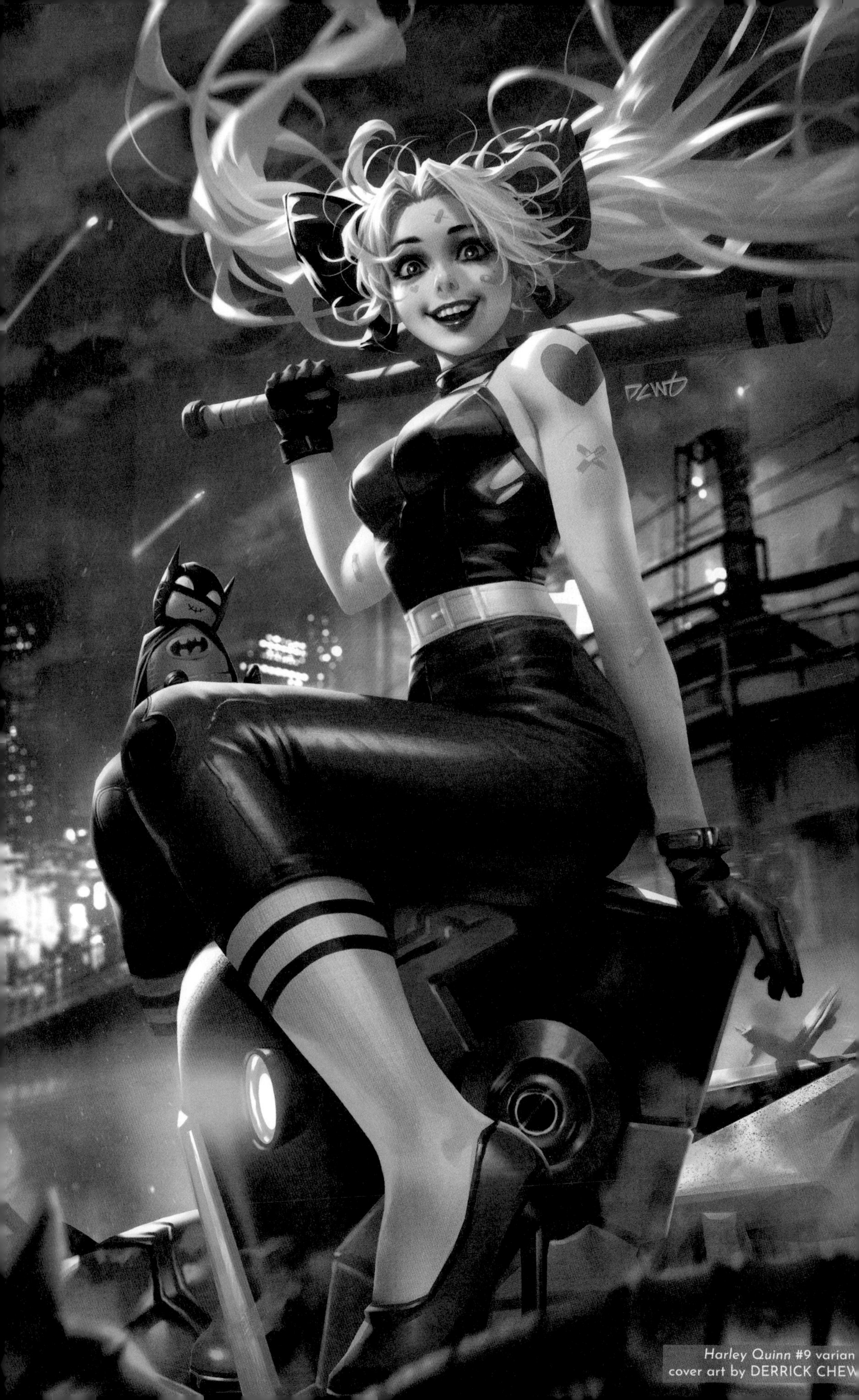

Harley Quinn #9 varian
cover art by DERRICK CHEW

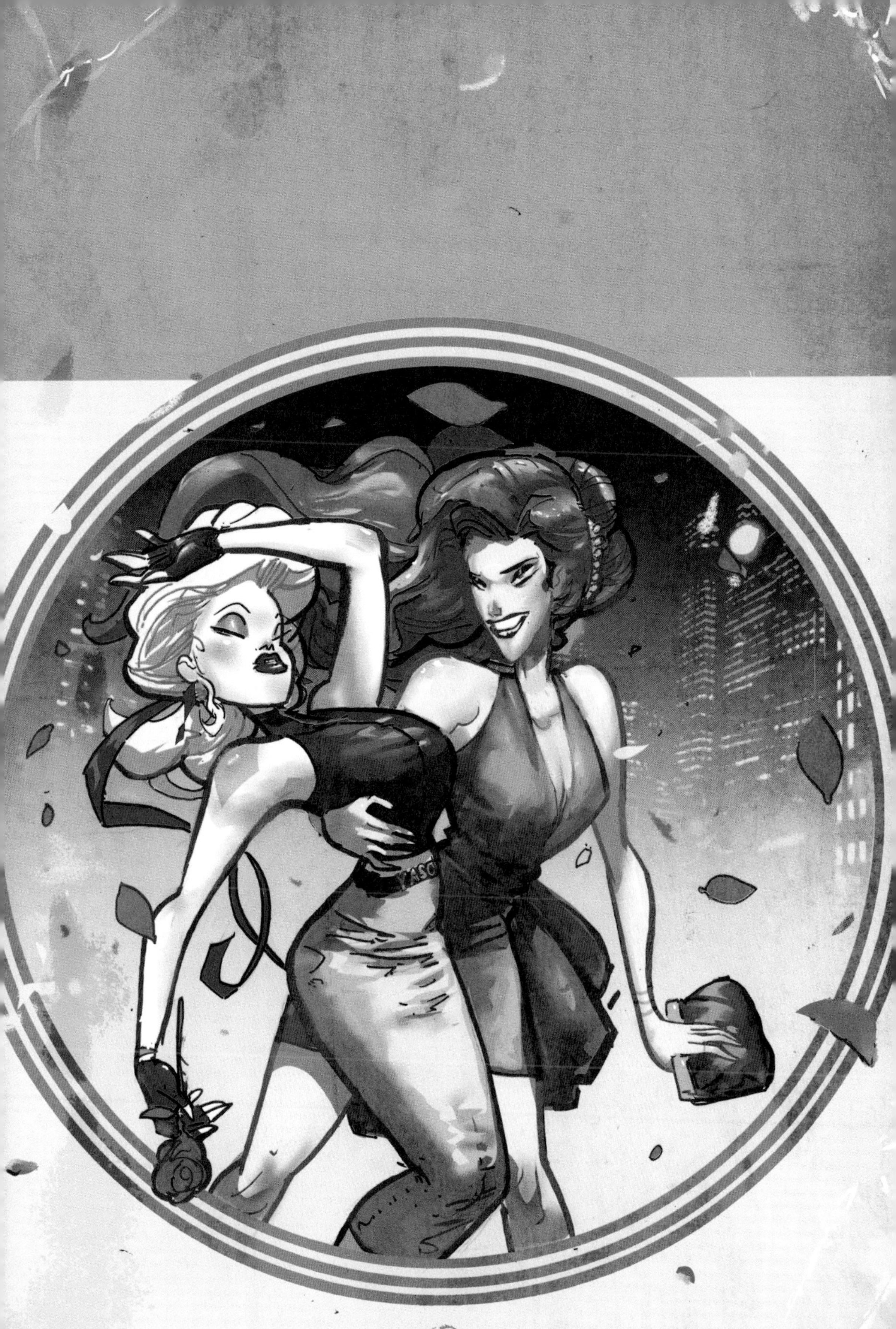

WAFFLE DOG PRESS

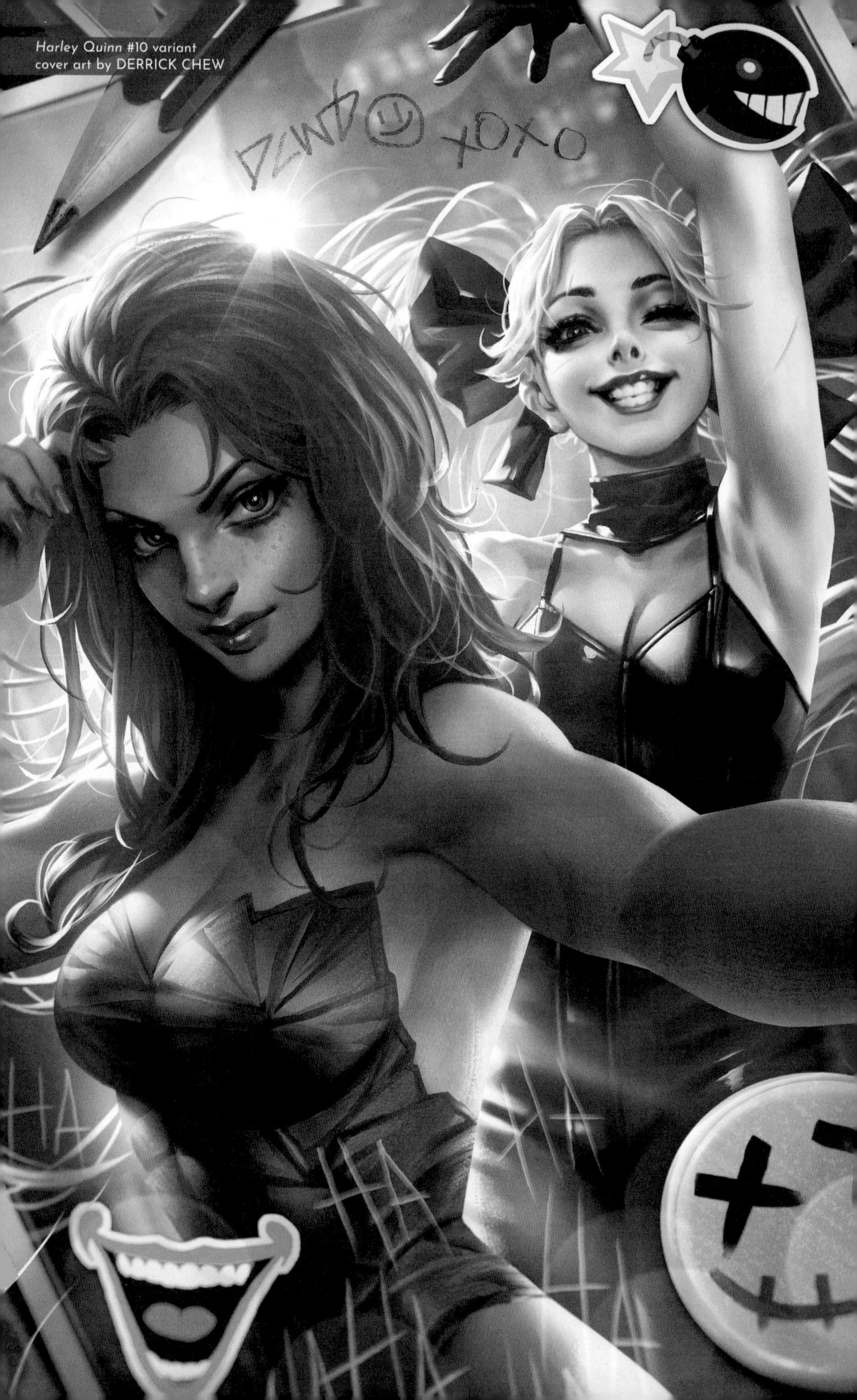
XOXO

Harley Quinn #10 variant
cover art by DERRICK CHEW

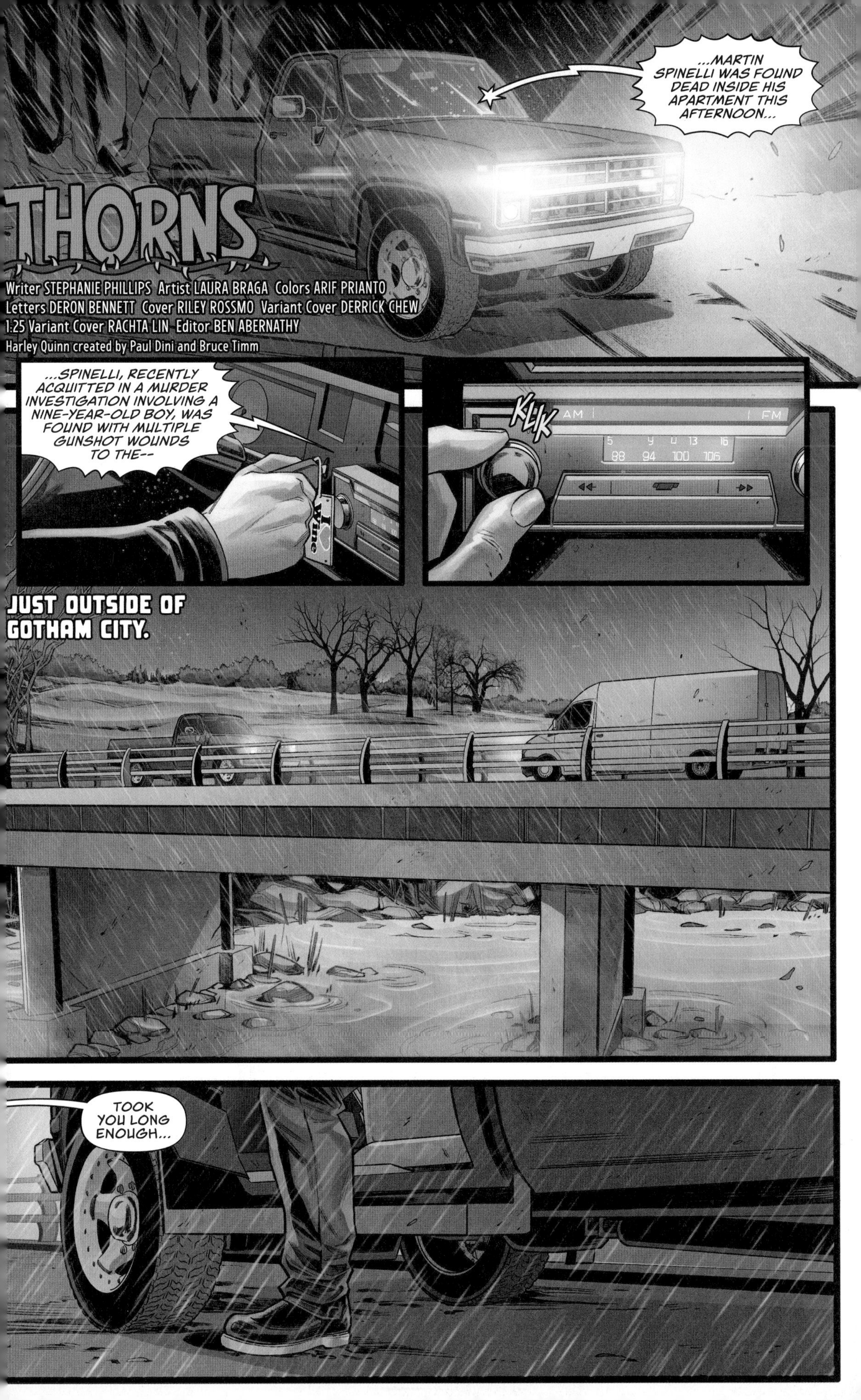
...MARTIN SPINELLI WAS FOUND DEAD INSIDE HIS APARTMENT THIS AFTERNOON...
THORNS
Writer STEPHANIE PHILLIPS Artist LAURA BRAGA Colors ARIF PRIANTO
Letters DERON BENNETT Cover RILEY ROSSMO Variant Cover DERRICK CHEW
1:25 Variant Cover RACHTA LIN Editor BEN ABERNATHY
Harley Quinn created by Paul Dini and Bruce Timm
...SPINELLI, RECENTLY ACQUITTED IN A MURDER INVESTIGATION INVOLVING A NINE-YEAR-OLD BOY, WAS FOUND WITH MULTIPLE GUNSHOT WOUNDS TO THE--
I Wine
KLIK
AM FM
JUST OUTSIDE OF GOTHAM CITY.
TOOK YOU LONG ENOUGH...

...I'VE BEEN WAITING IN THE *RAIN* FOR *TWENTY* MINUTES.

IT'S GOTHAM, ELI. IT *ALWAYS* RAINS.

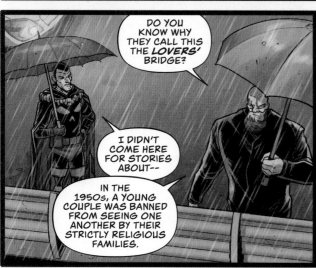

DO YOU KNOW WHY THEY CALL THIS THE *LOVERS'* BRIDGE?

I DIDN'T COME HERE FOR STORIES ABOUT--

IN THE 1950s, A YOUNG COUPLE WAS BANNED FROM SEEING ONE ANOTHER BY THEIR STRICTLY RELIGIOUS FAMILIES.

THEY MET HERE AT MIDNIGHT ON VALENTINE'S DAY AND TOOK THEIR OWN LIVES BY JUMPING HAND IN HAND INTO THE ROCKY WATER BELOW.

SINCE THEN, MANY YOUNG COUPLES HAVE JUMPED HERE TOGETHER... CHASING SOME *LEGEND* ABOUT ONLY *TRUE* LOVE PROTECTING YOU FROM THE CERTAIN DEATH WAITING BELOW.

HUGO, WE *NEED* TO TALK ABOUT *HARLEY.*

IVY'S BACK AND ALL THOSE... THOSE *GIRLS*... THEY *RUINED* MY CAUCUS OF CORRUPTION.

THEY RAN ME OVER WITH A *VAN!*

I *PAID* YOU TO HELP MANUFACTURE THAT DRUG AND IT'S ALL... *RUINED!*

I WANT MY MONEY BACK OR I'M GOING STRAIGHT TO GOTHAM P.D. AND I WILL TELL THEM EVERYTHING WE--

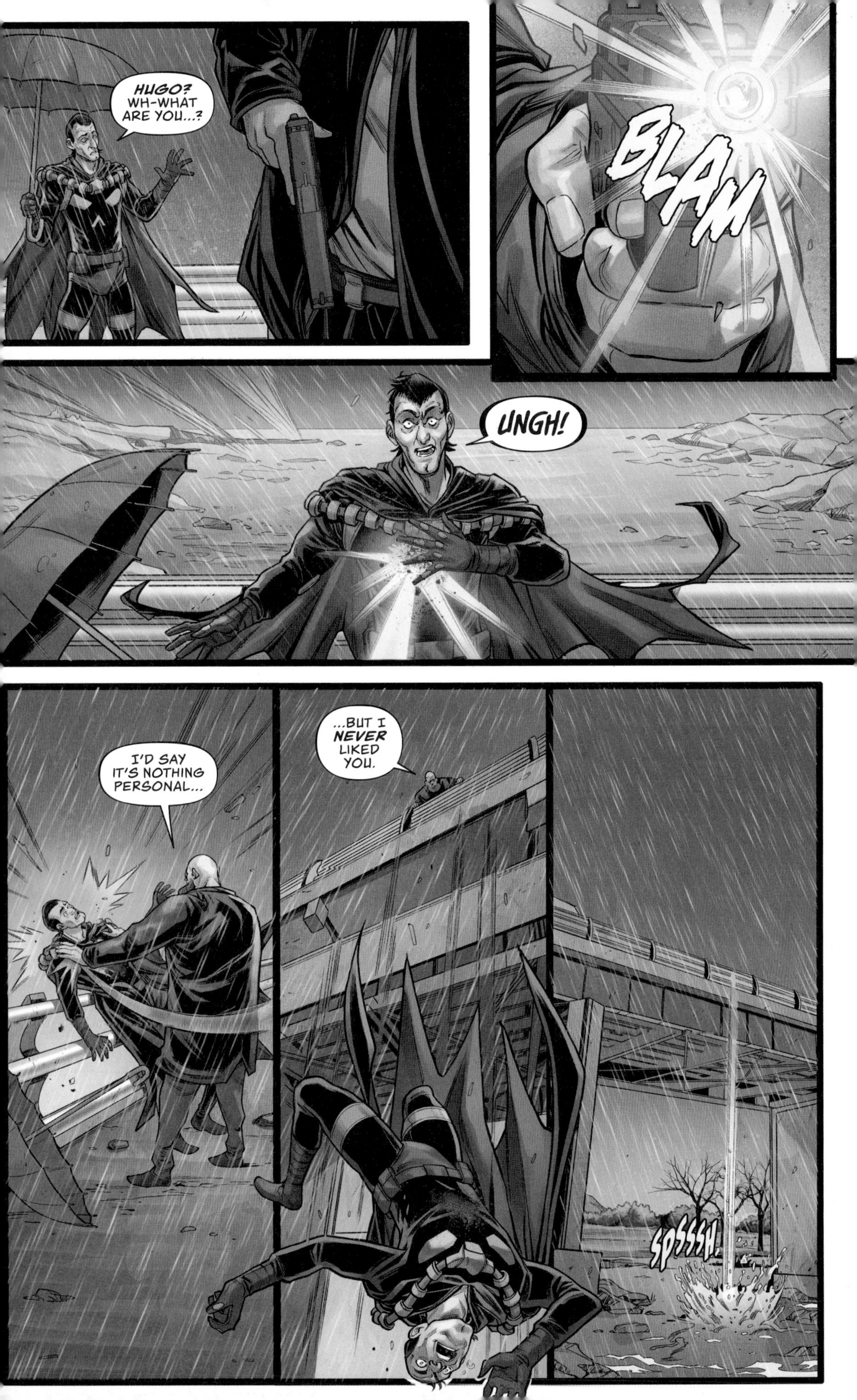
HUGO? WH-WHAT ARE YOU...?
BLAM
UNGH!
I'D SAY IT'S NOTHING PERSONAL...
...BUT I NEVER LIKED YOU.
SPSSSH

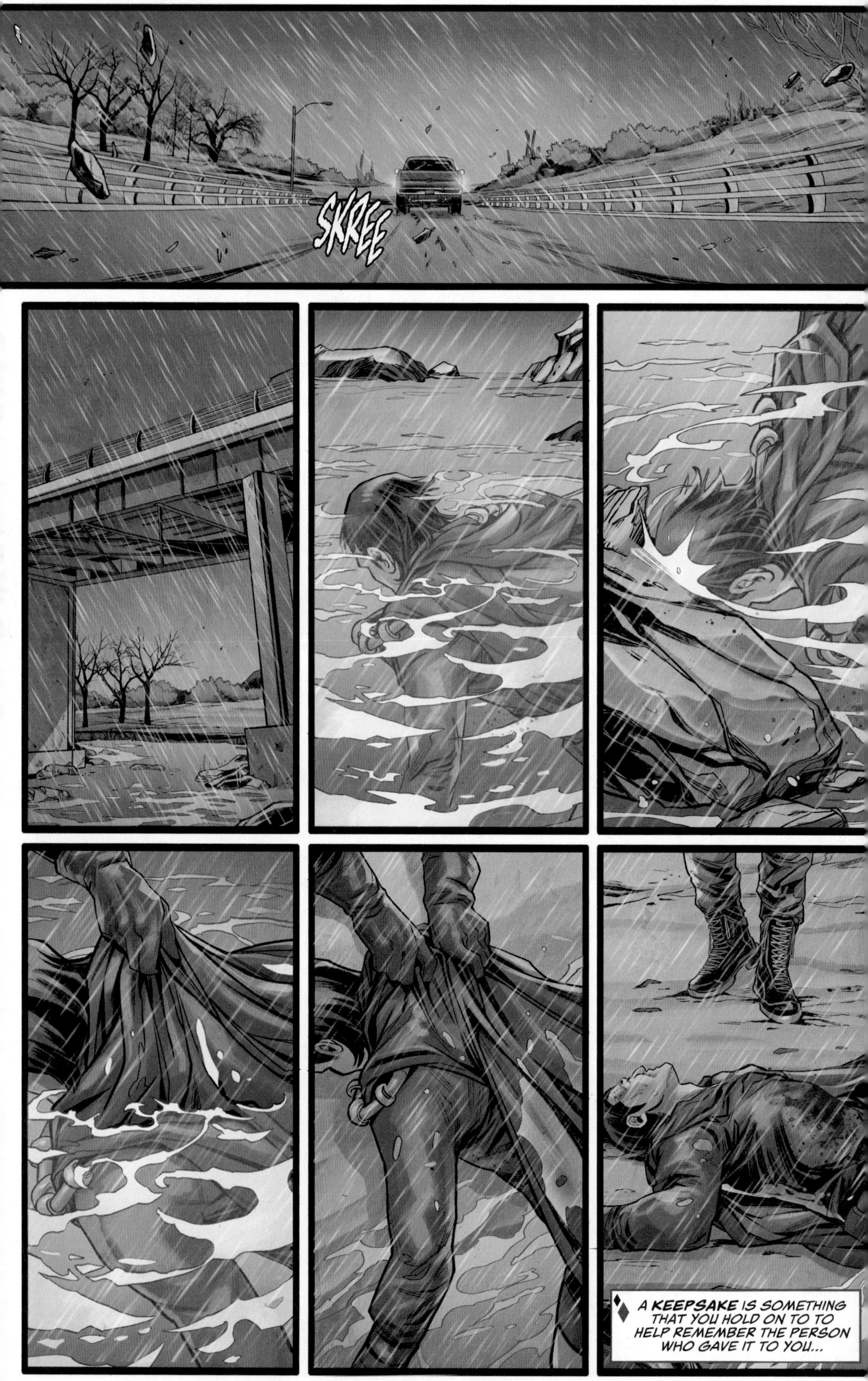
SKREE
A KEEPSAKE IS SOMETHING THAT YOU HOLD ON TO TO HELP REMEMBER THE PERSON WHO GAVE IT TO YOU...

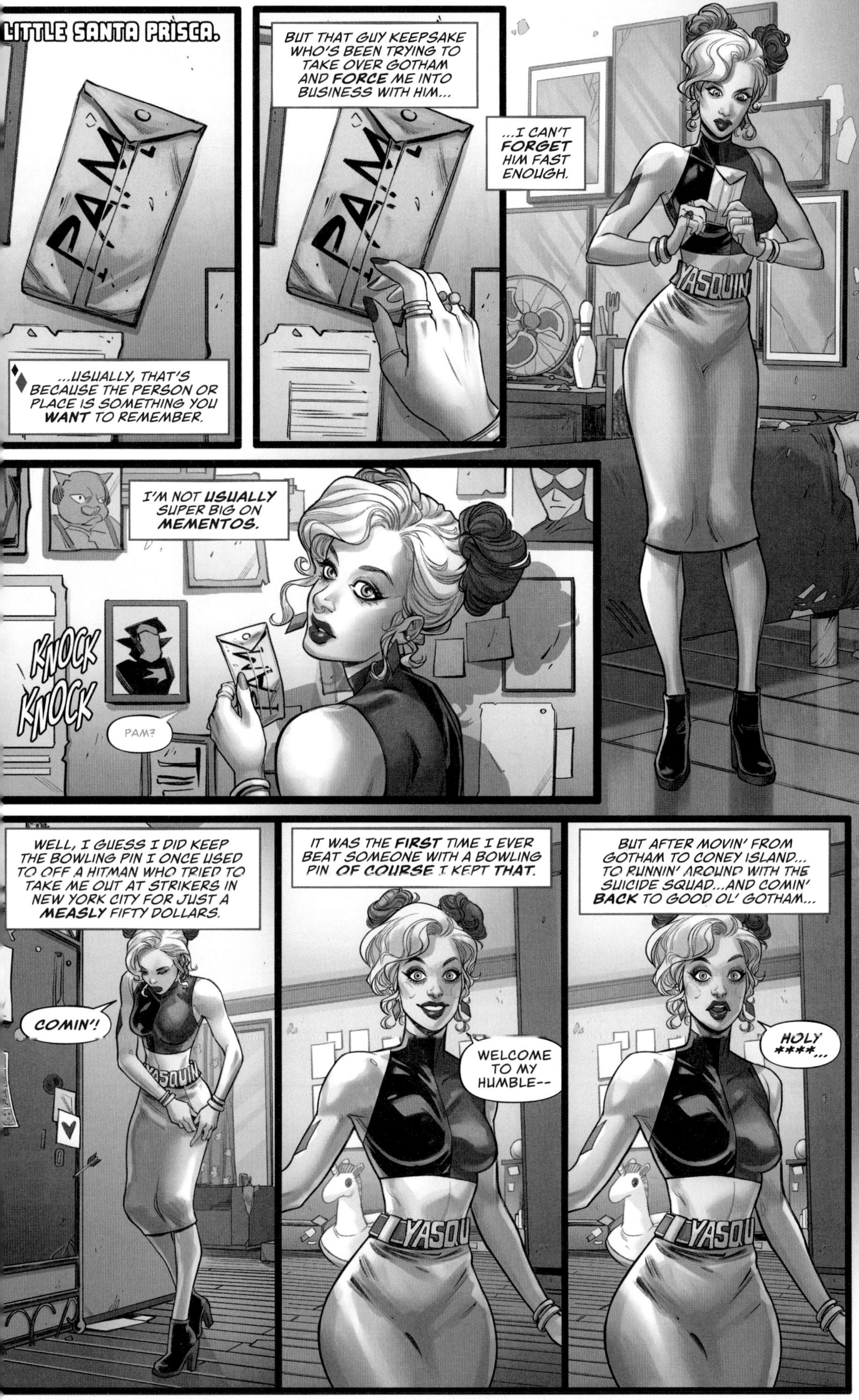
LITTLE SANTA PRISCA.
...USUALLY, THAT'S BECAUSE THE PERSON OR PLACE IS SOMETHING YOU WANT TO REMEMBER.
BUT THAT GUY KEEPSAKE WHO'S BEEN TRYING TO TAKE OVER GOTHAM AND FORCE ME INTO BUSINESS WITH HIM...
...I CAN'T FORGET HIM FAST ENOUGH.
I'M NOT USUALLY SUPER BIG ON MEMENTOS.
KNOCK KNOCK
PAM?
WELL, I GUESS I DID KEEP THE BOWLING PIN I ONCE USED TO OFF A HITMAN WHO TRIED TO TAKE ME OUT AT STRIKERS IN NEW YORK CITY FOR JUST A MEASLY FIFTY DOLLARS.
COMIN'!
IT WAS THE FIRST TIME I EVER BEAT SOMEONE WITH A BOWLING PIN OF COURSE I KEPT THAT.
WELCOME TO MY HUMBLE--
BUT AFTER MOVIN' FROM GOTHAM TO CONEY ISLAND... TO RUNNIN' AROUND WITH THE SUICIDE SQUAD...AND COMIN' BACK TO GOOD OL' GOTHAM...
HOLY ****...

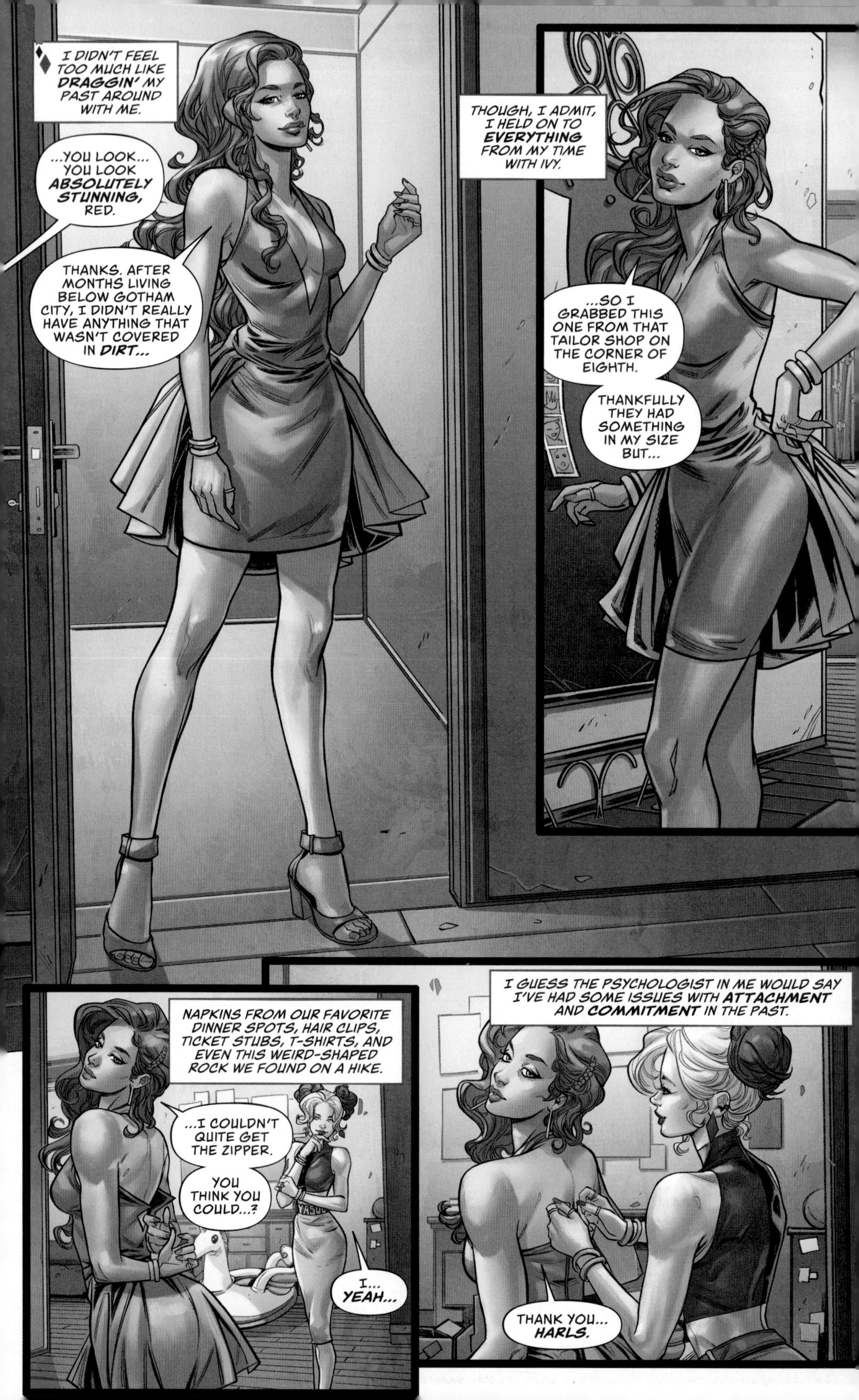
I DIDN'T FEEL TOO MUCH LIKE DRAGGIN' MY PAST AROUND WITH ME.
...YOU LOOK... YOU LOOK ABSOLUTELY STUNNING, RED.
THANKS. AFTER MONTHS LIVING BELOW GOTHAM CITY, I DIDN'T REALLY HAVE ANYTHING THAT WASN'T COVERED IN DIRT...
THOUGH, I ADMIT, I HELD ON TO EVERYTHING FROM MY TIME WITH IVY.
...SO I GRABBED THIS ONE FROM THAT TAILOR SHOP ON THE CORNER OF EIGHTH.
THANKFULLY THEY HAD SOMETHING IN MY SIZE BUT...
NAPKINS FROM OUR FAVORITE DINNER SPOTS, HAIR CLIPS, TICKET STUBS, T-SHIRTS, AND EVEN THIS WEIRD-SHAPED ROCK WE FOUND ON A HIKE.
...I COULDN'T QUITE GET THE ZIPPER.
YOU THINK YOU COULD...?
I... YEAH...
I GUESS THE PSYCHOLOGIST IN ME WOULD SAY I'VE HAD SOME ISSUES WITH ATTACHMENT AND COMMITMENT IN THE PAST.
THANK YOU... HARLS.

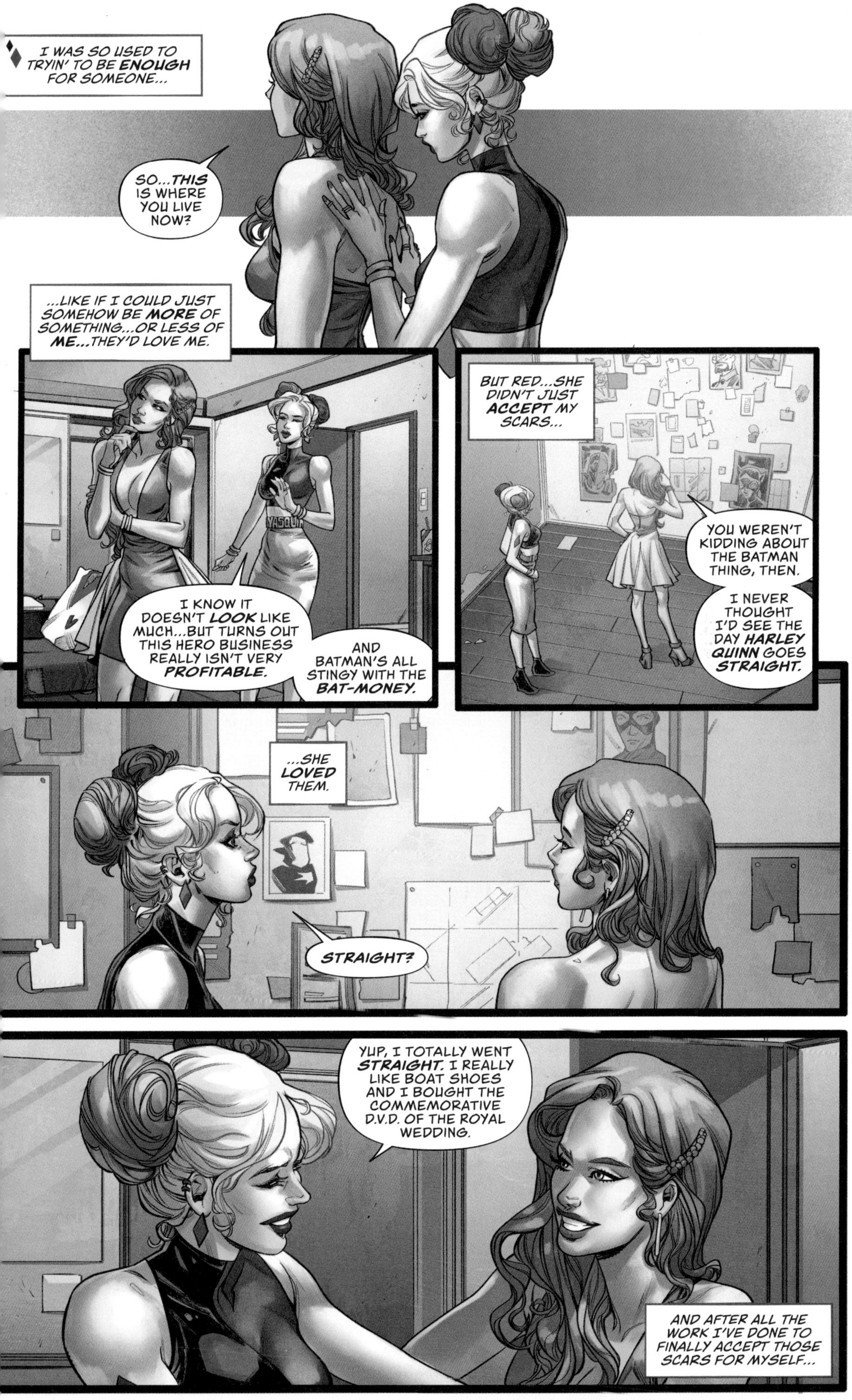
I WAS SO USED TO TRYIN' TO BE ENOUGH FOR SOMEONE...
SO...THIS IS WHERE YOU LIVE NOW?
...LIKE IF I COULD JUST SOMEHOW BE MORE OF SOMETHING...OR LESS OF ME...THEY'D LOVE ME.
I KNOW IT DOESN'T LOOK LIKE MUCH...BUT TURNS OUT THIS HERO BUSINESS REALLY ISN'T VERY PROFITABLE.
AND BATMAN'S ALL STINGY WITH THE BAT-MONEY.
BUT RED...SHE DIDN'T JUST ACCEPT MY SCARS...
YOU WEREN'T KIDDING ABOUT THE BATMAN THING, THEN.
I NEVER THOUGHT I'D SEE THE DAY HARLEY QUINN GOES STRAIGHT.
...SHE LOVED THEM.
STRAIGHT?
YUP, I TOTALLY WENT STRAIGHT. I REALLY LIKE BOAT SHOES AND I BOUGHT THE COMMEMORATIVE D.V.D. OF THE ROYAL WEDDING.
AND AFTER ALL THE WORK I'VE DONE TO FINALLY ACCEPT THOSE SCARS FOR MYSELF...

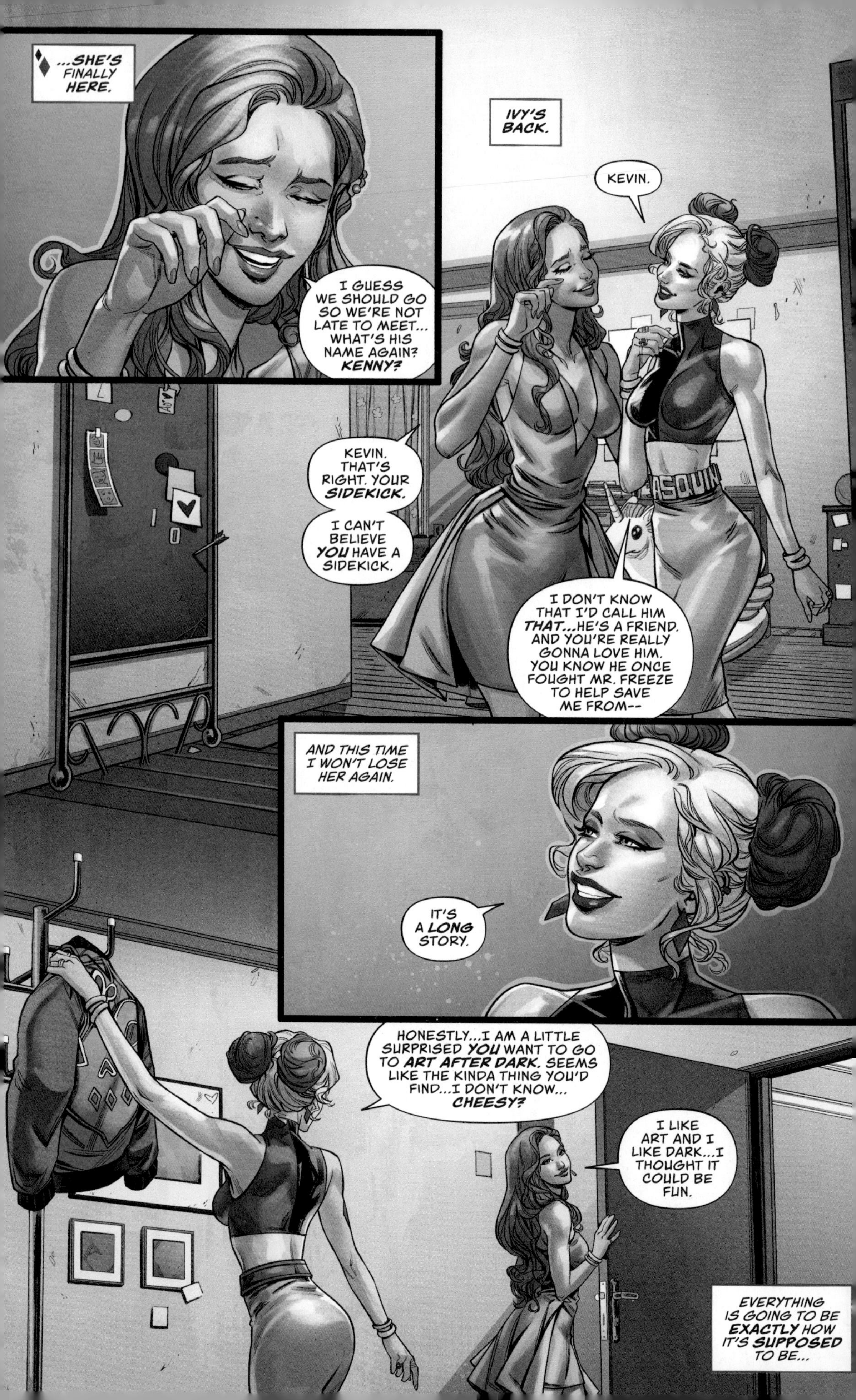
...SHE'S FINALLY HERE.
I GUESS WE SHOULD GO SO WE'RE NOT LATE TO MEET... WHAT'S HIS NAME AGAIN? KENNY?
IVY'S BACK.
KEVIN.
KEVIN. THAT'S RIGHT. YOUR SIDEKICK.
I CAN'T BELIEVE YOU HAVE A SIDEKICK.
I DON'T KNOW THAT I'D CALL HIM THAT...HE'S A FRIEND. AND YOU'RE REALLY GONNA LOVE HIM. YOU KNOW HE ONCE FOUGHT MR. FREEZE TO HELP SAVE ME FROM--
AND THIS TIME I WON'T LOSE HER AGAIN.
IT'S A LONG STORY.
HONESTLY...I AM A LITTLE SURPRISED YOU WANT TO GO TO ART AFTER DARK. SEEMS LIKE THE KINDA THING YOU'D FIND...I DON'T KNOW... CHEESY?
I LIKE ART AND I LIKE DARK...I THOUGHT IT COULD BE FUN.
EVERYTHING IS GOING TO BE EXACTLY HOW IT'S SUPPOSED TO BE...

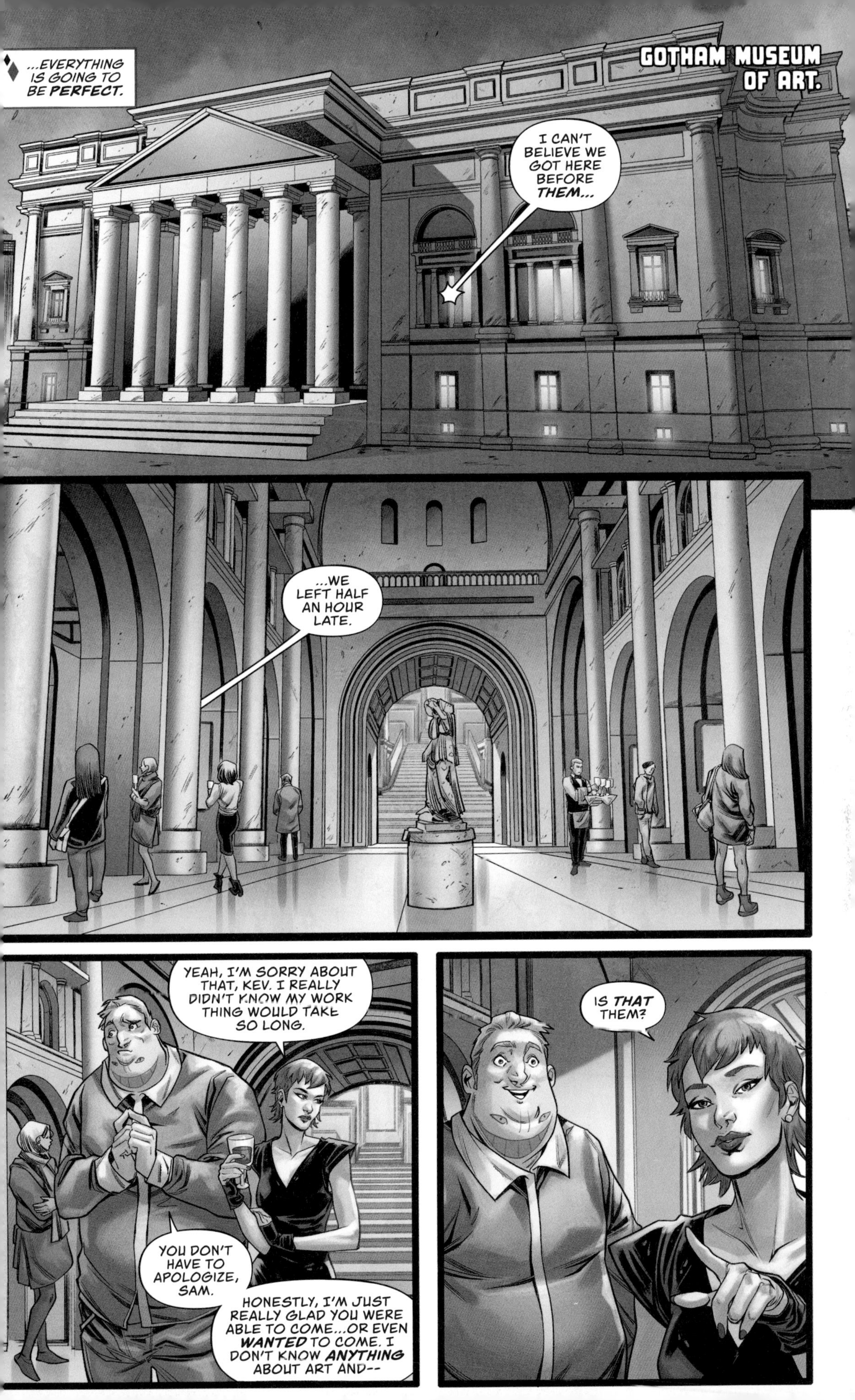
...EVERYTHING IS GOING TO BE PERFECT.
GOTHAM MUSEUM OF ART.
I CAN'T BELIEVE WE GOT HERE BEFORE THEM...
...WE LEFT HALF AN HOUR LATE.
YEAH, I'M SORRY ABOUT THAT, KEV. I REALLY DIDN'T KNOW MY WORK THING WOULD TAKE SO LONG.
YOU DON'T HAVE TO APOLOGIZE, SAM.
HONESTLY, I'M JUST REALLY GLAD YOU WERE ABLE TO COME...OR EVEN WANTED TO COME. I DON'T KNOW ANYTHING ABOUT ART AND--
IS THAT THEM?

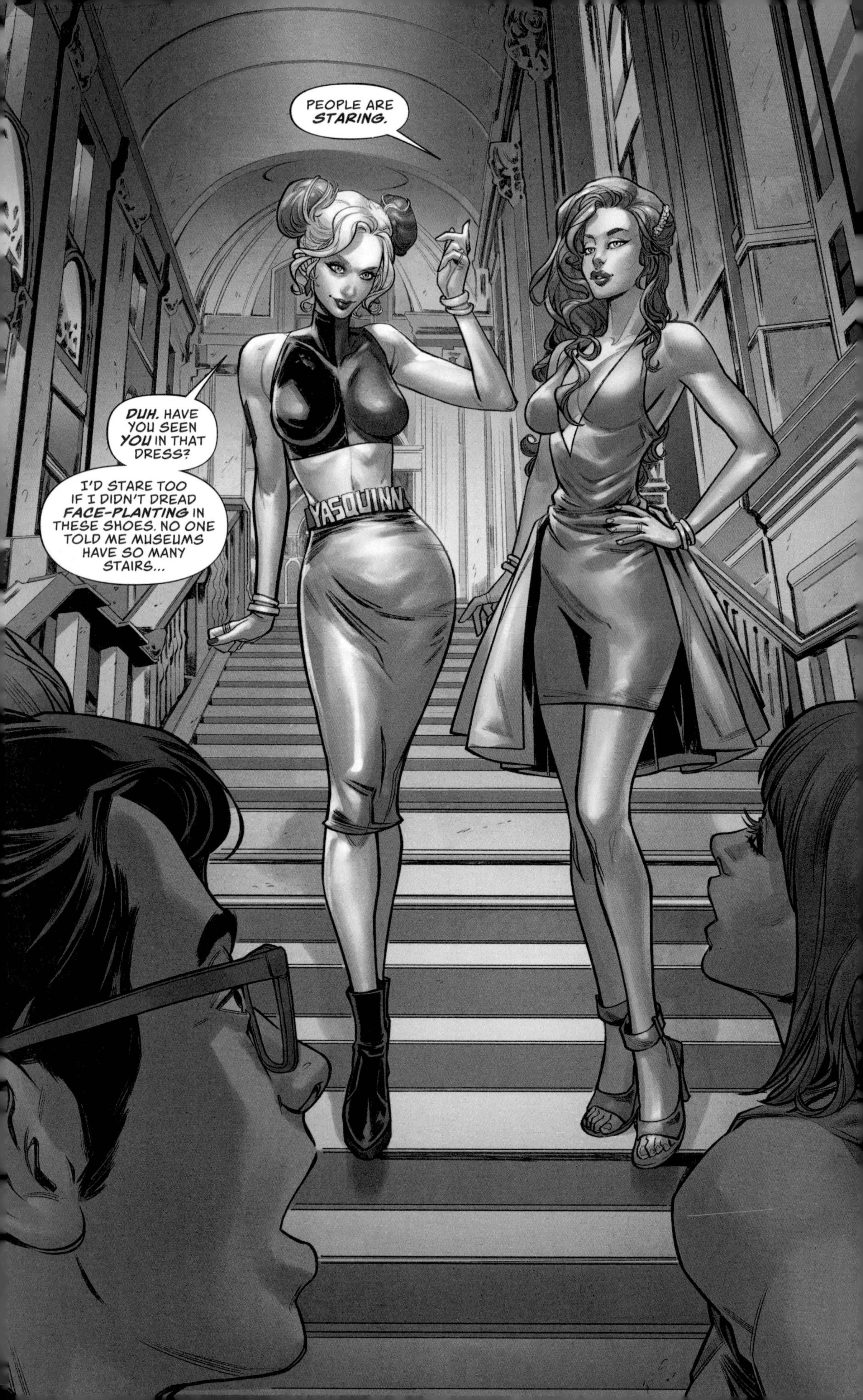
PEOPLE ARE STARING.
DUH. HAVE YOU SEEN YOU IN THAT DRESS?
I'D STARE TOO IF I DIDN'T DREAD FACE-PLANTING IN THESE SHOES. NO ONE TOLD ME MUSEUMS HAVE SO MANY STAIRS...
YASQUINN

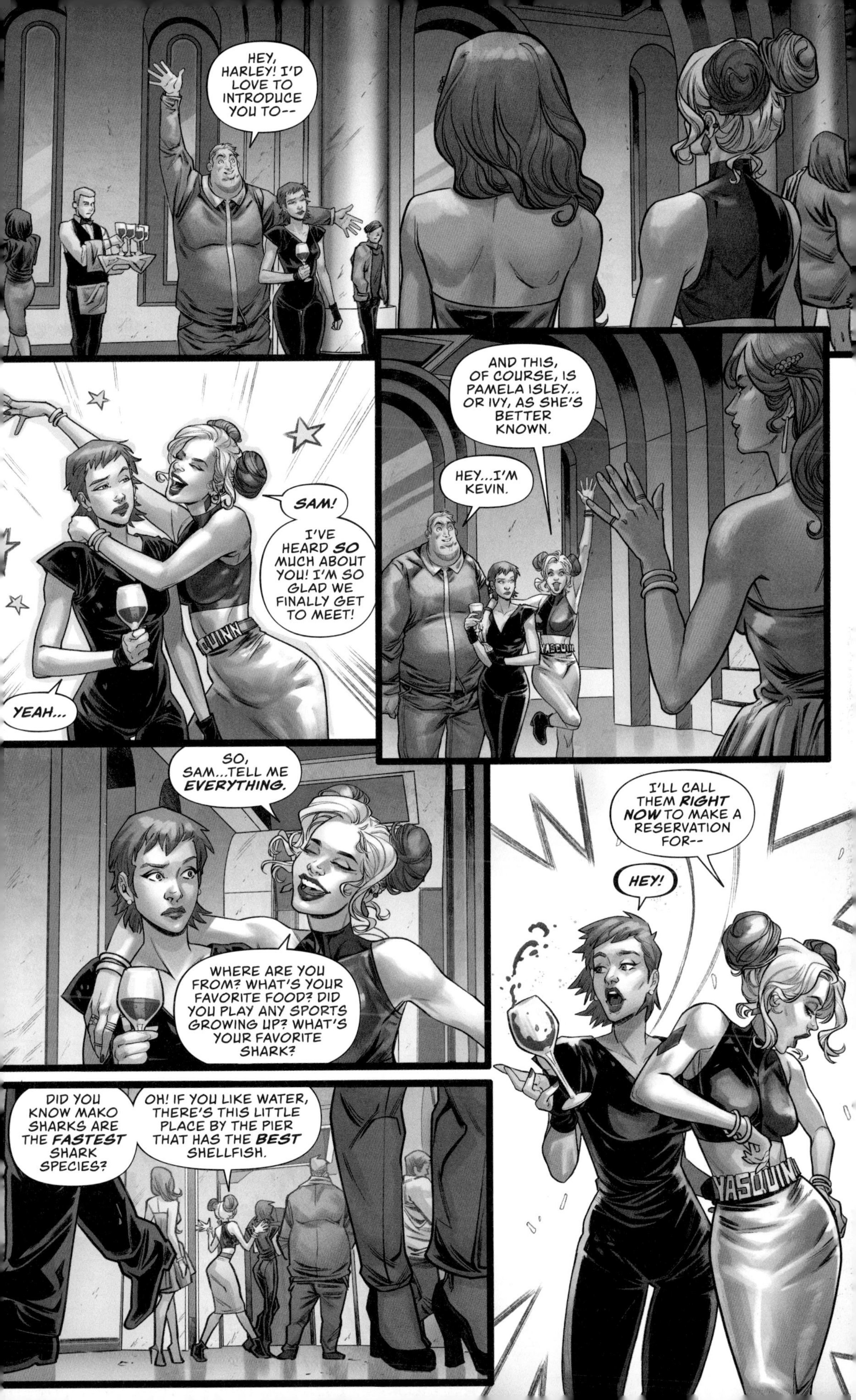
HEY, HARLEY! I'D LOVE TO INTRODUCE YOU TO--
SAM!
I'VE HEARD SO MUCH ABOUT YOU! I'M SO GLAD WE FINALLY GET TO MEET!
YEAH...
AND THIS, OF COURSE, IS PAMELA ISLEY... OR IVY, AS SHE'S BETTER KNOWN.
HEY...I'M KEVIN.
QUINN
SO, SAM...TELL ME EVERYTHING.
WHERE ARE YOU FROM? WHAT'S YOUR FAVORITE FOOD? DID YOU PLAY ANY SPORTS GROWING UP? WHAT'S YOUR FAVORITE SHARK?
DID YOU KNOW MAKO SHARKS ARE THE FASTEST SHARK SPECIES?
OH! IF YOU LIKE WATER, THERE'S THIS LITTLE PLACE BY THE PIER THAT HAS THE BEST SHELLFISH.
I'LL CALL THEM RIGHT NOW TO MAKE A RESERVATION FOR--
HEY!

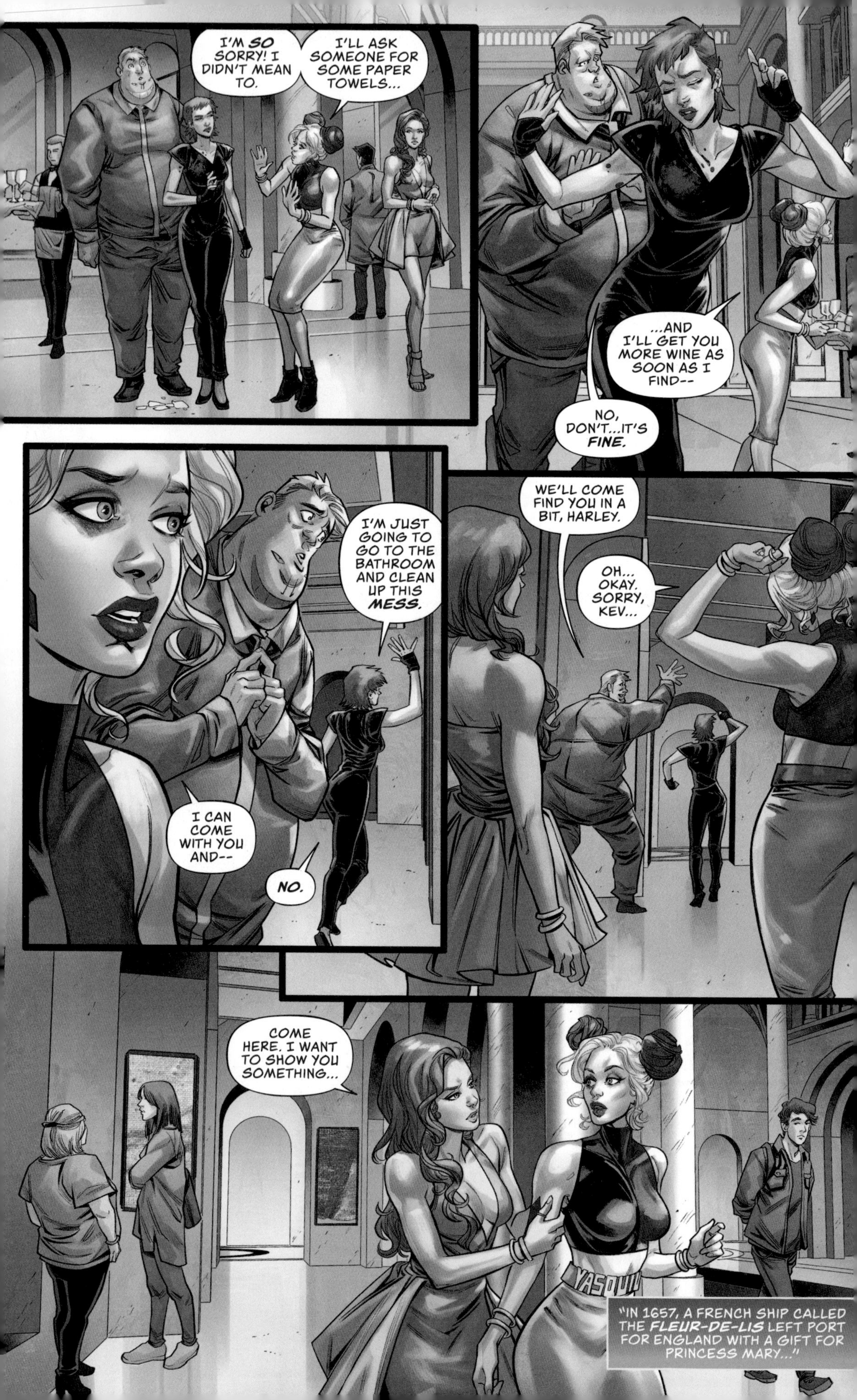

I'M SO SORRY! I DIDN'T MEAN TO.
I'LL ASK SOMEONE FOR SOME PAPER TOWELS...
...AND I'LL GET YOU MORE WINE AS SOON AS I FIND--
NO, DON'T...IT'S FINE.
I'M JUST GOING TO GO TO THE BATHROOM AND CLEAN UP THIS MESS.
I CAN COME WITH YOU AND--
NO.
WE'LL COME FIND YOU IN A BIT, HARLEY.
OH... OKAY. SORRY, KEV...
COME HERE. I WANT TO SHOW YOU SOMETHING...
"IN 1657, A FRENCH SHIP CALLED THE FLEUR-DE-LIS LEFT PORT FOR ENGLAND WITH A GIFT FOR PRINCESS MARY..."

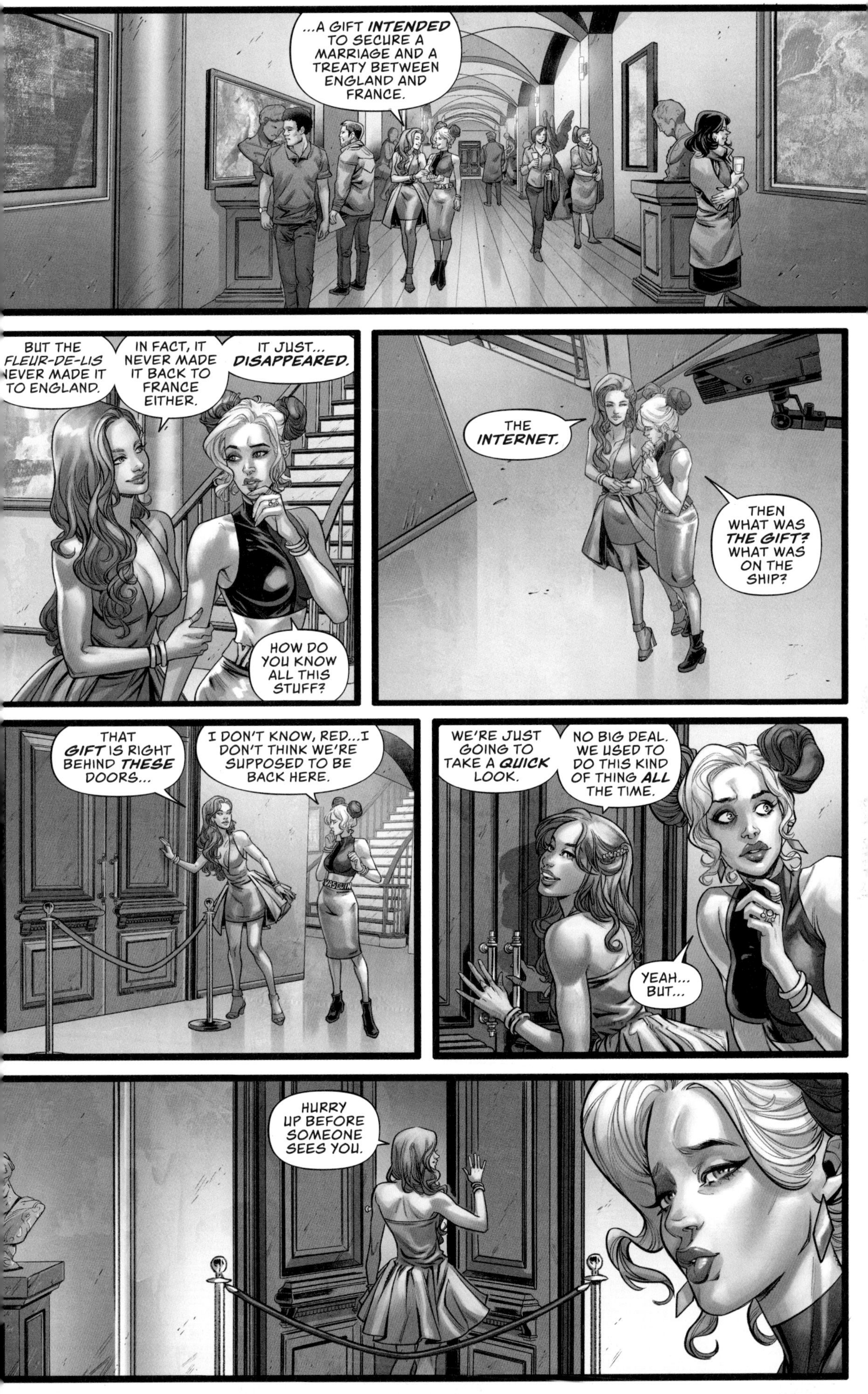
...A GIFT INTENDED TO SECURE A MARRIAGE AND A TREATY BETWEEN ENGLAND AND FRANCE.
BUT THE FLEUR-DE-LIS NEVER MADE IT TO ENGLAND.
IN FACT, IT NEVER MADE IT BACK TO FRANCE EITHER.
IT JUST... DISAPPEARED.
HOW DO YOU KNOW ALL THIS STUFF?
THE INTERNET.
THEN WHAT WAS THE GIFT? WHAT WAS ON THE SHIP?
THAT GIFT IS RIGHT BEHIND THESE DOORS...
I DON'T KNOW, RED...I DON'T THINK WE'RE SUPPOSED TO BE BACK HERE.
WE'RE JUST GOING TO TAKE A QUICK LOOK.
NO BIG DEAL. WE USED TO DO THIS KIND OF THING ALL THE TIME.
YEAH... BUT...
HURRY UP BEFORE SOMEONE SEES YOU.

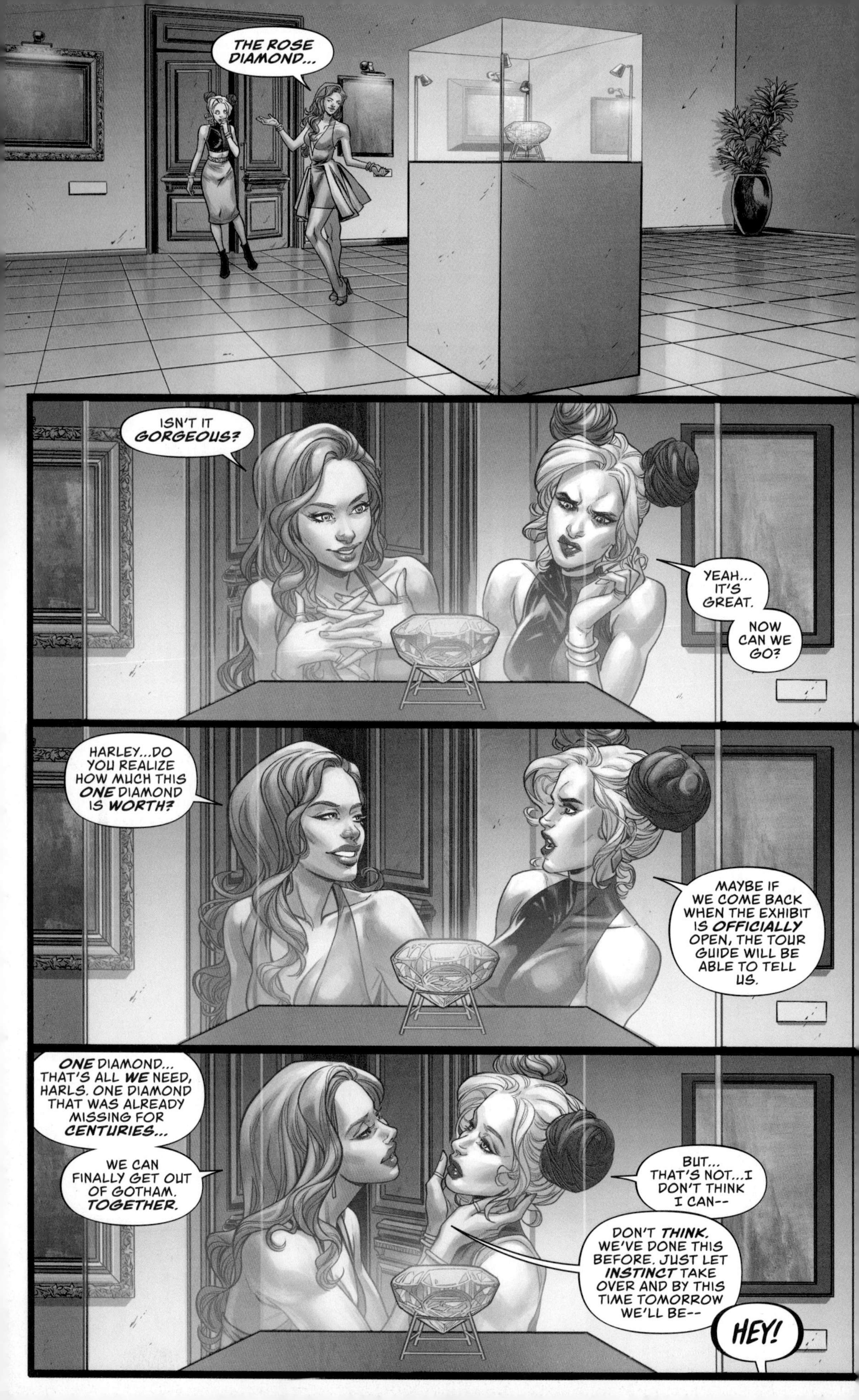
THE ROSE DIAMOND...
ISN'T IT GORGEOUS?
YEAH... IT'S GREAT.
NOW CAN WE GO?
HARLEY...DO YOU REALIZE HOW MUCH THIS ONE DIAMOND IS WORTH?
MAYBE IF WE COME BACK WHEN THE EXHIBIT IS OFFICIALLY OPEN, THE TOUR GUIDE WILL BE ABLE TO TELL US.
ONE DIAMOND... THAT'S ALL WE NEED, HARLS. ONE DIAMOND THAT WAS ALREADY MISSING FOR CENTURIES...
WE CAN FINALLY GET OUT OF GOTHAM. TOGETHER.
BUT... THAT'S NOT...I DON'T THINK I CAN--
DON'T THINK. WE'VE DONE THIS BEFORE. JUST LET INSTINCT TAKE OVER AND BY THIS TIME TOMORROW WE'LL BE--
HEY!

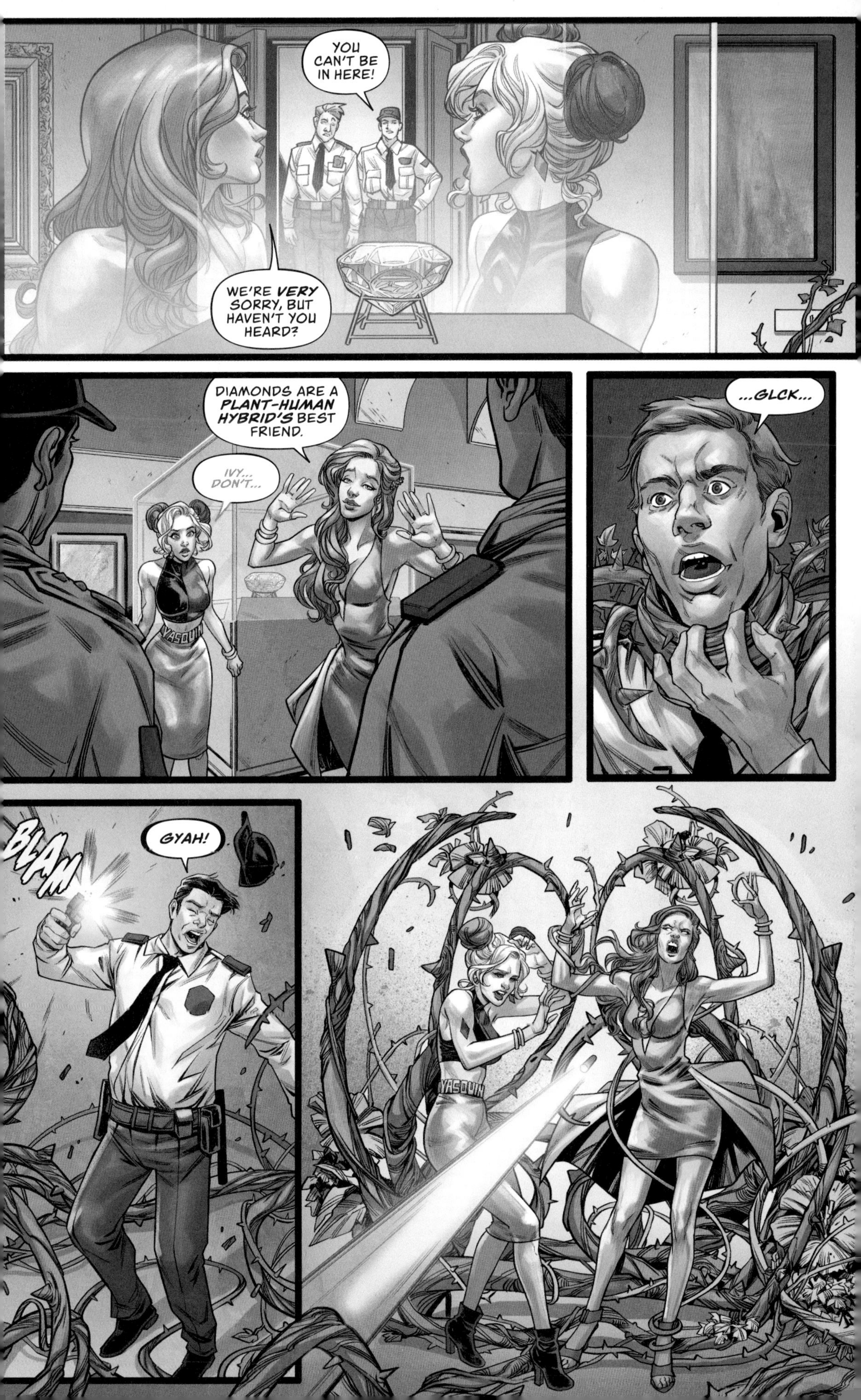

YOU CAN'T BE IN HERE!
WE'RE VERY SORRY, BUT HAVEN'T YOU HEARD?
DIAMONDS ARE A PLANT-HUMAN HYBRID'S BEST FRIEND.
IVY... DON'T...
YASQUIN
...GLCK...
BLAM
GYAH!
YASQUIN

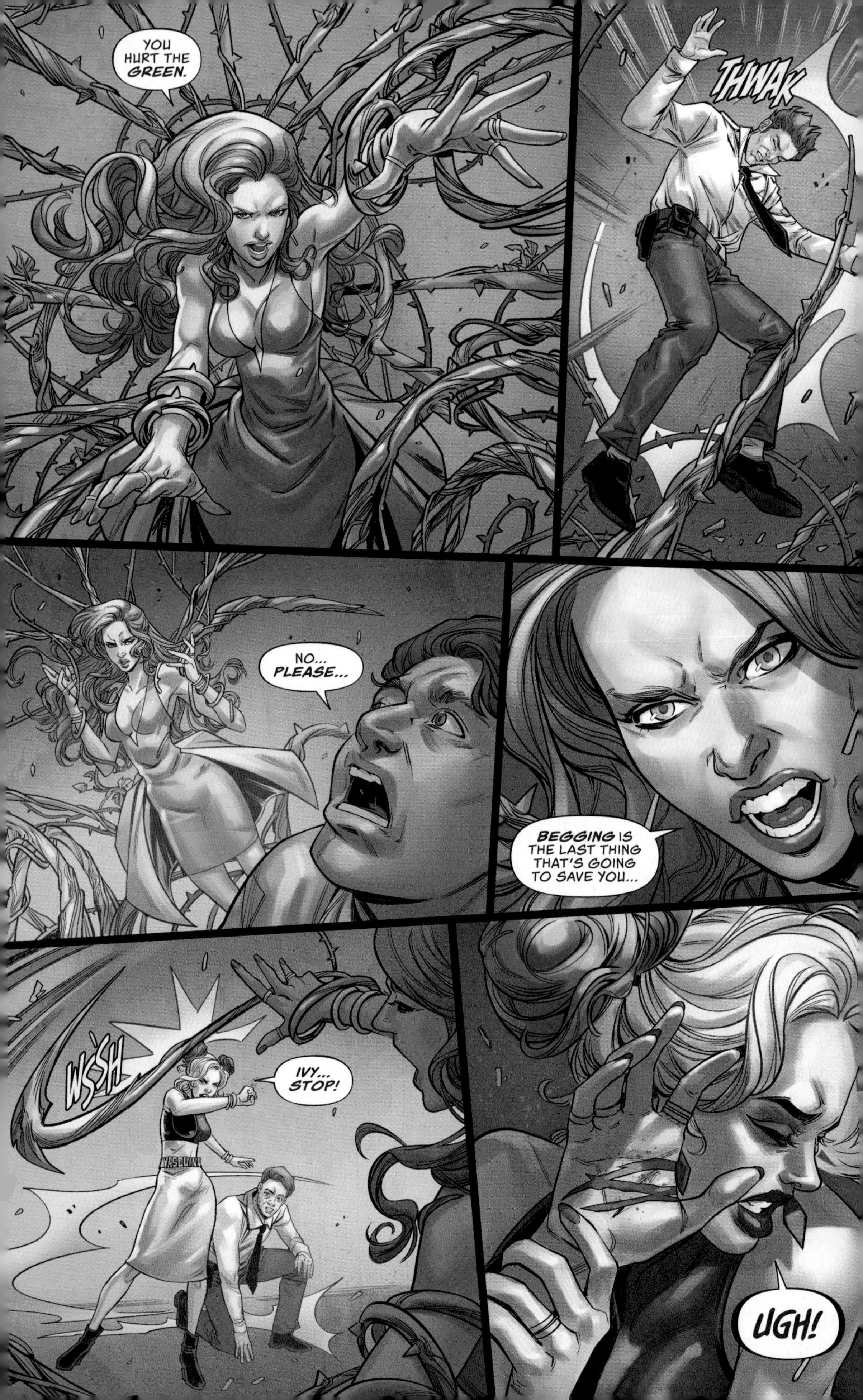
YOU HURT THE GREEN.
THWAK
NO... PLEASE...
BEGGING IS THE LAST THING THAT'S GOING TO SAVE YOU...
WSSH
IVY... STOP!
UGH!

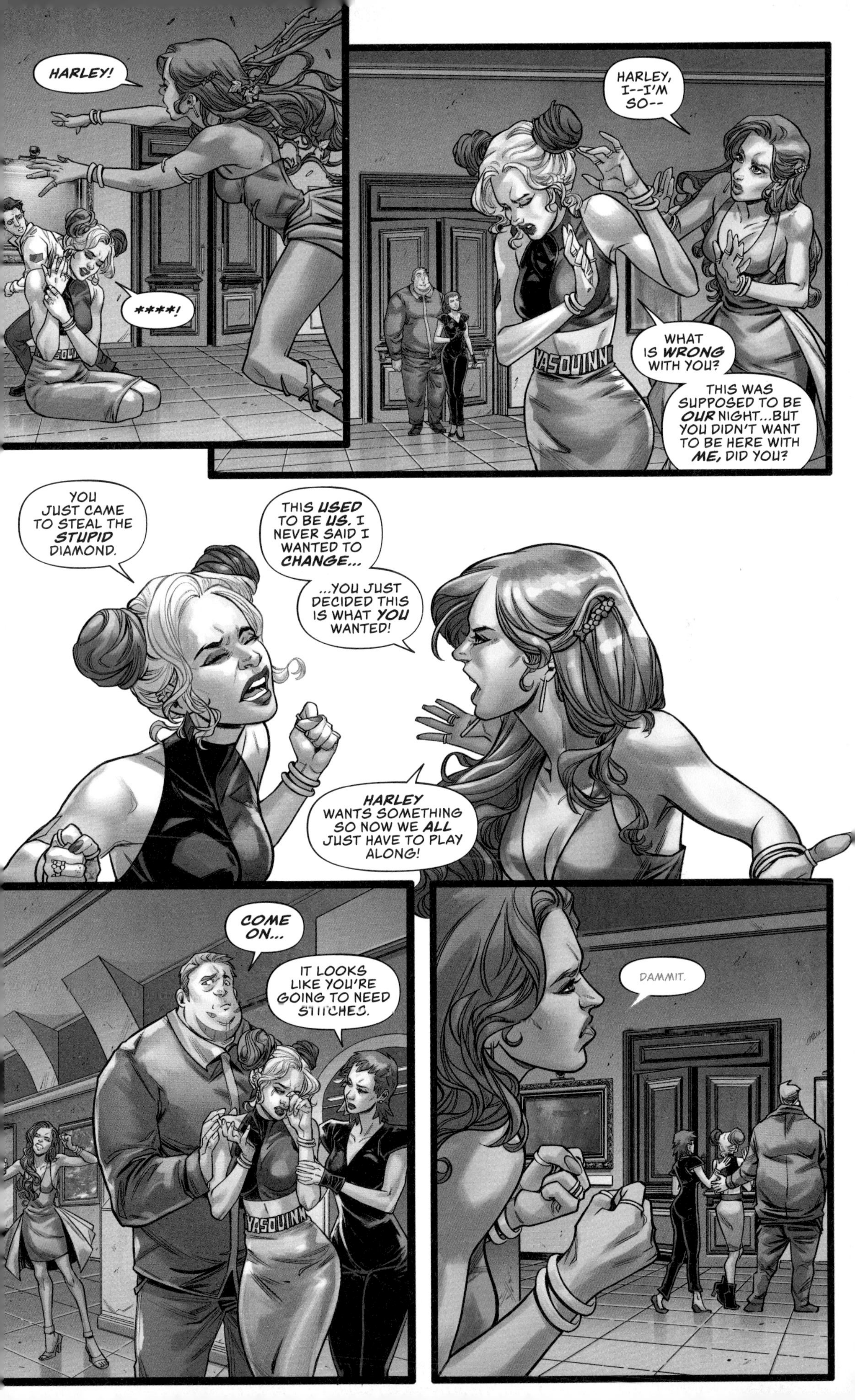

HARLEY!
****!
HARLEY, I--I'M SO--
WHAT IS WRONG WITH YOU?
THIS WAS SUPPOSED TO BE OUR NIGHT...BUT YOU DIDN'T WANT TO BE HERE WITH ME, DID YOU?
YOU JUST CAME TO STEAL THE STUPID DIAMOND.
THIS USED TO BE US. I NEVER SAID I WANTED TO CHANGE...
...YOU JUST DECIDED THIS IS WHAT YOU WANTED!
HARLEY WANTS SOMETHING SO NOW WE ALL JUST HAVE TO PLAY ALONG!
COME ON...
IT LOOKS LIKE YOU'RE GOING TO NEED STITCHES.
DAMMIT.

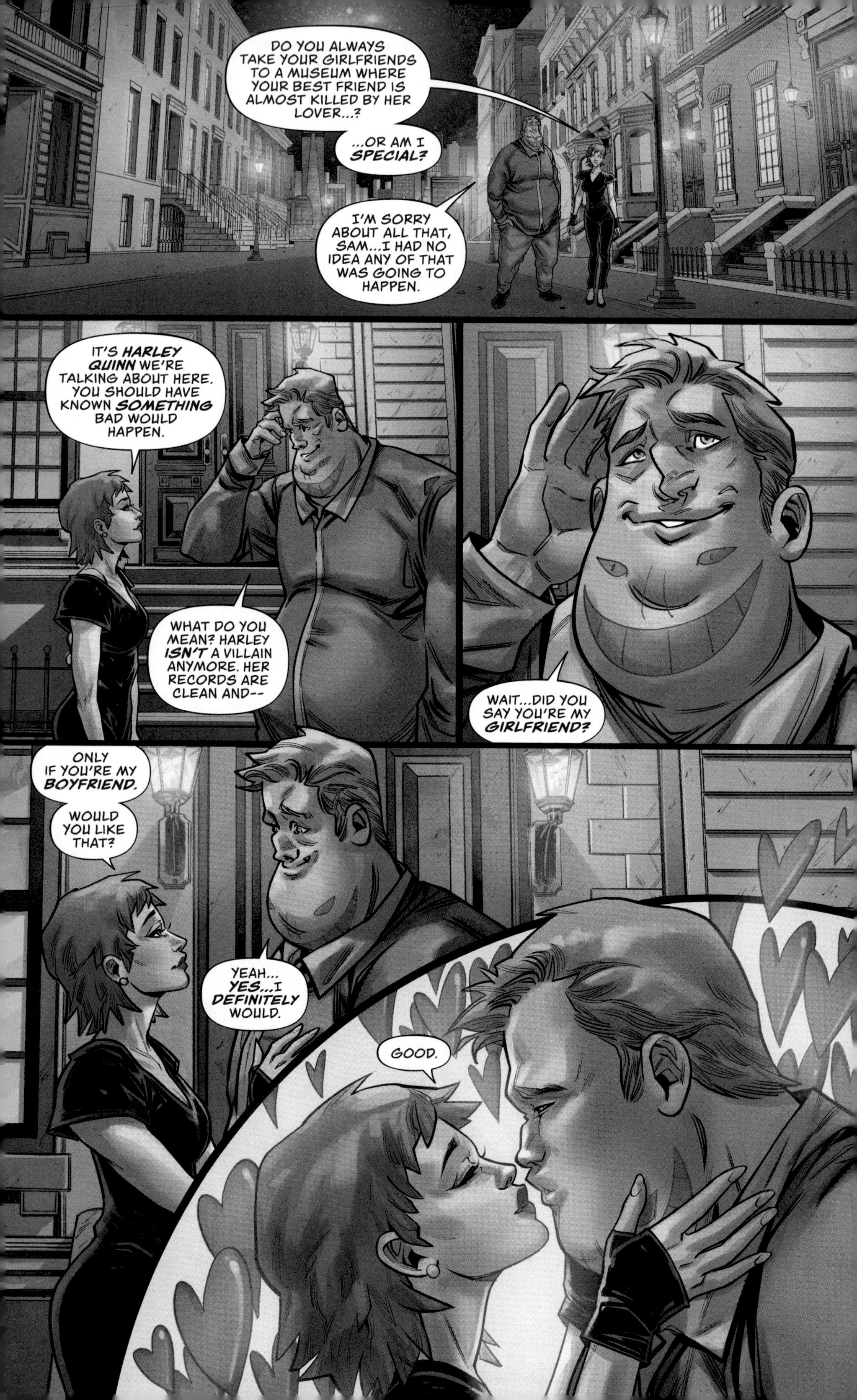
DO YOU ALWAYS TAKE YOUR GIRLFRIENDS TO A MUSEUM WHERE YOUR BEST FRIEND IS ALMOST KILLED BY HER LOVER...?
...OR AM I SPECIAL?
I'M SORRY ABOUT ALL THAT, SAM...I HAD NO IDEA ANY OF THAT WAS GOING TO HAPPEN.
IT'S HARLEY QUINN WE'RE TALKING ABOUT HERE. YOU SHOULD HAVE KNOWN SOMETHING BAD WOULD HAPPEN.
WHAT DO YOU MEAN? HARLEY ISN'T A VILLAIN ANYMORE. HER RECORDS ARE CLEAN AND--
WAIT...DID YOU SAY YOU'RE MY GIRLFRIEND?
ONLY IF YOU'RE MY BOYFRIEND.
WOULD YOU LIKE THAT?
YEAH... YES...I DEFINITELY WOULD.
GOOD.

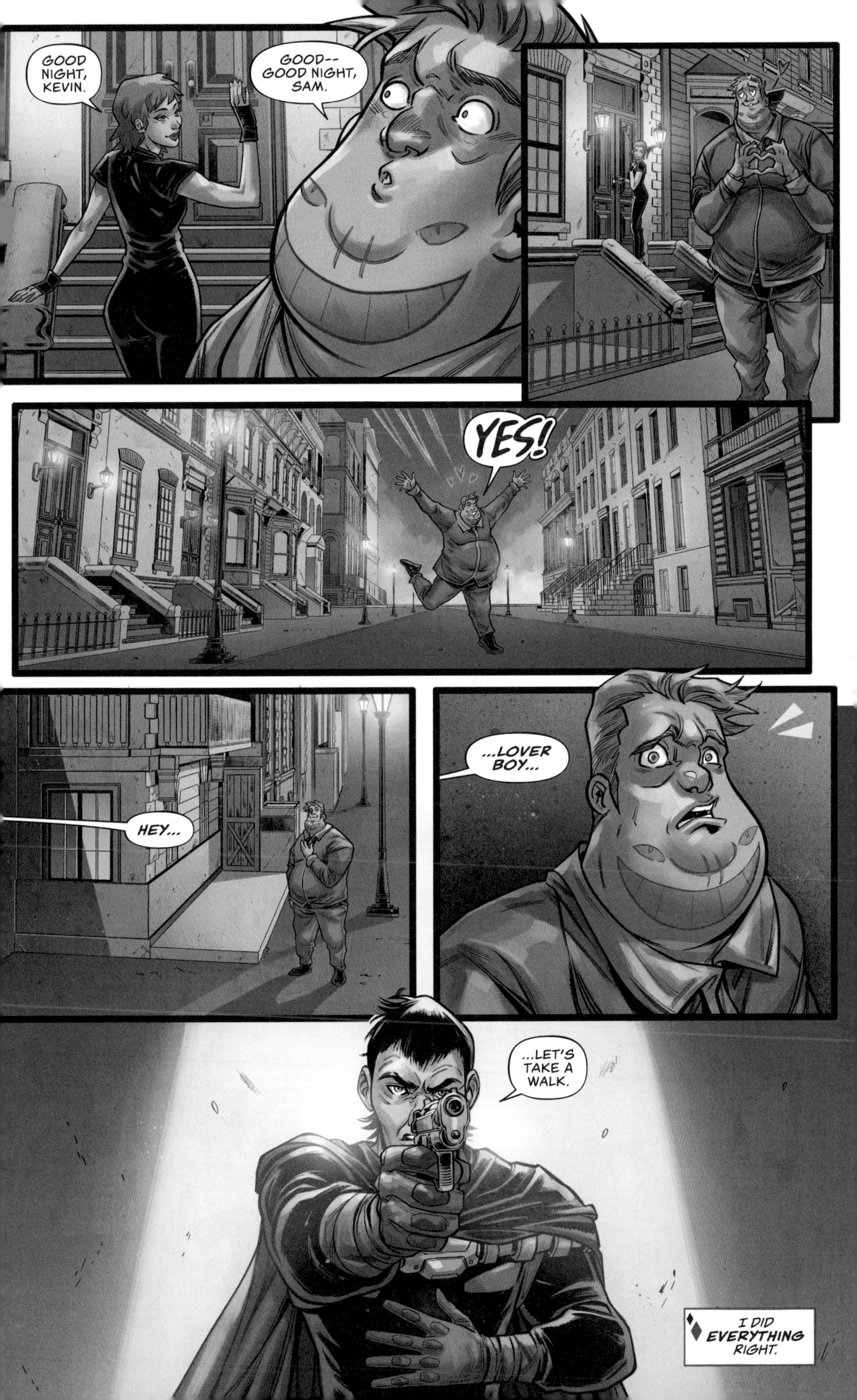
GOOD NIGHT, KEVIN.
GOOD-- GOOD NIGHT, SAM.
YES!
HEY...
...LOVER BOY...
...LET'S TAKE A WALK.
I DID EVERYTHING RIGHT.

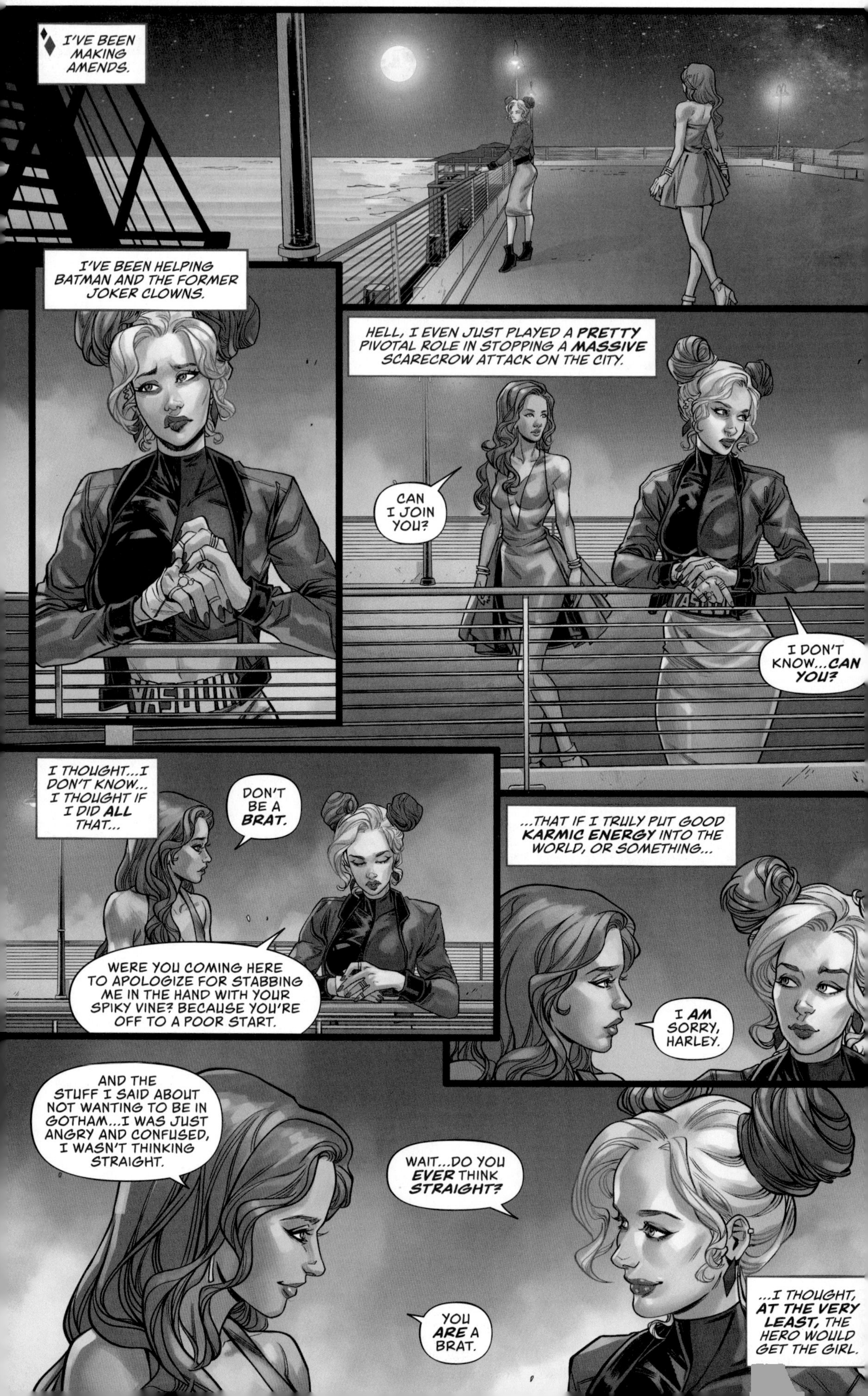
I'VE BEEN MAKING AMENDS.
I'VE BEEN HELPING BATMAN AND THE FORMER JOKER CLOWNS.
HELL, I EVEN JUST PLAYED A PRETTY PIVOTAL ROLE IN STOPPING A MASSIVE SCARECROW ATTACK ON THE CITY.
CAN I JOIN YOU?
I DON'T KNOW...CAN YOU?
I THOUGHT...I DON'T KNOW... I THOUGHT IF I DID ALL THAT...
DON'T BE A BRAT.
WERE YOU COMING HERE TO APOLOGIZE FOR STABBING ME IN THE HAND WITH YOUR SPIKY VINE? BECAUSE YOU'RE OFF TO A POOR START.
...THAT IF I TRULY PUT GOOD KARMIC ENERGY INTO THE WORLD, OR SOMETHING...
I AM SORRY, HARLEY.
AND THE STUFF I SAID ABOUT NOT WANTING TO BE IN GOTHAM...I WAS JUST ANGRY AND CONFUSED, I WASN'T THINKING STRAIGHT.
WAIT...DO YOU EVER THINK STRAIGHT?
YOU ARE A BRAT.
...I THOUGHT, AT THE VERY LEAST, THE HERO WOULD GET THE GIRL.

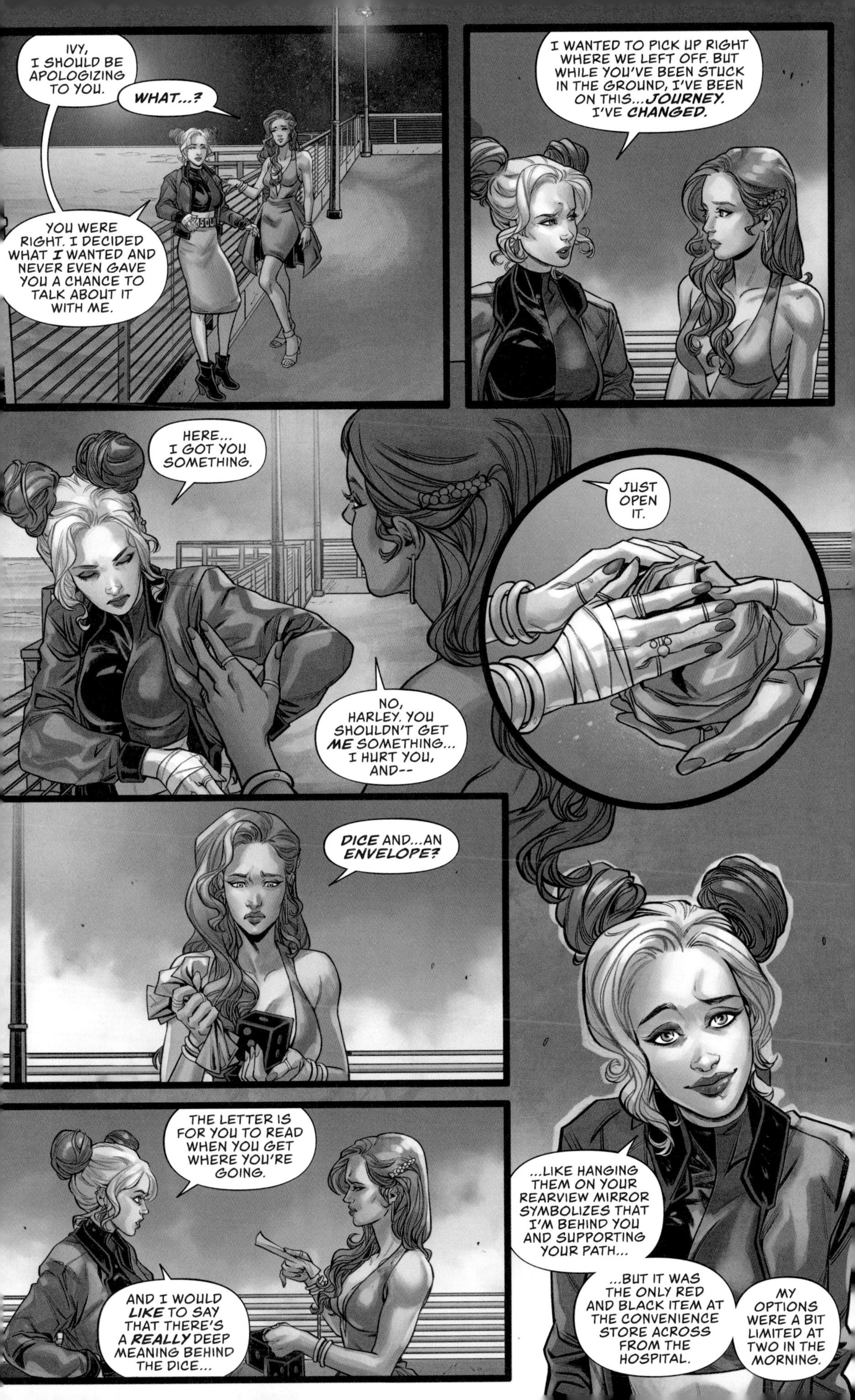
IVY, I SHOULD BE APOLOGIZING TO YOU.
WHAT...?
YOU WERE RIGHT. I DECIDED WHAT I WANTED AND NEVER EVEN GAVE YOU A CHANCE TO TALK ABOUT IT WITH ME.
I WANTED TO PICK UP RIGHT WHERE WE LEFT OFF. BUT WHILE YOU'VE BEEN STUCK IN THE GROUND, I'VE BEEN ON THIS...JOURNEY. I'VE CHANGED.
HERE... I GOT YOU SOMETHING.
NO, HARLEY. YOU SHOULDN'T GET ME SOMETHING... I HURT YOU, AND--
JUST OPEN IT.
DICE AND...AN ENVELOPE?
THE LETTER IS FOR YOU TO READ WHEN YOU GET WHERE YOU'RE GOING.
AND I WOULD LIKE TO SAY THAT THERE'S A REALLY DEEP MEANING BEHIND THE DICE...
...LIKE HANGING THEM ON YOUR REARVIEW MIRROR SYMBOLIZES THAT I'M BEHIND YOU AND SUPPORTING YOUR PATH...
...BUT IT WAS THE ONLY RED AND BLACK ITEM AT THE CONVENIENCE STORE ACROSS FROM THE HOSPITAL.
MY OPTIONS WERE A BIT LIMITED AT TWO IN THE MORNING.

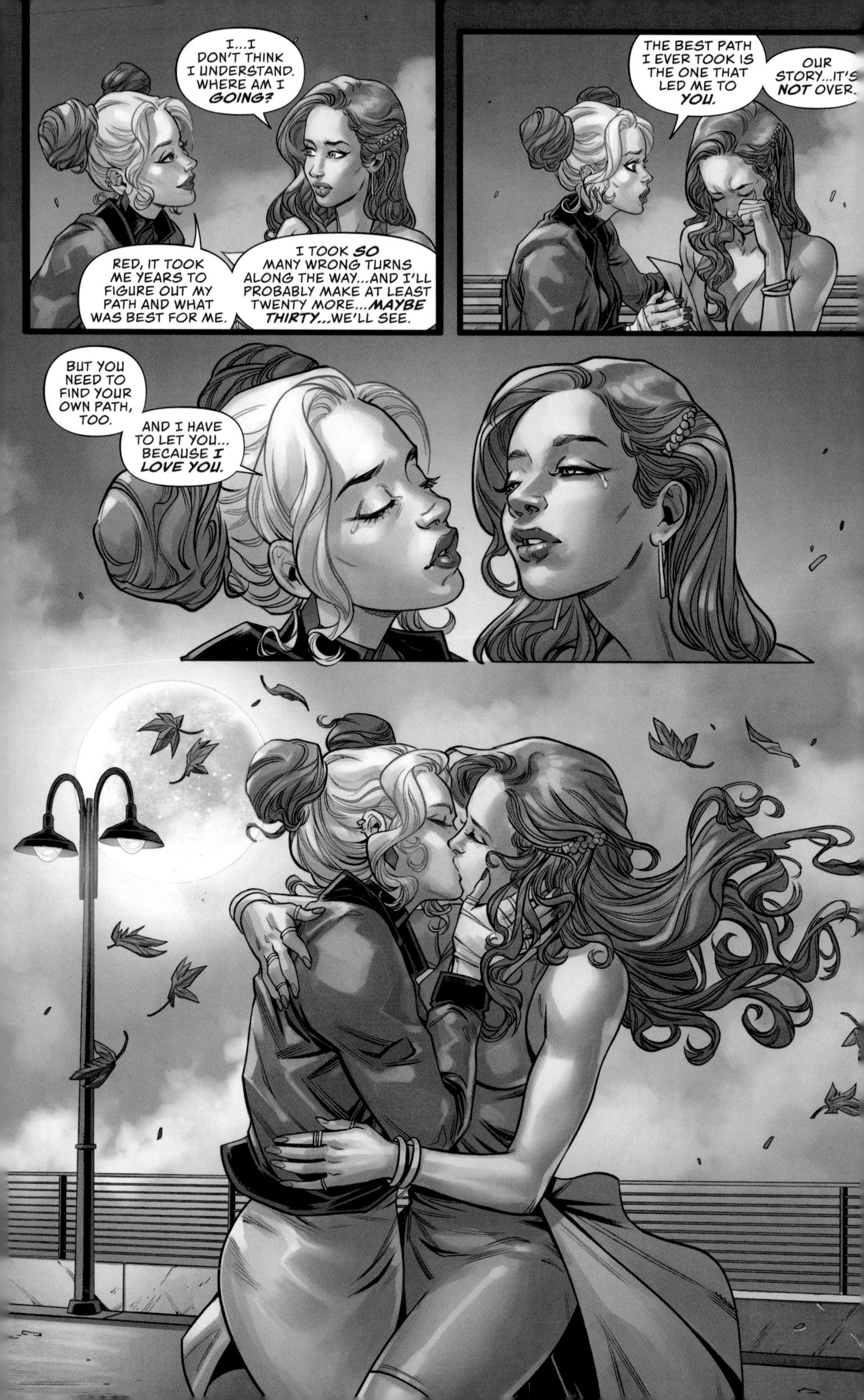
I...I DON'T THINK I UNDERSTAND. WHERE AM I *GOING?*
RED, IT TOOK ME YEARS TO FIGURE OUT MY PATH AND WHAT WAS BEST FOR ME.
I TOOK *SO* MANY WRONG TURNS ALONG THE WAY...AND I'LL PROBABLY MAKE AT LEAST TWENTY MORE...*MAYBE THIRTY...*WE'LL SEE.
THE BEST PATH I EVER TOOK IS THE ONE THAT LED ME TO *YOU.*
OUR STORY...IT'S *NOT* OVER.
BUT YOU NEED TO FIND YOUR OWN PATH, TOO.
AND I HAVE TO LET YOU... BECAUSE *I LOVE YOU.*

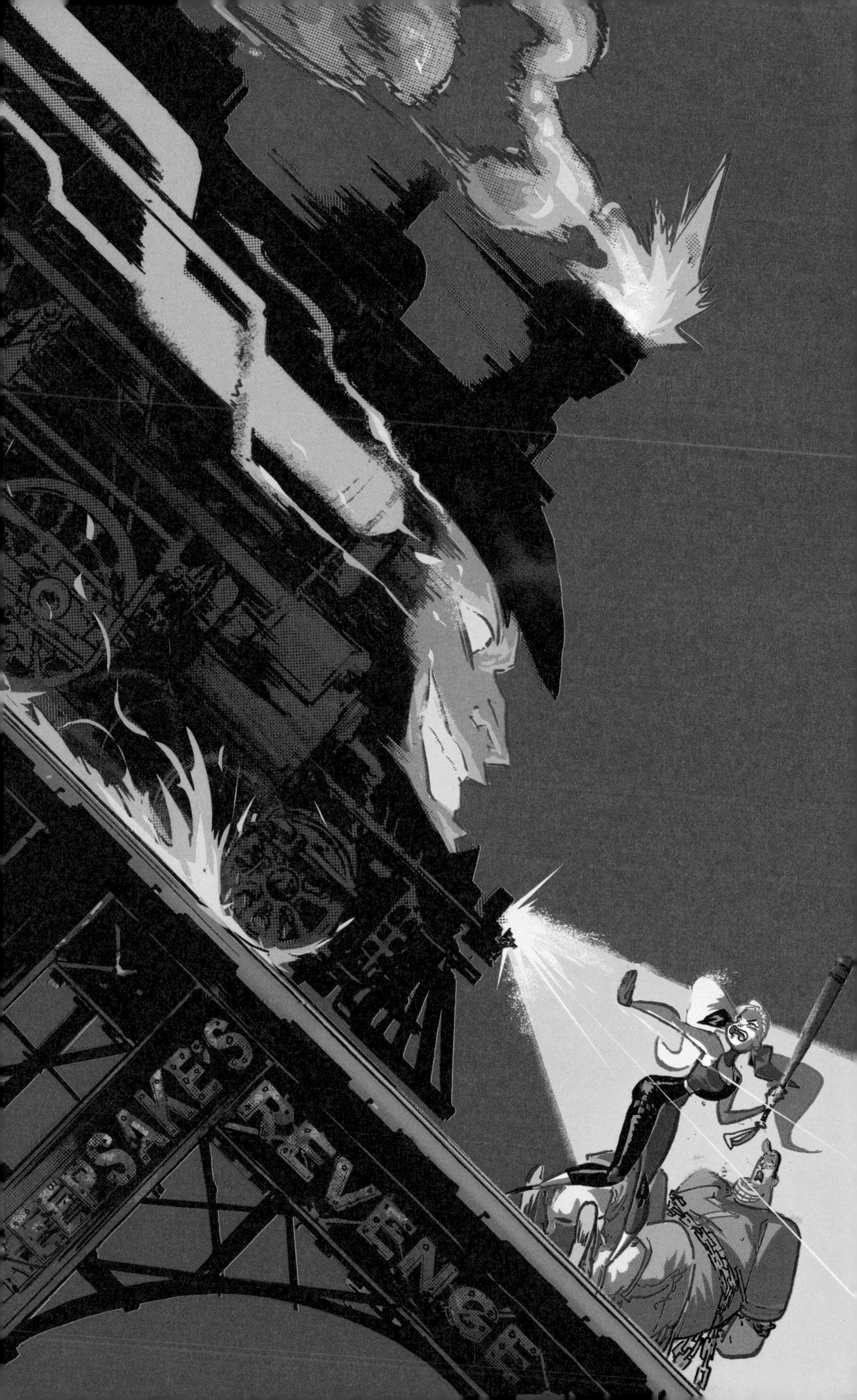
SAKE'S REVENGE

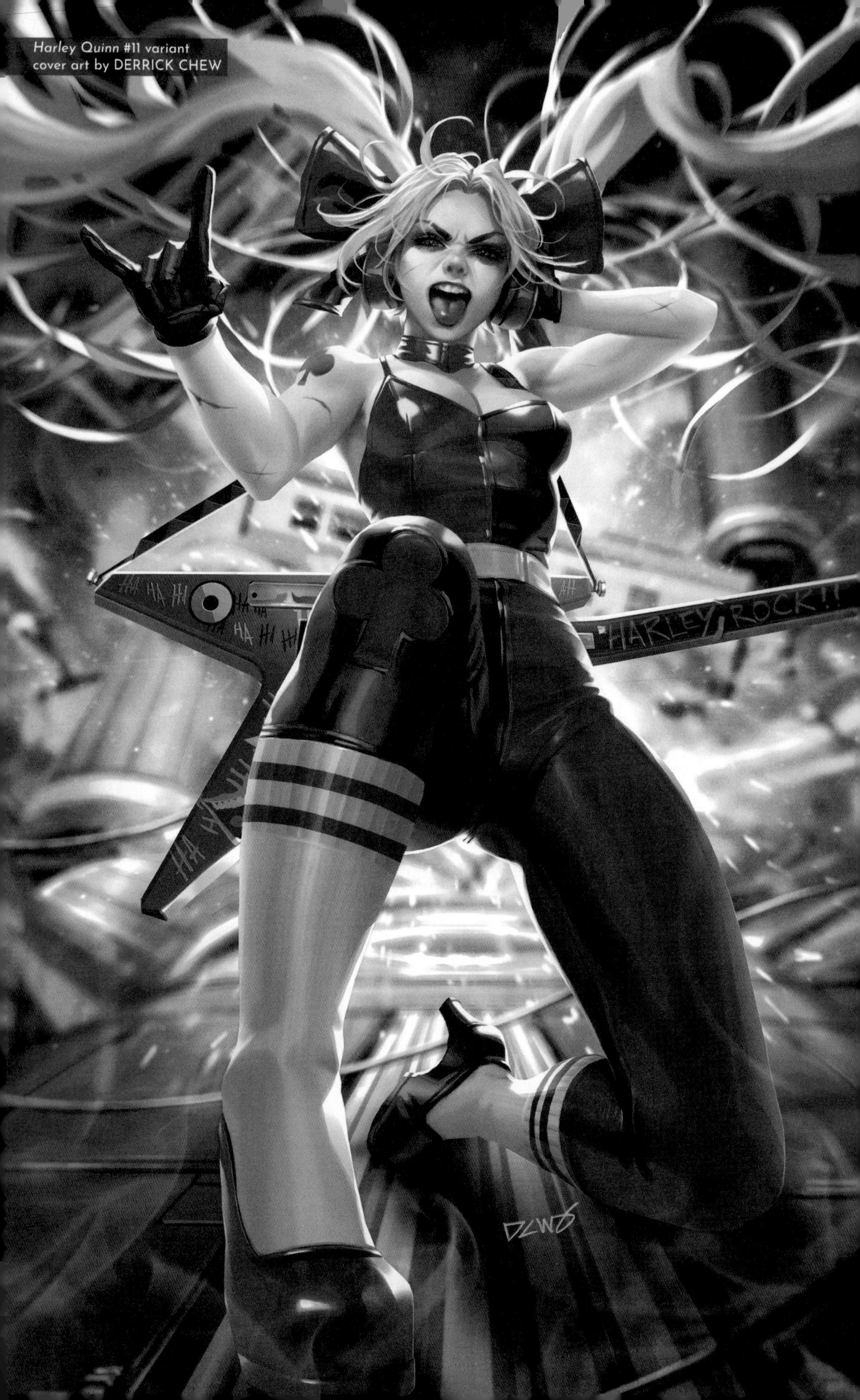
HARLEY ROCK!!

Harley Quinn #11 variant
cover art by DERRICK CHEW

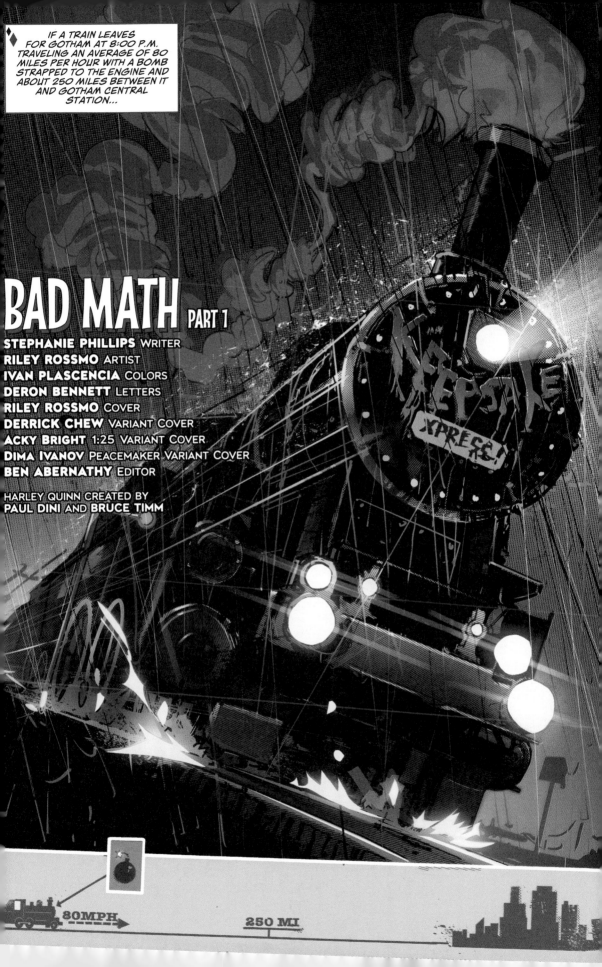

IF A TRAIN LEAVES FOR GOTHAM AT 8:00 P.M. TRAVELING AN AVERAGE OF 80 MILES PER HOUR WITH A BOMB STRAPPED TO THE ENGINE AND ABOUT 250 MILES BETWEEN IT AND GOTHAM CENTRAL STATION...

BAD MATH PART 1

STEPHANIE PHILLIPS WRITER

RILEY ROSSMO ARTIST

IVAN PLASCENCIA COLORS

DERON BENNETT LETTERS

RILEY ROSSMO COVER

DERRICK CHEW VARIANT COVER

ACKY BRIGHT 1:25 VARIANT COVER

DIMA IVANOV PEACEMAKER VARIANT COVER

BEN ABERNATHY EDITOR

HARLEY QUINN CREATED BY
PAUL DINI AND **BRUCE TIMM**

80MPH

250 MI

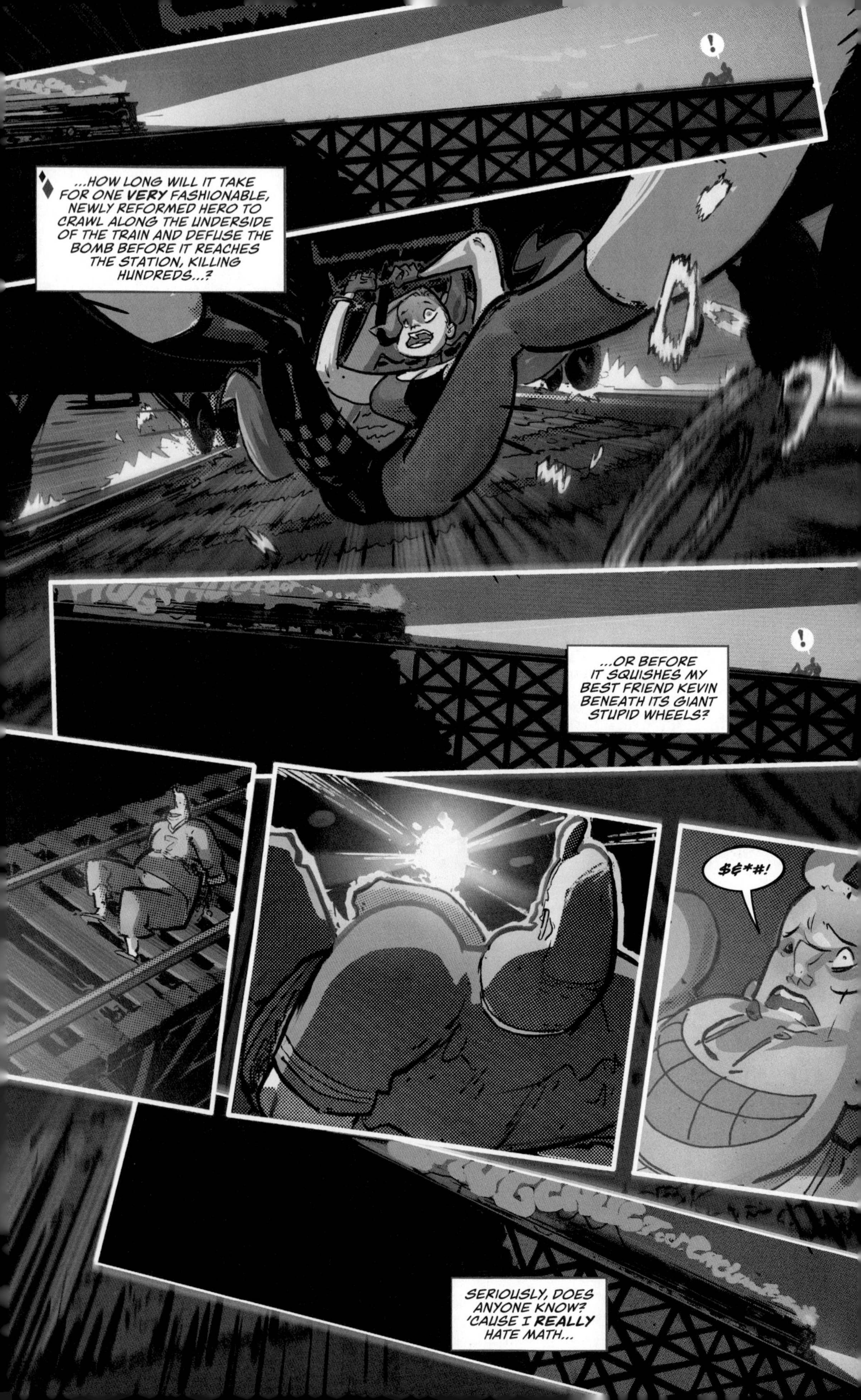
!
...HOW LONG WILL IT TAKE FOR ONE VERY FASHIONABLE, NEWLY REFORMED HERO TO CRAWL ALONG THE UNDERSIDE OF THE TRAIN AND DEFUSE THE BOMB BEFORE IT REACHES THE STATION, KILLING HUNDREDS...?
!
...OR BEFORE IT SQUISHES MY BEST FRIEND KEVIN BENEATH ITS GIANT STUPID WHEELS?
$¢*#!
SERIOUSLY, DOES ANYONE KNOW? 'CAUSE I REALLY HATE MATH...

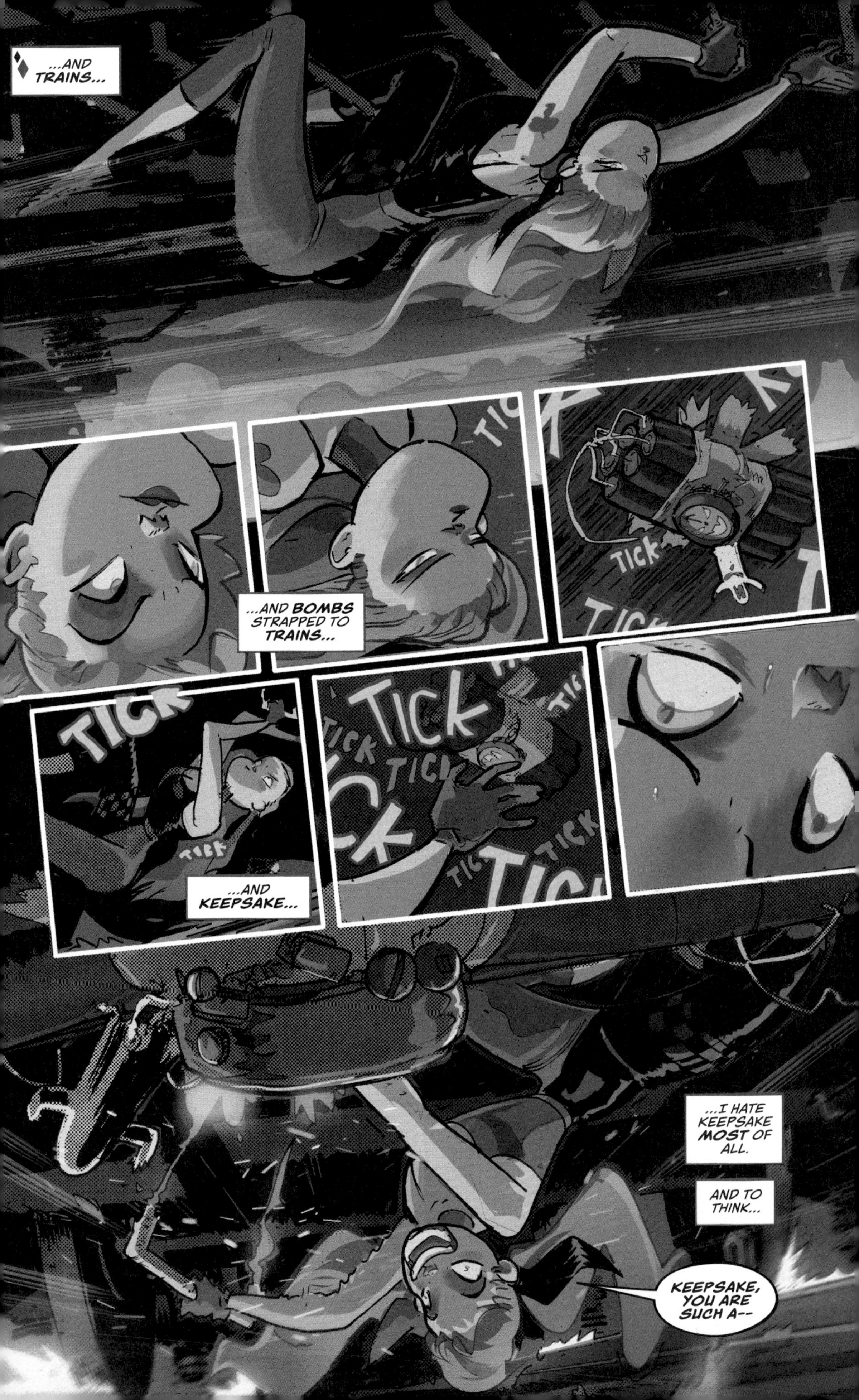

...AND TRAINS...
TICK
TICK
...AND BOMBS STRAPPED TO TRAINS...
TICK
TICK
...AND KEEPSAKE...
TICK
TICK
TICK
TICK
...I HATE KEEPSAKE MOST OF ALL.
AND TO THINK...
KEEPSAKE, YOU ARE SUCH A--

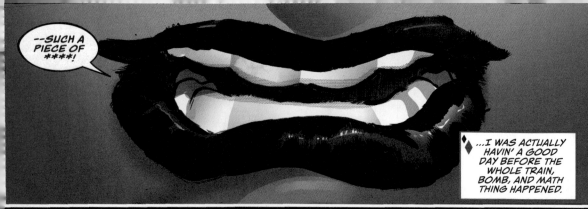

--SUCH A PIECE OF ****!

◆ ...I WAS ACTUALLY HAVIN' A GOOD DAY BEFORE THE WHOLE TRAIN, BOMB, AND MATH THING HAPPENED.

KEEPSAKE USED MY *MIND* LIKE IT WAS...LIKE IT WAS SOME KINDA *SANDBOX* FOR HIM TO MESS AROUND IN.

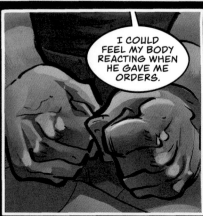

I COULD FEEL MY BODY REACTING WHEN HE GAVE ME ORDERS.

NO MATTER HOW MUCH I *TRIED* TO *NOT* DO WHAT HE SAID...

...I-- I HAD *NO* CONTROL...

EVEN CHANGED MY NAME... BLANE...

...I CAN'T...

FIVE HOURS EARLIER. GOTHAM.

YOU DON'T HAVE TO...IT'S OVER NOW.

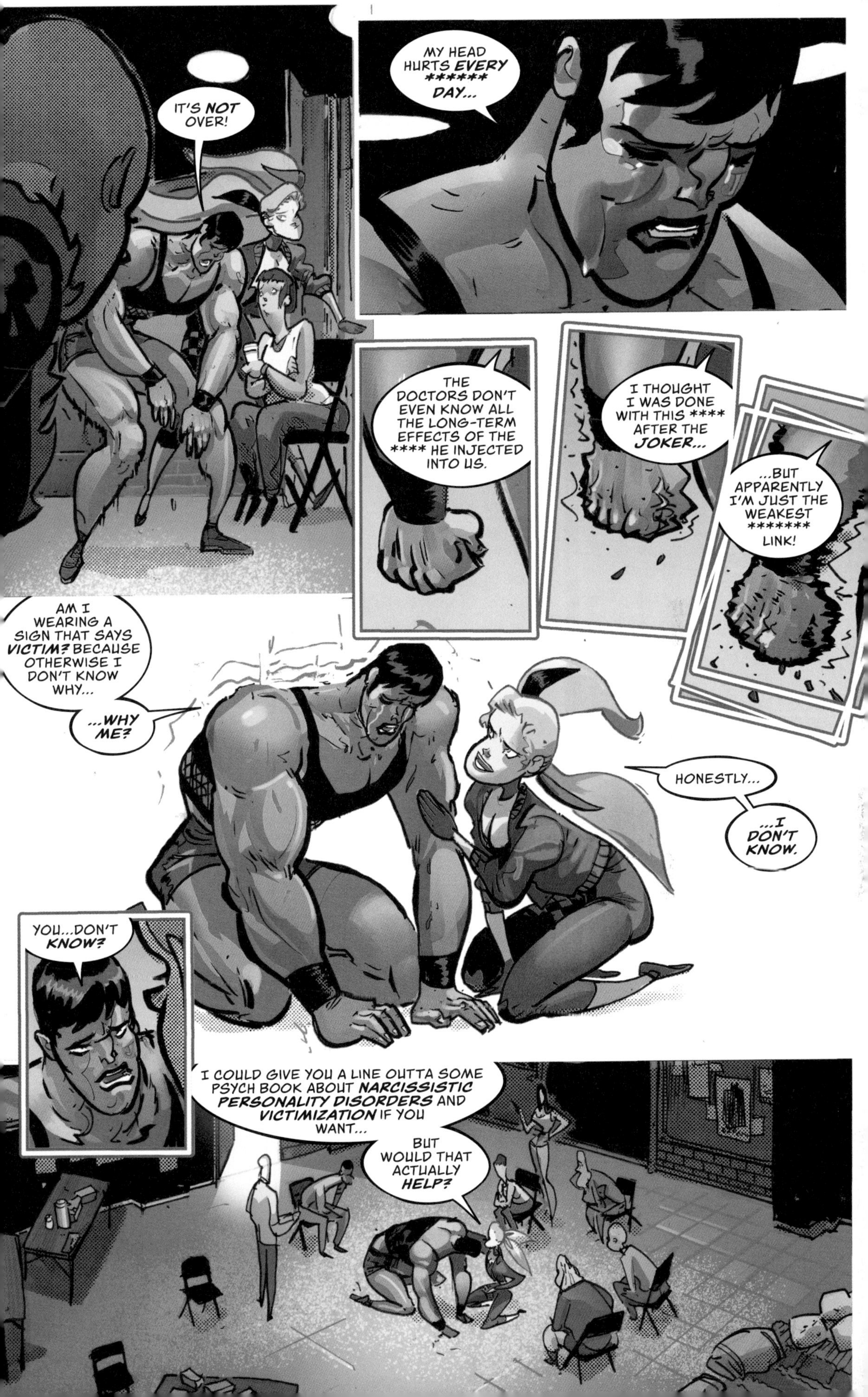
IT'S NOT OVER!
MY HEAD HURTS EVERY ****** DAY...
THE DOCTORS DON'T EVEN KNOW ALL THE LONG-TERM EFFECTS OF THE **** HE INJECTED INTO US.
I THOUGHT I WAS DONE WITH THIS **** AFTER THE JOKER...
...BUT APPARENTLY I'M JUST THE WEAKEST ******* LINK!
AM I WEARING A SIGN THAT SAYS VICTIM? BECAUSE OTHERWISE I DON'T KNOW WHY...
...WHY ME?
HONESTLY...
...I DON'T KNOW.
YOU...DON'T KNOW?
I COULD GIVE YOU A LINE OUTTA SOME PSYCH BOOK ABOUT NARCISSISTIC PERSONALITY DISORDERS AND VICTIMIZATION IF YOU WANT...
BUT WOULD THAT ACTUALLY HELP?

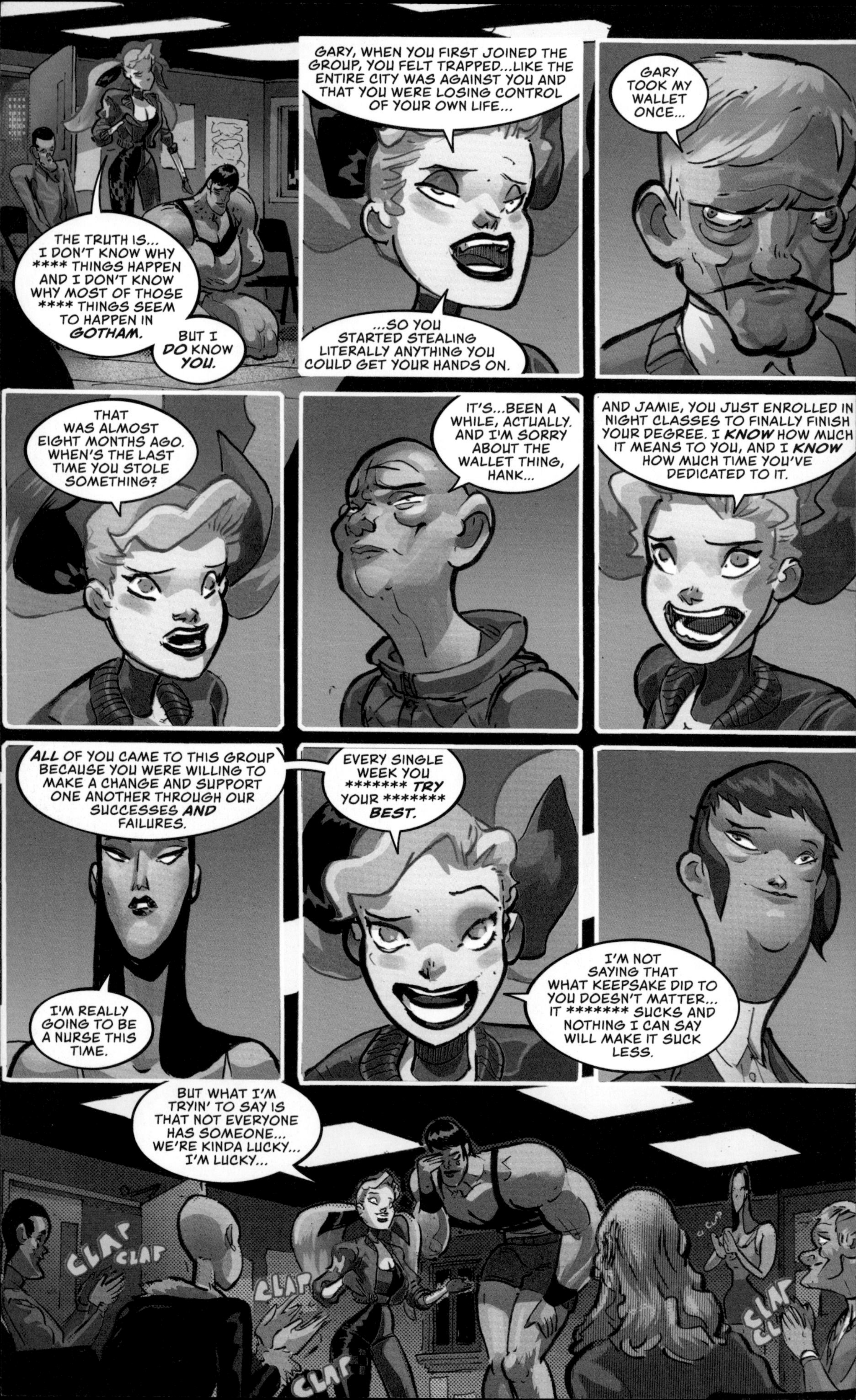
THE TRUTH IS... I DON'T KNOW WHY **** THINGS HAPPEN AND I DON'T KNOW WHY MOST OF THOSE **** THINGS SEEM TO HAPPEN IN GOTHAM.
BUT I DO KNOW YOU.
GARY, WHEN YOU FIRST JOINED THE GROUP, YOU FELT TRAPPED...LIKE THE ENTIRE CITY WAS AGAINST YOU AND THAT YOU WERE LOSING CONTROL OF YOUR OWN LIFE...
...SO YOU STARTED STEALING LITERALLY ANYTHING YOU COULD GET YOUR HANDS ON.
GARY TOOK MY WALLET ONCE...
THAT WAS ALMOST EIGHT MONTHS AGO. WHEN'S THE LAST TIME YOU STOLE SOMETHING?
IT'S...BEEN A WHILE, ACTUALLY. AND I'M SORRY ABOUT THE WALLET THING, HANK...
AND JAMIE, YOU JUST ENROLLED IN NIGHT CLASSES TO FINALLY FINISH YOUR DEGREE. I KNOW HOW MUCH IT MEANS TO YOU, AND I KNOW HOW MUCH TIME YOU'VE DEDICATED TO IT.
ALL OF YOU CAME TO THIS GROUP BECAUSE YOU WERE WILLING TO MAKE A CHANGE AND SUPPORT ONE ANOTHER THROUGH OUR SUCCESSES AND FAILURES.
I'M REALLY GOING TO BE A NURSE THIS TIME.
EVERY SINGLE WEEK YOU ******* TRY YOUR ******* BEST.
I'M NOT SAYING THAT WHAT KEEPSAKE DID TO YOU DOESN'T MATTER... IT ******* SUCKS AND NOTHING I CAN SAY WILL MAKE IT SUCK LESS.
BUT WHAT I'M TRYIN' TO SAY IS THAT NOT EVERYONE HAS SOMEONE... WE'RE KINDA LUCKY... I'M LUCKY...
CLAP CLAP
CLAP
CLAP
CLAP CLAP

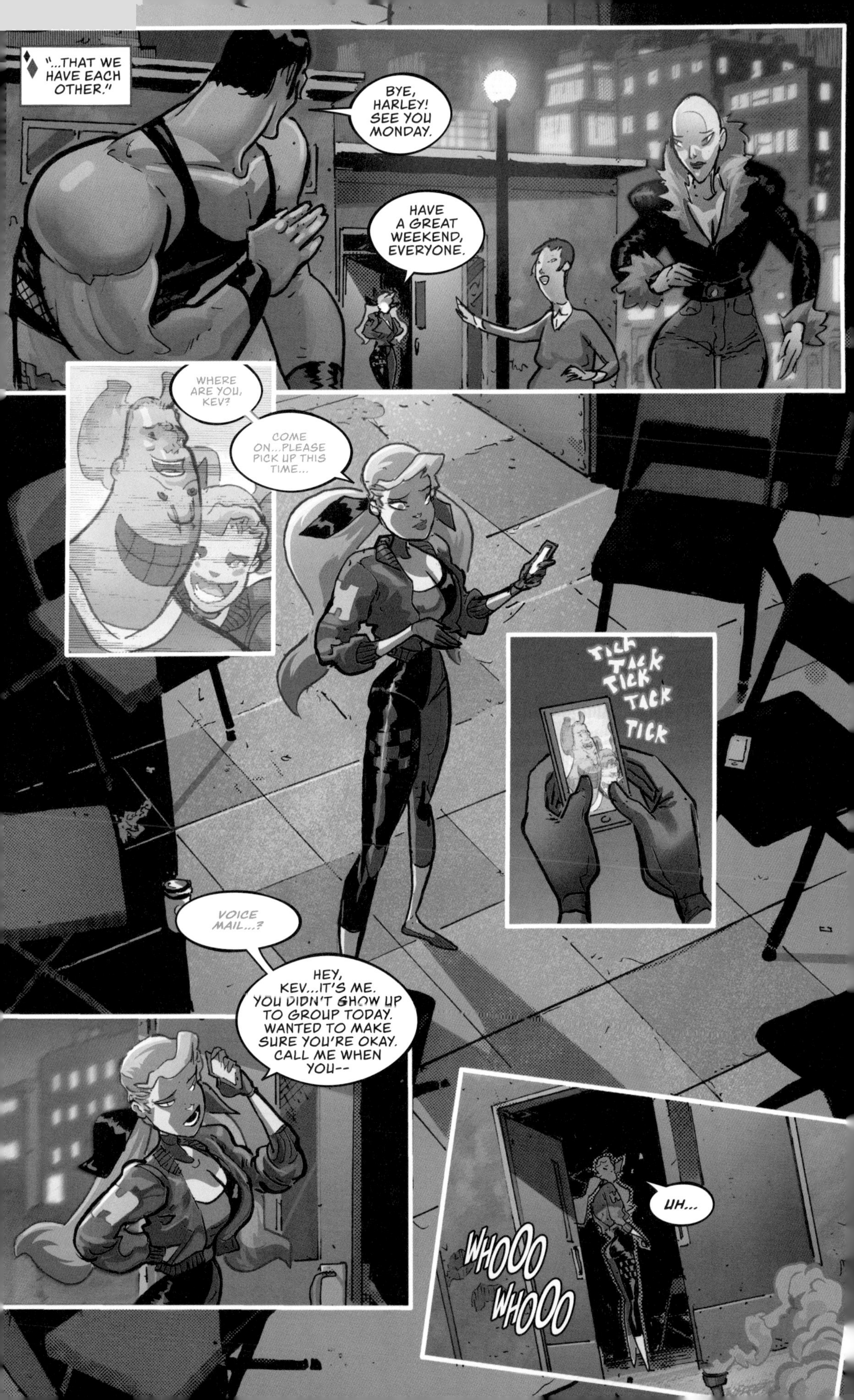
"...THAT WE HAVE EACH OTHER."
BYE, HARLEY! SEE YOU MONDAY.
HAVE A GREAT WEEKEND, EVERYONE.
WHERE ARE YOU, KEV?
COME ON...PLEASE PICK UP THIS TIME...
TICK TACK TICK TACK TICK
VOICE MAIL...?
HEY, KEV...IT'S ME. YOU DIDN'T SHOW UP TO GROUP TODAY. WANTED TO MAKE SURE YOU'RE OKAY. CALL ME WHEN YOU--
UH...
WHOOO WHOOO

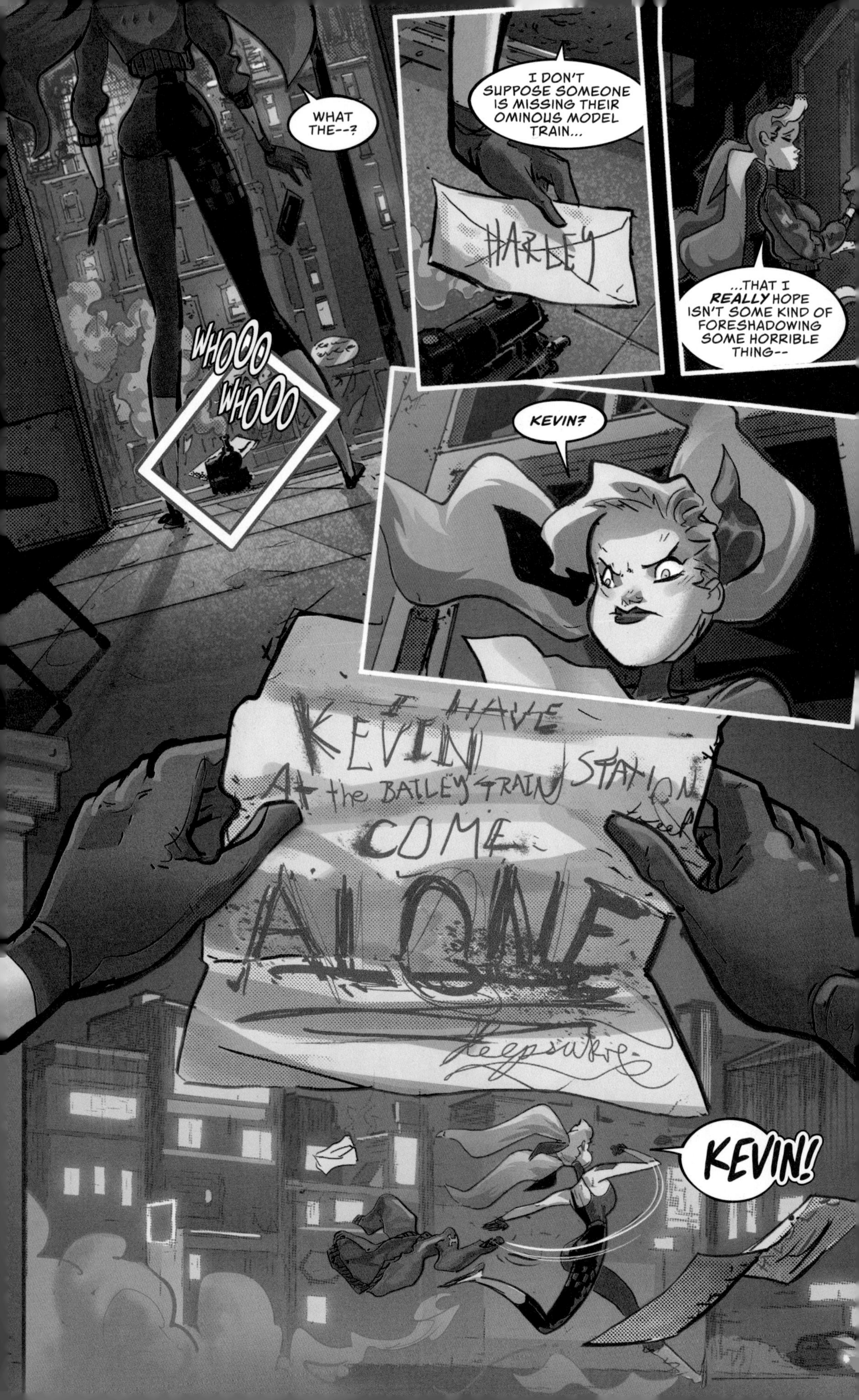

WHAT THE--?
WHOOO WHOOO
I DON'T SUPPOSE SOMEONE IS MISSING THEIR OMINOUS MODEL TRAIN...
HARLEY
...THAT I REALLY HOPE ISN'T SOME KIND OF FORESHADOWING SOME HORRIBLE THING--
KEVIN?
I HAVE KEVIN At the BAILEY TRAIN STATION
COME ALONE
KEVIN!

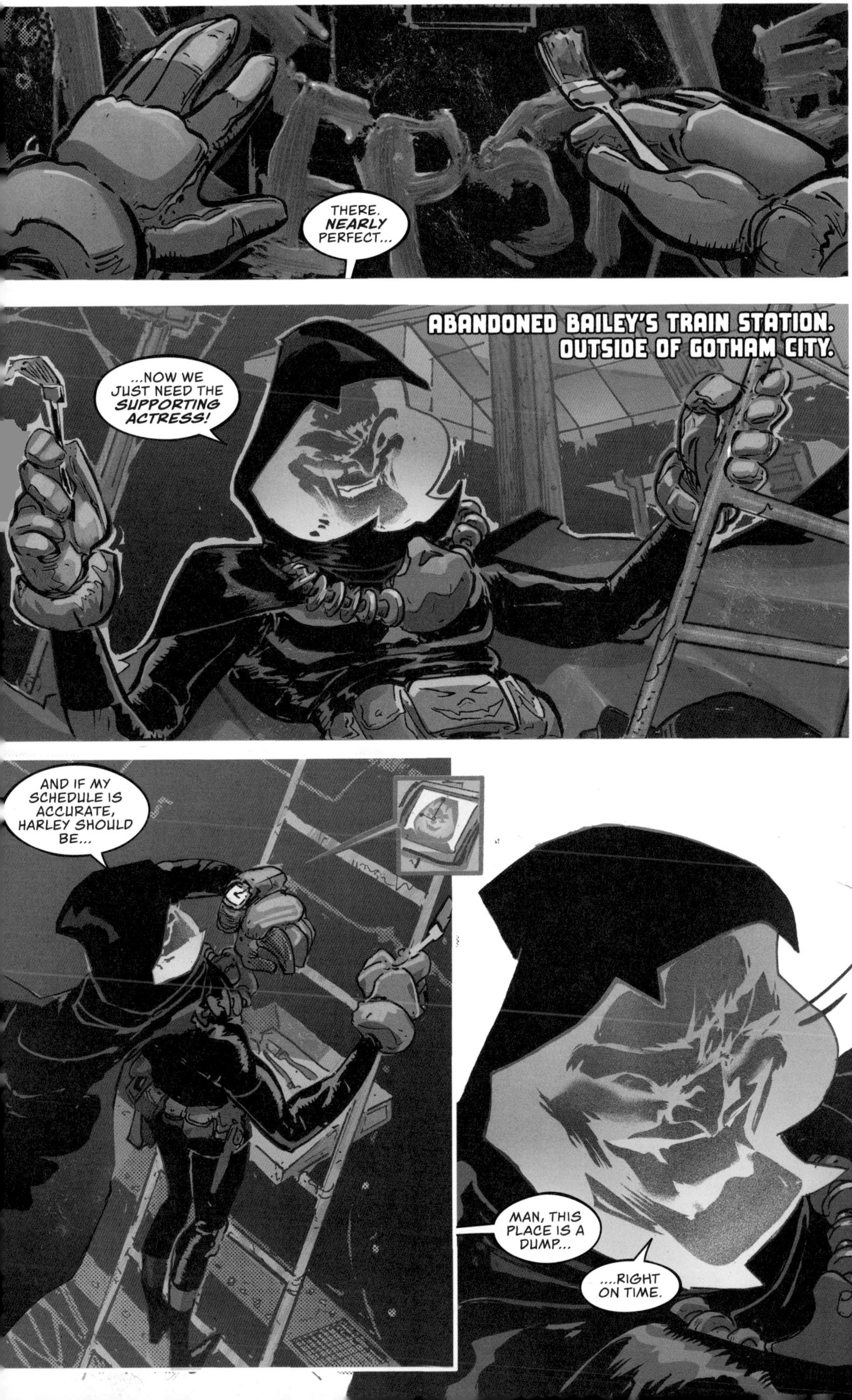
THERE. NEARLY PERFECT...
ABANDONED BAILEY'S TRAIN STATION. OUTSIDE OF GOTHAM CITY.
...NOW WE JUST NEED THE SUPPORTING ACTRESS!
AND IF MY SCHEDULE IS ACCURATE, HARLEY SHOULD BE...
MAN, THIS PLACE IS A DUMP...
....RIGHT ON TIME.

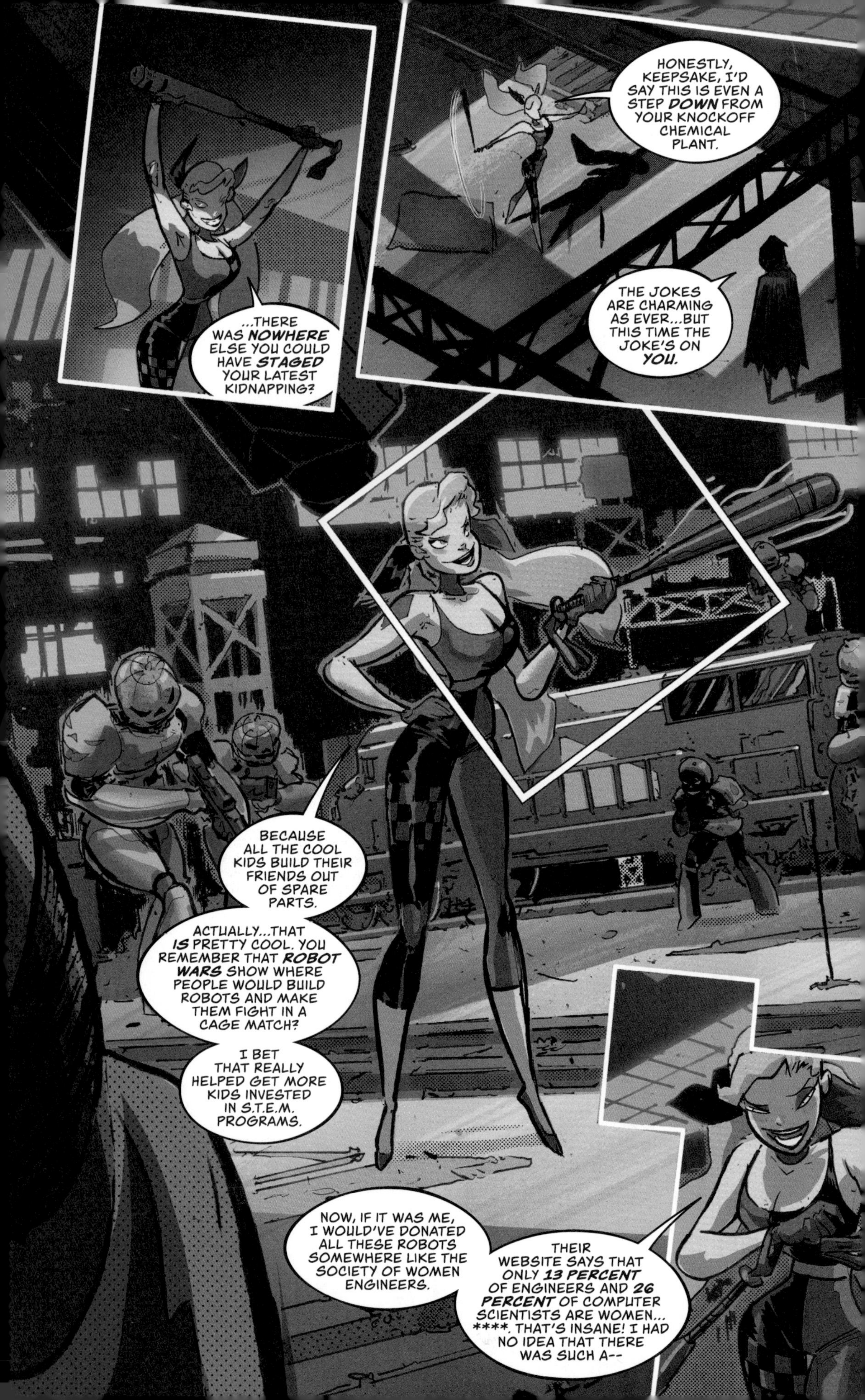

HONESTLY, KEEPSAKE, I'D SAY THIS IS EVEN A STEP DOWN FROM YOUR KNOCKOFF CHEMICAL PLANT.
...THERE WAS NOWHERE ELSE YOU COULD HAVE STAGED YOUR LATEST KIDNAPPING?
THE JOKES ARE CHARMING AS EVER...BUT THIS TIME THE JOKE'S ON YOU.
BECAUSE ALL THE COOL KIDS BUILD THEIR FRIENDS OUT OF SPARE PARTS.
ACTUALLY...THAT IS PRETTY COOL. YOU REMEMBER THAT ROBOT WARS SHOW WHERE PEOPLE WOULD BUILD ROBOTS AND MAKE THEM FIGHT IN A CAGE MATCH?
I BET THAT REALLY HELPED GET MORE KIDS INVESTED IN S.T.E.M. PROGRAMS.
NOW, IF IT WAS ME, I WOULD'VE DONATED ALL THESE ROBOTS SOMEWHERE LIKE THE SOCIETY OF WOMEN ENGINEERS.
THEIR WEBSITE SAYS THAT ONLY 13 PERCENT OF ENGINEERS AND 26 PERCENT OF COMPUTER SCIENTISTS ARE WOMEN... ****. THAT'S INSANE! I HAD NO IDEA THAT THERE WAS SUCH A--

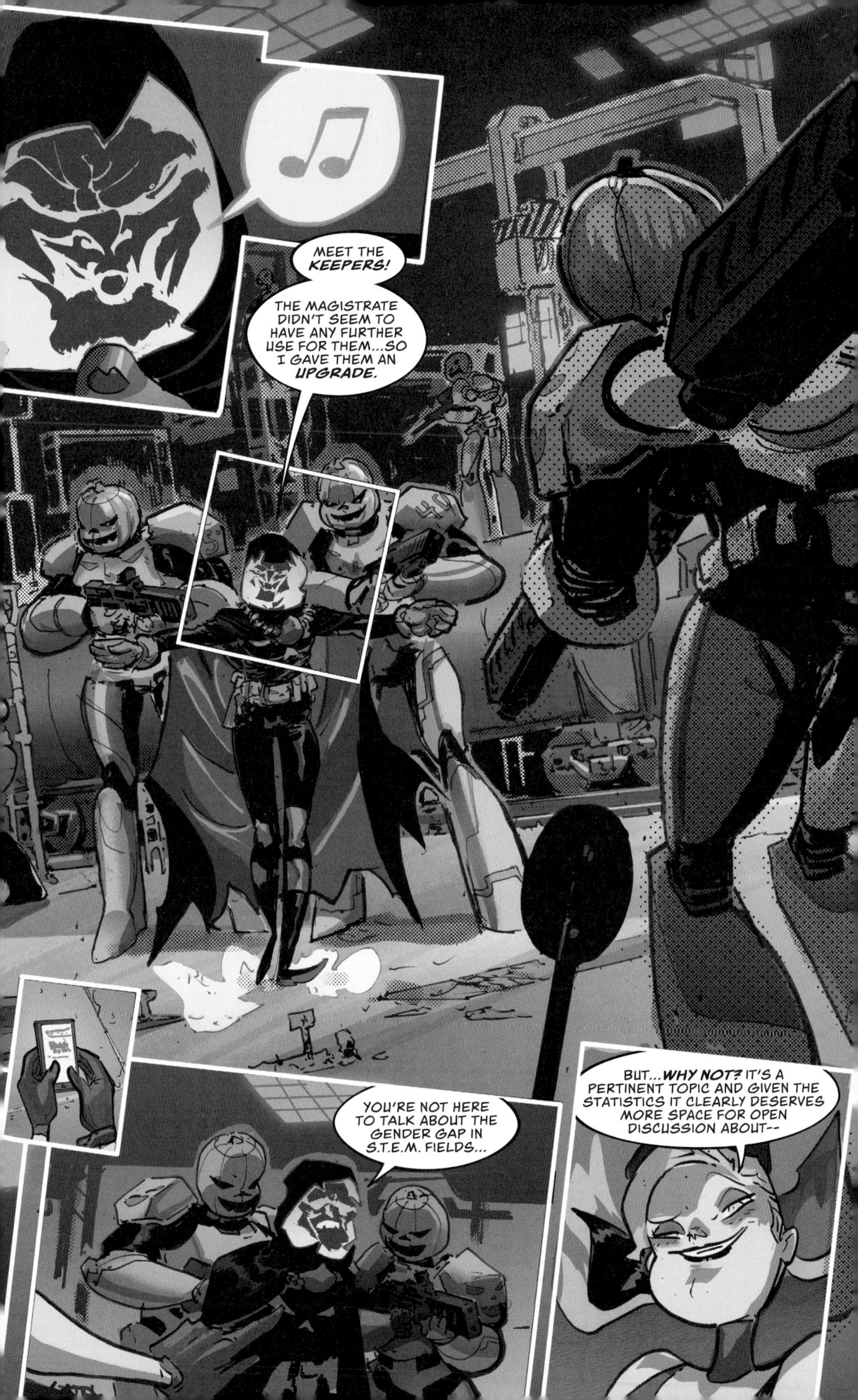
♫
MEET THE KEEPERS!
THE MAGISTRATE DIDN'T SEEM TO HAVE ANY FURTHER USE FOR THEM...SO I GAVE THEM AN UPGRADE.
YOU'RE NOT HERE TO TALK ABOUT THE GENDER GAP IN S.T.E.M. FIELDS...
BUT...WHY NOT? IT'S A PERTINENT TOPIC AND GIVEN THE STATISTICS IT CLEARLY DESERVES MORE SPACE FOR OPEN DISCUSSION ABOUT--

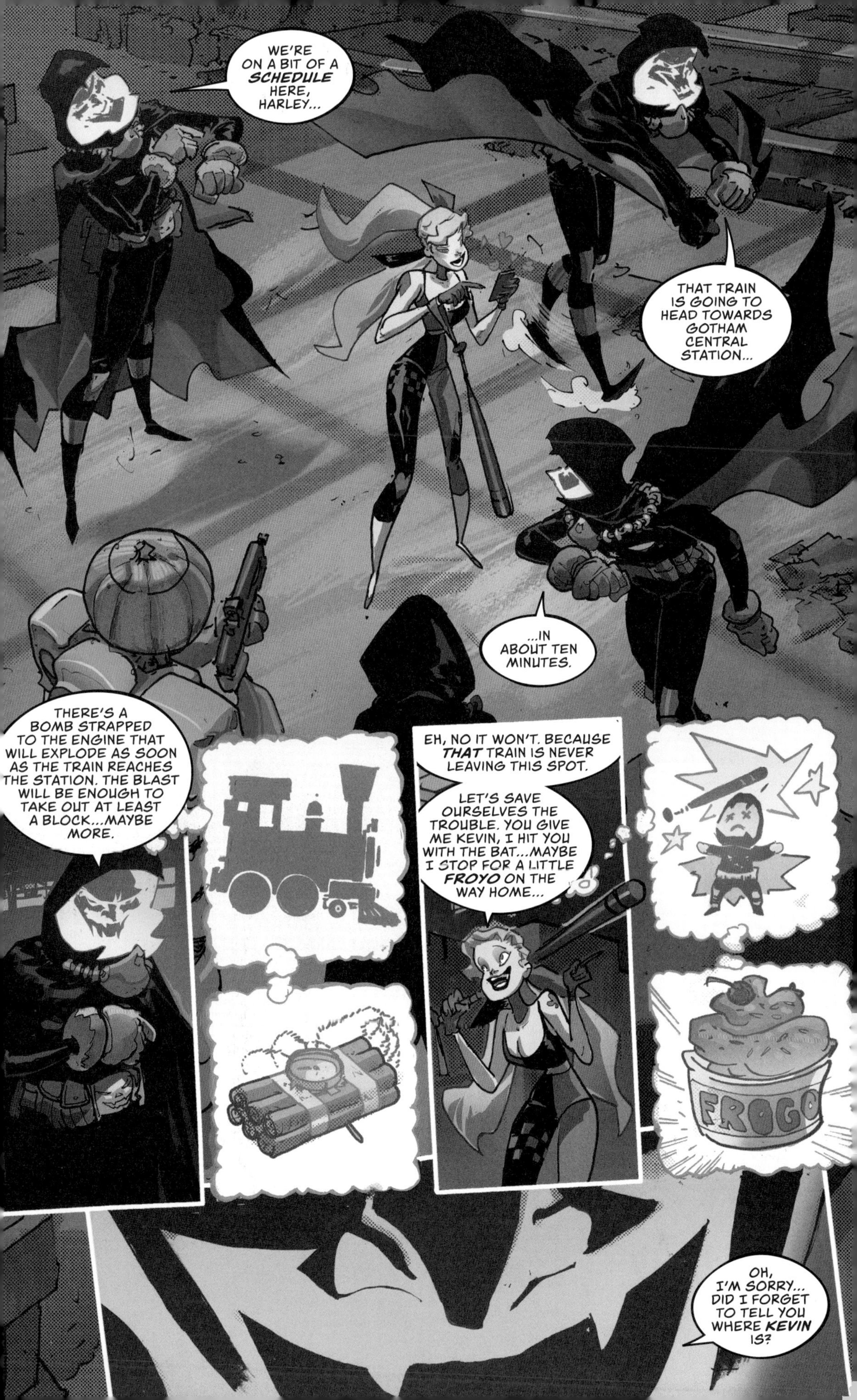
WE'RE ON A BIT OF A *SCHEDULE* HERE, HARLEY...
THAT TRAIN IS GOING TO HEAD TOWARDS GOTHAM CENTRAL STATION...
...IN ABOUT TEN MINUTES.
THERE'S A BOMB STRAPPED TO THE ENGINE THAT WILL EXPLODE AS SOON AS THE TRAIN REACHES THE STATION. THE BLAST WILL BE ENOUGH TO TAKE OUT AT LEAST A BLOCK...MAYBE MORE.
EH, NO IT WON'T. BECAUSE *THAT* TRAIN IS NEVER LEAVING THIS SPOT.
LET'S SAVE OURSELVES THE TROUBLE. YOU GIVE ME KEVIN, I HIT YOU WITH THE BAT...MAYBE I STOP FOR A LITTLE *FROYO* ON THE WAY HOME...
FROGO
OH, I'M SORRY... DID I FORGET TO TELL YOU WHERE *KEVIN* IS?

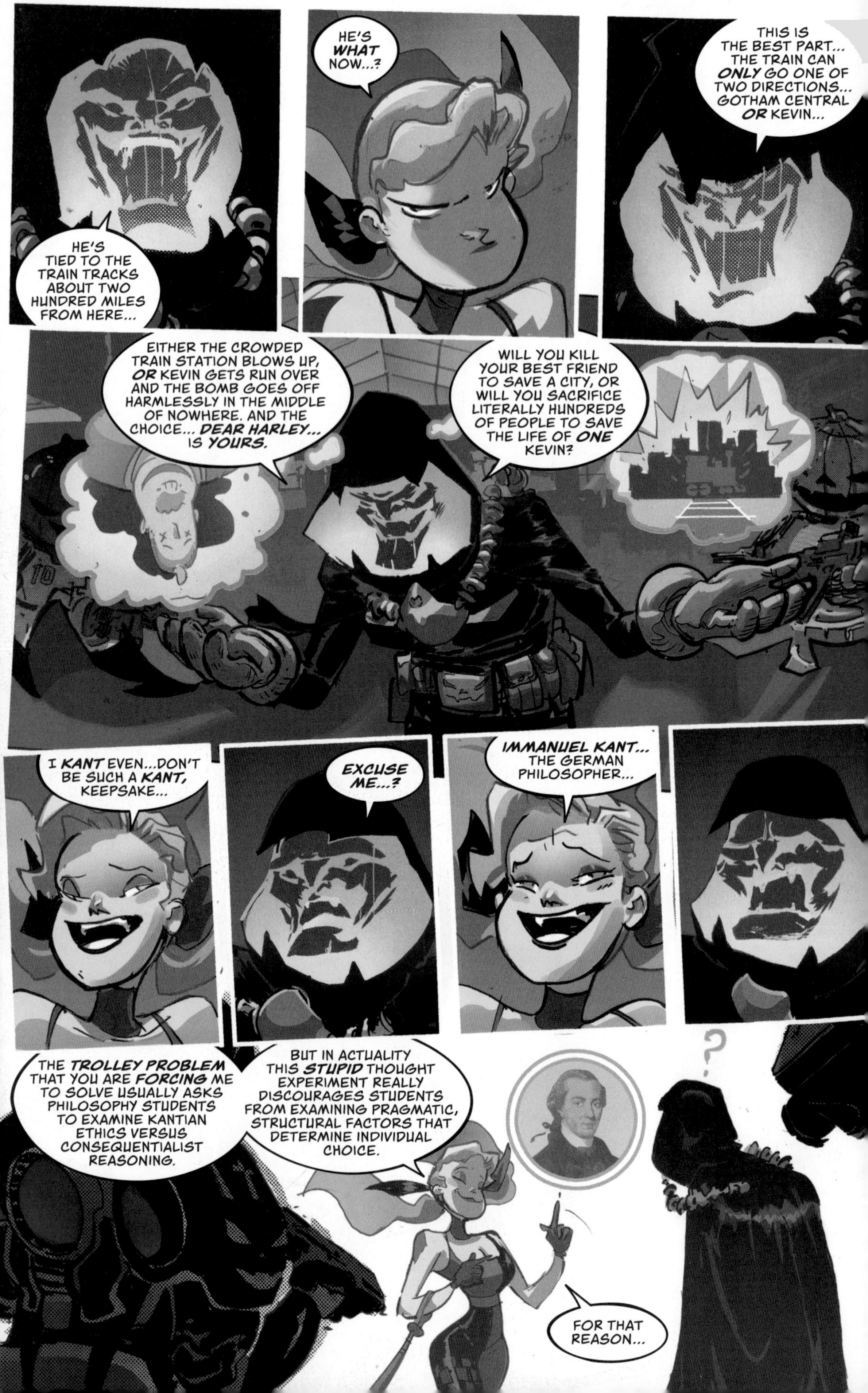
HE'S TIED TO THE TRAIN TRACKS ABOUT TWO HUNDRED MILES FROM HERE...
HE'S WHAT NOW...?
THIS IS THE BEST PART... THE TRAIN CAN ONLY GO ONE OF TWO DIRECTIONS... GOTHAM CENTRAL OR KEVIN...
EITHER THE CROWDED TRAIN STATION BLOWS UP, OR KEVIN GETS RUN OVER AND THE BOMB GOES OFF HARMLESSLY IN THE MIDDLE OF NOWHERE. AND THE CHOICE... DEAR HARLEY... IS YOURS.
WILL YOU KILL YOUR BEST FRIEND TO SAVE A CITY, OR WILL YOU SACRIFICE LITERALLY HUNDREDS OF PEOPLE TO SAVE THE LIFE OF ONE KEVIN?
I KANT EVEN...DON'T BE SUCH A KANT, KEEPSAKE...
EXCUSE ME...?
IMMANUEL KANT... THE GERMAN PHILOSOPHER...
THE TROLLEY PROBLEM THAT YOU ARE FORCING ME TO SOLVE USUALLY ASKS PHILOSOPHY STUDENTS TO EXAMINE KANTIAN ETHICS VERSUS CONSEQUENTIALIST REASONING.
BUT IN ACTUALITY THIS STUPID THOUGHT EXPERIMENT REALLY DISCOURAGES STUDENTS FROM EXAMINING PRAGMATIC, STRUCTURAL FACTORS THAT DETERMINE INDIVIDUAL CHOICE.
?
FOR THAT REASON...

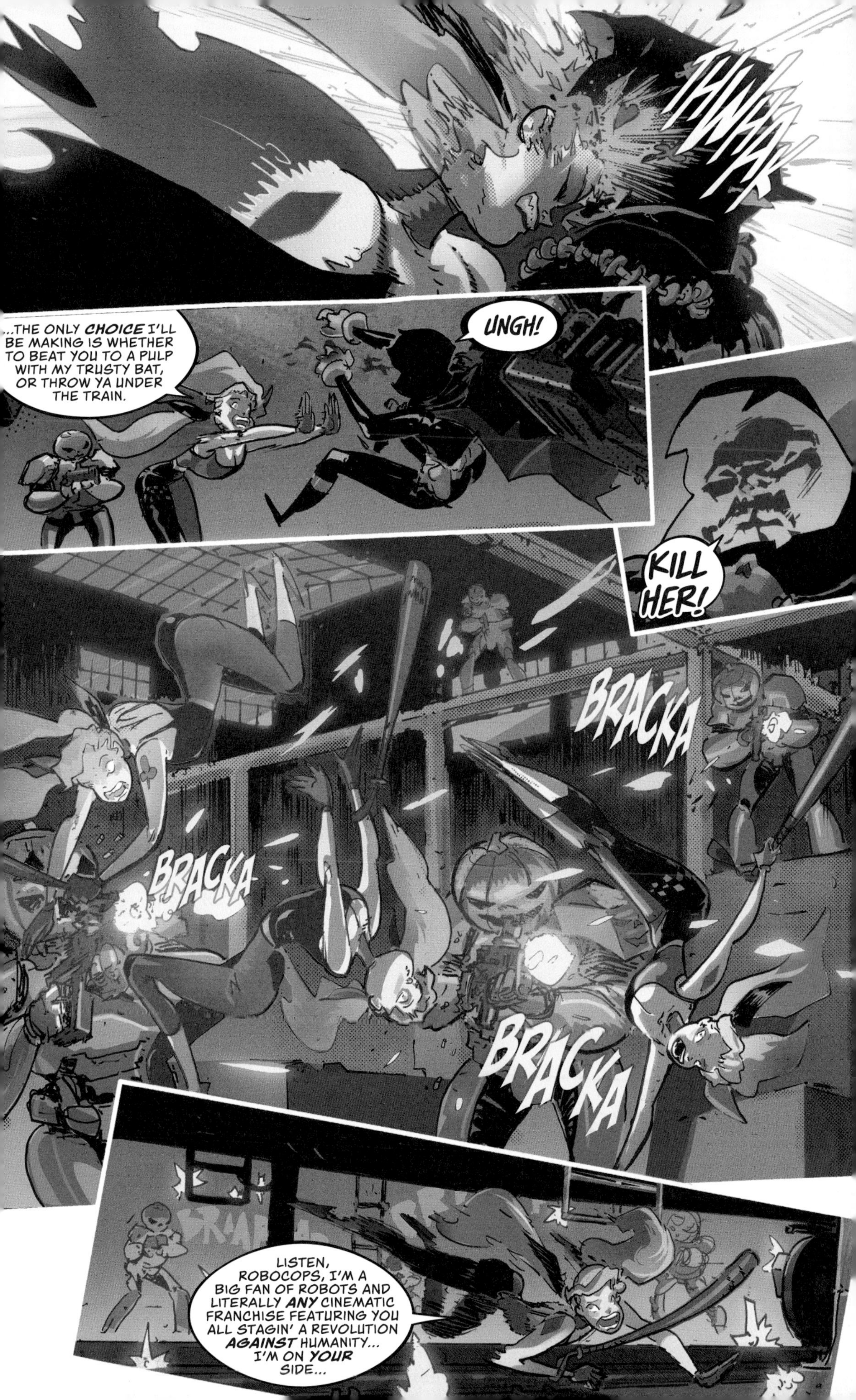
THWAK
...THE ONLY CHOICE I'LL BE MAKING IS WHETHER TO BEAT YOU TO A PULP WITH MY TRUSTY BAT, OR THROW YA UNDER THE TRAIN.
UNGH!
KILL HER!
BRACKA
BRACKA
BRACKA
LISTEN, ROBOCOPS, I'M A BIG FAN OF ROBOTS AND LITERALLY ANY CINEMATIC FRANCHISE FEATURING YOU ALL STAGIN' A REVOLUTION AGAINST HUMANITY... I'M ON YOUR SIDE...

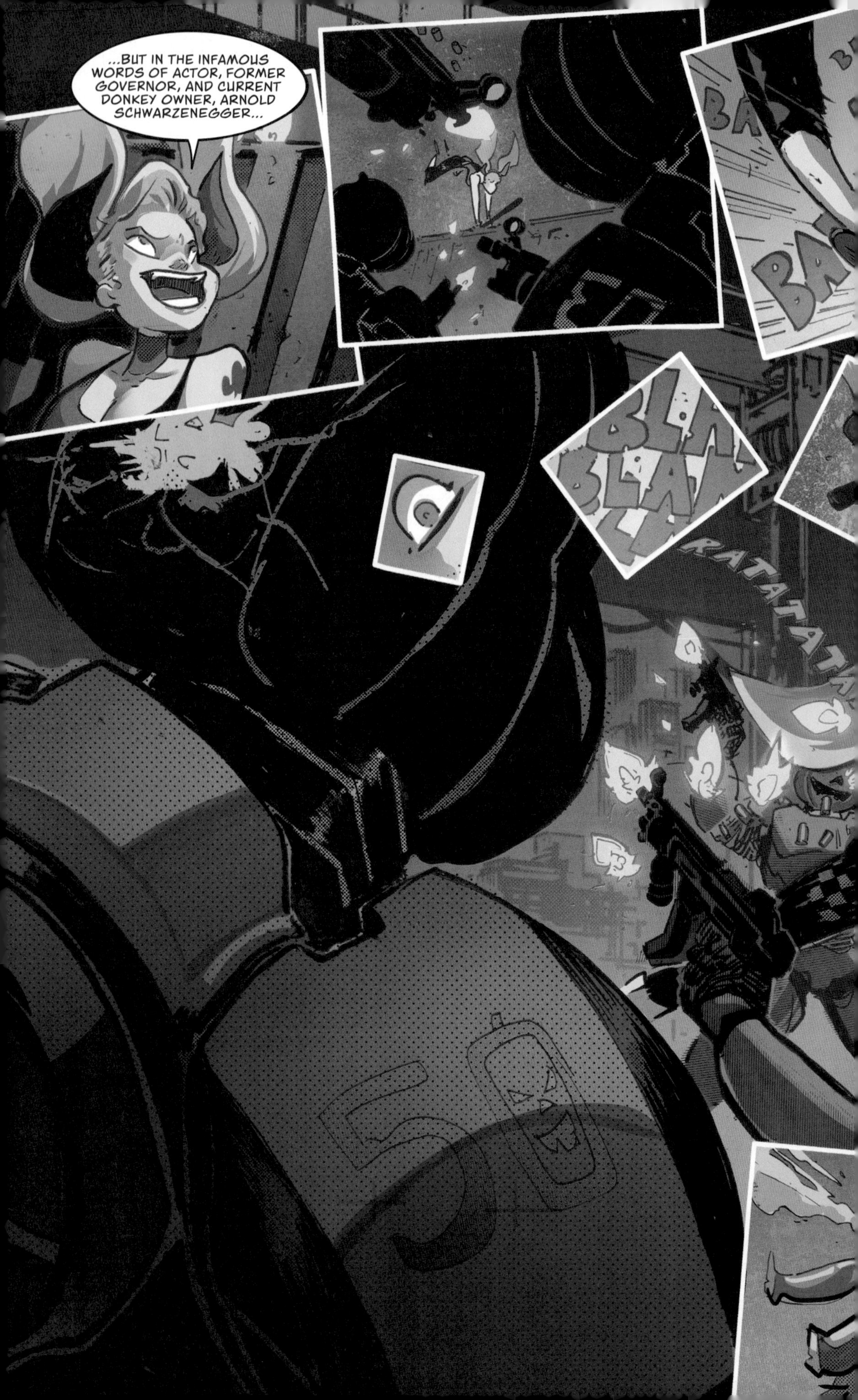
...BUT IN THE INFAMOUS WORDS OF ACTOR, FORMER GOVERNOR, AND CURRENT DONKEY OWNER, ARNOLD SCHWARZENEGGER...

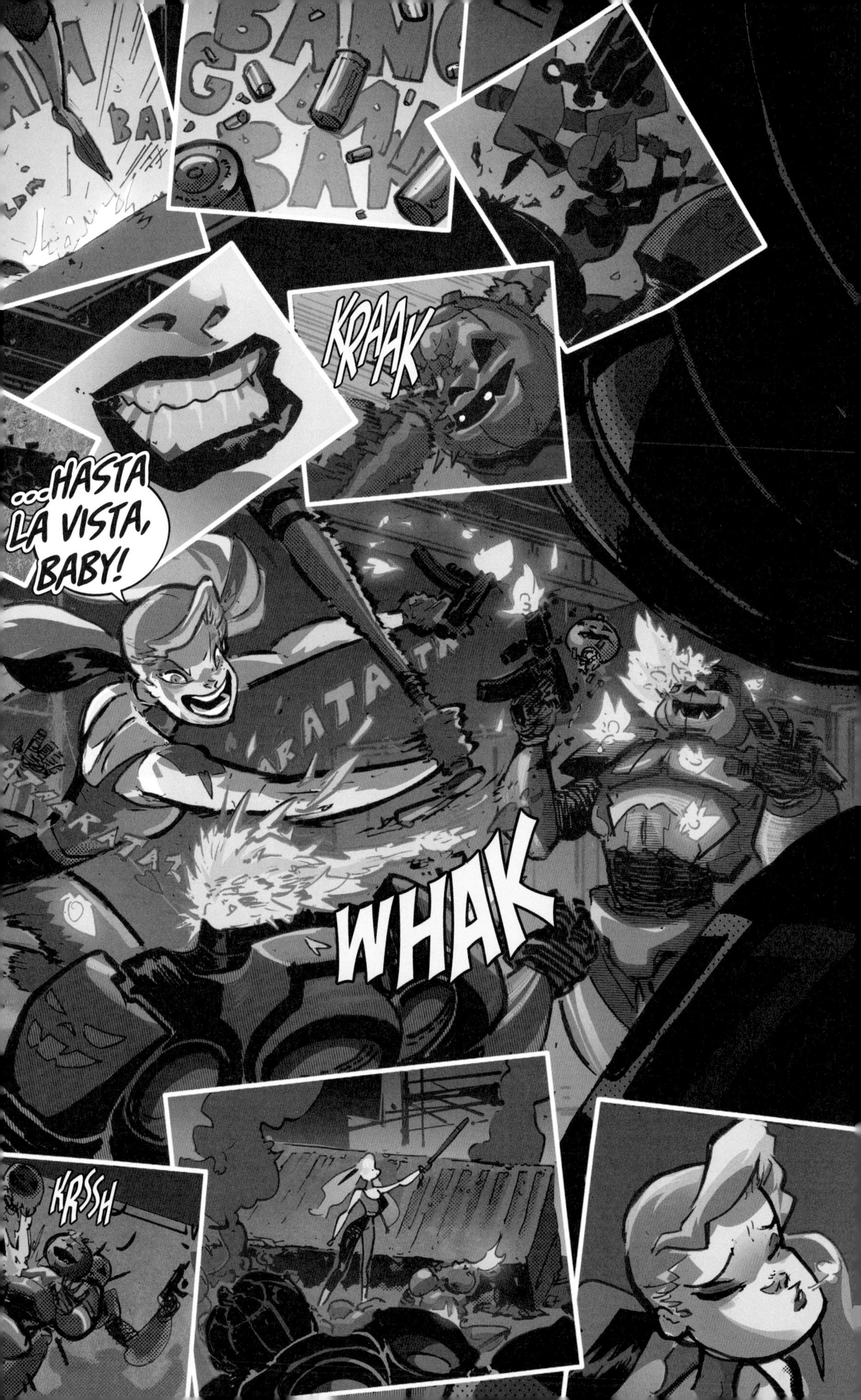
KRAAK
...HASTA LA VISTA, BABY!
WHAK
KRSSH

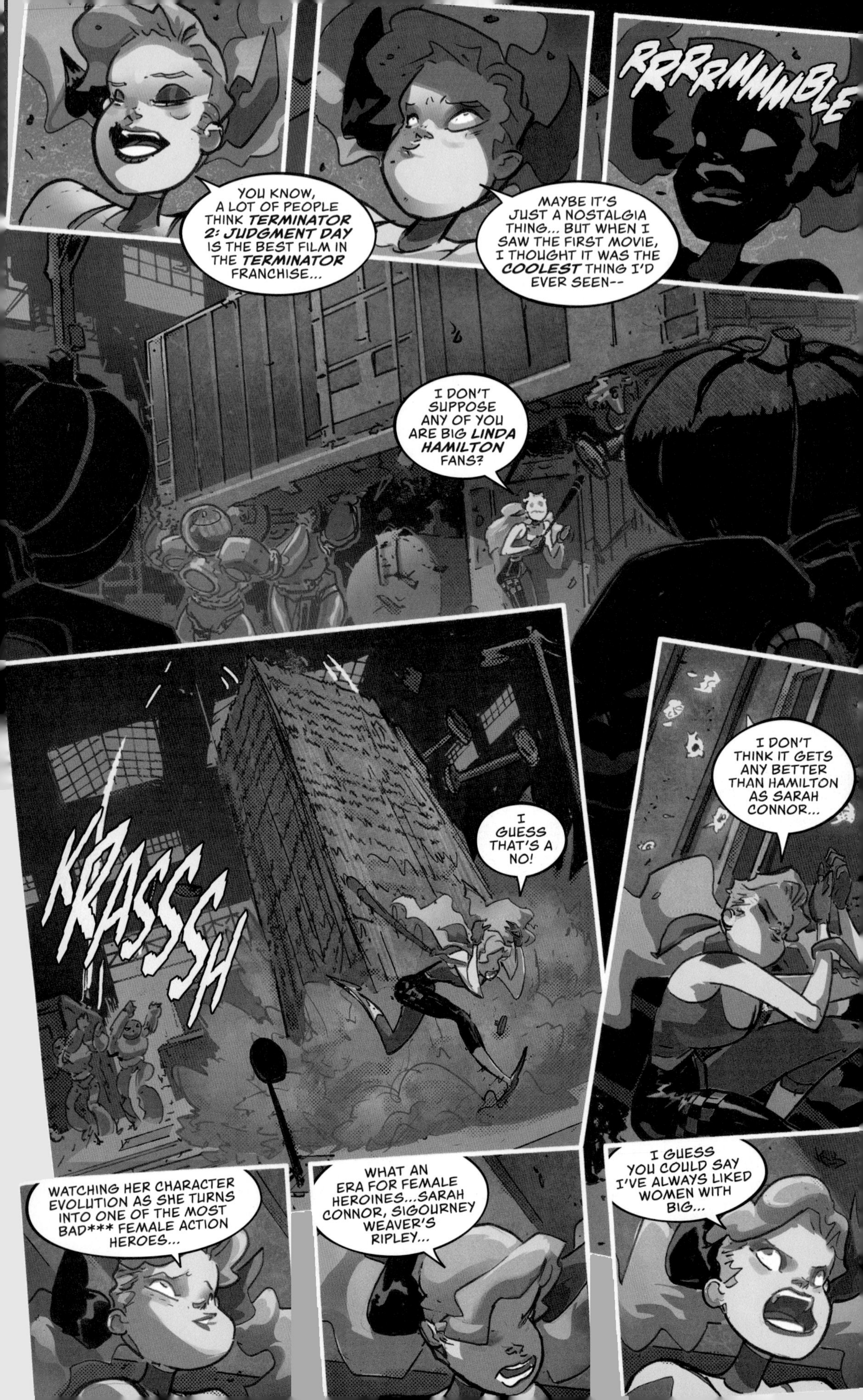

YOU KNOW, A LOT OF PEOPLE THINK TERMINATOR 2: JUDGMENT DAY IS THE BEST FILM IN THE TERMINATOR FRANCHISE...
MAYBE IT'S JUST A NOSTALGIA THING... BUT WHEN I SAW THE FIRST MOVIE, I THOUGHT IT WAS THE COOLEST THING I'D EVER SEEN--
RRRRMMMMBLE
I DON'T SUPPOSE ANY OF YOU ARE BIG LINDA HAMILTON FANS?
KRASSSH
I GUESS THAT'S A NO!
I DON'T THINK IT GETS ANY BETTER THAN HAMILTON AS SARAH CONNOR...
WATCHING HER CHARACTER EVOLUTION AS SHE TURNS INTO ONE OF THE MOST BAD*** FEMALE ACTION HEROES...
WHAT AN ERA FOR FEMALE HEROINES...SARAH CONNOR, SIGOURNEY WEAVER'S RIPLEY...
I GUESS YOU COULD SAY I'VE ALWAYS LIKED WOMEN WITH BIG...

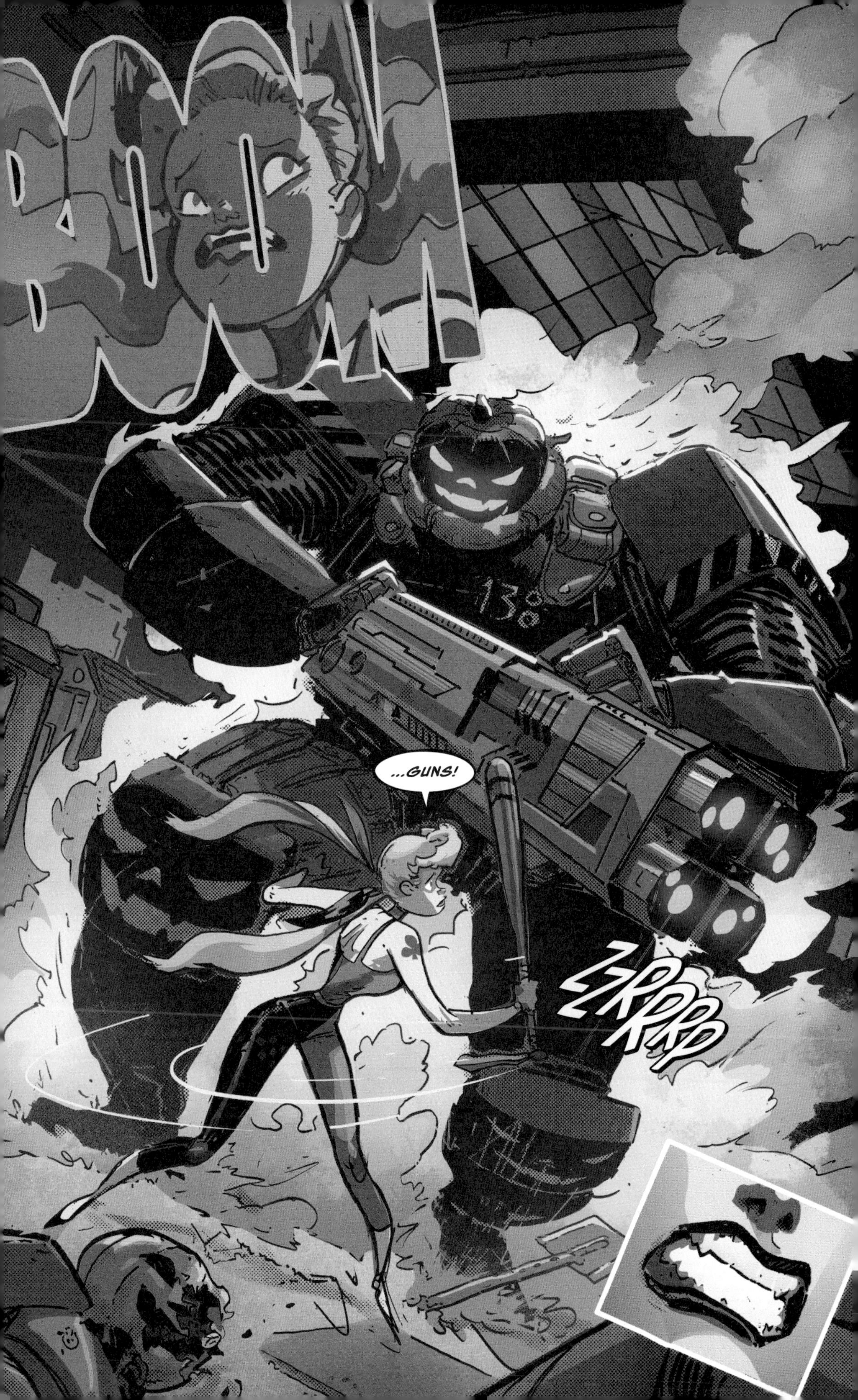
BRAAM
...GUNS!
ZZRRRP

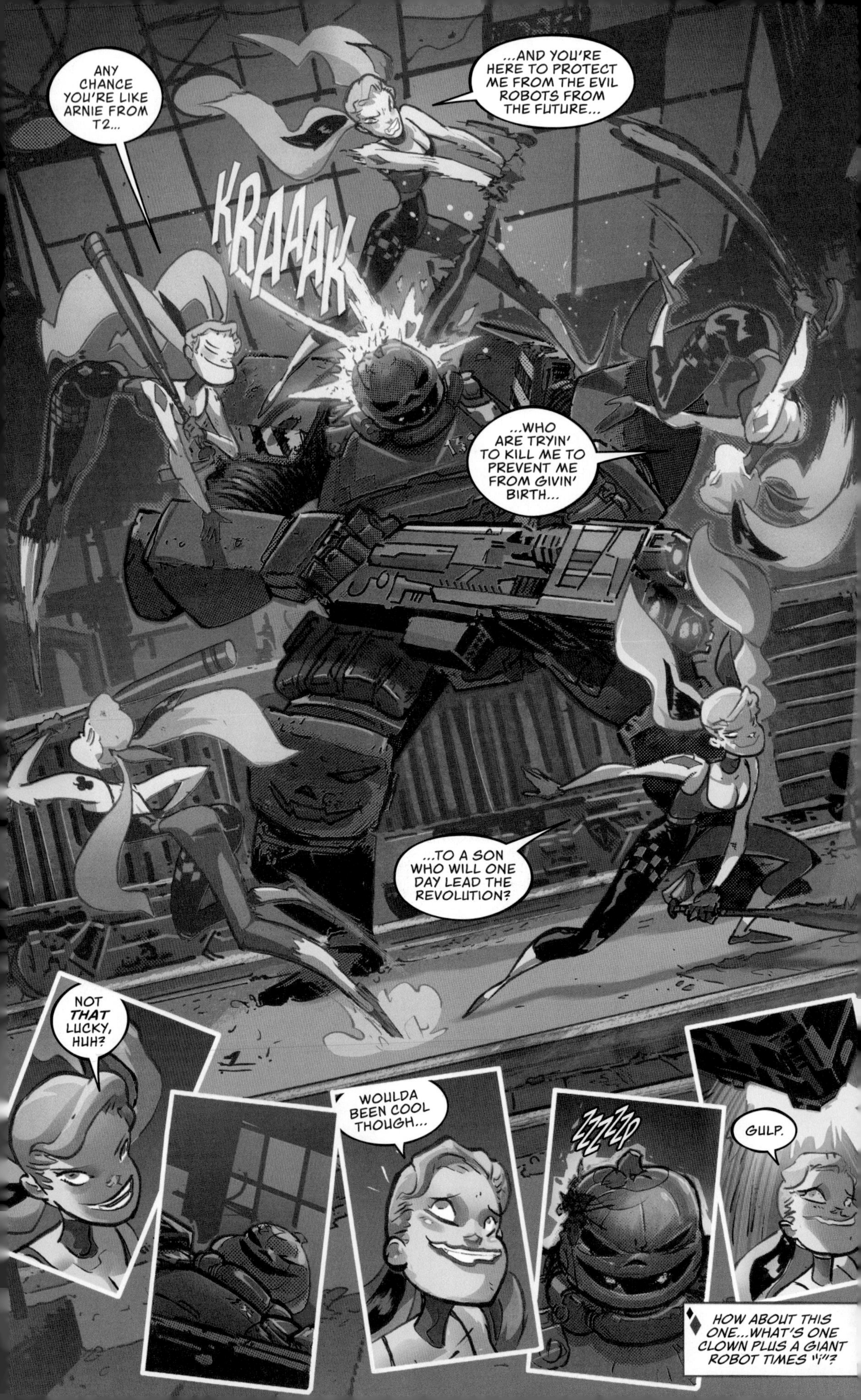
ANY CHANCE YOU'RE LIKE ARNIE FROM T2...
...AND YOU'RE HERE TO PROTECT ME FROM THE EVIL ROBOTS FROM THE FUTURE...
KRAAAK
...WHO ARE TRYIN' TO KILL ME TO PREVENT ME FROM GIVIN' BIRTH...
...TO A SON WHO WILL ONE DAY LEAD THE REVOLUTION?
NOT *THAT* LUCKY, HUH?
WOULDA BEEN COOL THOUGH...
ZZZZZP
GULP.
HOW ABOUT THIS ONE...WHAT'S ONE CLOWN PLUS A GIANT ROBOT TIMES "i"?

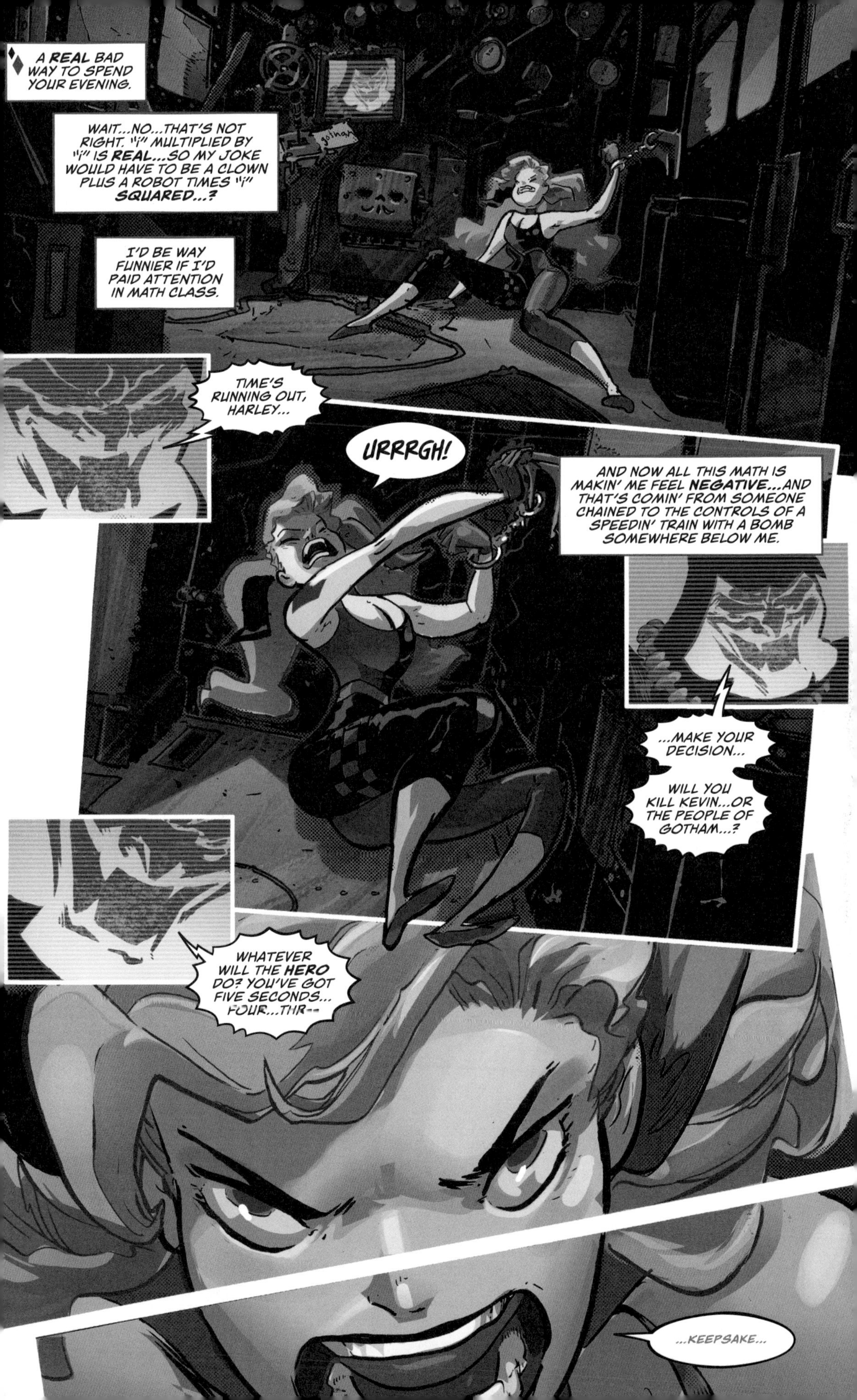
A REAL BAD WAY TO SPEND YOUR EVENING.
WAIT...NO...THAT'S NOT RIGHT. "i" MULTIPLIED BY "i" IS REAL...SO MY JOKE WOULD HAVE TO BE A CLOWN PLUS A ROBOT TIMES "i" SQUARED...?
I'D BE WAY FUNNIER IF I'D PAID ATTENTION IN MATH CLASS.
TIME'S RUNNING OUT, HARLEY...
URRRGH!
AND NOW ALL THIS MATH IS MAKIN' ME FEEL NEGATIVE...AND THAT'S COMIN' FROM SOMEONE CHAINED TO THE CONTROLS OF A SPEEDIN' TRAIN WITH A BOMB SOMEWHERE BELOW ME.
...MAKE YOUR DECISION...
WILL YOU KILL KEVIN...OR THE PEOPLE OF GOTHAM...?
WHATEVER WILL THE HERO DO? YOU'VE GOT FIVE SECONDS... FOUR...THR--
...KEEPSAKE...

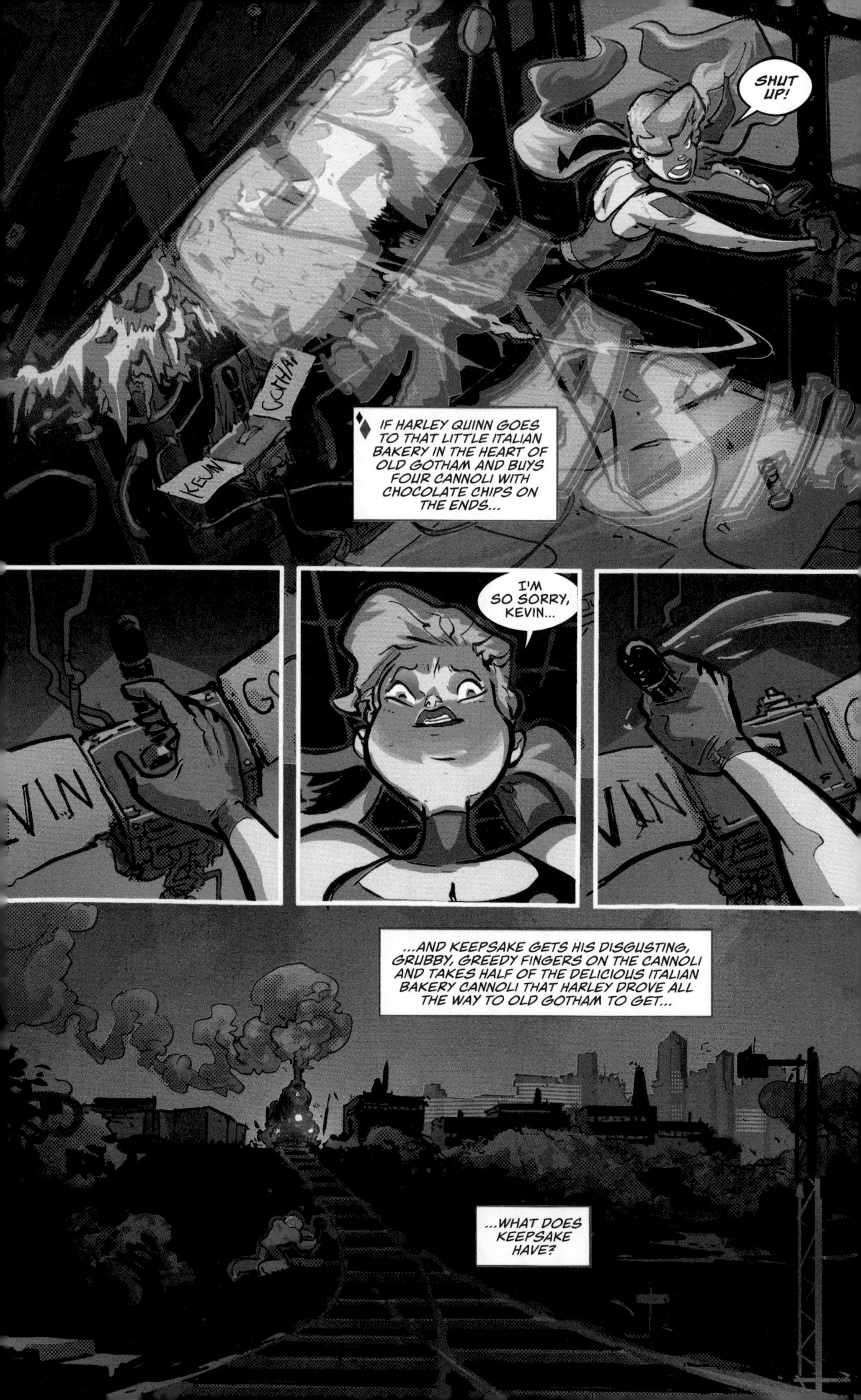
SHUT UP!
GOTHAM
KEVIN
IF HARLEY QUINN GOES TO THAT LITTLE ITALIAN BAKERY IN THE HEART OF OLD GOTHAM AND BUYS FOUR CANNOLI WITH CHOCOLATE CHIPS ON THE ENDS...
I'M SO SORRY, KEVIN...
...AND KEEPSAKE GETS HIS DISGUSTING, GRUBBY, GREEDY FINGERS ON THE CANNOLI AND TAKES HALF OF THE DELICIOUS ITALIAN BAKERY CANNOLI THAT HARLEY DROVE ALL THE WAY TO OLD GOTHAM TO GET...
...WHAT DOES KEEPSAKE HAVE?

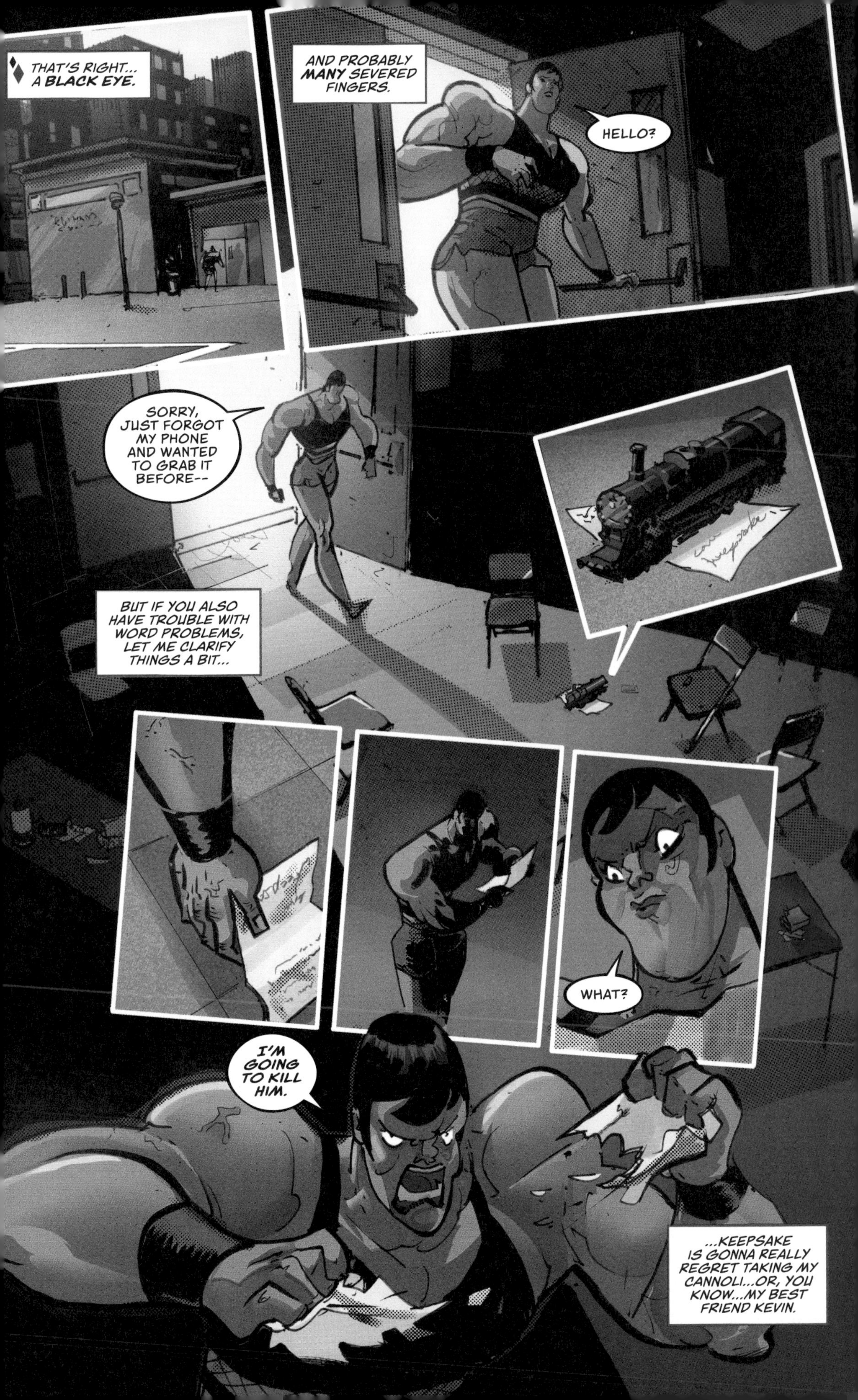
THAT'S RIGHT... A BLACK EYE.
AND PROBABLY MANY SEVERED FINGERS.
HELLO?
SORRY, JUST FORGOT MY PHONE AND WANTED TO GRAB IT BEFORE--
BUT IF YOU ALSO HAVE TROUBLE WITH WORD PROBLEMS, LET ME CLARIFY THINGS A BIT...
WHAT?
I'M GOING TO KILL HIM.
...KEEPSAKE IS GONNA REALLY REGRET TAKING MY CANNOLI...OR, YOU KNOW...MY BEST FRIEND KEVIN.

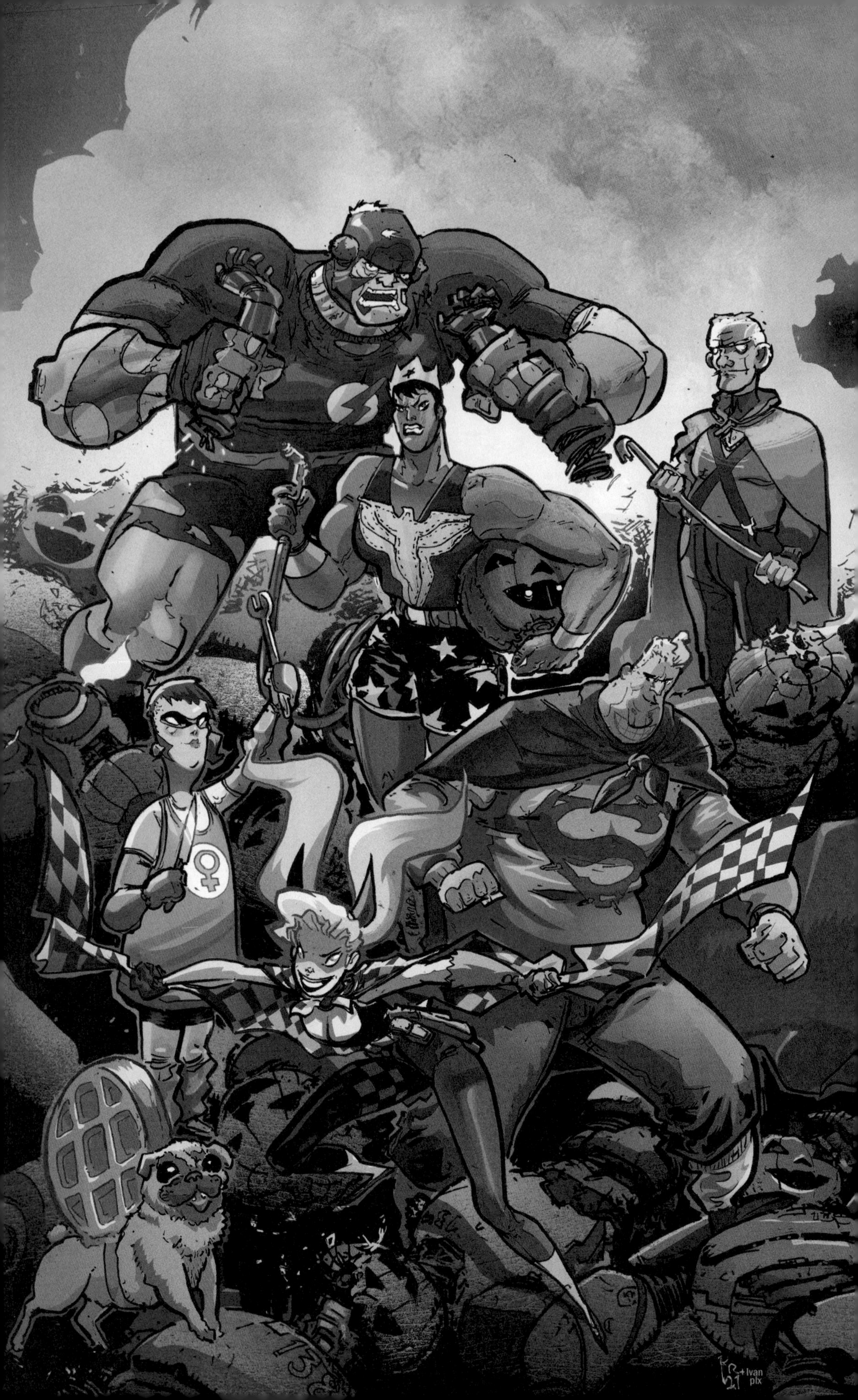

TWO WEEKS AGO.

"...AND TONIGHT, THE INVESTIGATION INTO THE MYSTERIOUS DEATH OF MARTIN SPINELLI IS **STILL** ONGOING IN GOTHAM CITY..."

"SPINELLI WAS FOUND DEAD INSIDE HIS APARTMENT JUST **HOURS** AFTER HE WAS ACQUITTED OF THE MURDER OF A NINE-YEAR-OLD BOY."

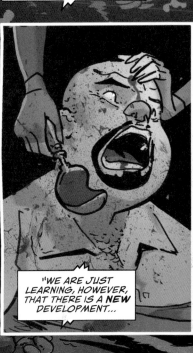

"THE BODY OF NINE-YEAR-OLD JEFFREY DUNN HAS NEVER BEEN FOUND..."

"...THAT LACK OF PHYSICAL EVIDENCE **SERIOUSLY** DAMAGED THE PROSECUTION'S CASE."

"WE ARE JUST LEARNING, HOWEVER, THAT THERE IS A **NEW** DEVELOPMENT..."

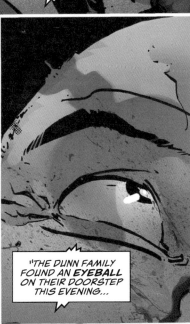

"...AN EYEBALL THAT AUTHORITIES TELL US **IS** A MATCH TO MARTIN SPINELLI..."

"...AN ABSOLUTELY **SHOCKING** DEVELOPMENT, FRANKLY..."

"THE DUNN FAMILY FOUND AN **EYEBALL** ON THEIR DOORSTEP THIS EVENING..."

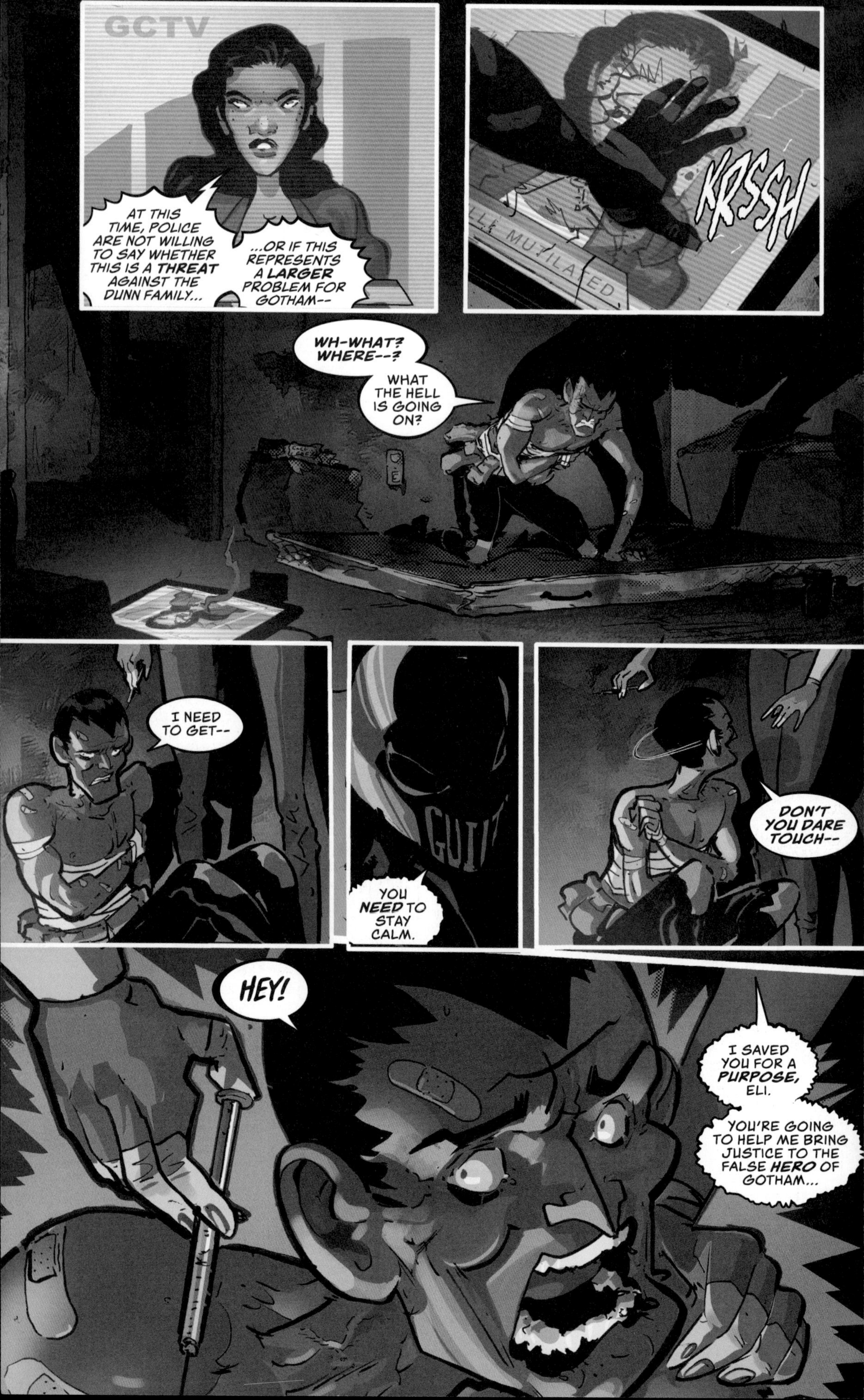
GCTV
AT THIS TIME, POLICE ARE NOT WILLING TO SAY WHETHER THIS IS A **THREAT** AGAINST THE DUNN FAMILY...
...OR IF THIS REPRESENTS A **LARGER** PROBLEM FOR GOTHAM--
KRSSH
WH-WHAT? WHERE--?
WHAT THE HELL IS GOING ON?
I NEED TO GET--
YOU **NEED** TO STAY CALM.
DON'T YOU DARE TOUCH--
HEY!
I SAVED YOU FOR A **PURPOSE,** ELI.
YOU'RE GOING TO HELP ME BRING JUSTICE TO THE FALSE **HERO** OF GOTHAM...

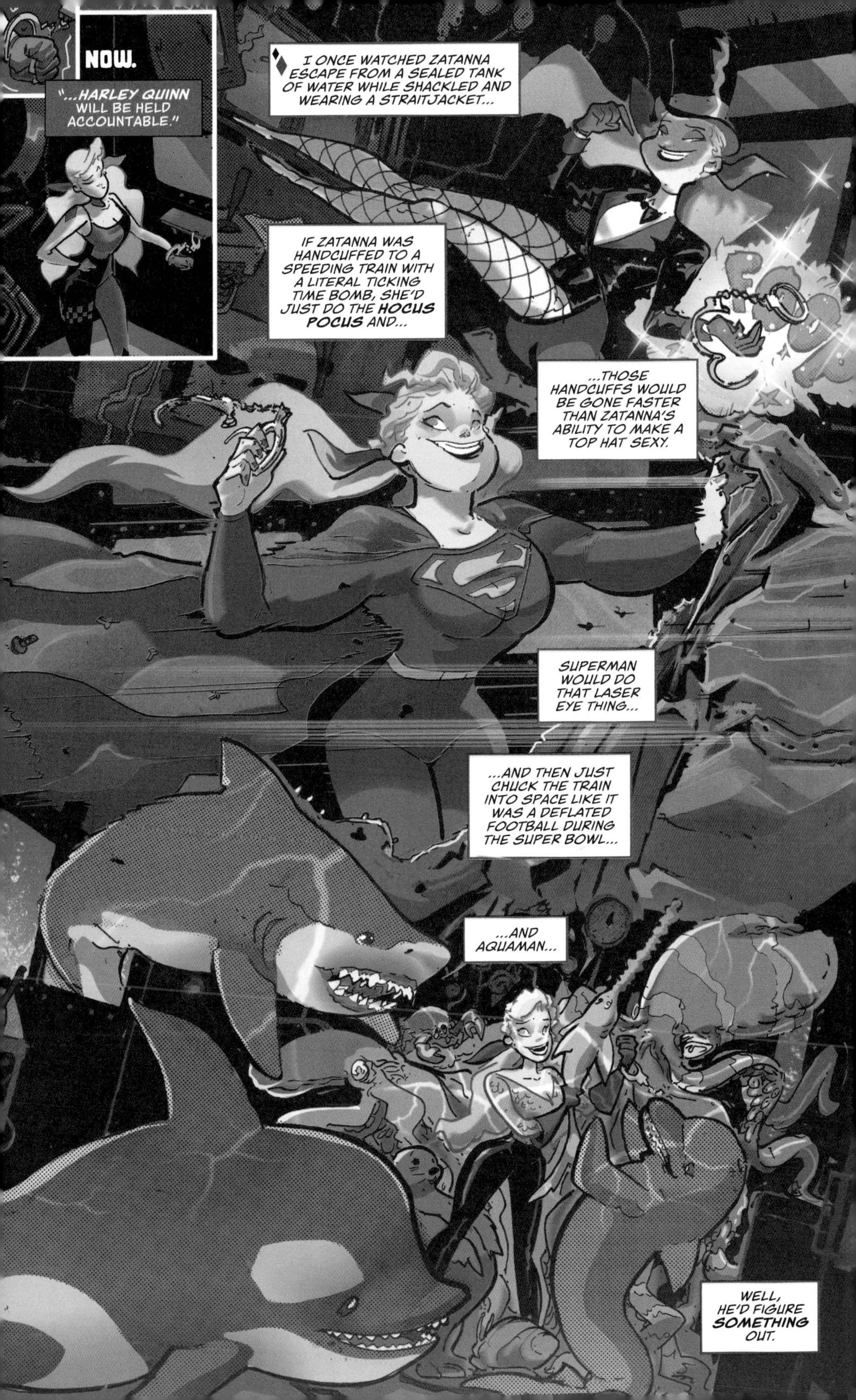
NOW.
"...HARLEY QUINN WILL BE HELD ACCOUNTABLE."
I ONCE WATCHED ZATANNA ESCAPE FROM A SEALED TANK OF WATER WHILE SHACKLED AND WEARING A STRAITJACKET...
IF ZATANNA WAS HANDCUFFED TO A SPEEDING TRAIN WITH A LITERAL TICKING TIME BOMB, SHE'D JUST DO THE HOCUS POCUS AND...
...THOSE HANDCUFFS WOULD BE GONE FASTER THAN ZATANNA'S ABILITY TO MAKE A TOP HAT SEXY.
SUPERMAN WOULD DO THAT LASER EYE THING...
...AND THEN JUST CHUCK THE TRAIN INTO SPACE LIKE IT WAS A DEFLATED FOOTBALL DURING THE SUPER BOWL...
...AND AQUAMAN...
WELL, HE'D FIGURE SOMETHING OUT.

BAD MATH PART 2

STEPHANIE PHILLIPS WRITER
RILEY ROSSMO ARTIST
IVAN PLASCENCIA COLORS
ANDWORLD DESIGN LETTERS
RILEY ROSSMO COVER
DERRICK CHEW VARIANT COVER
RIAN GONZALES 1:25 VARIANT COVER
BEN ABERNATHY EDITOR

HARLEY QUINN CREATED BY
PAUL DINI AND **BRUCE TIMM**

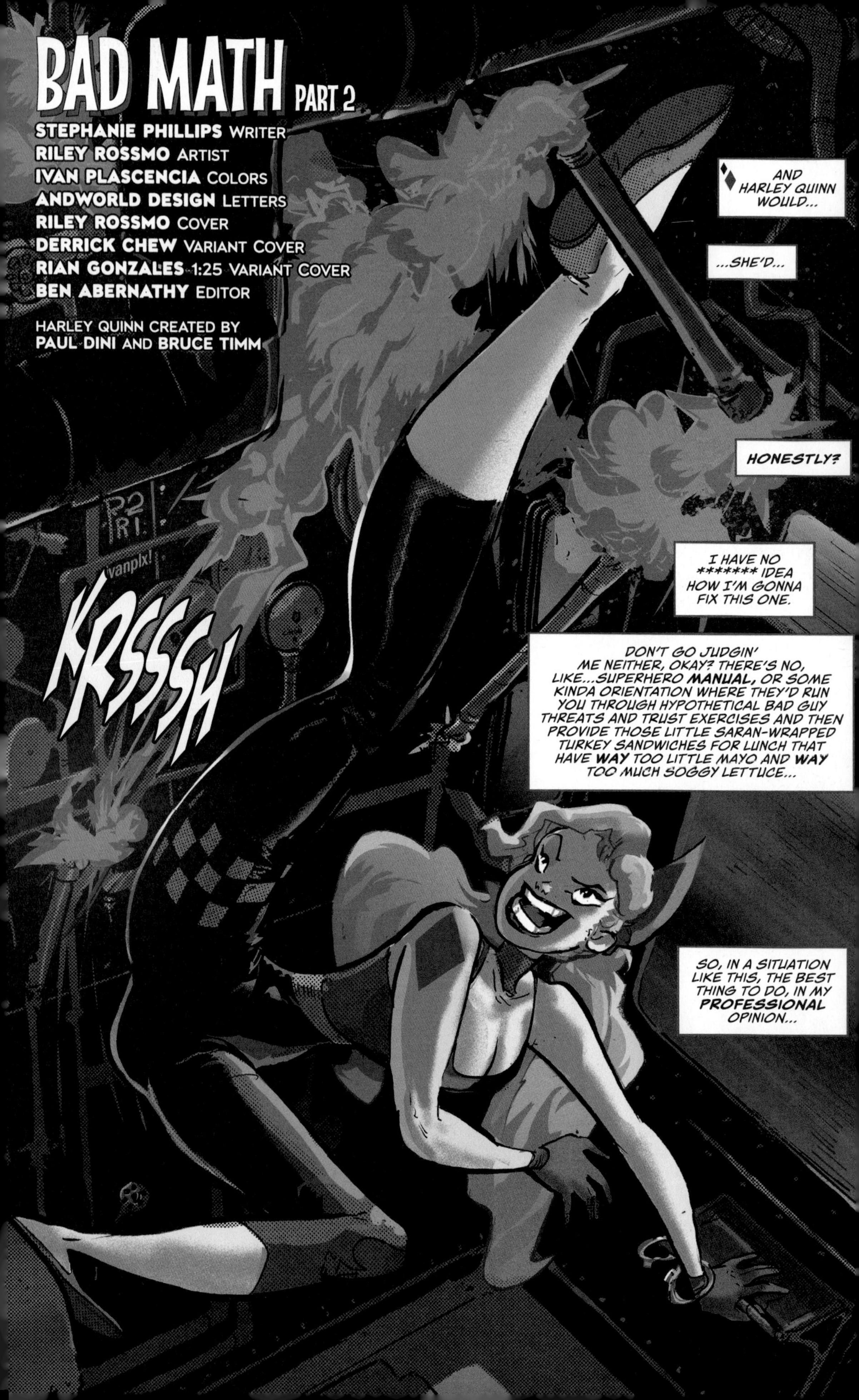
AND HARLEY QUINN WOULD...
...SHE'D...
HONESTLY?
I HAVE NO ******* IDEA HOW I'M GONNA FIX THIS ONE.
KRSSSH
DON'T GO JUDGIN' ME NEITHER, OKAY? THERE'S NO, LIKE...SUPERHERO MANUAL, OR SOME KINDA ORIENTATION WHERE THEY'D RUN YOU THROUGH HYPOTHETICAL BAD GUY THREATS AND TRUST EXERCISES AND THEN PROVIDE THOSE LITTLE SARAN-WRAPPED TURKEY SANDWICHES FOR LUNCH THAT HAVE WAY TOO LITTLE MAYO AND WAY TOO MUCH SOGGY LETTUCE...
SO, IN A SITUATION LIKE THIS, THE BEST THING TO DO, IN MY PROFESSIONAL OPINION...

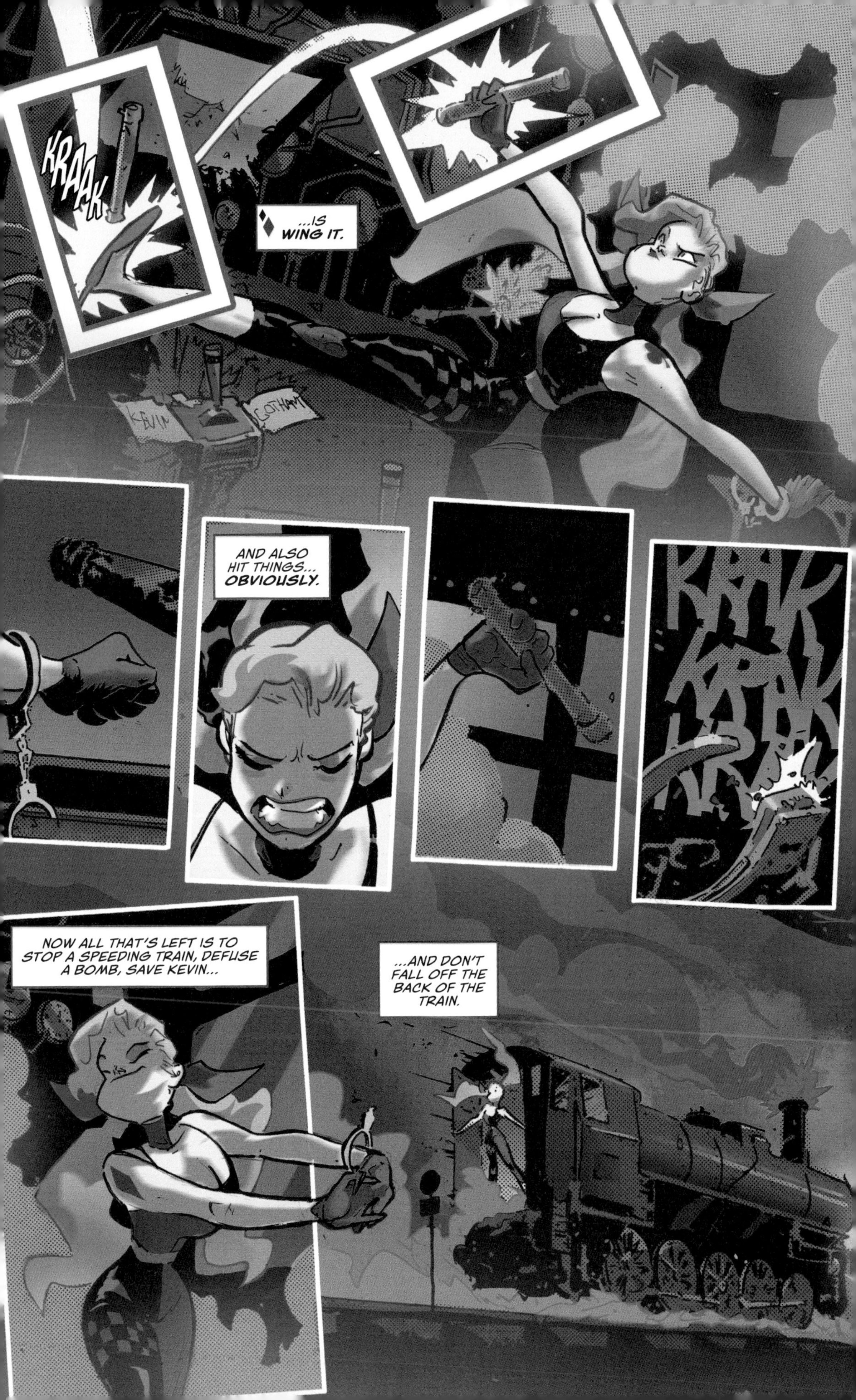
KRAAK
...IS WING IT.
AND ALSO HIT THINGS... OBVIOUSLY.
NOW ALL THAT'S LEFT IS TO STOP A SPEEDING TRAIN, DEFUSE A BOMB, SAVE KEVIN...
...AND DON'T FALL OFF THE BACK OF THE TRAIN.

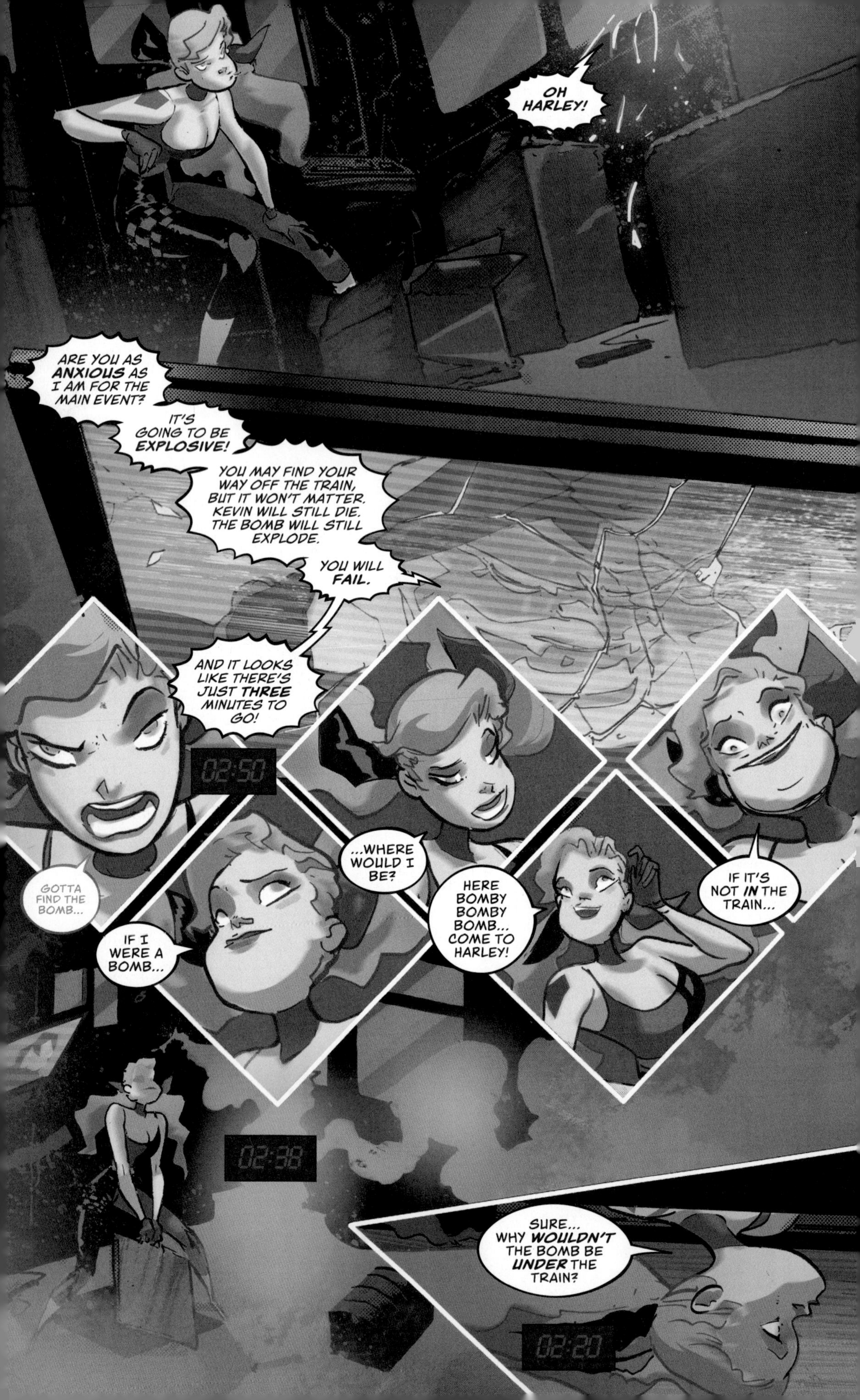
OH HARLEY!
ARE YOU AS **ANXIOUS** AS I AM FOR THE MAIN EVENT?
IT'S GOING TO BE **EXPLOSIVE!**
YOU MAY FIND YOUR WAY OFF THE TRAIN, BUT IT WON'T MATTER. KEVIN WILL STILL DIE. THE BOMB WILL STILL EXPLODE.
YOU WILL **FAIL.**
AND IT LOOKS LIKE THERE'S JUST **THREE** MINUTES TO GO!
02:50
GOTTA FIND THE BOMB...
IF I WERE A BOMB...
...WHERE WOULD I BE?
HERE BOMBY BOMBY BOMB... COME TO HARLEY!
IF IT'S NOT **IN** THE TRAIN...
02:38
SURE... WHY **WOULDN'T** THE BOMB BE **UNDER** THE TRAIN?
02:20

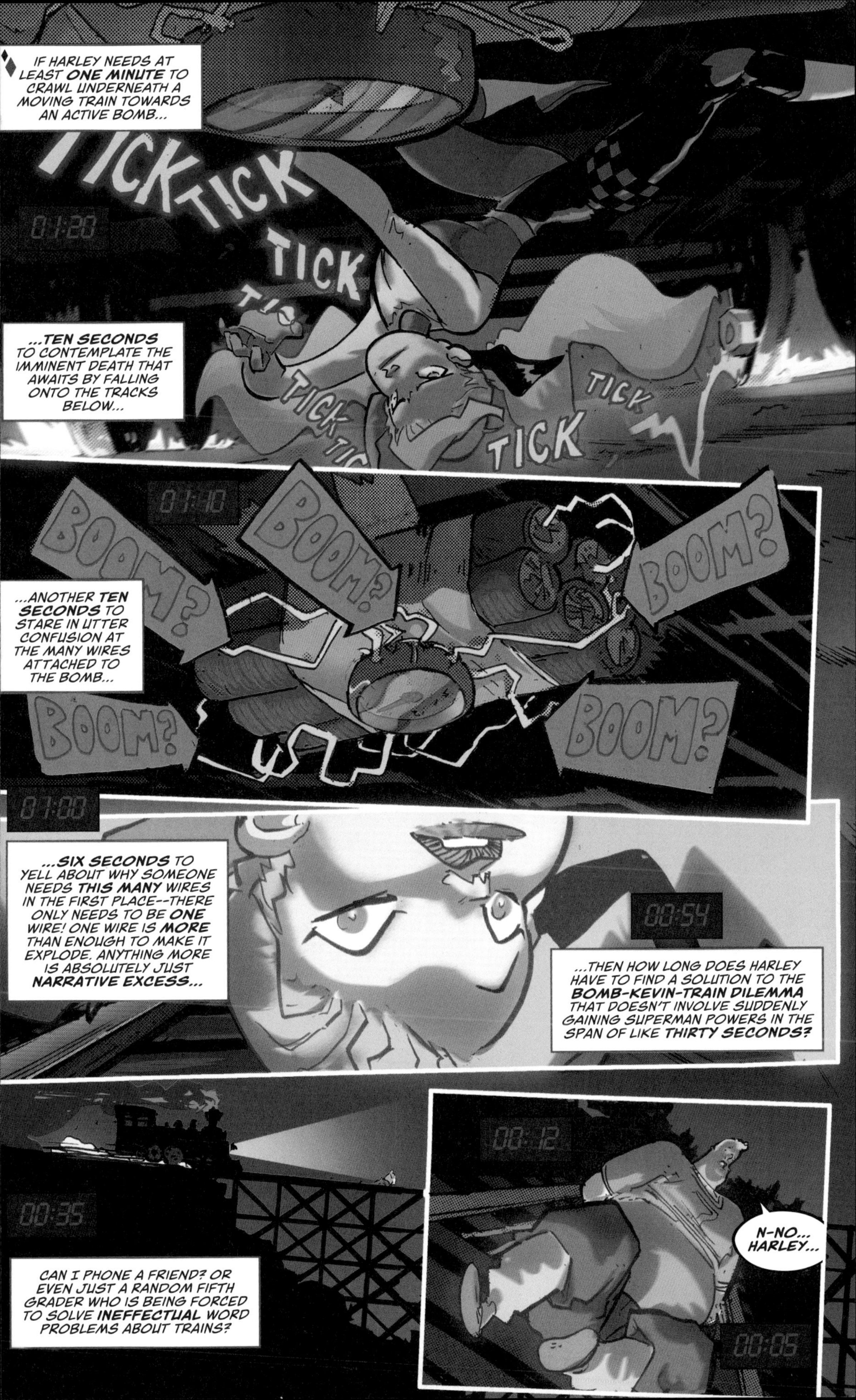
IF HARLEY NEEDS AT LEAST ONE MINUTE TO CRAWL UNDERNEATH A MOVING TRAIN TOWARDS AN ACTIVE BOMB...
TICK TICK TICK
01:20
...TEN SECONDS TO CONTEMPLATE THE IMMINENT DEATH THAT AWAITS BY FALLING ONTO THE TRACKS BELOW...
TICK TICK TICK
01:10
BOOM? BOOM? BOOM? BOOM? BOOM?
...ANOTHER TEN SECONDS TO STARE IN UTTER CONFUSION AT THE MANY WIRES ATTACHED TO THE BOMB...
01:00
...SIX SECONDS TO YELL ABOUT WHY SOMEONE NEEDS THIS MANY WIRES IN THE FIRST PLACE--THERE ONLY NEEDS TO BE ONE WIRE! ONE WIRE IS MORE THAN ENOUGH TO MAKE IT EXPLODE. ANYTHING MORE IS ABSOLUTELY JUST NARRATIVE EXCESS...
00:54
...THEN HOW LONG DOES HARLEY HAVE TO FIND A SOLUTION TO THE BOMB-KEVIN-TRAIN DILEMMA THAT DOESN'T INVOLVE SUDDENLY GAINING SUPERMAN POWERS IN THE SPAN OF LIKE THIRTY SECONDS?
00:35
CAN I PHONE A FRIEND? OR EVEN JUST A RANDOM FIFTH GRADER WHO IS BEING FORCED TO SOLVE INEFFECTUAL WORD PROBLEMS ABOUT TRAINS?
00:12
N-NO... HARLEY...
00:05

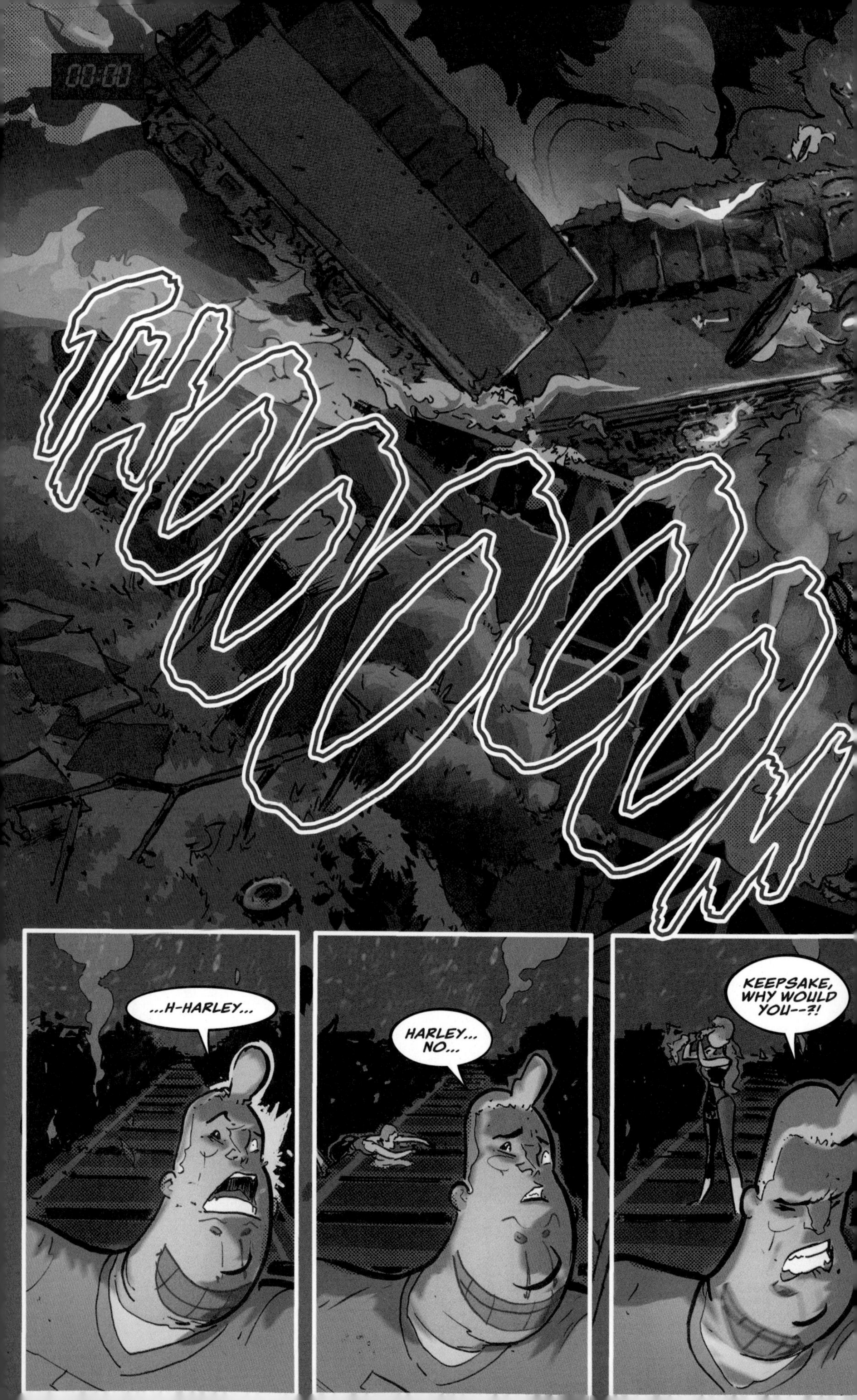
00:00
...H-HARLEY...
HARLEY... NO...
KEEPSAKE, WHY WOULD YOU--?!

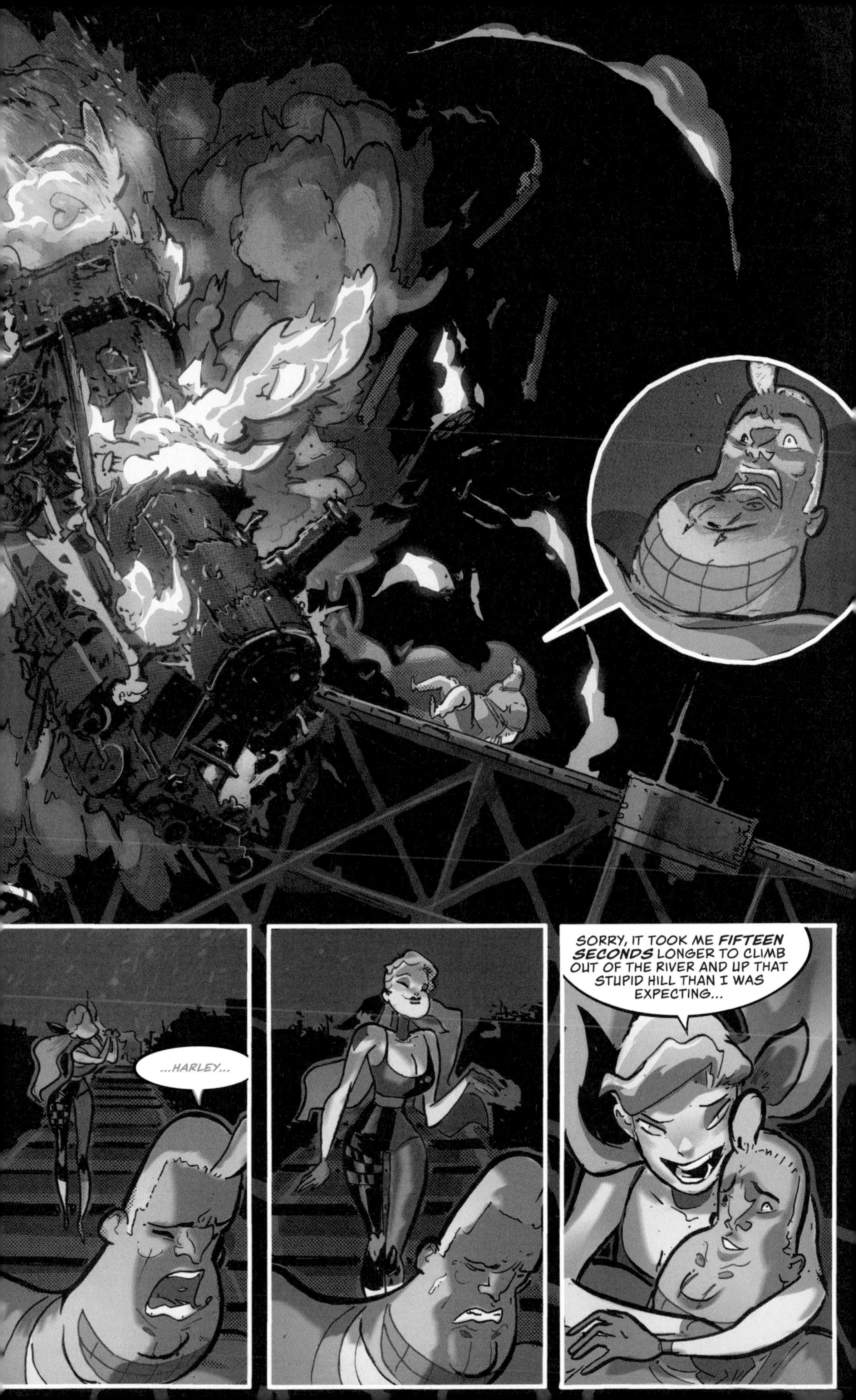
...HARLEY...
SORRY, IT TOOK ME FIFTEEN SECONDS LONGER TO CLIMB OUT OF THE RIVER AND UP THAT STUPID HILL THAN I WAS EXPECTING...

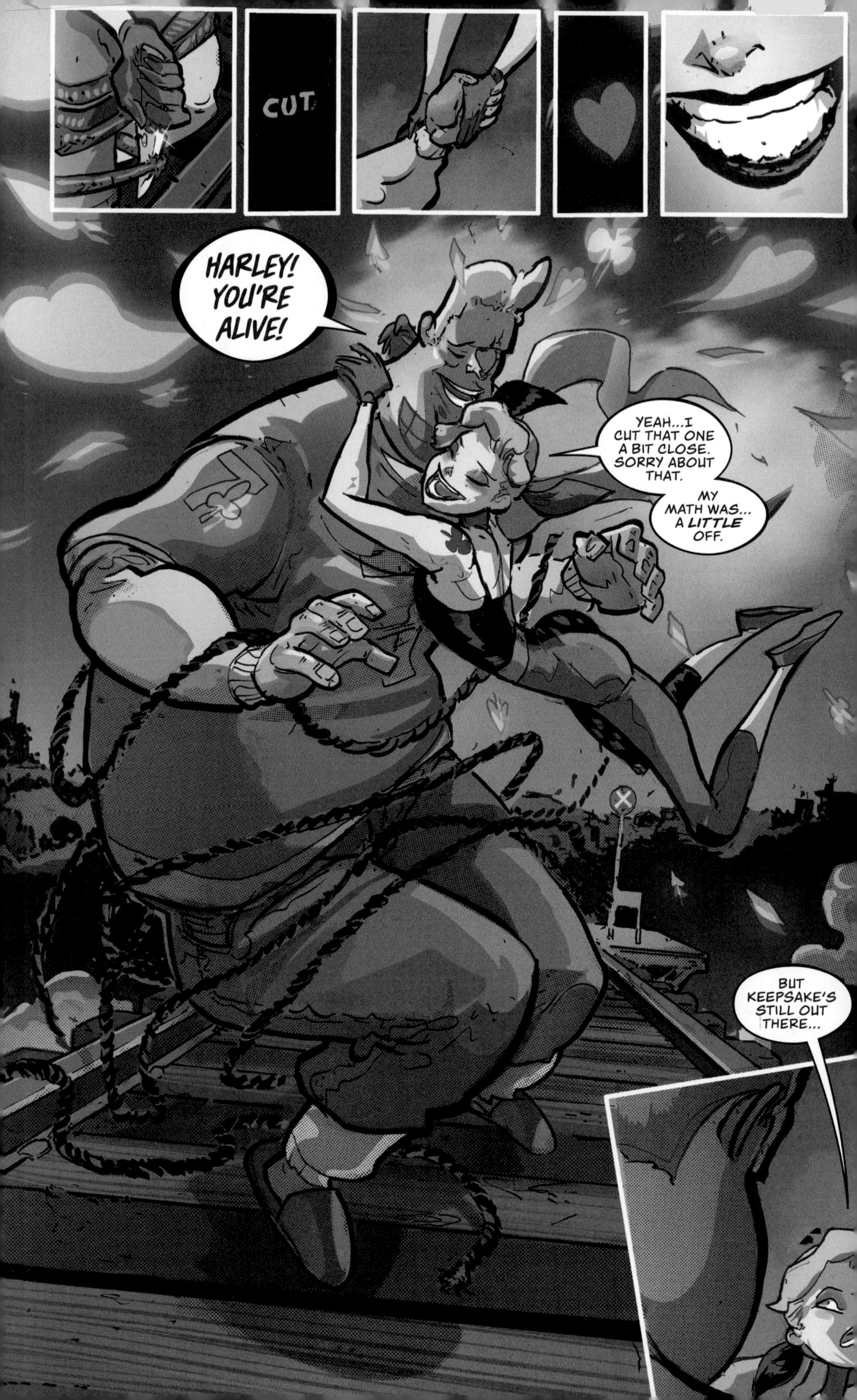
CUT
HARLEY! YOU'RE ALIVE!
YEAH...I CUT THAT ONE A BIT CLOSE. SORRY ABOUT THAT.
MY MATH WAS... A LITTLE OFF.
BUT KEEPSAKE'S STILL OUT THERE...

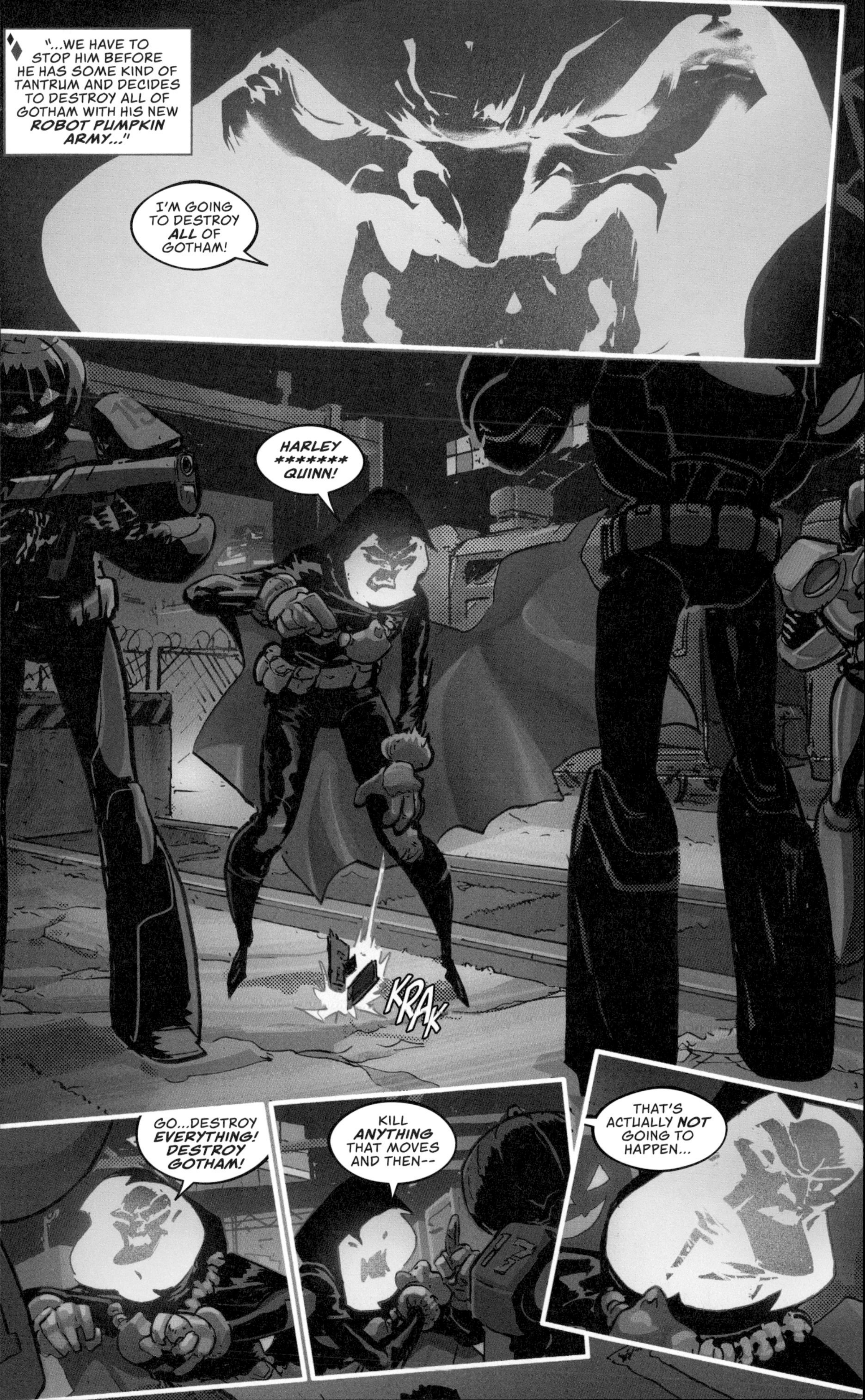

"...WE HAVE TO STOP HIM BEFORE HE HAS SOME KIND OF TANTRUM AND DECIDES TO DESTROY ALL OF GOTHAM WITH HIS NEW ROBOT PUMPKIN ARMY..."
I'M GOING TO DESTROY ALL OF GOTHAM!
HARLEY ******* QUINN!
KRAK
GO...DESTROY EVERYTHING! DESTROY GOTHAM!
KILL ANYTHING THAT MOVES AND THEN--
THAT'S ACTUALLY NOT GOING TO HAPPEN...

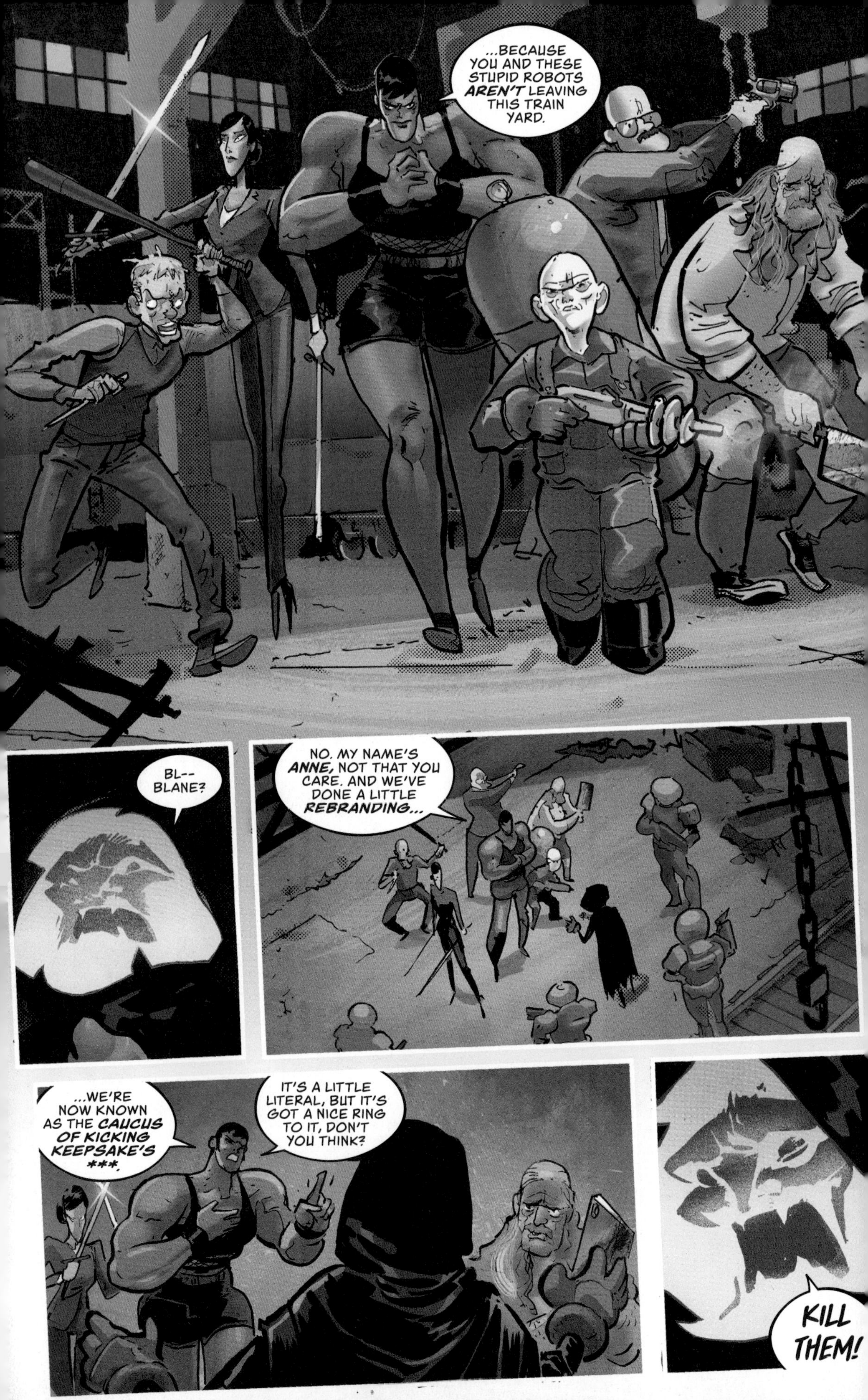

...BECAUSE YOU AND THESE STUPID ROBOTS AREN'T LEAVING THIS TRAIN YARD.
BL-- BLANE?
NO. MY NAME'S ANNE, NOT THAT YOU CARE. AND WE'VE DONE A LITTLE REBRANDING...
...WE'RE NOW KNOWN AS THE CAUCUS OF KICKING KEEPSAKE'S ***.
IT'S A LITTLE LITERAL, BUT IT'S GOT A NICE RING TO IT, DON'T YOU THINK?
KILL THEM!

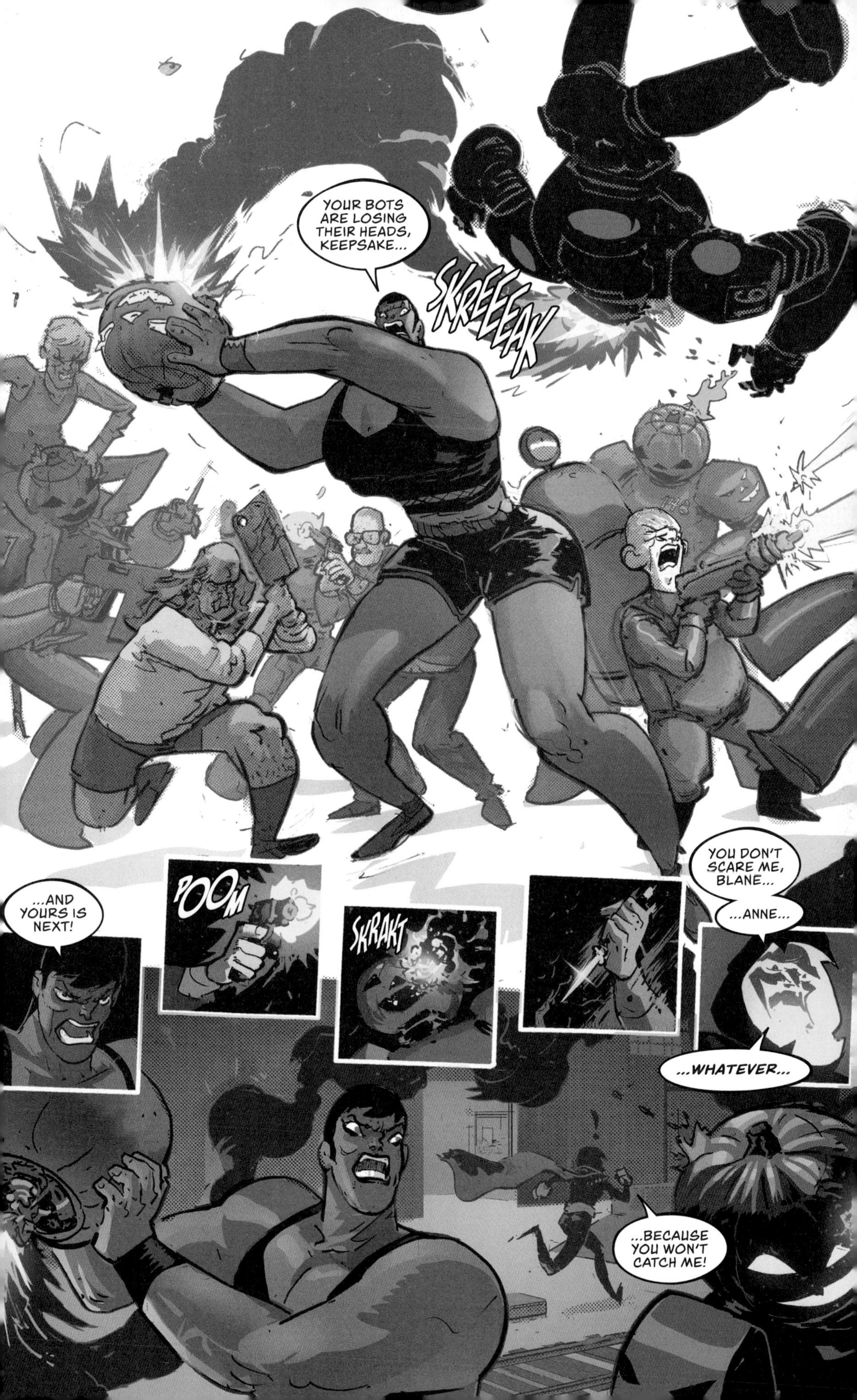
YOUR BOTS ARE LOSING THEIR HEADS, KEEPSAKE...
SKREEEEAK
...AND YOURS IS NEXT!
POOM
SKRAKT
YOU DON'T SCARE ME, BLANE...
...ANNE...
...WHATEVER...
...BECAUSE YOU WON'T CATCH ME!

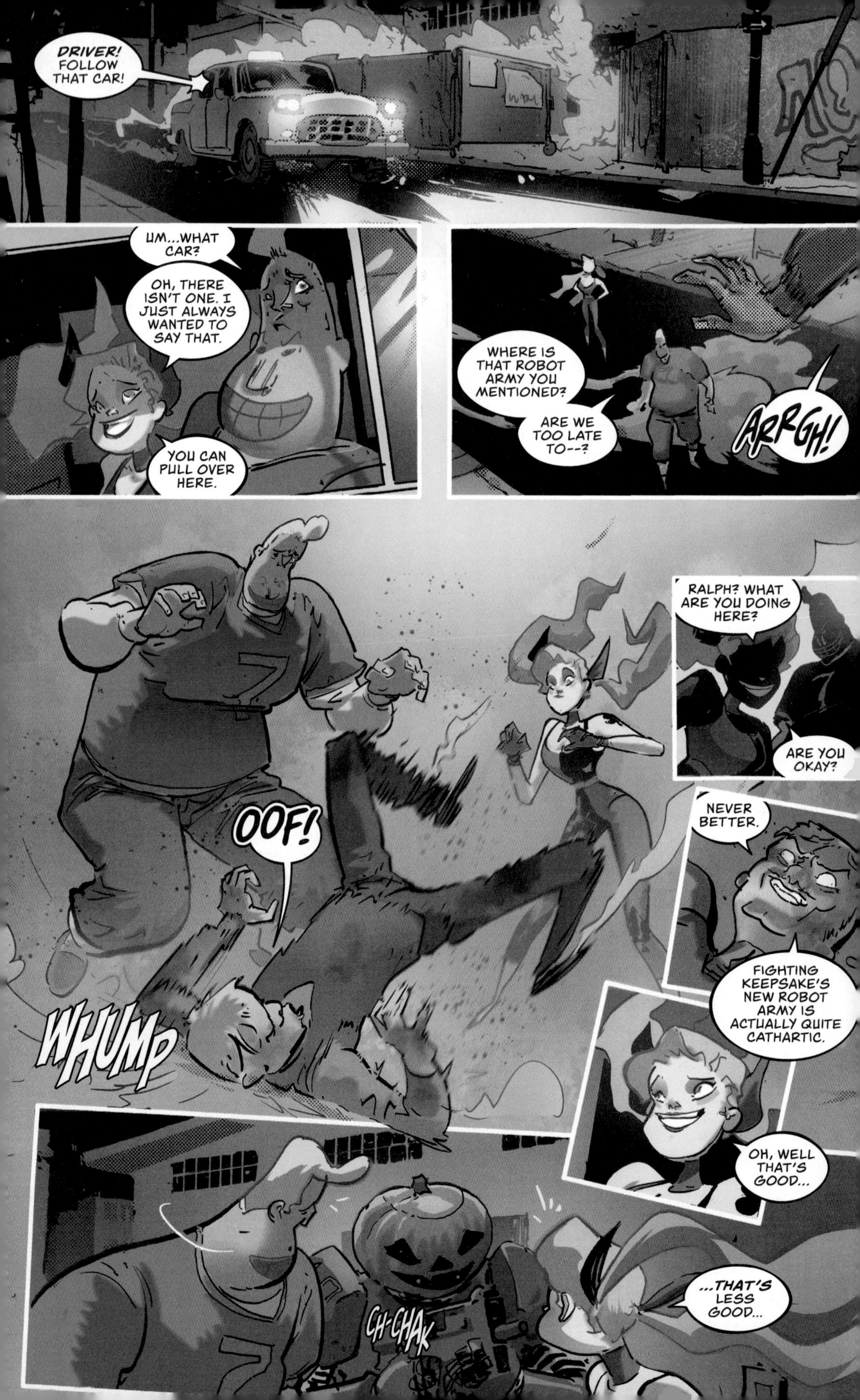
DRIVER! FOLLOW THAT CAR!
UM...WHAT CAR?
OH, THERE ISN'T ONE. I JUST ALWAYS WANTED TO SAY THAT.
YOU CAN PULL OVER HERE.
WHERE IS THAT ROBOT ARMY YOU MENTIONED?
ARE WE TOO LATE TO--?
ARRGH!
OOF!
WHUMP
RALPH? WHAT ARE YOU DOING HERE?
ARE YOU OKAY?
NEVER BETTER.
FIGHTING KEEPSAKE'S NEW ROBOT ARMY IS ACTUALLY QUITE CATHARTIC.
OH, WELL THAT'S GOOD...
CH-CHAK
...THAT'S LESS GOOD...

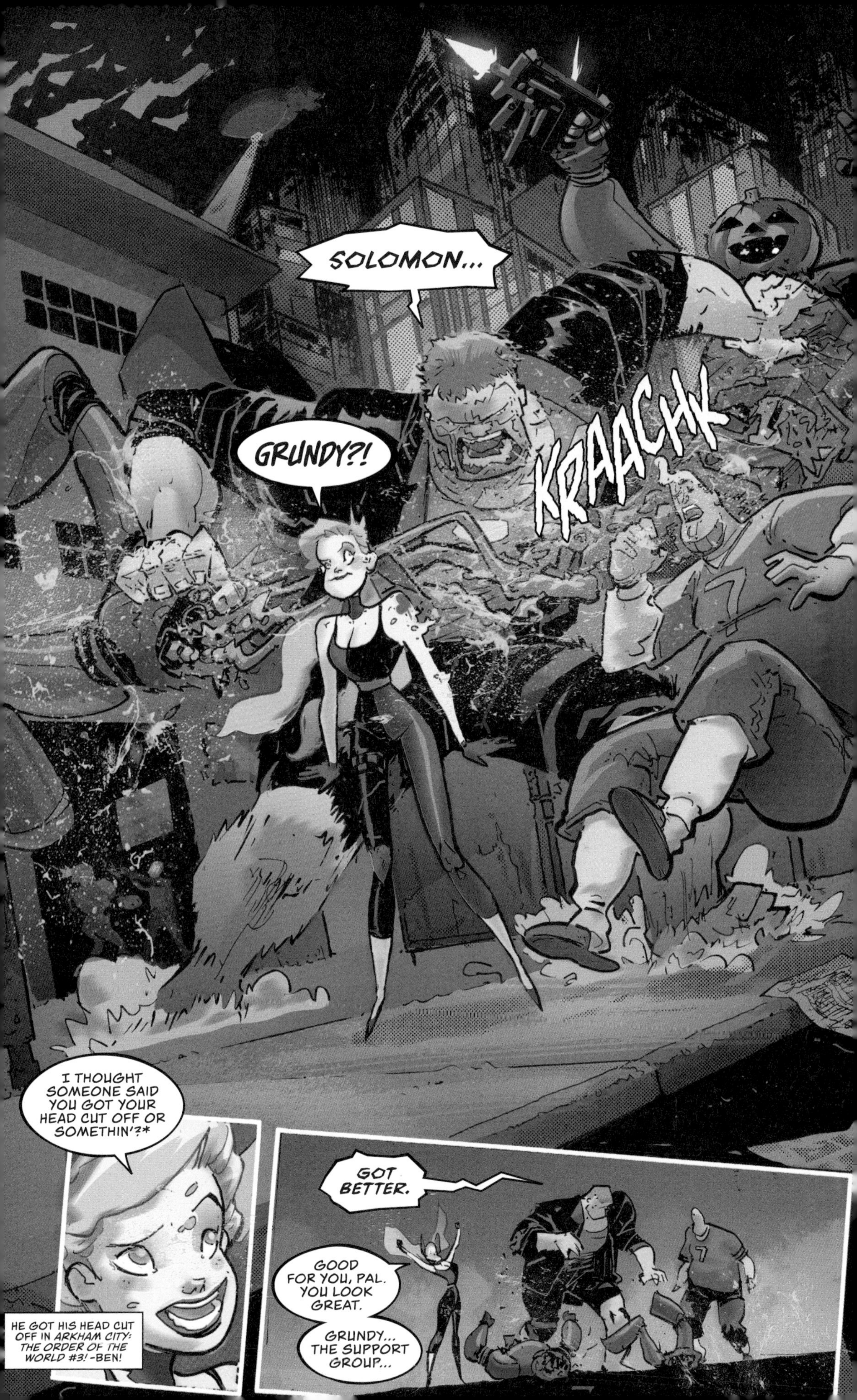
SOLOMON...
GRUNDY?!
KRAACHK
I THOUGHT SOMEONE SAID YOU GOT YOUR HEAD CUT OFF OR SOMETHIN'?*
HE GOT HIS HEAD CUT OFF IN *ARKHAM CITY: THE ORDER OF THE WORLD #3!* -BEN!
GOT BETTER.
GOOD FOR YOU, PAL. YOU LOOK GREAT.
GRUNDY... THE SUPPORT GROUP...

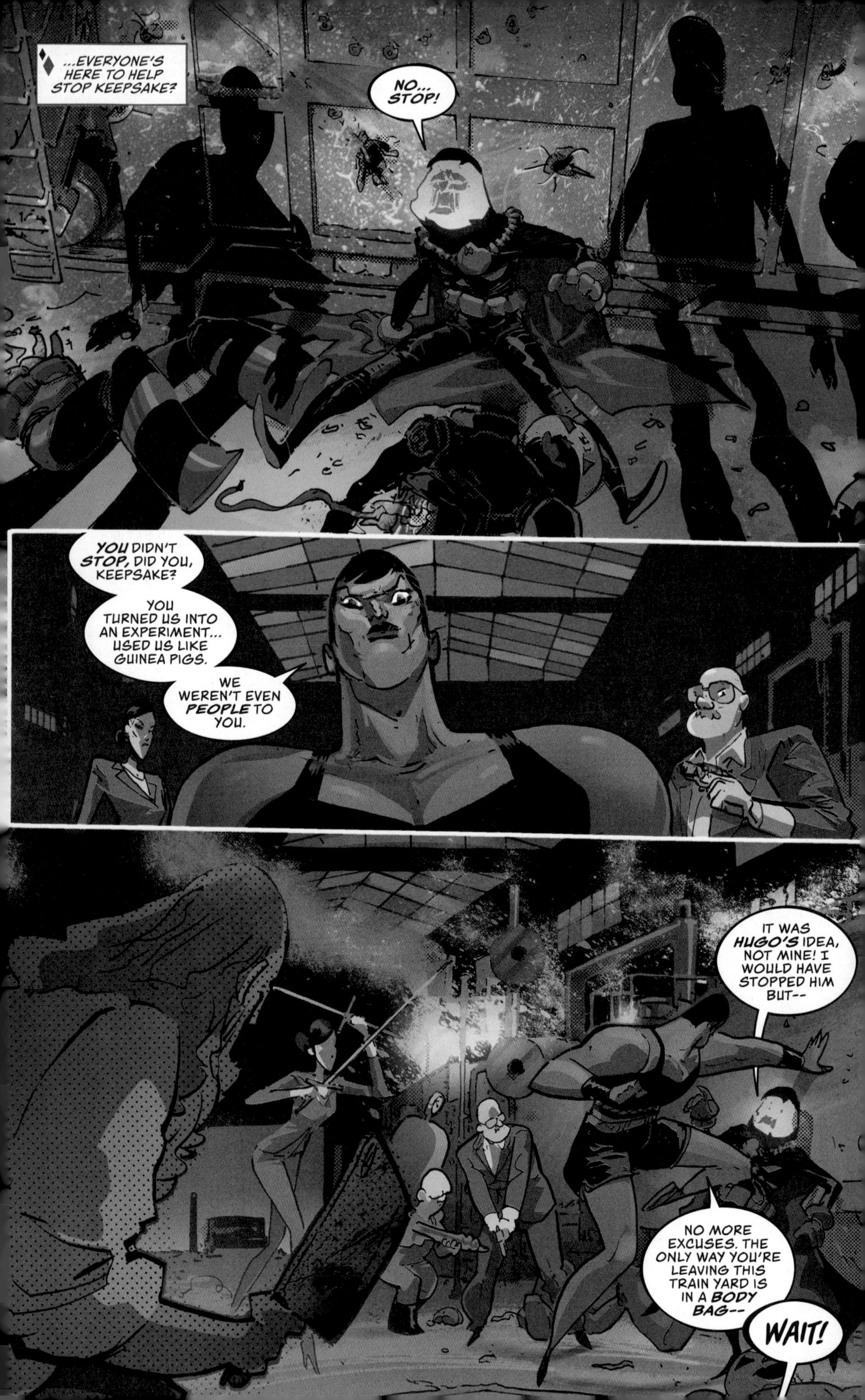
...EVERYONE'S HERE TO HELP STOP KEEPSAKE?
NO... STOP!
YOU DIDN'T STOP, DID YOU, KEEPSAKE?
YOU TURNED US INTO AN EXPERIMENT... USED US LIKE GUINEA PIGS.
WE WEREN'T EVEN PEOPLE TO YOU.
IT WAS HUGO'S IDEA, NOT MINE! I WOULD HAVE STOPPED HIM BUT--
NO MORE EXCUSES. THE ONLY WAY YOU'RE LEAVING THIS TRAIN YARD IS IN A BODY BAG--
WAIT!

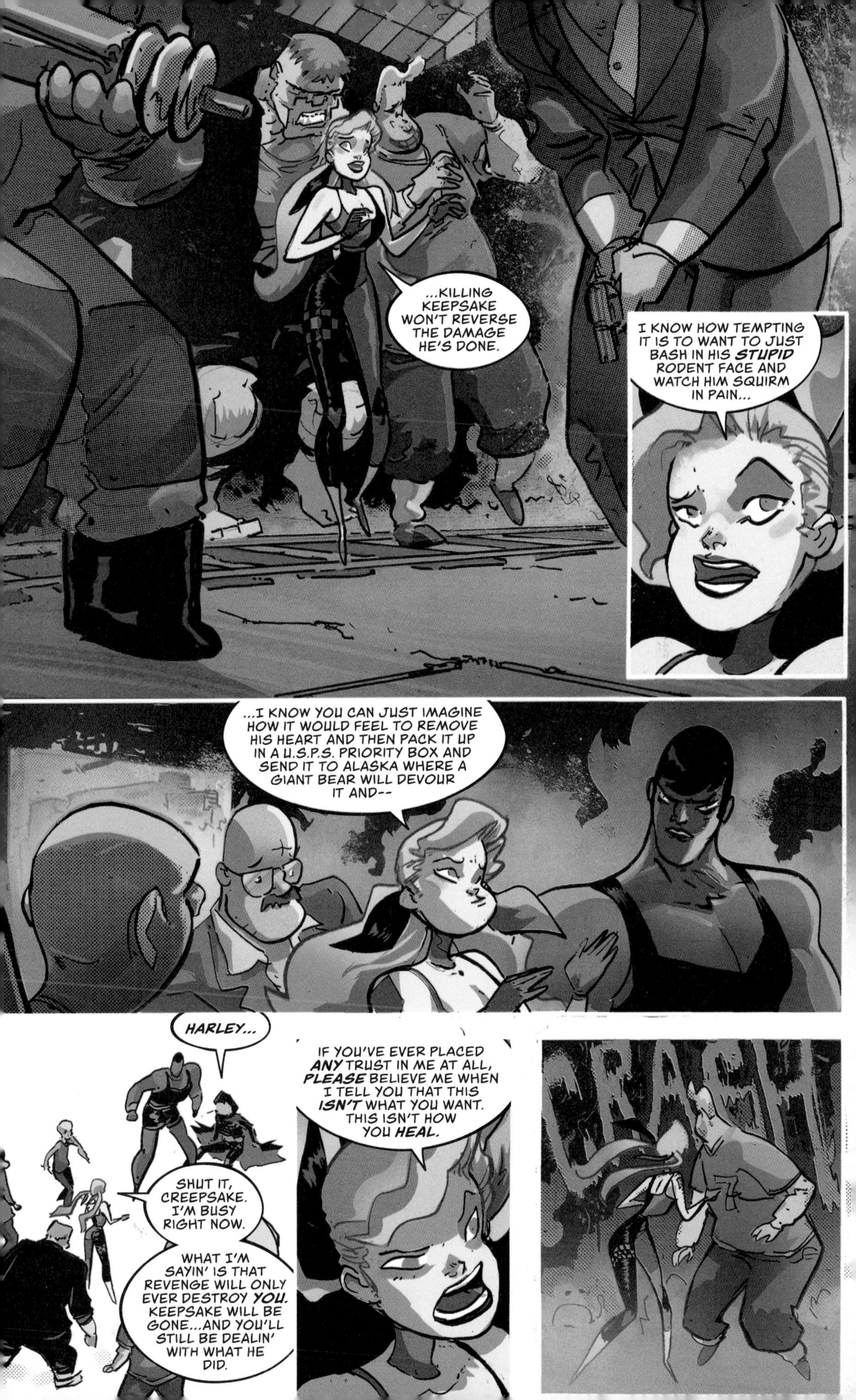
...KILLING KEEPSAKE WON'T REVERSE THE DAMAGE HE'S DONE.
I KNOW HOW TEMPTING IT IS TO WANT TO JUST BASH IN HIS STUPID RODENT FACE AND WATCH HIM SQUIRM IN PAIN...
...I KNOW YOU CAN JUST IMAGINE HOW IT WOULD FEEL TO REMOVE HIS HEART AND THEN PACK IT UP IN A U.S.P.S. PRIORITY BOX AND SEND IT TO ALASKA WHERE A GIANT BEAR WILL DEVOUR IT AND--
HARLEY...
SHUT IT, CREEPSAKE. I'M BUSY RIGHT NOW.
WHAT I'M SAYIN' IS THAT REVENGE WILL ONLY EVER DESTROY YOU. KEEPSAKE WILL BE GONE...AND YOU'LL STILL BE DEALIN' WITH WHAT HE DID.
IF YOU'VE EVER PLACED ANY TRUST IN ME AT ALL, PLEASE BELIEVE ME WHEN I TELL YOU THAT THIS ISN'T WHAT YOU WANT. THIS ISN'T HOW YOU HEAL.

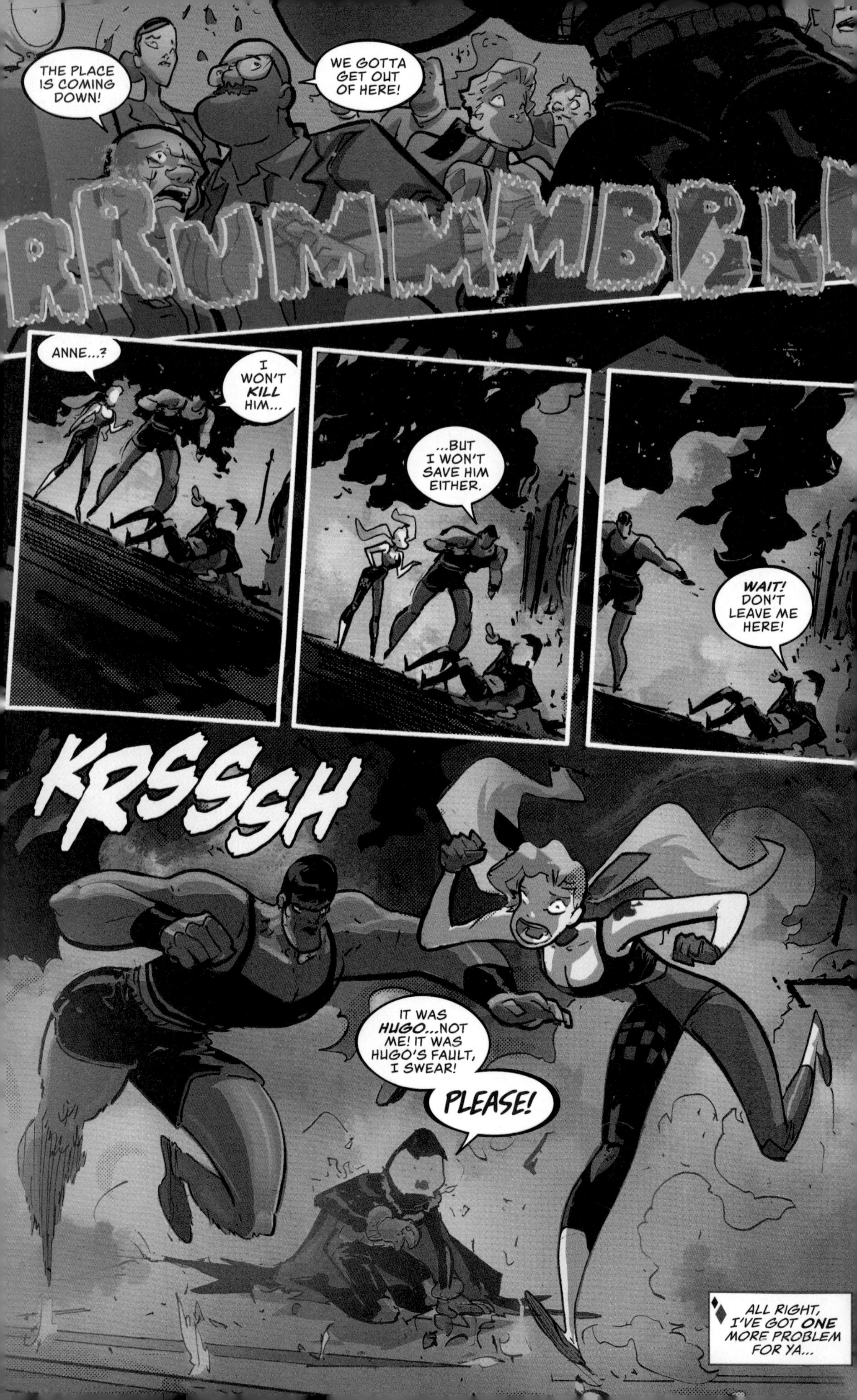
THE PLACE IS COMING DOWN!
WE GOTTA GET OUT OF HERE!
ANNE...?
I WON'T KILL HIM...
...BUT I WON'T SAVE HIM EITHER.
WAIT! DON'T LEAVE ME HERE!
KRSSSH
IT WAS HUGO...NOT ME! IT WAS HUGO'S FAULT, I SWEAR!
PLEASE!
ALL RIGHT, I'VE GOT ONE MORE PROBLEM FOR YA...

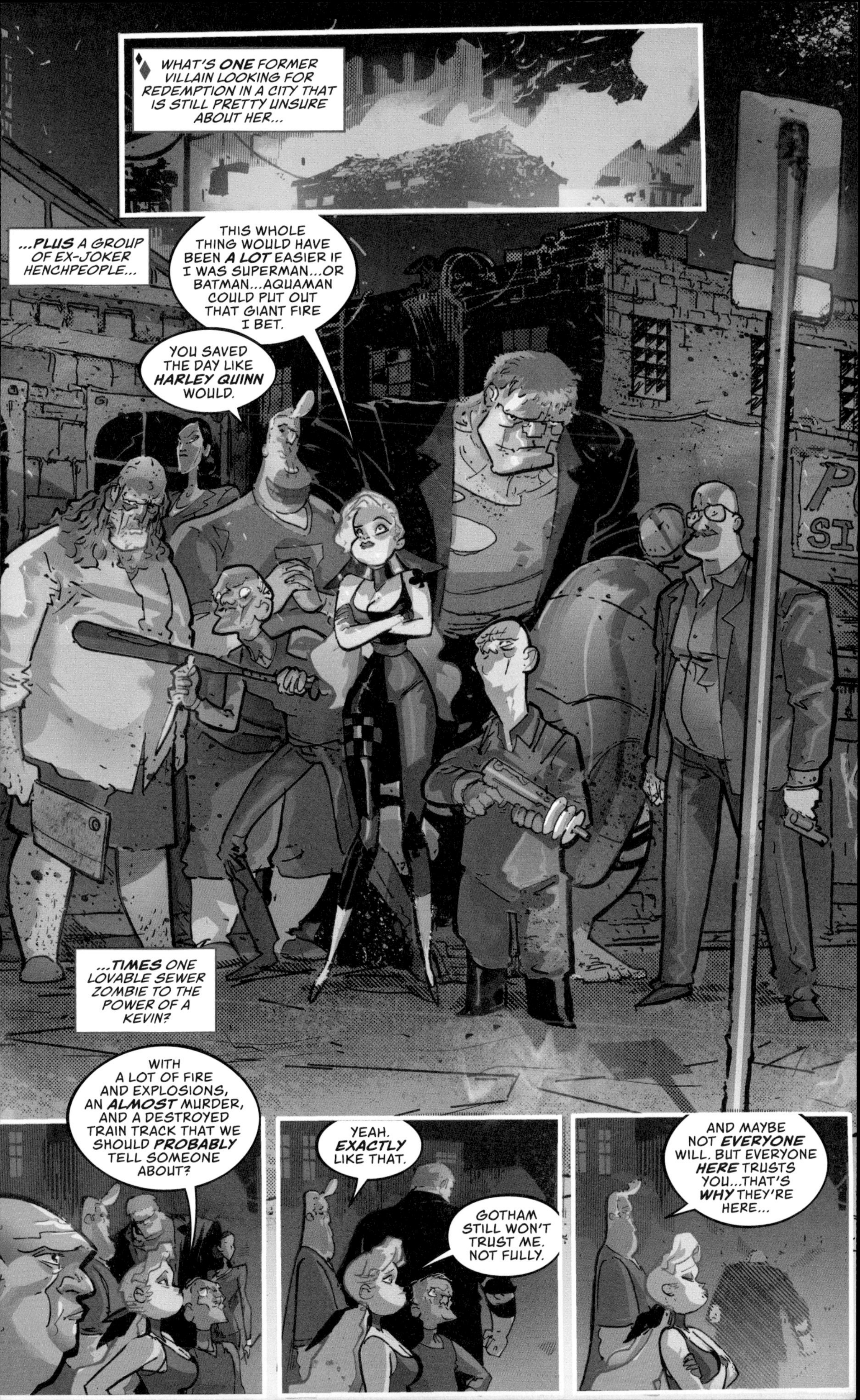
WHAT'S ONE FORMER VILLAIN LOOKING FOR REDEMPTION IN A CITY THAT IS STILL PRETTY UNSURE ABOUT HER...
...PLUS A GROUP OF EX-JOKER HENCHPEOPLE...
THIS WHOLE THING WOULD HAVE BEEN A LOT EASIER IF I WAS SUPERMAN...OR BATMAN...AQUAMAN COULD PUT OUT THAT GIANT FIRE I BET.
YOU SAVED THE DAY LIKE HARLEY QUINN WOULD.
...TIMES ONE LOVABLE SEWER ZOMBIE TO THE POWER OF A KEVIN?
WITH A LOT OF FIRE AND EXPLOSIONS, AN ALMOST MURDER, AND A DESTROYED TRAIN TRACK THAT WE SHOULD PROBABLY TELL SOMEONE ABOUT?
YEAH. EXACTLY LIKE THAT.
GOTHAM STILL WON'T TRUST ME. NOT FULLY.
AND MAYBE NOT EVERYONE WILL. BUT EVERYONE HERE TRUSTS YOU...THAT'S WHY THEY'RE HERE...

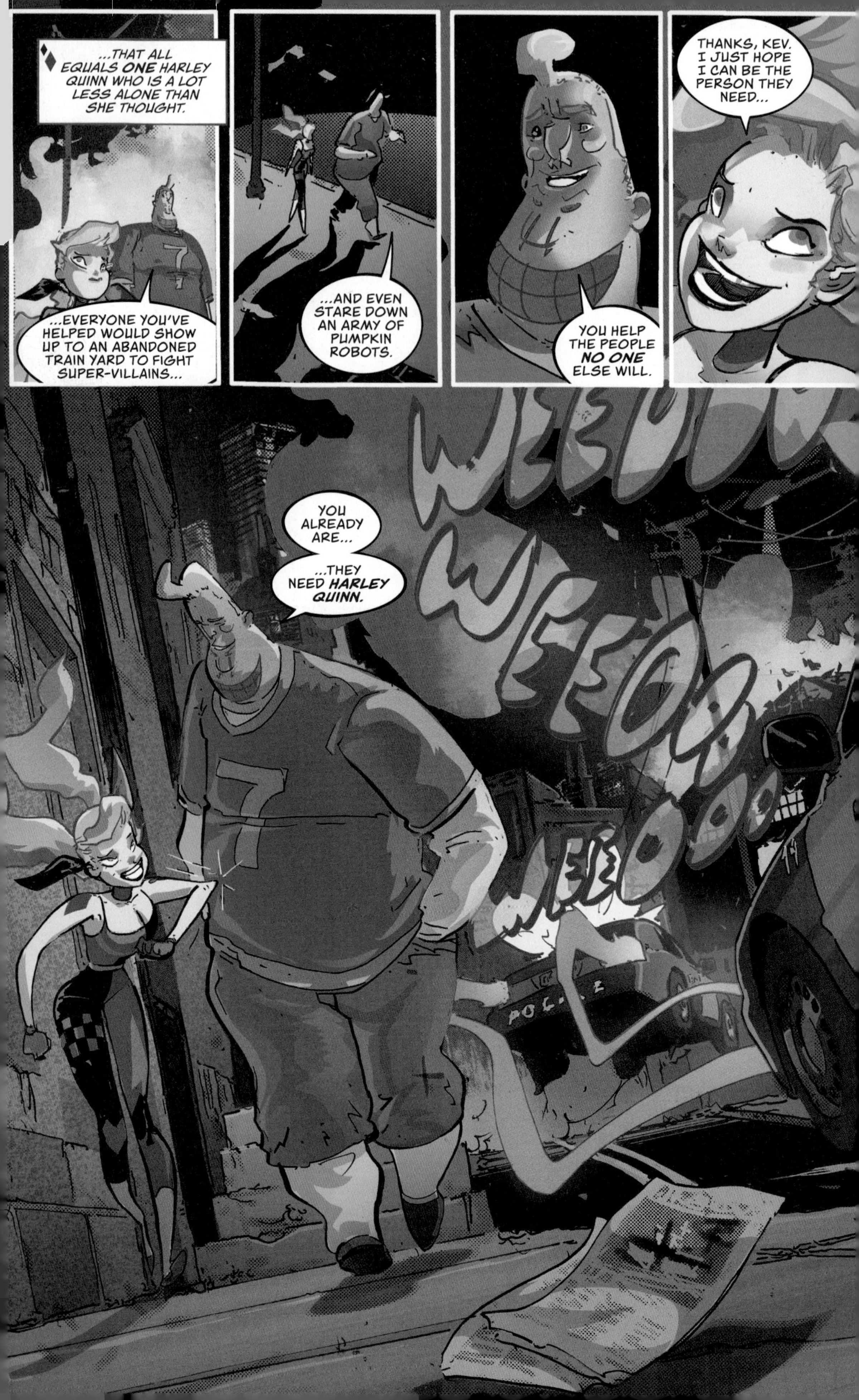
...THAT ALL EQUALS ONE HARLEY QUINN WHO IS A LOT LESS ALONE THAN SHE THOUGHT.
...EVERYONE YOU'VE HELPED WOULD SHOW UP TO AN ABANDONED TRAIN YARD TO FIGHT SUPER-VILLAINS...
...AND EVEN STARE DOWN AN ARMY OF PUMPKIN ROBOTS.
YOU HELP THE PEOPLE NO ONE ELSE WILL.
THANKS, KEV. I JUST HOPE I CAN BE THE PERSON THEY NEED...
YOU ALREADY ARE...
...THEY NEED HARLEY QUINN.
POLICE

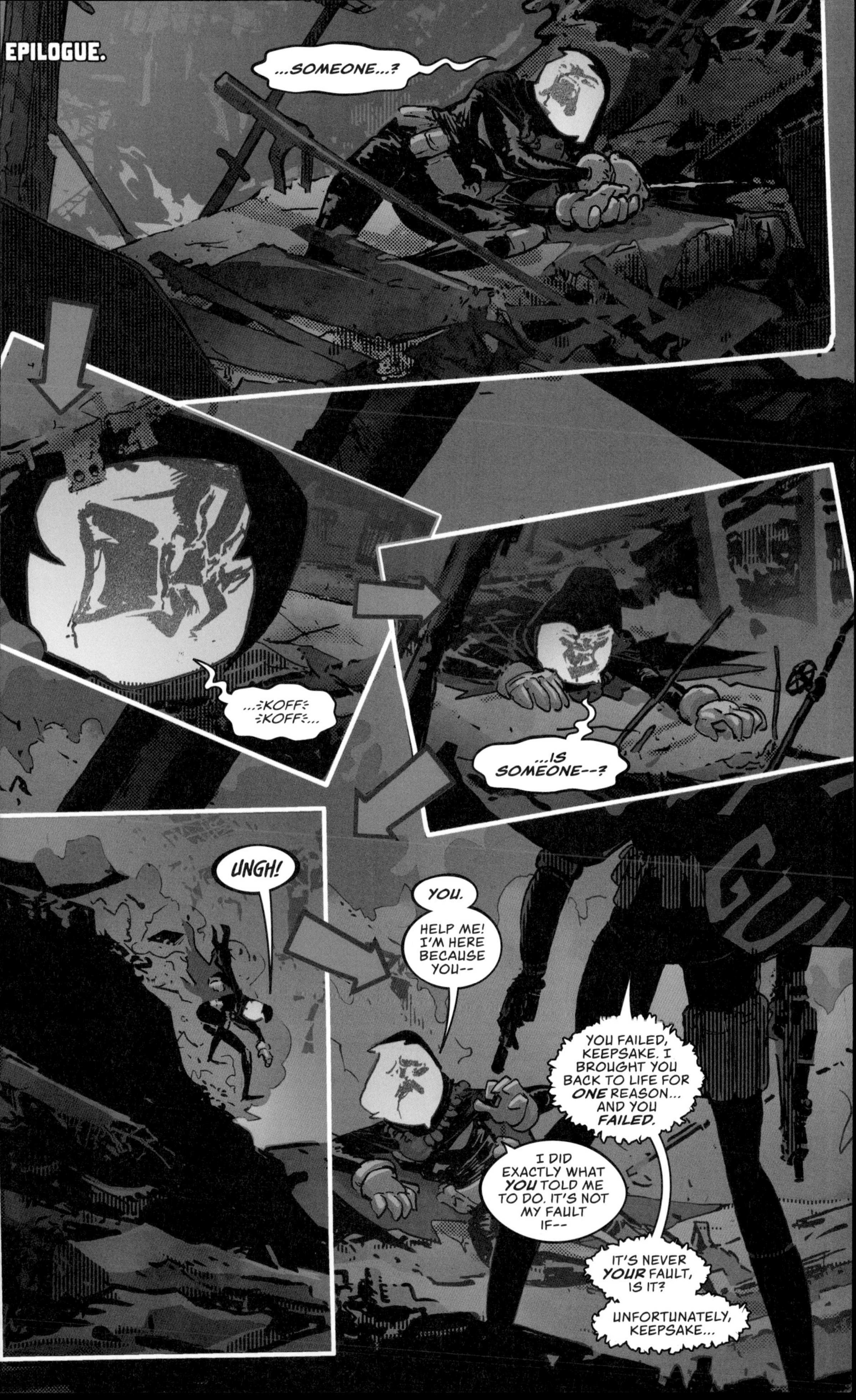
EPILOGUE.
...SOMEONE...?
...KOFF KOFF...
...IS SOMEONE--?
UNGH!
YOU.
HELP ME! I'M HERE BECAUSE YOU--
YOU FAILED, KEEPSAKE. I BROUGHT YOU BACK TO LIFE FOR ONE REASON... AND YOU FAILED.
I DID EXACTLY WHAT YOU TOLD ME TO DO. IT'S NOT MY FAULT IF--
IT'S NEVER YOUR FAULT, IS IT?
UNFORTUNATELY, KEEPSAKE...

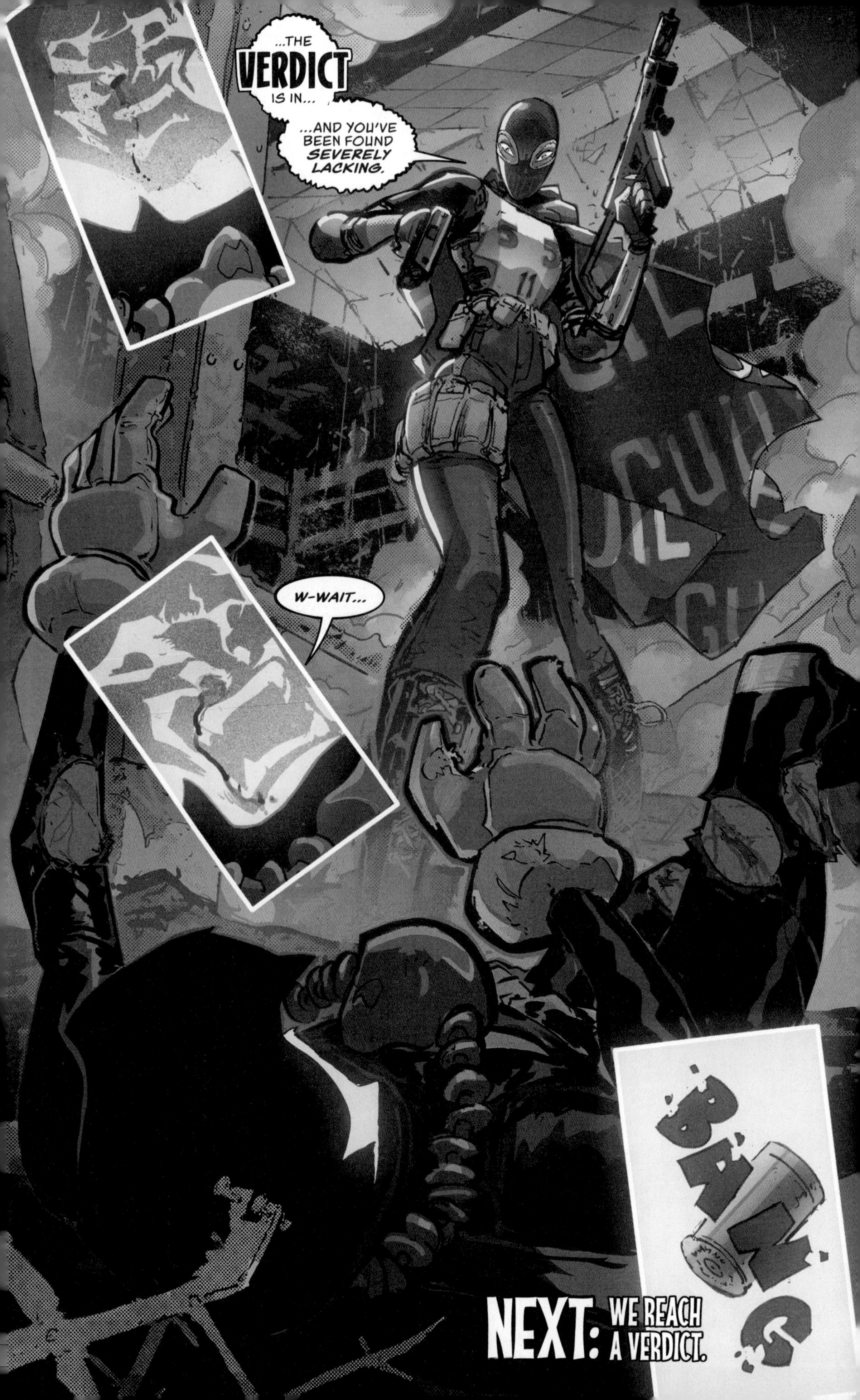
...THE VERDICT IS IN...
...AND YOU'VE BEEN FOUND SEVERELY LACKING.
W-WAIT...
BANG
NEXT: WE REACH A VERDICT.

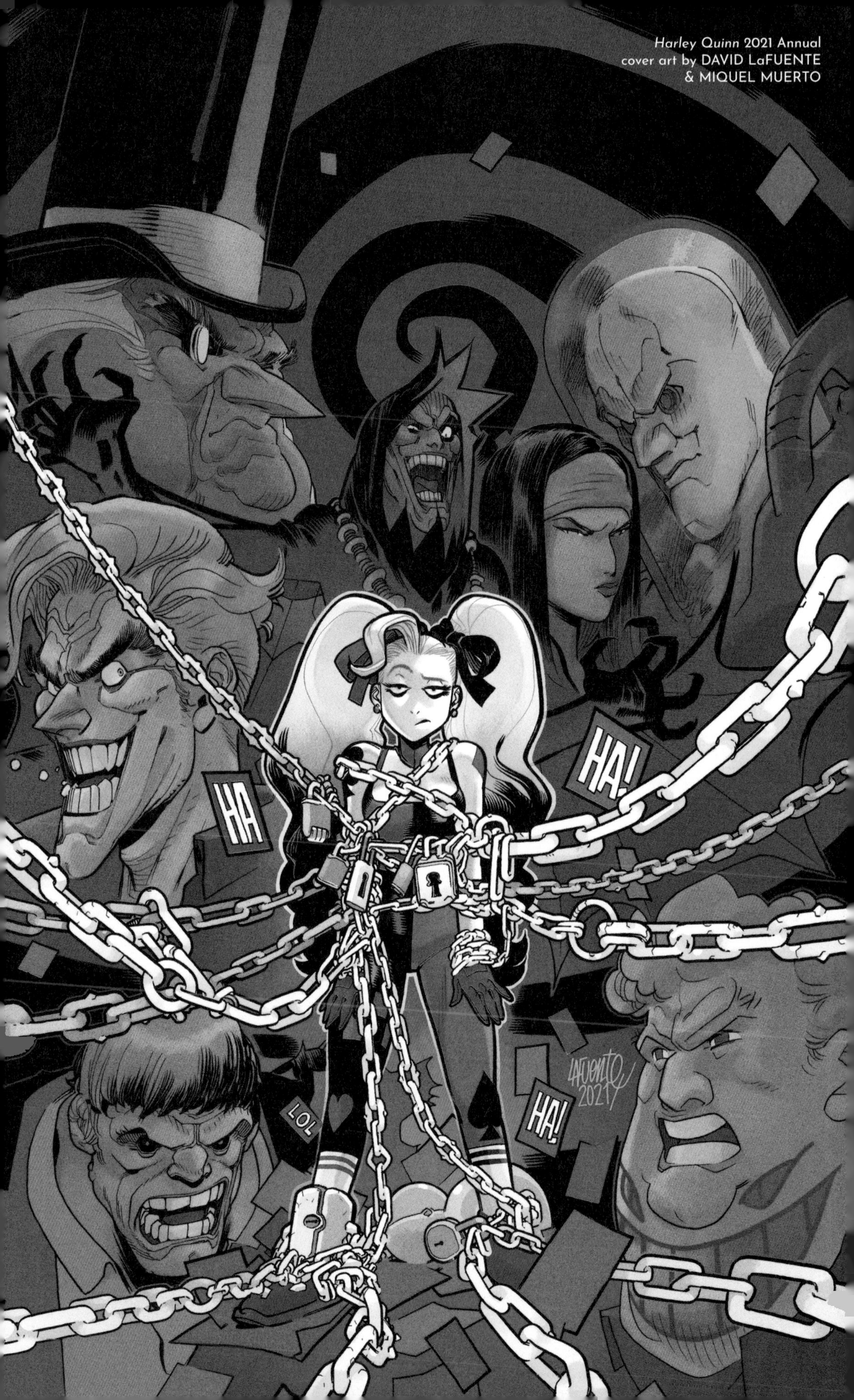
HA!
HA
LOL
HA!

Harley Quinn 2021 Annual
cover art by DAVID LaFUENTE
& MIQUEL MUERTO

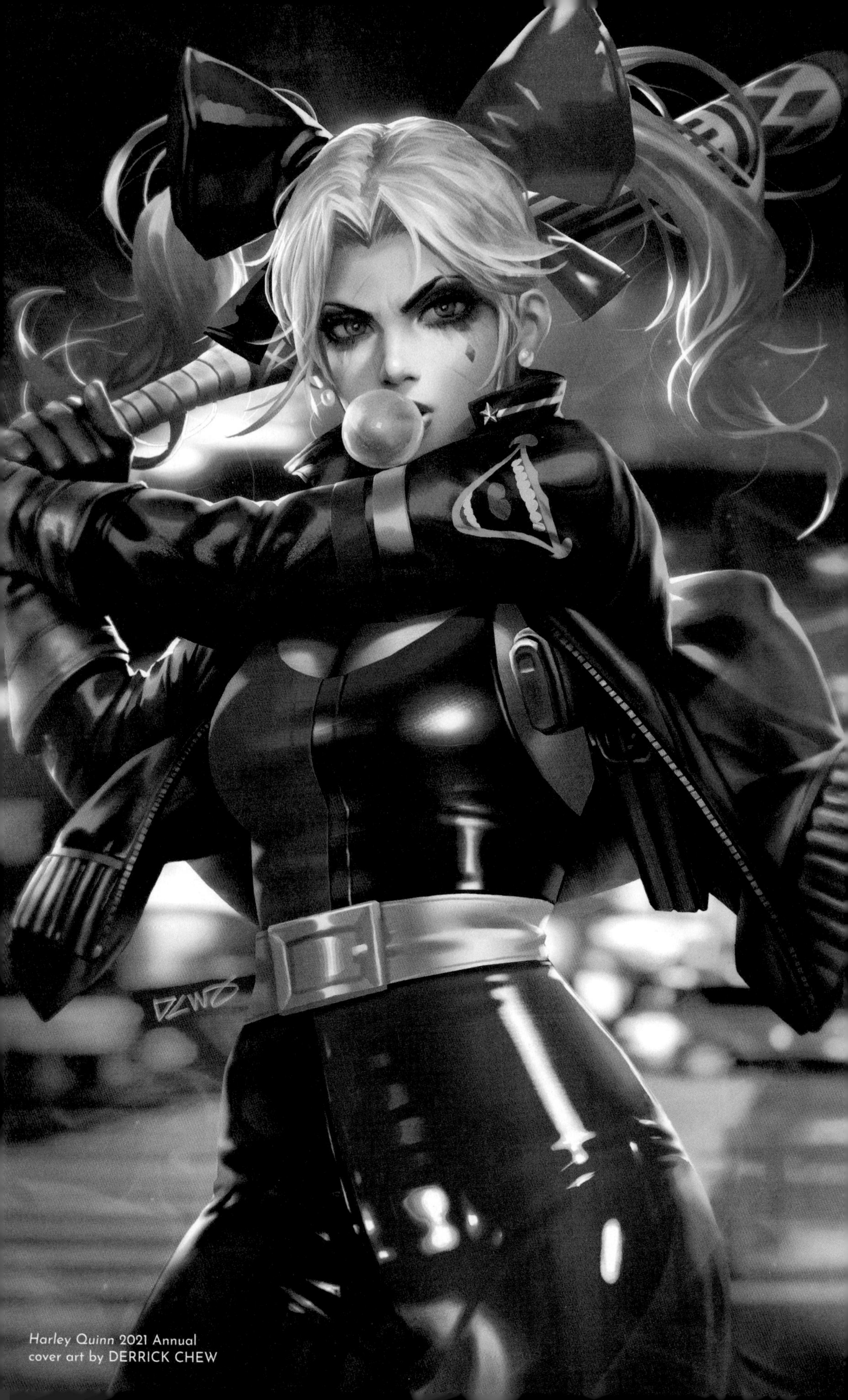

Harley Quinn 2021 Annual
cover art by DERRICK CHEW

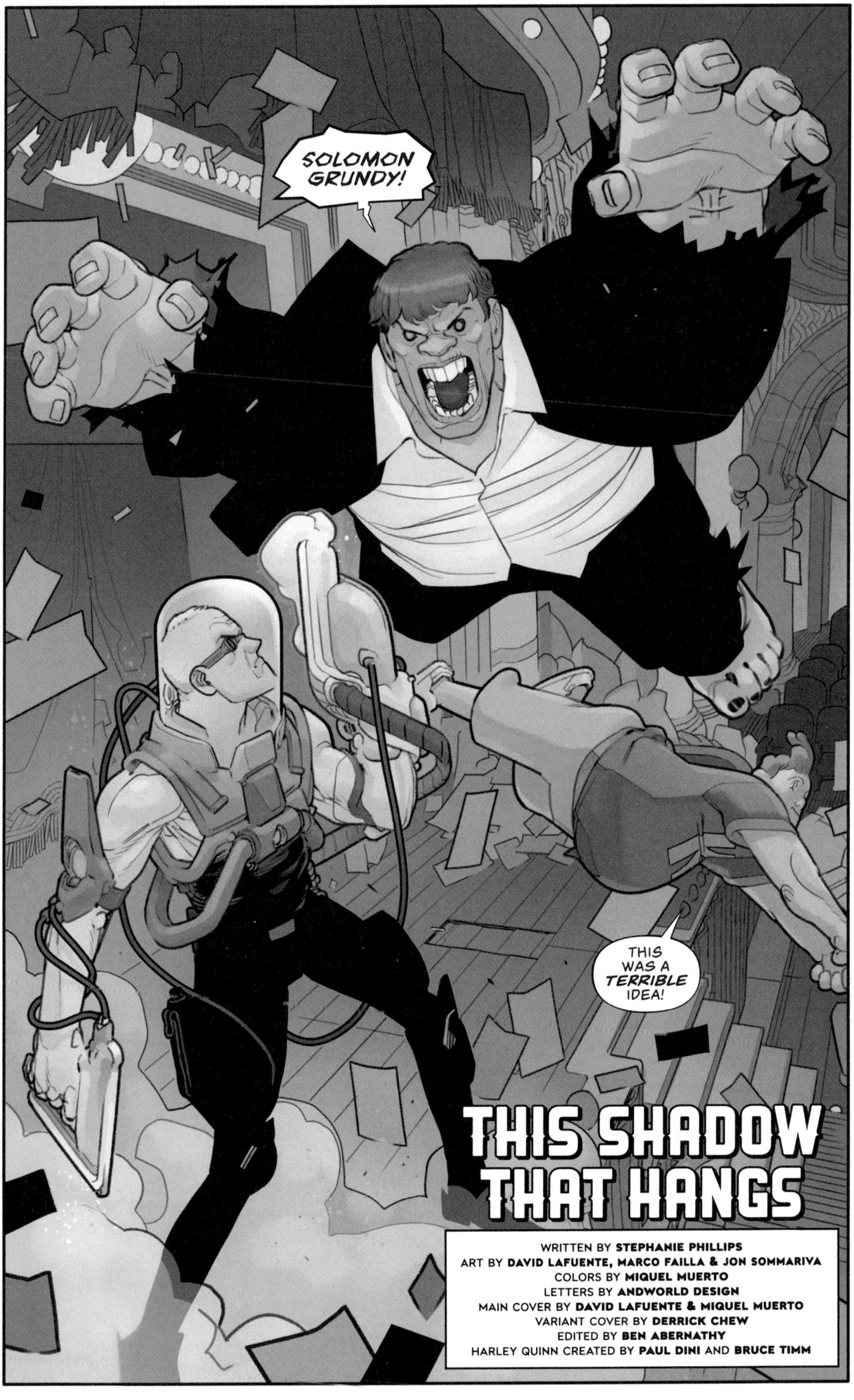
SOLOMON GRUNDY!
THIS WAS A TERRIBLE IDEA!

THIS SHADOW THAT HANGS

WRITTEN BY **STEPHANIE PHILLIPS**
ART BY **DAVID LAFUENTE, MARCO FAILLA & JON SOMMARIVA**
COLORS BY **MIQUEL MUERTO**
LETTERS BY **ANDWORLD DESIGN**
MAIN COVER BY **DAVID LAFUENTE & MIQUEL MUERTO**
VARIANT COVER BY **DERRICK CHEW**
EDITED BY **BEN ABERNATHY**
HARLEY QUINN CREATED BY **PAUL DINI** AND **BRUCE TIMM**

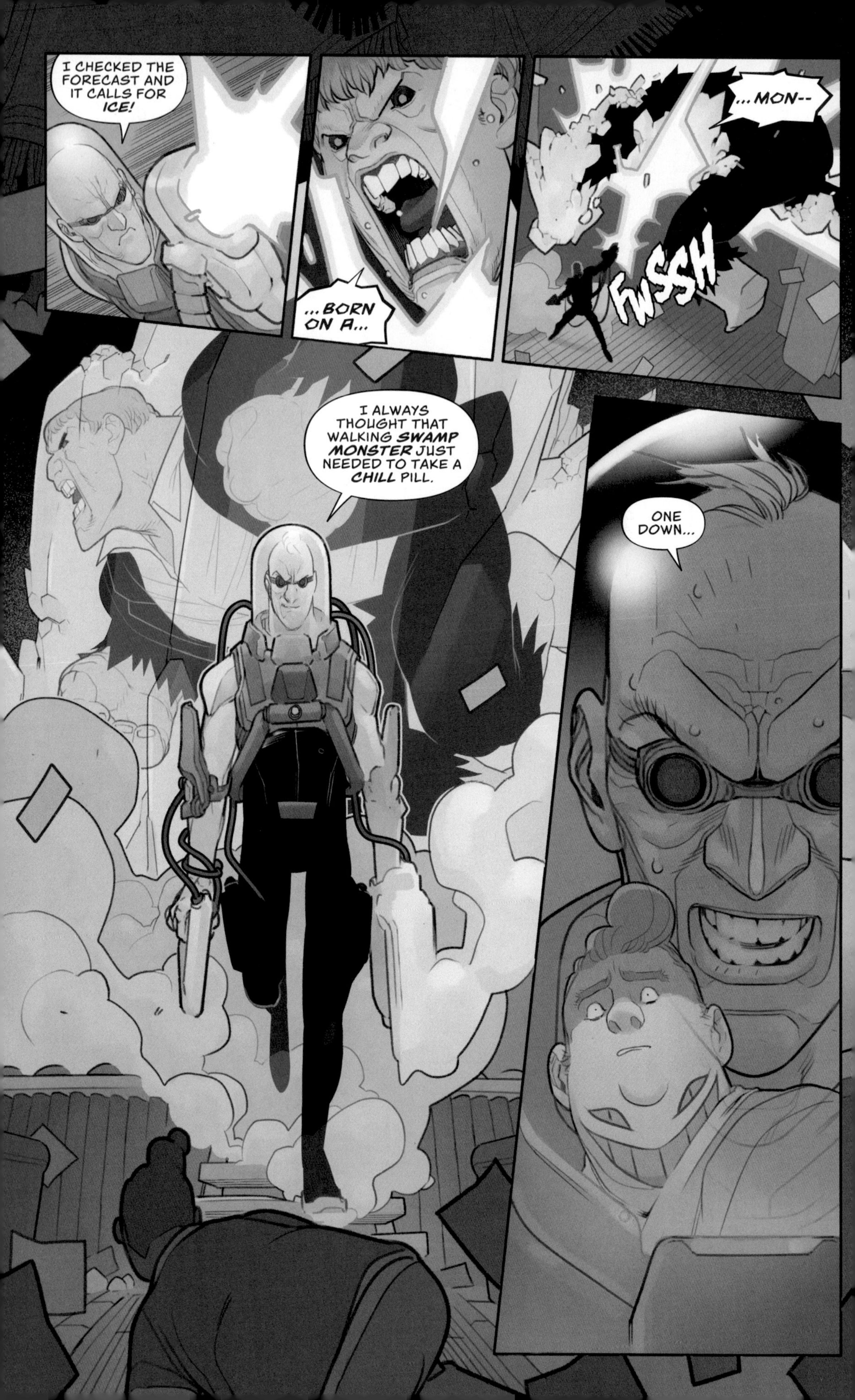
I CHECKED THE FORECAST AND IT CALLS FOR ICE!
...BORN ON A...
...MON--
FWSSH
I ALWAYS THOUGHT THAT WALKING SWAMP MONSTER JUST NEEDED TO TAKE A CHILL PILL.
ONE DOWN...

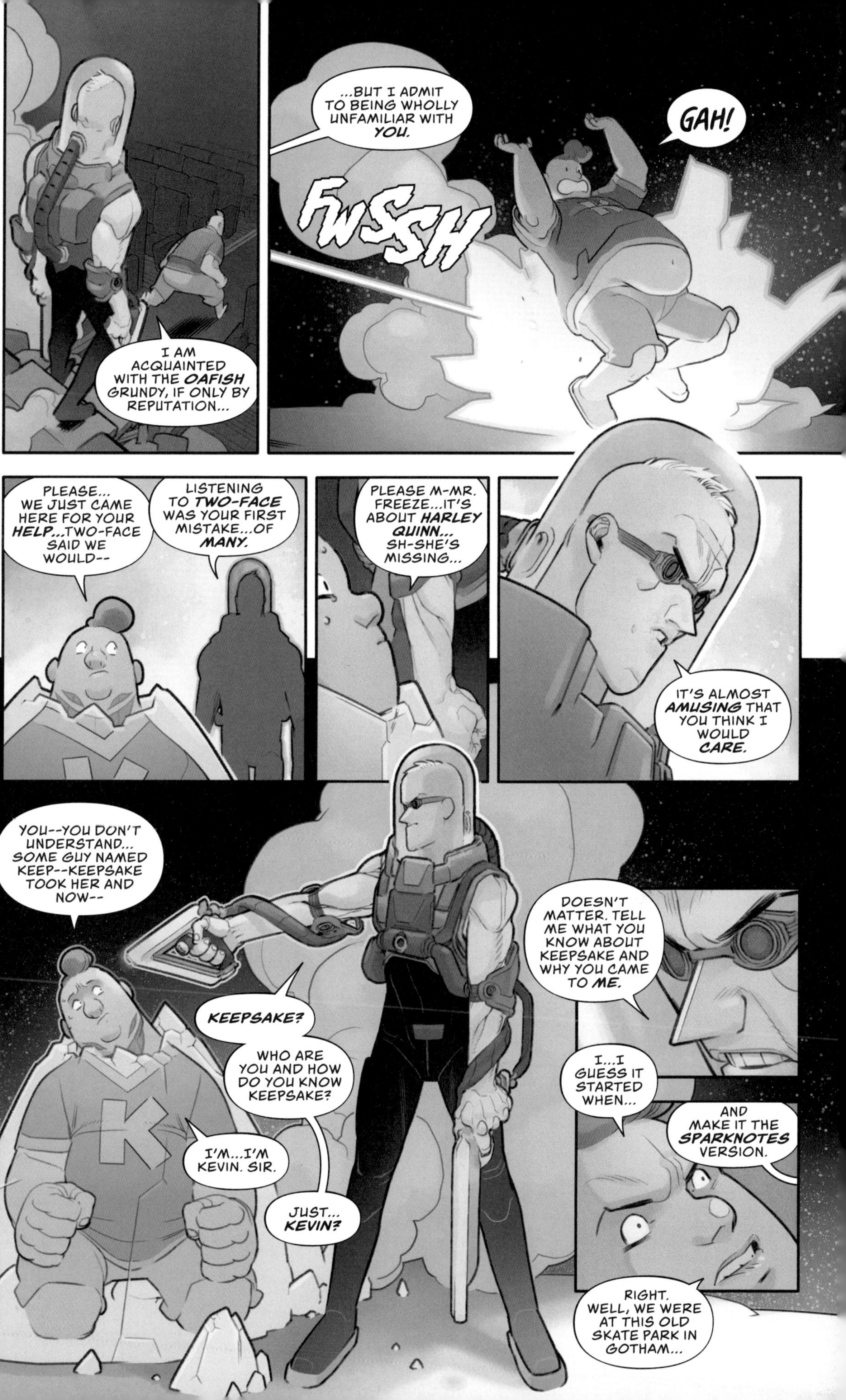
I AM ACQUAINTED WITH THE OAFISH GRUNDY, IF ONLY BY REPUTATION...
...BUT I ADMIT TO BEING WHOLLY UNFAMILIAR WITH YOU.
FWSSH
GAH!
PLEASE... WE JUST CAME HERE FOR YOUR HELP...TWO-FACE SAID WE WOULD--
LISTENING TO TWO-FACE WAS YOUR FIRST MISTAKE...OF MANY.
PLEASE M-MR. FREEZE...IT'S ABOUT HARLEY QUINN... SH-SHE'S MISSING...
IT'S ALMOST AMUSING THAT YOU THINK I WOULD CARE.
YOU--YOU DON'T UNDERSTAND... SOME GUY NAMED KEEP--KEEPSAKE TOOK HER AND NOW--
KEEPSAKE?
WHO ARE YOU AND HOW DO YOU KNOW KEEPSAKE?
I'M...I'M KEVIN. SIR.
JUST... KEVIN?
DOESN'T MATTER. TELL ME WHAT YOU KNOW ABOUT KEEPSAKE AND WHY YOU CAME TO ME.
I...I GUESS IT STARTED WHEN...
AND MAKE IT THE SPARKNOTES VERSION.
RIGHT. WELL, WE WERE AT THIS OLD SKATE PARK IN GOTHAM...

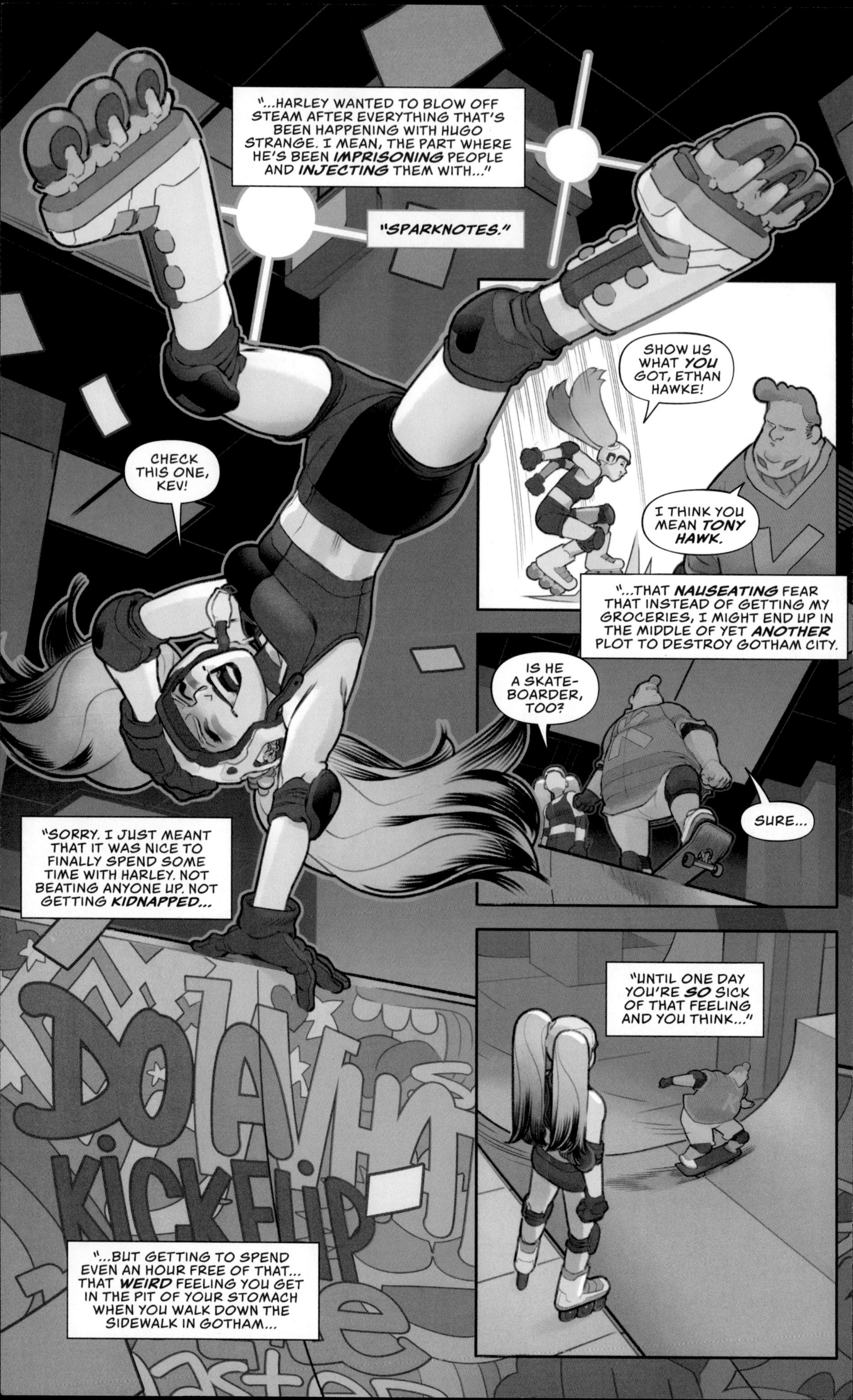
"...HARLEY WANTED TO BLOW OFF STEAM AFTER EVERYTHING THAT'S BEEN HAPPENING WITH HUGO STRANGE. I MEAN, THE PART WHERE HE'S BEEN IMPRISONING PEOPLE AND INJECTING THEM WITH..."
"SPARKNOTES."
CHECK THIS ONE, KEV!
SHOW US WHAT YOU GOT, ETHAN HAWKE!
I THINK YOU MEAN TONY HAWK.
"...THAT NAUSEATING FEAR THAT INSTEAD OF GETTING MY GROCERIES, I MIGHT END UP IN THE MIDDLE OF YET ANOTHER PLOT TO DESTROY GOTHAM CITY.
IS HE A SKATE-BOARDER, TOO?
SURE...
"SORRY. I JUST MEANT THAT IT WAS NICE TO FINALLY SPEND SOME TIME WITH HARLEY. NOT BEATING ANYONE UP. NOT GETTING KIDNAPPED...
"UNTIL ONE DAY YOU'RE SO SICK OF THAT FEELING AND YOU THINK..."
KICKFLIP
"...BUT GETTING TO SPEND EVEN AN HOUR FREE OF THAT... THAT WEIRD FEELING YOU GET IN THE PIT OF YOUR STOMACH WHEN YOU WALK DOWN THE SIDEWALK IN GOTHAM...

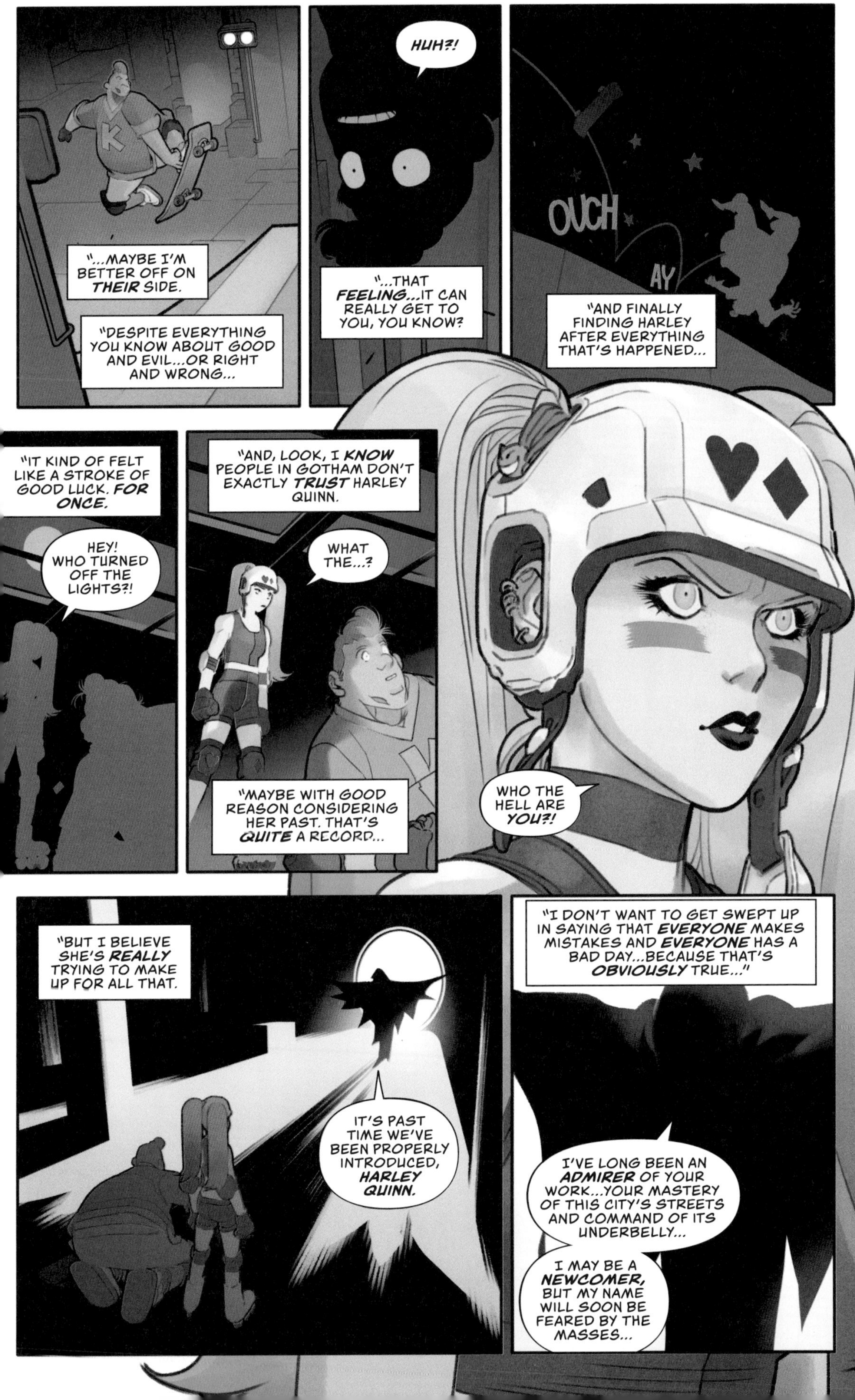
"...MAYBE I'M BETTER OFF ON THEIR SIDE.
"DESPITE EVERYTHING YOU KNOW ABOUT GOOD AND EVIL...OR RIGHT AND WRONG...
HUH?!
"...THAT FEELING...IT CAN REALLY GET TO YOU, YOU KNOW?
OUCH
AY
"AND FINALLY FINDING HARLEY AFTER EVERYTHING THAT'S HAPPENED...
"IT KIND OF FELT LIKE A STROKE OF GOOD LUCK. FOR ONCE.
HEY! WHO TURNED OFF THE LIGHTS?!
"AND, LOOK, I KNOW PEOPLE IN GOTHAM DON'T EXACTLY TRUST HARLEY QUINN.
WHAT THE...?
"MAYBE WITH GOOD REASON CONSIDERING HER PAST. THAT'S QUITE A RECORD...
WHO THE HELL ARE YOU?!
"BUT I BELIEVE SHE'S REALLY TRYING TO MAKE UP FOR ALL THAT.
IT'S PAST TIME WE'VE BEEN PROPERLY INTRODUCED, HARLEY QUINN.
"I DON'T WANT TO GET SWEPT UP IN SAYING THAT EVERYONE MAKES MISTAKES AND EVERYONE HAS A BAD DAY...BECAUSE THAT'S OBVIOUSLY TRUE..."
I'VE LONG BEEN AN ADMIRER OF YOUR WORK...YOUR MASTERY OF THIS CITY'S STREETS AND COMMAND OF ITS UNDERBELLY...
I MAY BE A NEWCOMER, BUT MY NAME WILL SOON BE FEARED BY THE MASSES...

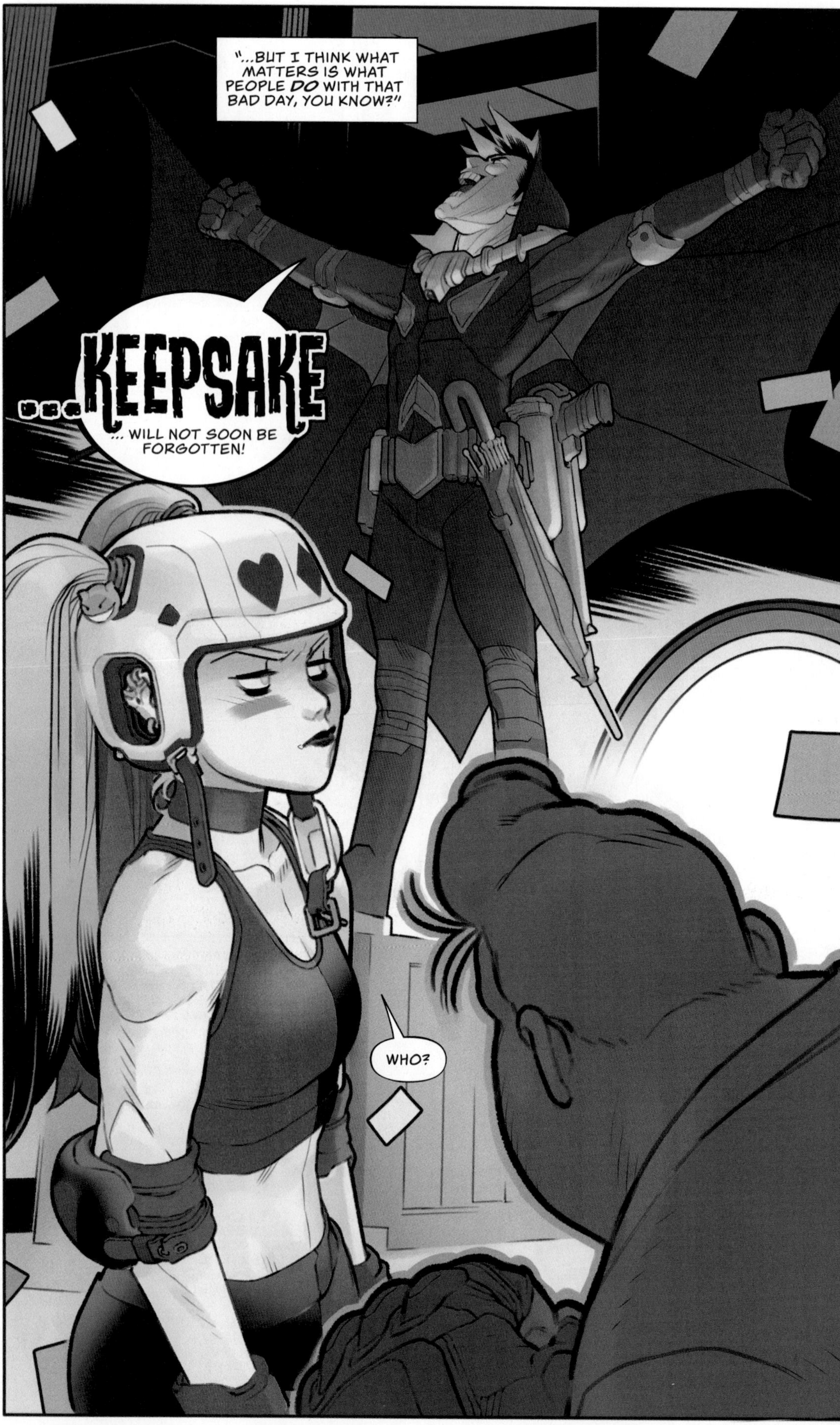
"...BUT I THINK WHAT MATTERS IS WHAT PEOPLE DO WITH THAT BAD DAY, YOU KNOW?"
...KEEPSAKE ...WILL NOT SOON BE FORGOTTEN!
WHO?

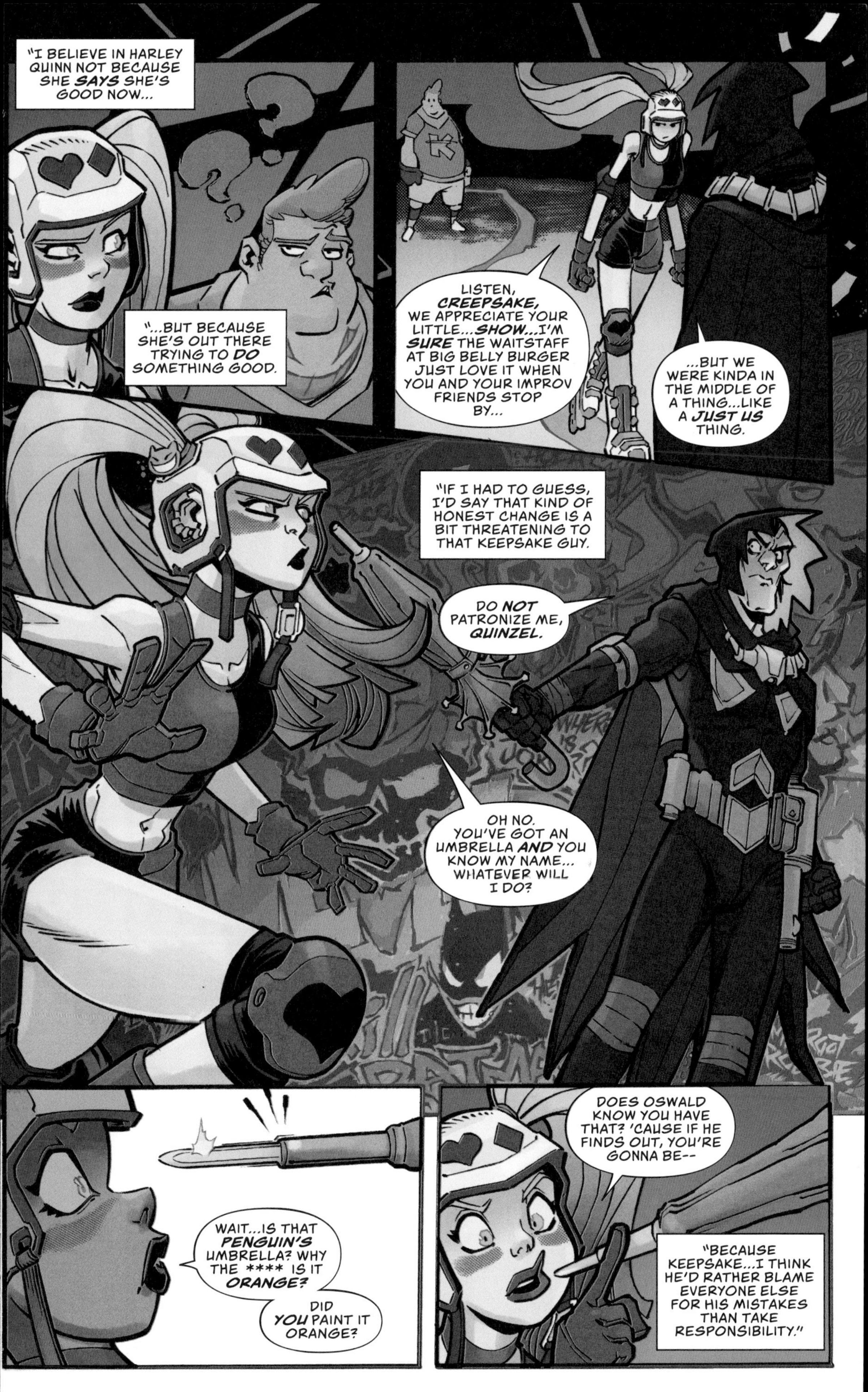
"I BELIEVE IN HARLEY QUINN NOT BECAUSE SHE SAYS SHE'S GOOD NOW...
"...BUT BECAUSE SHE'S OUT THERE TRYING TO DO SOMETHING GOOD.
LISTEN, CREEPSAKE, WE APPRECIATE YOUR LITTLE...SHOW...I'M SURE THE WAITSTAFF AT BIG BELLY BURGER JUST LOVE IT WHEN YOU AND YOUR IMPROV FRIENDS STOP BY...
...BUT WE WERE KINDA IN THE MIDDLE OF A THING...LIKE A JUST US THING.
"IF I HAD TO GUESS, I'D SAY THAT KIND OF HONEST CHANGE IS A BIT THREATENING TO THAT KEEPSAKE GUY.
DO NOT PATRONIZE ME, QUINZEL.
OH NO. YOU'VE GOT AN UMBRELLA AND YOU KNOW MY NAME... WHATEVER WILL I DO?
WAIT...IS THAT PENGUIN'S UMBRELLA? WHY THE **** IS IT ORANGE?
DID YOU PAINT IT ORANGE?
DOES OSWALD KNOW YOU HAVE THAT? 'CAUSE IF HE FINDS OUT, YOU'RE GONNA BE--
"BECAUSE KEEPSAKE...I THINK HE'D RATHER BLAME EVERYONE ELSE FOR HIS MISTAKES THAN TAKE RESPONSIBILITY."

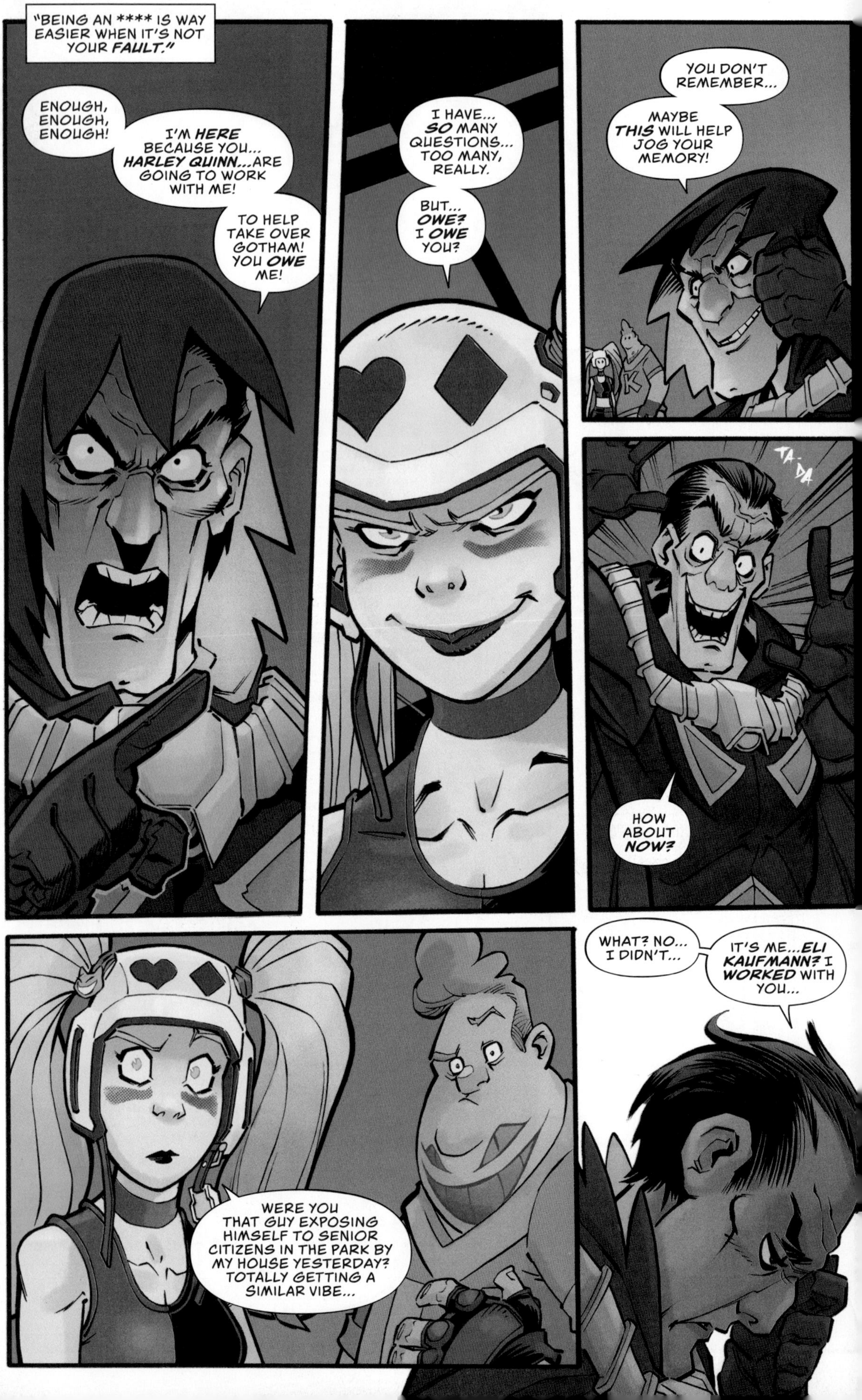
"BEING AN **** IS WAY EASIER WHEN IT'S NOT YOUR FAULT."
ENOUGH, ENOUGH, ENOUGH!
I'M HERE BECAUSE YOU... HARLEY QUINN...ARE GOING TO WORK WITH ME!
TO HELP TAKE OVER GOTHAM! YOU OWE ME!
I HAVE... SO MANY QUESTIONS... TOO MANY, REALLY.
BUT... OWE? I OWE YOU?
YOU DON'T REMEMBER...
MAYBE THIS WILL HELP JOG YOUR MEMORY!
TA-DA
HOW ABOUT NOW?
WERE YOU THAT GUY EXPOSING HIMSELF TO SENIOR CITIZENS IN THE PARK BY MY HOUSE YESTERDAY? TOTALLY GETTING A SIMILAR VIBE...
WHAT? NO... I DIDN'T...
IT'S ME...ELI KAUFMANN? I WORKED WITH YOU...

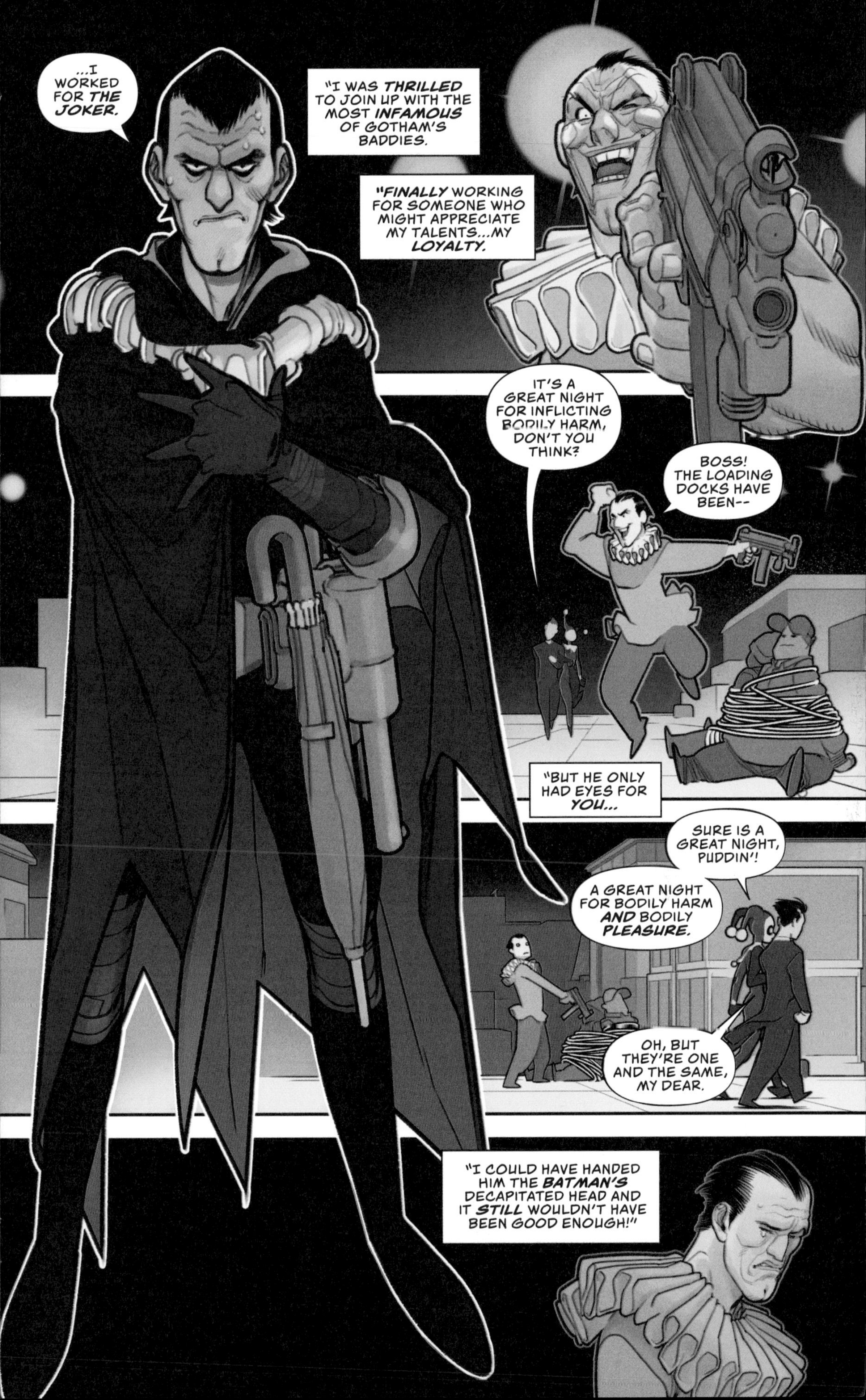
...I WORKED FOR THE JOKER.
"I WAS THRILLED TO JOIN UP WITH THE MOST INFAMOUS OF GOTHAM'S BADDIES.
"FINALLY WORKING FOR SOMEONE WHO MIGHT APPRECIATE MY TALENTS...MY LOYALTY.
IT'S A GREAT NIGHT FOR INFLICTING BODILY HARM, DON'T YOU THINK?
BOSS! THE LOADING DOCKS HAVE BEEN--
"BUT HE ONLY HAD EYES FOR YOU...
SURE IS A GREAT NIGHT, PUDDIN'!
A GREAT NIGHT FOR BODILY HARM AND BODILY PLEASURE.
OH, BUT THEY'RE ONE AND THE SAME, MY DEAR.
"I COULD HAVE HANDED HIM THE BATMAN'S DECAPITATED HEAD AND IT STILL WOULDN'T HAVE BEEN GOOD ENOUGH!"

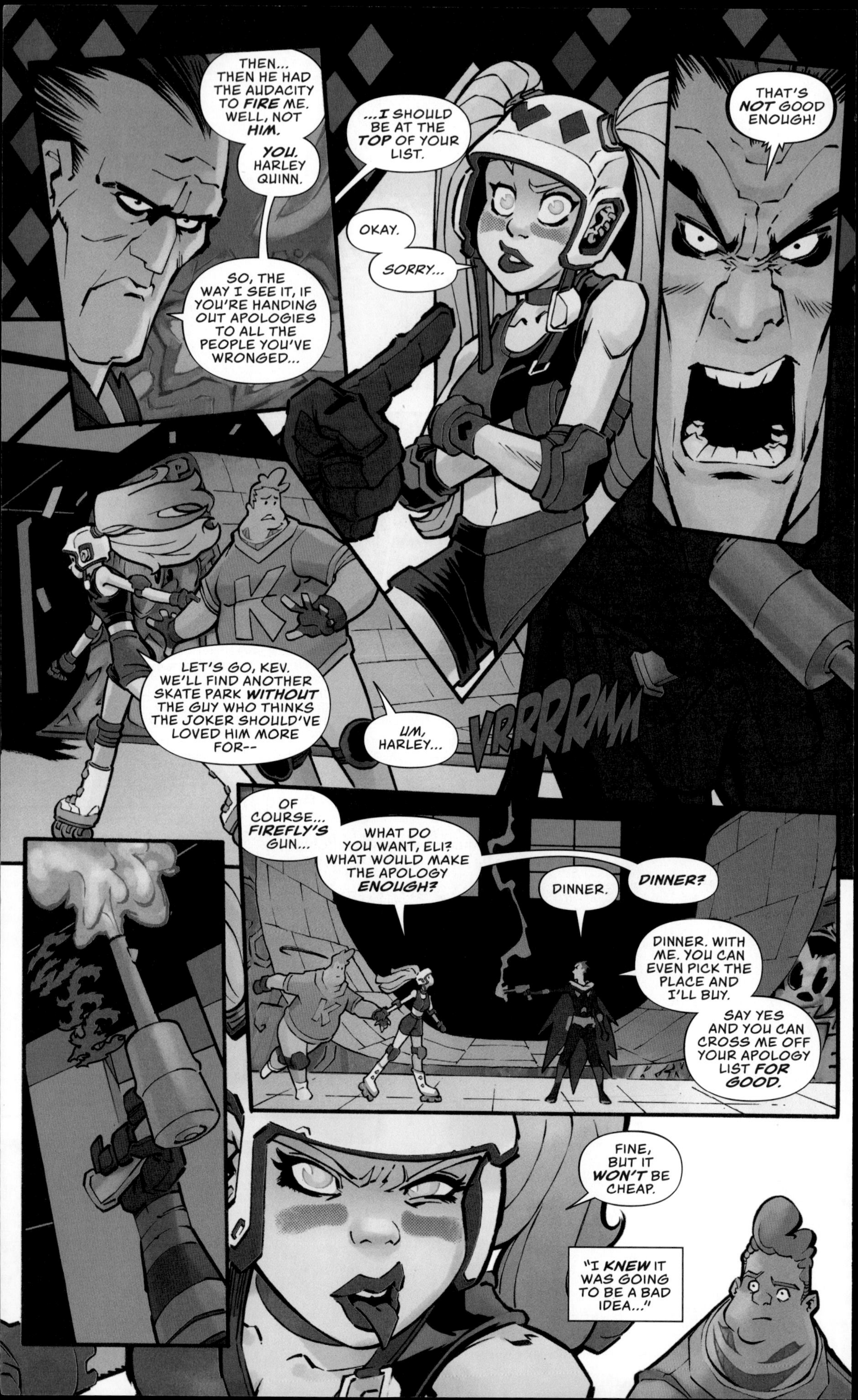
THEN... THEN HE HAD THE AUDACITY TO FIRE ME. WELL, NOT HIM.
YOU. HARLEY QUINN.
SO, THE WAY I SEE IT, IF YOU'RE HANDING OUT APOLOGIES TO ALL THE PEOPLE YOU'VE WRONGED...
...I SHOULD BE AT THE TOP OF YOUR LIST.
OKAY.
SORRY...
THAT'S NOT GOOD ENOUGH!
LET'S GO, KEV. WE'LL FIND ANOTHER SKATE PARK WITHOUT THE GUY WHO THINKS THE JOKER SHOULD'VE LOVED HIM MORE FOR--
UM, HARLEY...
VRRRRMM
OF COURSE... FIREFLY'S GUN...
WHAT DO YOU WANT, ELI? WHAT WOULD MAKE THE APOLOGY ENOUGH?
DINNER.
DINNER?
DINNER. WITH ME. YOU CAN EVEN PICK THE PLACE AND I'LL BUY.
SAY YES AND YOU CAN CROSS ME OFF YOUR APOLOGY LIST FOR GOOD.
FINE, BUT IT WON'T BE CHEAP.
"I KNEW IT WAS GOING TO BE A BAD IDEA..."

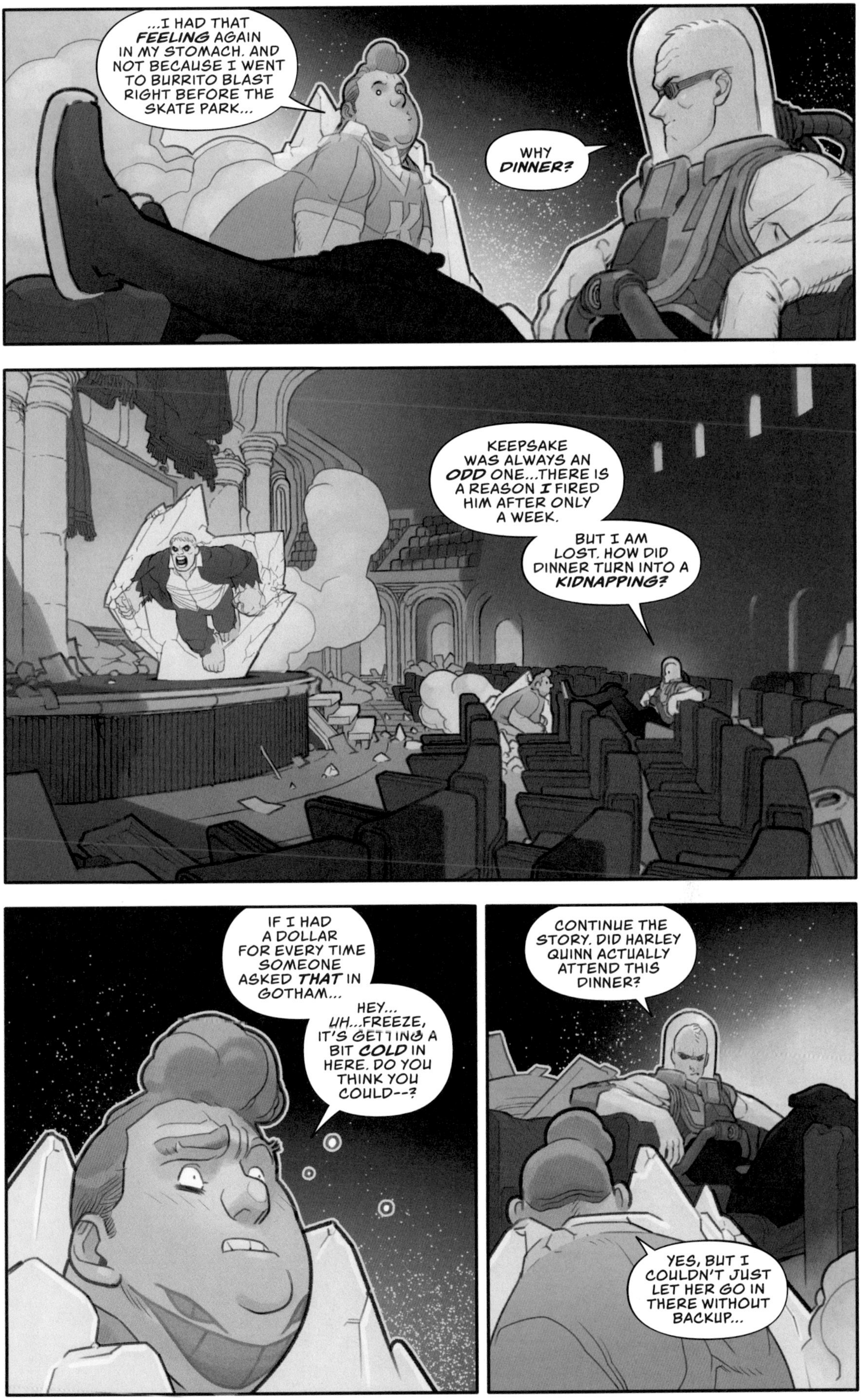
...I HAD THAT FEELING AGAIN IN MY STOMACH. AND NOT BECAUSE I WENT TO BURRITO BLAST RIGHT BEFORE THE SKATE PARK...
WHY DINNER?
KEEPSAKE WAS ALWAYS AN ODD ONE...THERE IS A REASON I FIRED HIM AFTER ONLY A WEEK.
BUT I AM LOST. HOW DID DINNER TURN INTO A KIDNAPPING?
IF I HAD A DOLLAR FOR EVERY TIME SOMEONE ASKED THAT IN GOTHAM...
HEY... UH...FREEZE, IT'S GETTING A BIT COLD IN HERE. DO YOU THINK YOU COULD--?
CONTINUE THE STORY. DID HARLEY QUINN ACTUALLY ATTEND THIS DINNER?
YES, BUT I COULDN'T JUST LET HER GO IN THERE WITHOUT BACKUP...

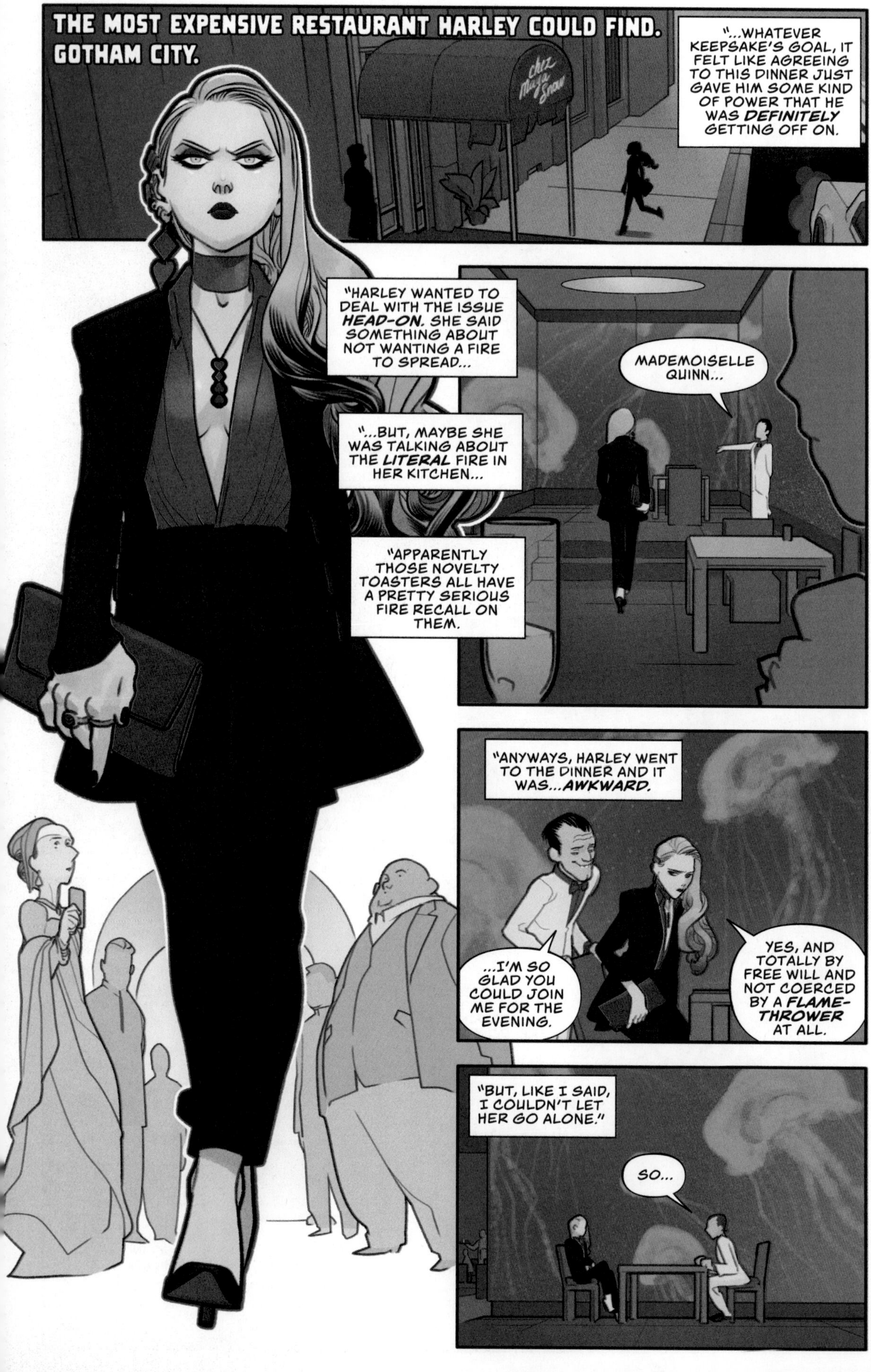
THE MOST EXPENSIVE RESTAURANT HARLEY COULD FIND. GOTHAM CITY.
"...WHATEVER KEEPSAKE'S GOAL, IT FELT LIKE AGREEING TO THIS DINNER JUST GAVE HIM SOME KIND OF POWER THAT HE WAS DEFINITELY GETTING OFF ON.
"HARLEY WANTED TO DEAL WITH THE ISSUE HEAD-ON. SHE SAID SOMETHING ABOUT NOT WANTING A FIRE TO SPREAD...
"...BUT, MAYBE SHE WAS TALKING ABOUT THE LITERAL FIRE IN HER KITCHEN...
"APPARENTLY THOSE NOVELTY TOASTERS ALL HAVE A PRETTY SERIOUS FIRE RECALL ON THEM.
MADEMOISELLE QUINN...
"ANYWAYS, HARLEY WENT TO THE DINNER AND IT WAS...AWKWARD.
...I'M SO GLAD YOU COULD JOIN ME FOR THE EVENING.
YES, AND TOTALLY BY FREE WILL AND NOT COERCED BY A FLAME-THROWER AT ALL.
"BUT, LIKE I SAID, I COULDN'T LET HER GO ALONE."
SO...

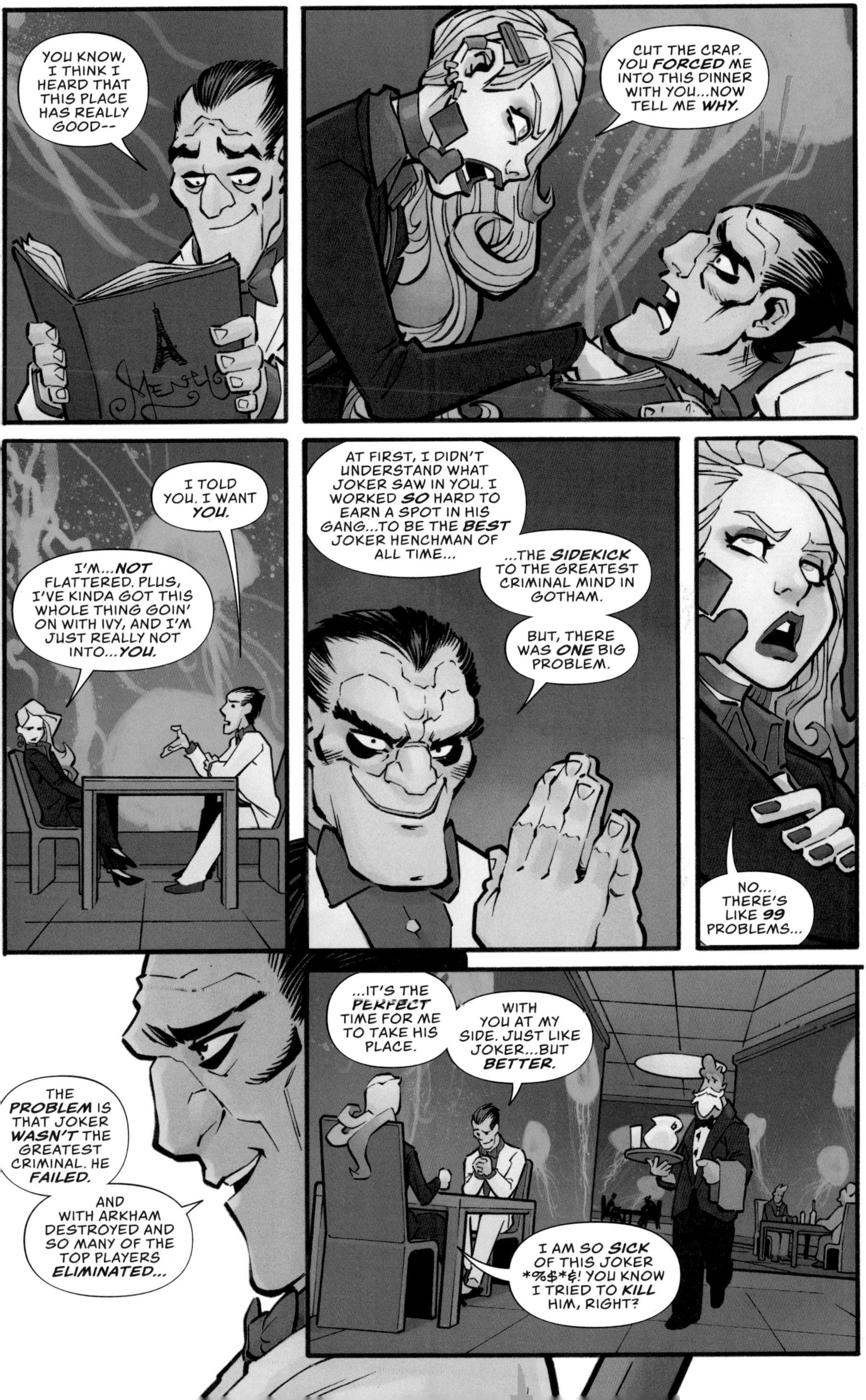
YOU KNOW, I THINK I HEARD THAT THIS PLACE HAS REALLY GOOD--
CUT THE CRAP. YOU FORCED ME INTO THIS DINNER WITH YOU...NOW TELL ME WHY.
I TOLD YOU. I WANT YOU.
I'M...NOT FLATTERED. PLUS, I'VE KINDA GOT THIS WHOLE THING GOIN' ON WITH IVY, AND I'M JUST REALLY NOT INTO...YOU.
AT FIRST, I DIDN'T UNDERSTAND WHAT JOKER SAW IN YOU. I WORKED SO HARD TO EARN A SPOT IN HIS GANG...TO BE THE BEST JOKER HENCHMAN OF ALL TIME...
...THE SIDEKICK TO THE GREATEST CRIMINAL MIND IN GOTHAM.
BUT, THERE WAS ONE BIG PROBLEM.
NO... THERE'S LIKE 99 PROBLEMS...
THE PROBLEM IS THAT JOKER WASN'T THE GREATEST CRIMINAL. HE FAILED.
AND WITH ARKHAM DESTROYED AND SO MANY OF THE TOP PLAYERS ELIMINATED...
...IT'S THE PERFECT TIME FOR ME TO TAKE HIS PLACE.
WITH YOU AT MY SIDE. JUST LIKE JOKER...BUT BETTER.
I AM SO SICK OF THIS JOKER *%$*&! YOU KNOW I TRIED TO KILL HIM, RIGHT?

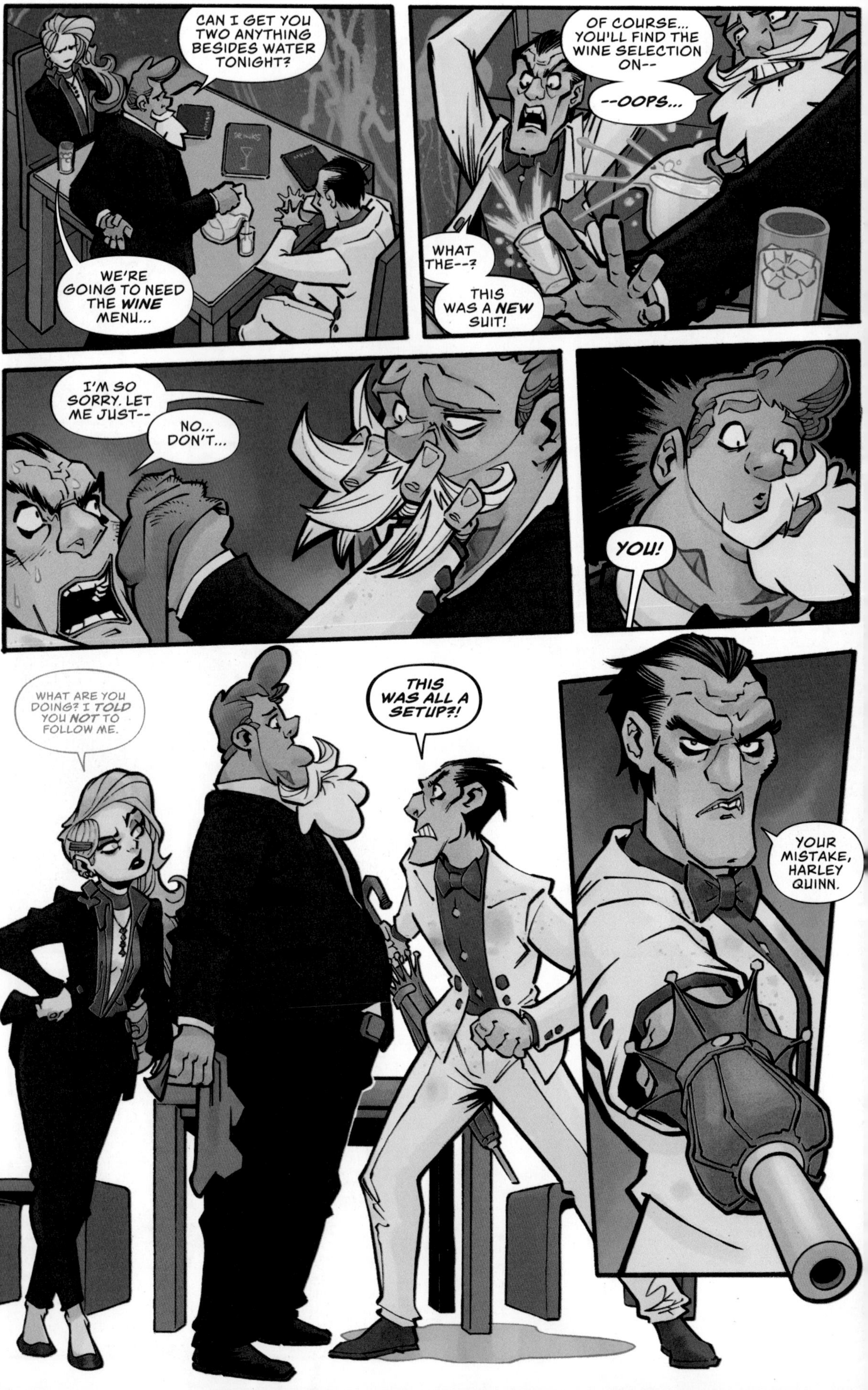
CAN I GET YOU TWO ANYTHING BESIDES WATER TONIGHT?
WE'RE GOING TO NEED THE *WINE* MENU...
OF COURSE... YOU'LL FIND THE WINE SELECTION ON--
--OOPS...
WHAT THE--?
THIS WAS A *NEW* SUIT!
I'M SO SORRY. LET ME JUST--
NO... DON'T...
YOU!
WHAT ARE YOU DOING? I *TOLD* YOU *NOT* TO FOLLOW ME.
THIS WAS ALL A SETUP?!
YOUR MISTAKE, HARLEY QUINN.

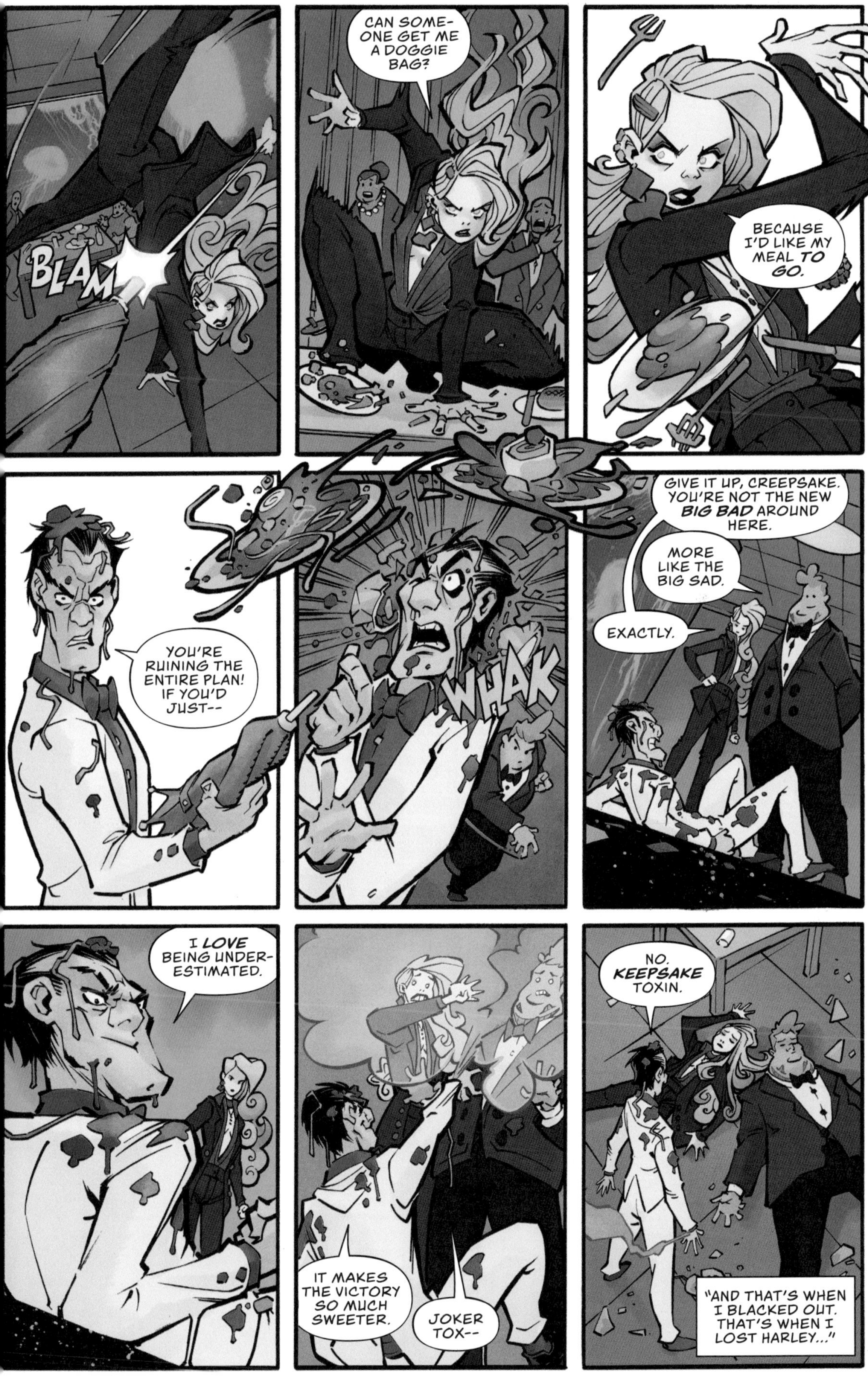
BLAM
CAN SOME-ONE GET ME A DOGGIE BAG?
BECAUSE I'D LIKE MY MEAL TO GO.
YOU'RE RUINING THE ENTIRE PLAN! IF YOU'D JUST--
WHAK
GIVE IT UP, CREEPSAKE. YOU'RE NOT THE NEW BIG BAD AROUND HERE.
MORE LIKE THE BIG SAD.
EXACTLY.
I LOVE BEING UNDER-ESTIMATED.
IT MAKES THE VICTORY SO MUCH SWEETER.
JOKER TOX--
NO. KEEPSAKE TOXIN.
"AND THAT'S WHEN I BLACKED OUT. THAT'S WHEN I LOST HARLEY..."

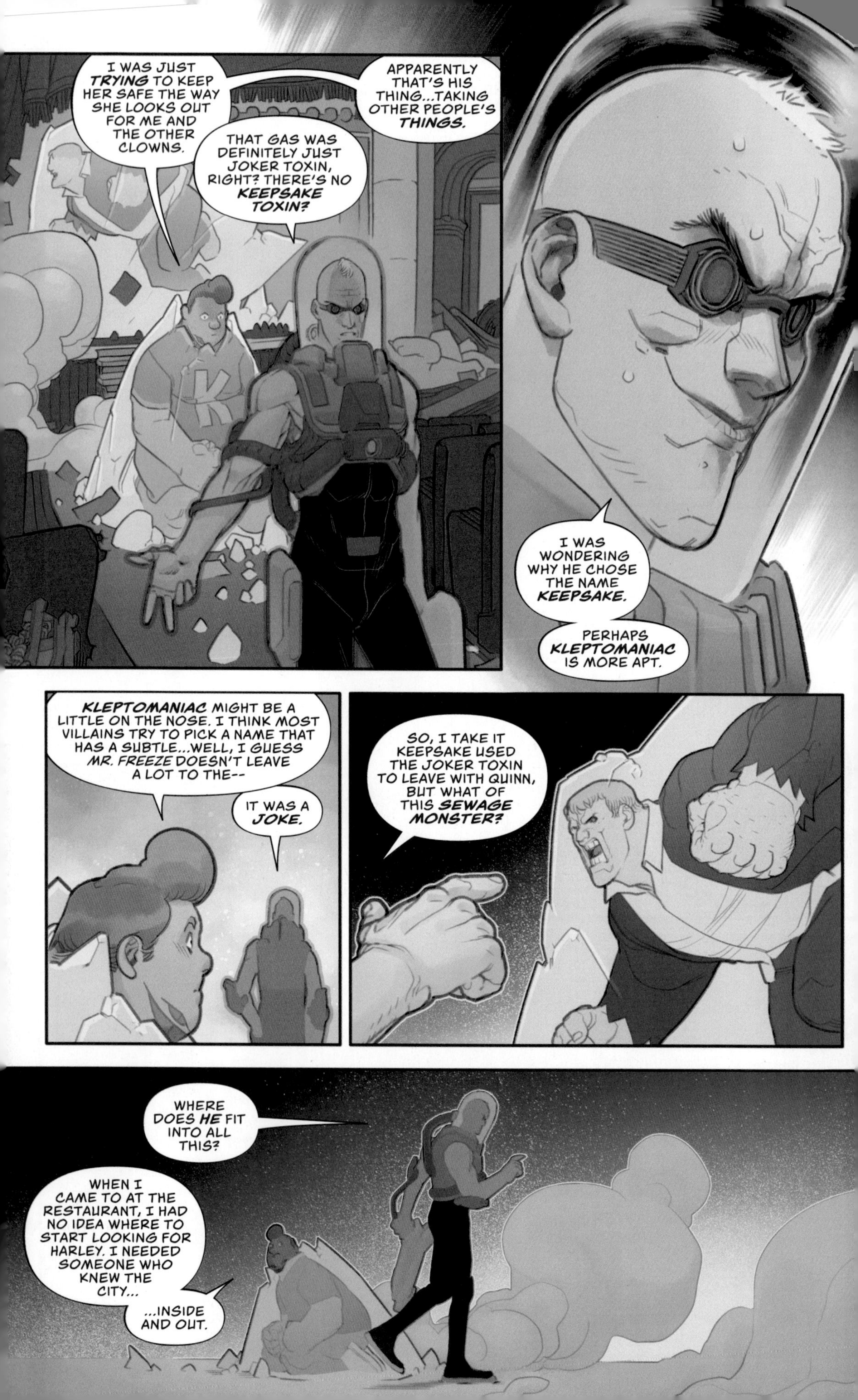
I WAS JUST TRYING TO KEEP HER SAFE THE WAY SHE LOOKS OUT FOR ME AND THE OTHER CLOWNS.
APPARENTLY THAT'S HIS THING...TAKING OTHER PEOPLE'S THINGS.
THAT GAS WAS DEFINITELY JUST JOKER TOXIN, RIGHT? THERE'S NO KEEPSAKE TOXIN?
I WAS WONDERING WHY HE CHOSE THE NAME KEEPSAKE.
PERHAPS KLEPTOMANIAC IS MORE APT.
KLEPTOMANIAC MIGHT BE A LITTLE ON THE NOSE. I THINK MOST VILLAINS TRY TO PICK A NAME THAT HAS A SUBTLE...WELL, I GUESS MR. FREEZE DOESN'T LEAVE A LOT TO THE--
IT WAS A JOKE.
SO, I TAKE IT KEEPSAKE USED THE JOKER TOXIN TO LEAVE WITH QUINN, BUT WHAT OF THIS SEWAGE MONSTER?
WHERE DOES HE FIT INTO ALL THIS?
WHEN I CAME TO AT THE RESTAURANT, I HAD NO IDEA WHERE TO START LOOKING FOR HARLEY. I NEEDED SOMEONE WHO KNEW THE CITY...
...INSIDE AND OUT.

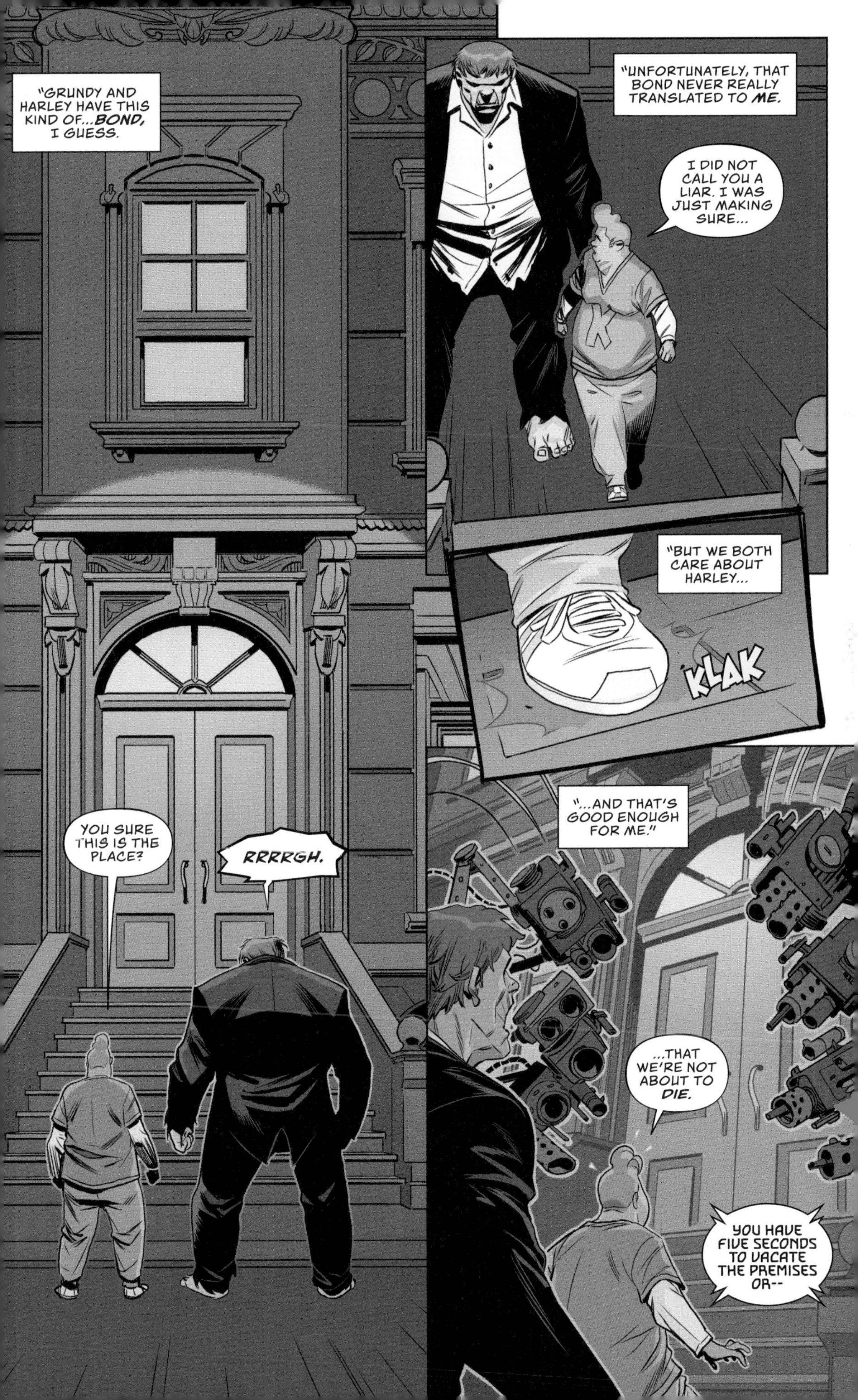
"GRUNDY AND HARLEY HAVE THIS KIND OF...BOND, I GUESS.
YOU SURE THIS IS THE PLACE?
RRRRGH.
"UNFORTUNATELY, THAT BOND NEVER REALLY TRANSLATED TO ME.
I DID NOT CALL YOU A LIAR. I WAS JUST MAKING SURE...
"BUT WE BOTH CARE ABOUT HARLEY...
KLAK
"...AND THAT'S GOOD ENOUGH FOR ME."
...THAT WE'RE NOT ABOUT TO DIE.
YOU HAVE FIVE SECONDS TO VACATE THE PREMISES OR--

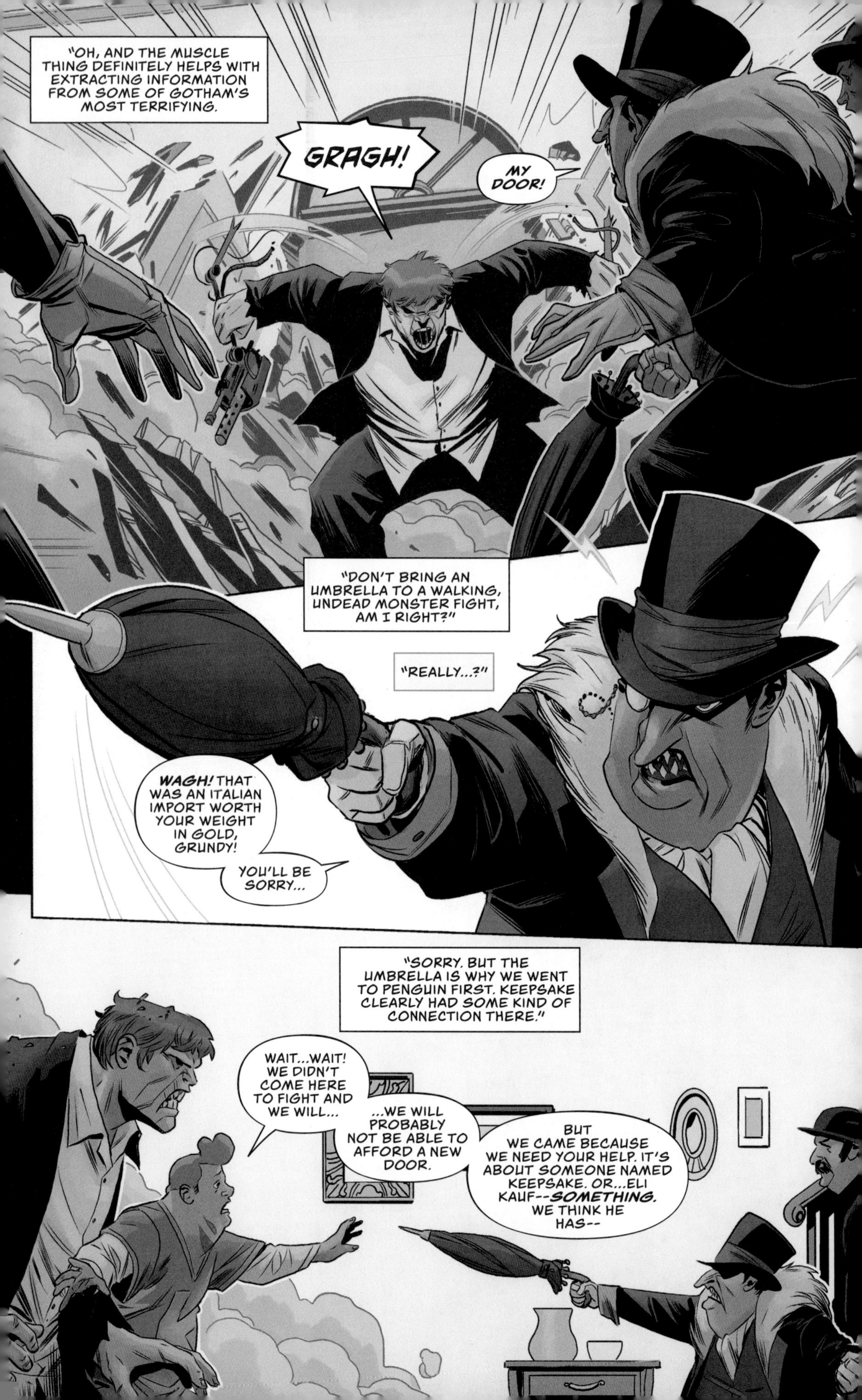
"OH, AND THE MUSCLE THING DEFINITELY HELPS WITH EXTRACTING INFORMATION FROM SOME OF GOTHAM'S MOST TERRIFYING.
GRAGH!
MY DOOR!
"DON'T BRING AN UMBRELLA TO A WALKING, UNDEAD MONSTER FIGHT, AM I RIGHT?"
"REALLY...?"
WAGH! THAT WAS AN ITALIAN IMPORT WORTH YOUR WEIGHT IN GOLD, GRUNDY!
YOU'LL BE SORRY...
"SORRY. BUT THE UMBRELLA IS WHY WE WENT TO PENGUIN FIRST. KEEPSAKE CLEARLY HAD SOME KIND OF CONNECTION THERE."
WAIT...WAIT! WE DIDN'T COME HERE TO FIGHT AND WE WILL...
...WE WILL PROBABLY NOT BE ABLE TO AFFORD A NEW DOOR.
BUT WE CAME BECAUSE WE NEED YOUR HELP. IT'S ABOUT SOMEONE NAMED KEEPSAKE. OR...ELI KAUF--SOMETHING. WE THINK HE HAS--

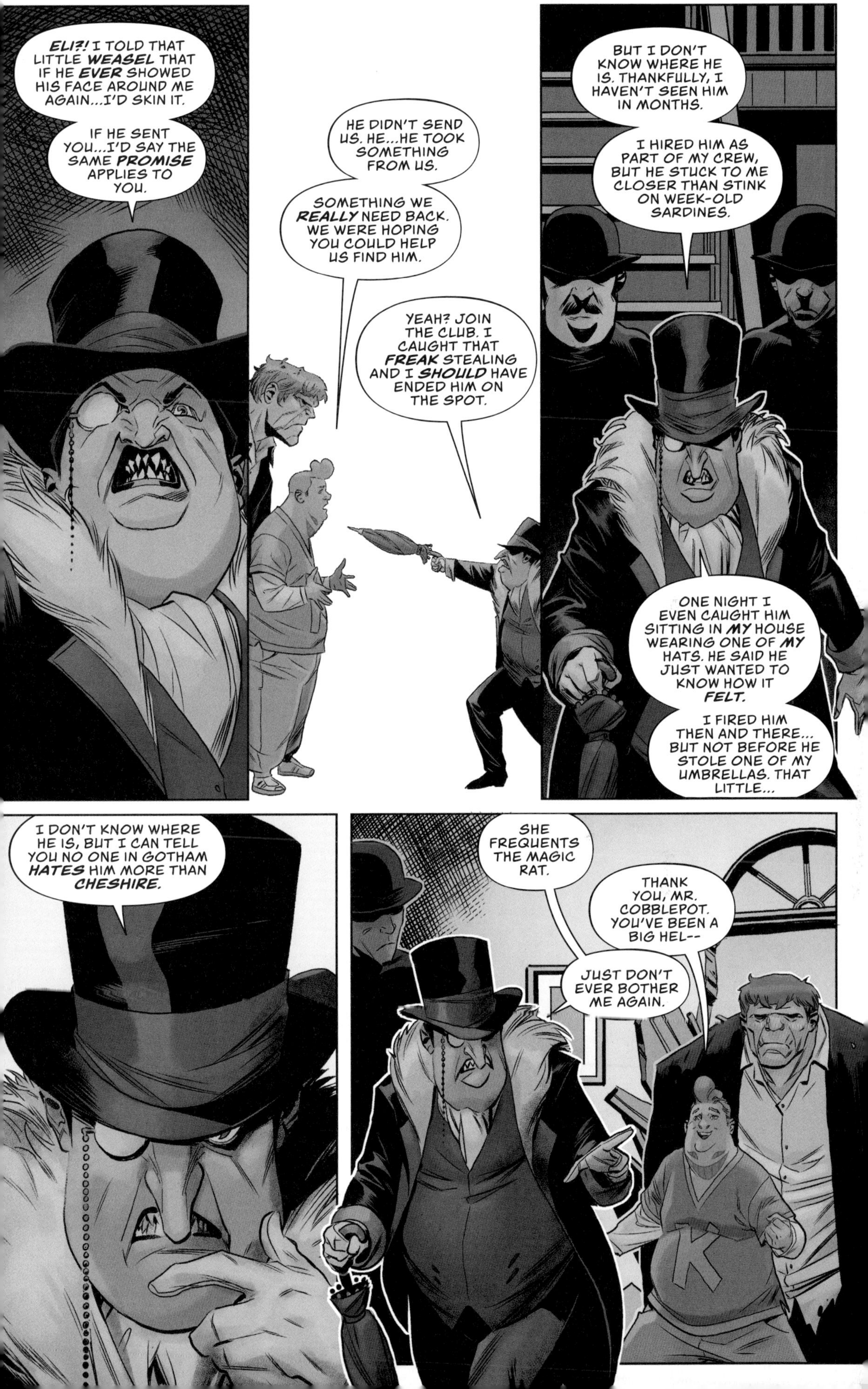
ELI?! I TOLD THAT LITTLE WEASEL THAT IF HE EVER SHOWED HIS FACE AROUND ME AGAIN...I'D SKIN IT.
IF HE SENT YOU...I'D SAY THE SAME PROMISE APPLIES TO YOU.
HE DIDN'T SEND US. HE...HE TOOK SOMETHING FROM US.
SOMETHING WE REALLY NEED BACK. WE WERE HOPING YOU COULD HELP US FIND HIM.
YEAH? JOIN THE CLUB. I CAUGHT THAT FREAK STEALING AND I SHOULD HAVE ENDED HIM ON THE SPOT.
BUT I DON'T KNOW WHERE HE IS. THANKFULLY, I HAVEN'T SEEN HIM IN MONTHS.
I HIRED HIM AS PART OF MY CREW, BUT HE STUCK TO ME CLOSER THAN STINK ON WEEK-OLD SARDINES.
ONE NIGHT I EVEN CAUGHT HIM SITTING IN MY HOUSE WEARING ONE OF MY HATS. HE SAID HE JUST WANTED TO KNOW HOW IT FELT.
I FIRED HIM THEN AND THERE... BUT NOT BEFORE HE STOLE ONE OF MY UMBRELLAS. THAT LITTLE...
I DON'T KNOW WHERE HE IS, BUT I CAN TELL YOU NO ONE IN GOTHAM HATES HIM MORE THAN CHESHIRE.
SHE FREQUENTS THE MAGIC RAT.
THANK YOU, MR. COBBLEPOT. YOU'VE BEEN A BIG HEL--
JUST DON'T EVER BOTHER ME AGAIN.

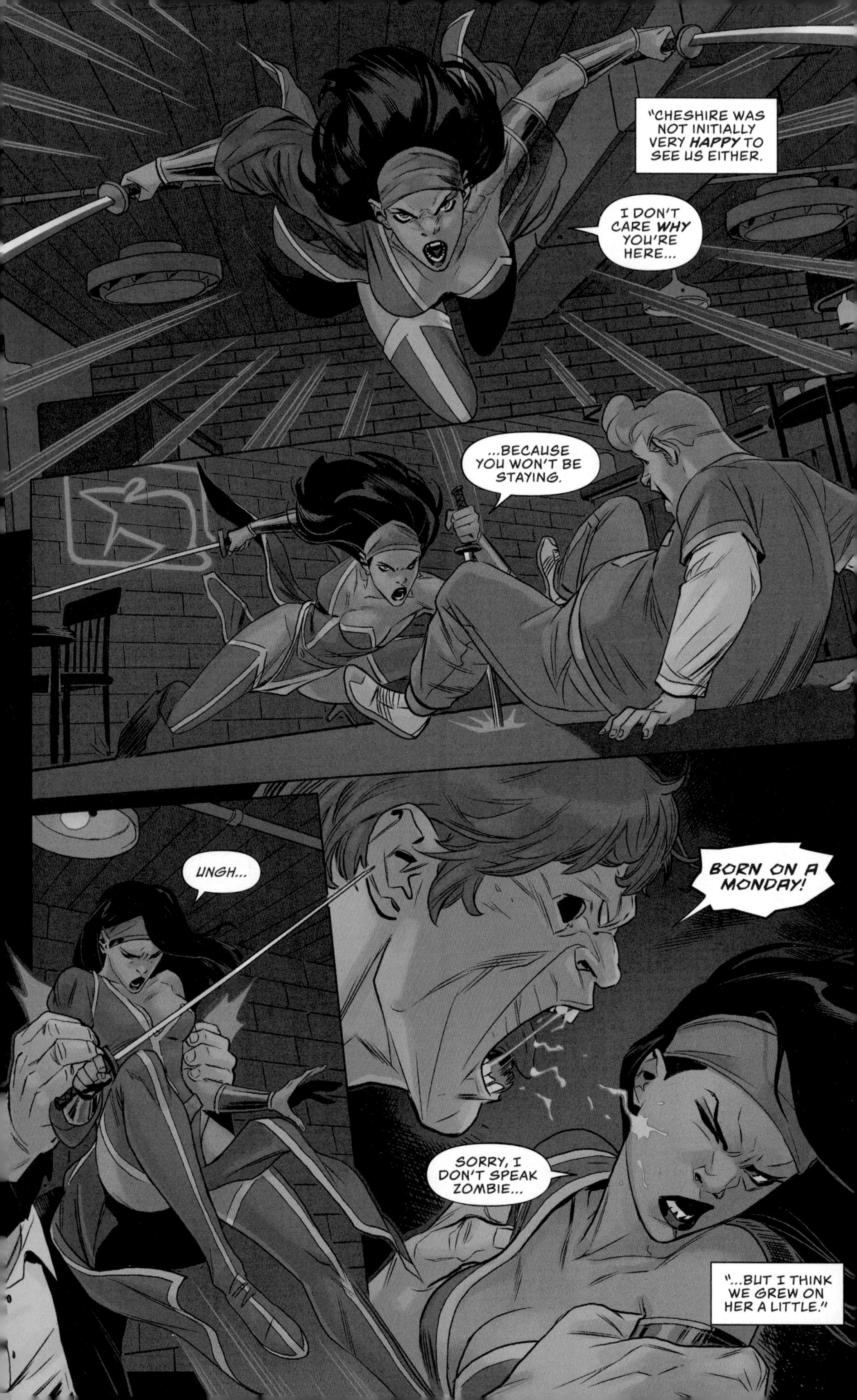
"CHESHIRE WAS NOT INITIALLY VERY *HAPPY* TO SEE US EITHER.
I DON'T CARE *WHY* YOU'RE HERE...
...BECAUSE YOU WON'T BE STAYING.
UNGH...
BORN ON A MONDAY!
SORRY, I DON'T SPEAK ZOMBIE...
"...BUT I THINK WE GREW ON HER A LITTLE."

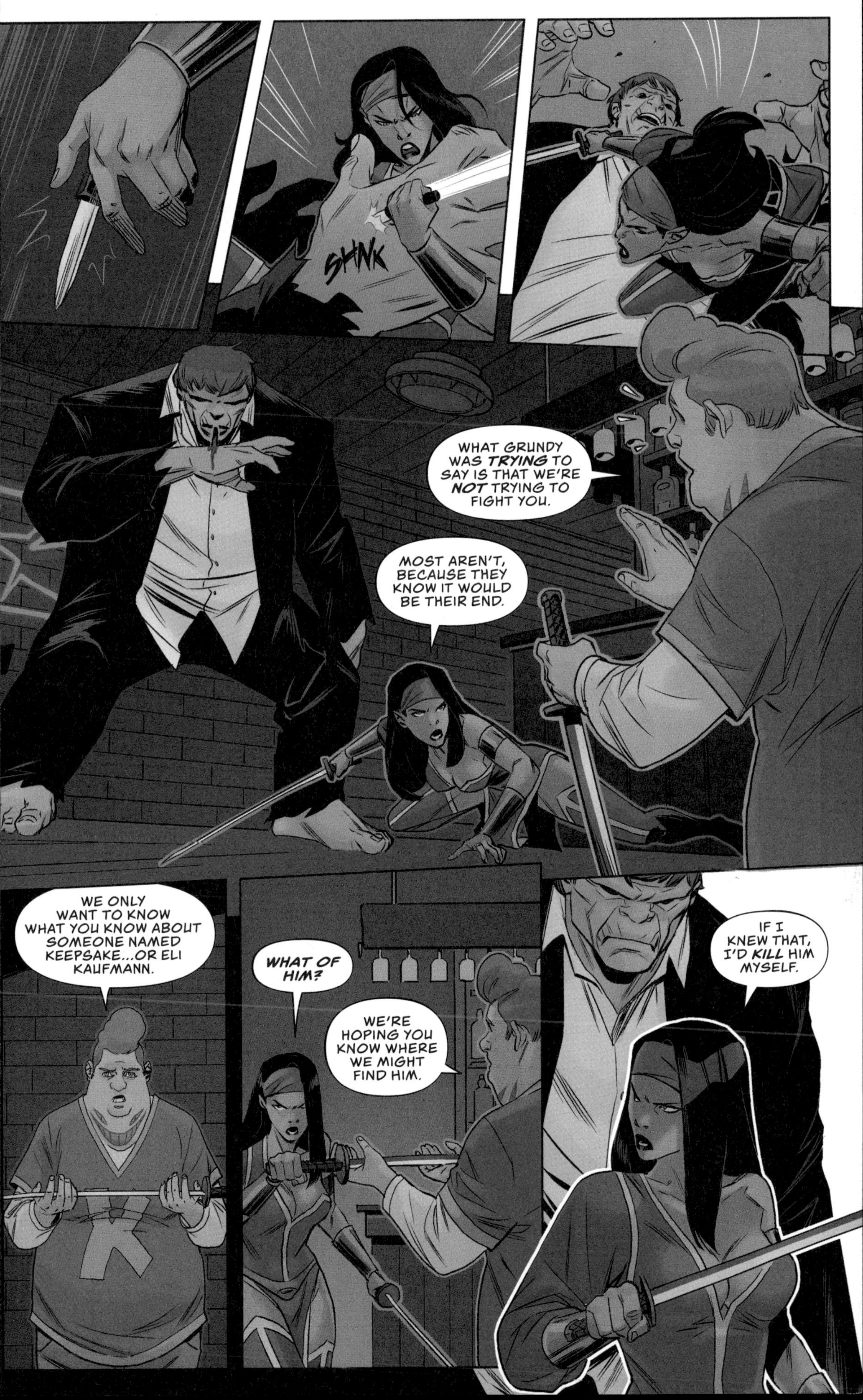
SHNK
WHAT GRUNDY WAS TRYING TO SAY IS THAT WE'RE NOT TRYING TO FIGHT YOU.
MOST AREN'T, BECAUSE THEY KNOW IT WOULD BE THEIR END.
WE ONLY WANT TO KNOW WHAT YOU KNOW ABOUT SOMEONE NAMED KEEPSAKE...OR ELI KAUFMANN.
WHAT OF HIM?
WE'RE HOPING YOU KNOW WHERE WE MIGHT FIND HIM.
IF I KNEW THAT, I'D KILL HIM MYSELF.

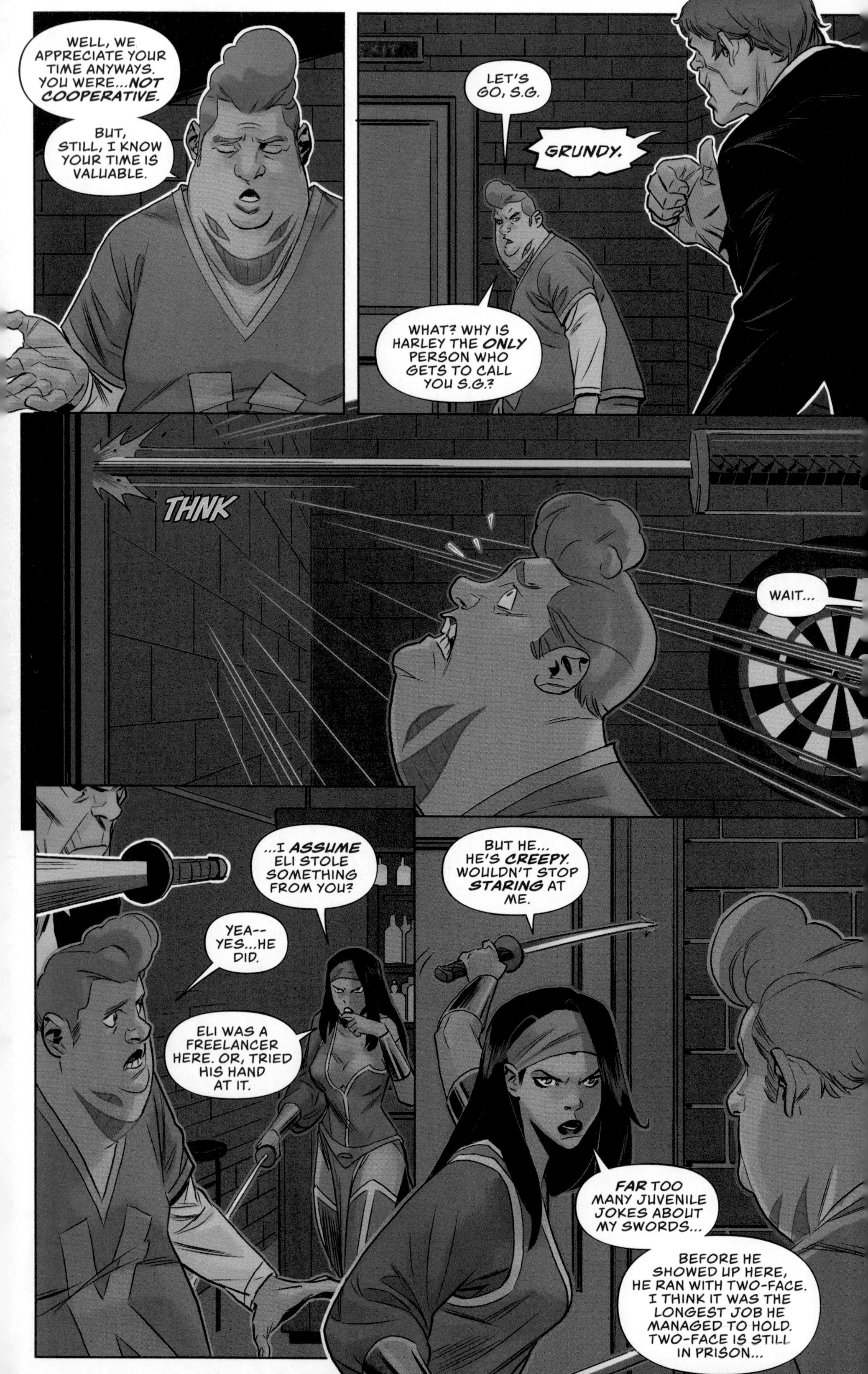
WELL, WE APPRECIATE YOUR TIME ANYWAYS. YOU WERE...*NOT COOPERATIVE.*
BUT, STILL, I KNOW YOUR TIME IS VALUABLE.
LET'S GO, S.G.
GRUNDY.
WHAT? WHY IS HARLEY THE *ONLY* PERSON WHO GETS TO CALL YOU S.G.?
THNK
WAIT...
...I *ASSUME* ELI STOLE SOMETHING FROM YOU?
YEA-- YES...HE DID.
ELI WAS A FREELANCER HERE. OR, TRIED HIS HAND AT IT.
BUT HE... HE'S *CREEPY.* WOULDN'T STOP *STARING* AT ME.
FAR TOO MANY JUVENILE JOKES ABOUT MY SWORDS...
BEFORE HE SHOWED UP HERE, HE RAN WITH TWO-FACE. I THINK IT WAS THE LONGEST JOB HE MANAGED TO HOLD. TWO-FACE IS STILL IN PRISON...

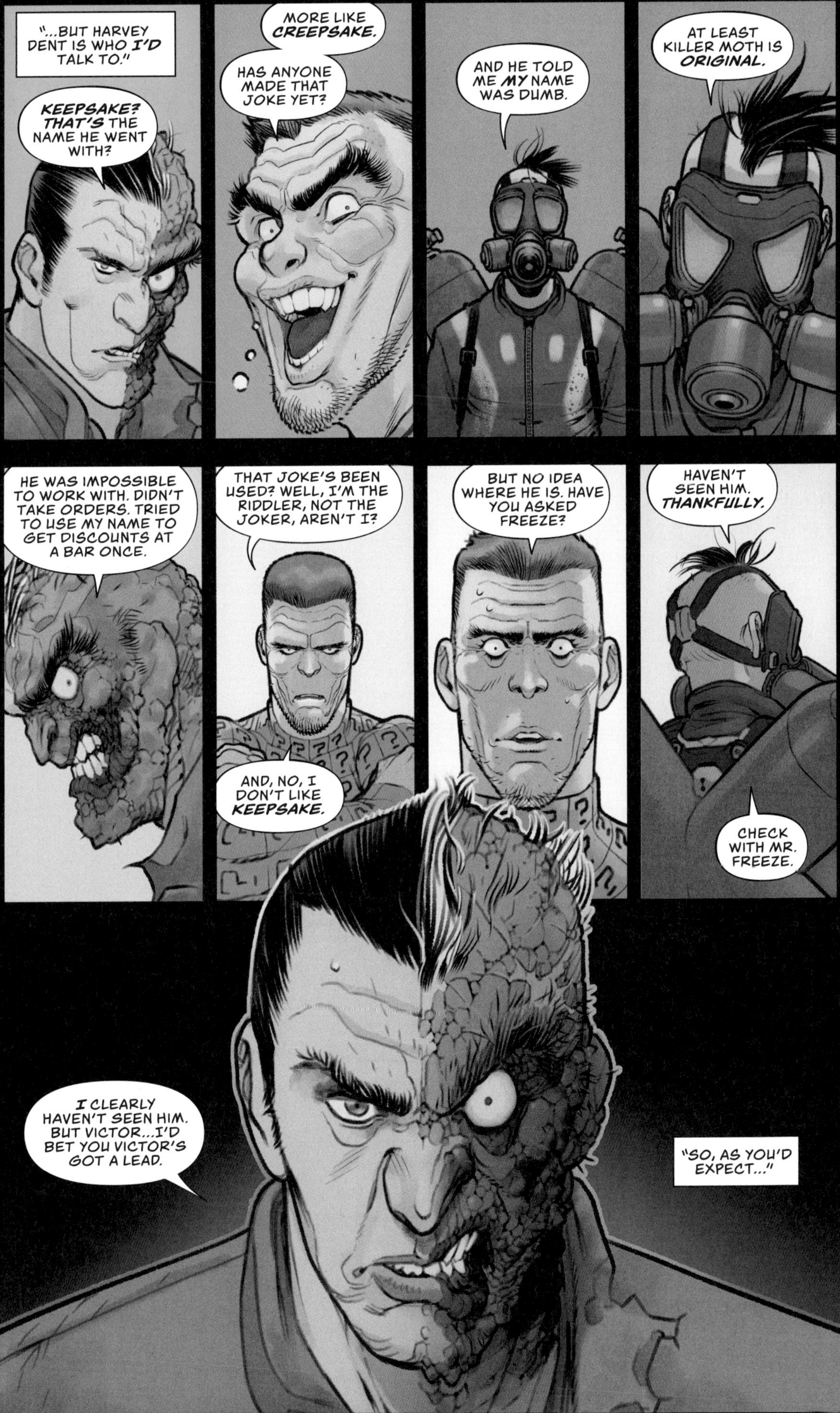
"...BUT HARVEY DENT IS WHO I'D TALK TO."
KEEPSAKE? THAT'S THE NAME HE WENT WITH?
MORE LIKE CREEPSAKE.
HAS ANYONE MADE THAT JOKE YET?
AND HE TOLD ME MY NAME WAS DUMB.
AT LEAST KILLER MOTH IS ORIGINAL.
HE WAS IMPOSSIBLE TO WORK WITH. DIDN'T TAKE ORDERS. TRIED TO USE MY NAME TO GET DISCOUNTS AT A BAR ONCE.
THAT JOKE'S BEEN USED? WELL, I'M THE RIDDLER, NOT THE JOKER, AREN'T I?
AND, NO, I DON'T LIKE KEEPSAKE.
BUT NO IDEA WHERE HE IS. HAVE YOU ASKED FREEZE?
HAVEN'T SEEN HIM. THANKFULLY.
CHECK WITH MR. FREEZE.
I CLEARLY HAVEN'T SEEN HIM. BUT VICTOR...I'D BET YOU VICTOR'S GOT A LEAD.
"SO, AS YOU'D EXPECT..."

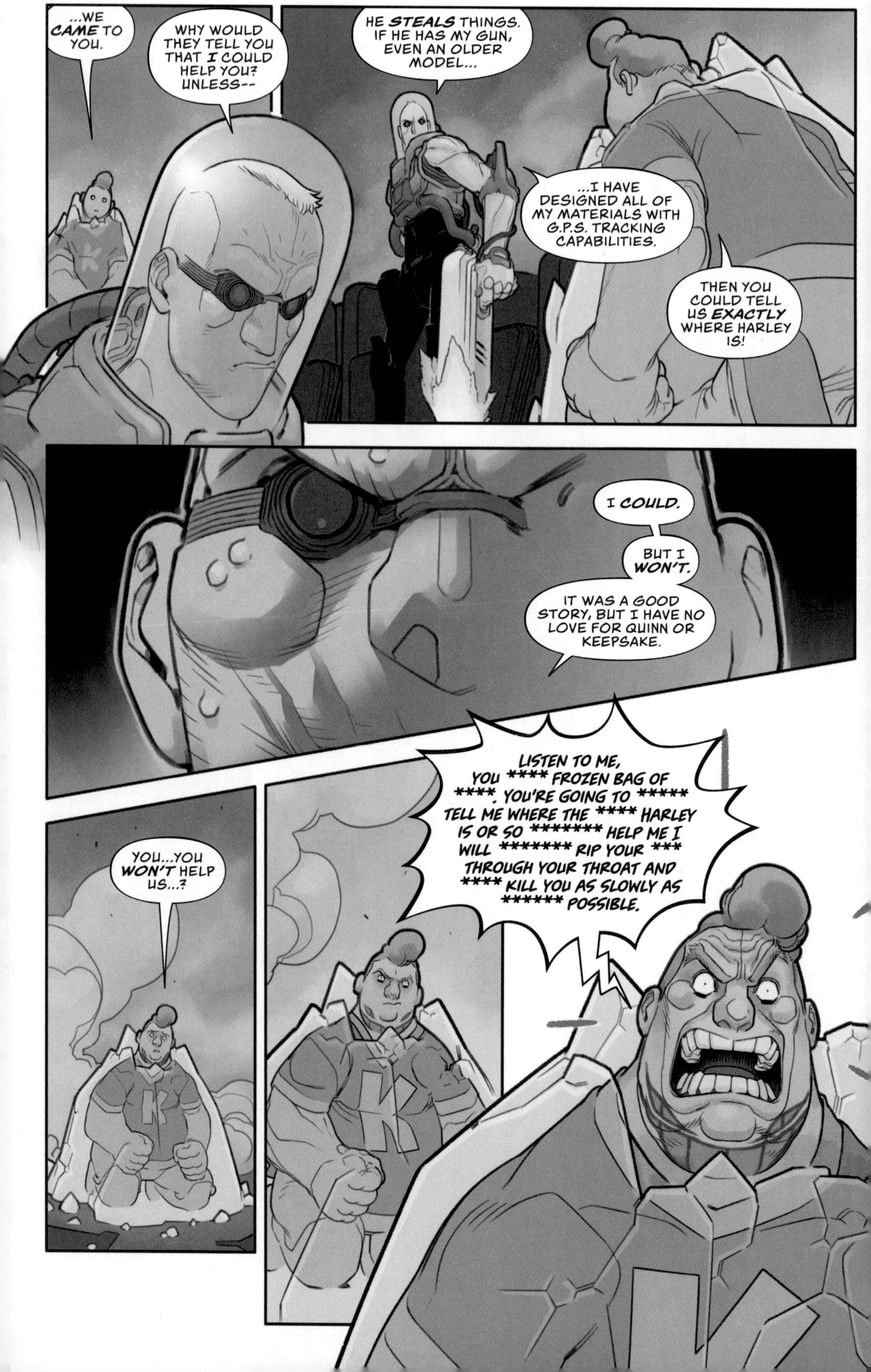
...WE CAME TO YOU.
WHY WOULD THEY TELL YOU THAT I COULD HELP YOU? UNLESS--
HE STEALS THINGS. IF HE HAS MY GUN, EVEN AN OLDER MODEL...
...I HAVE DESIGNED ALL OF MY MATERIALS WITH G.P.S. TRACKING CAPABILITIES.
THEN YOU COULD TELL US EXACTLY WHERE HARLEY IS!
I COULD.
BUT I WON'T.
IT WAS A GOOD STORY, BUT I HAVE NO LOVE FOR QUINN OR KEEPSAKE.
YOU...YOU WON'T HELP US...?
LISTEN TO ME, YOU **** FROZEN BAG OF ****. YOU'RE GOING TO ***** TELL ME WHERE THE **** HARLEY IS OR SO ******* HELP ME I WILL ******* RIP YOUR *** THROUGH YOUR THROAT AND **** KILL YOU AS SLOWLY AS ****** POSSIBLE.

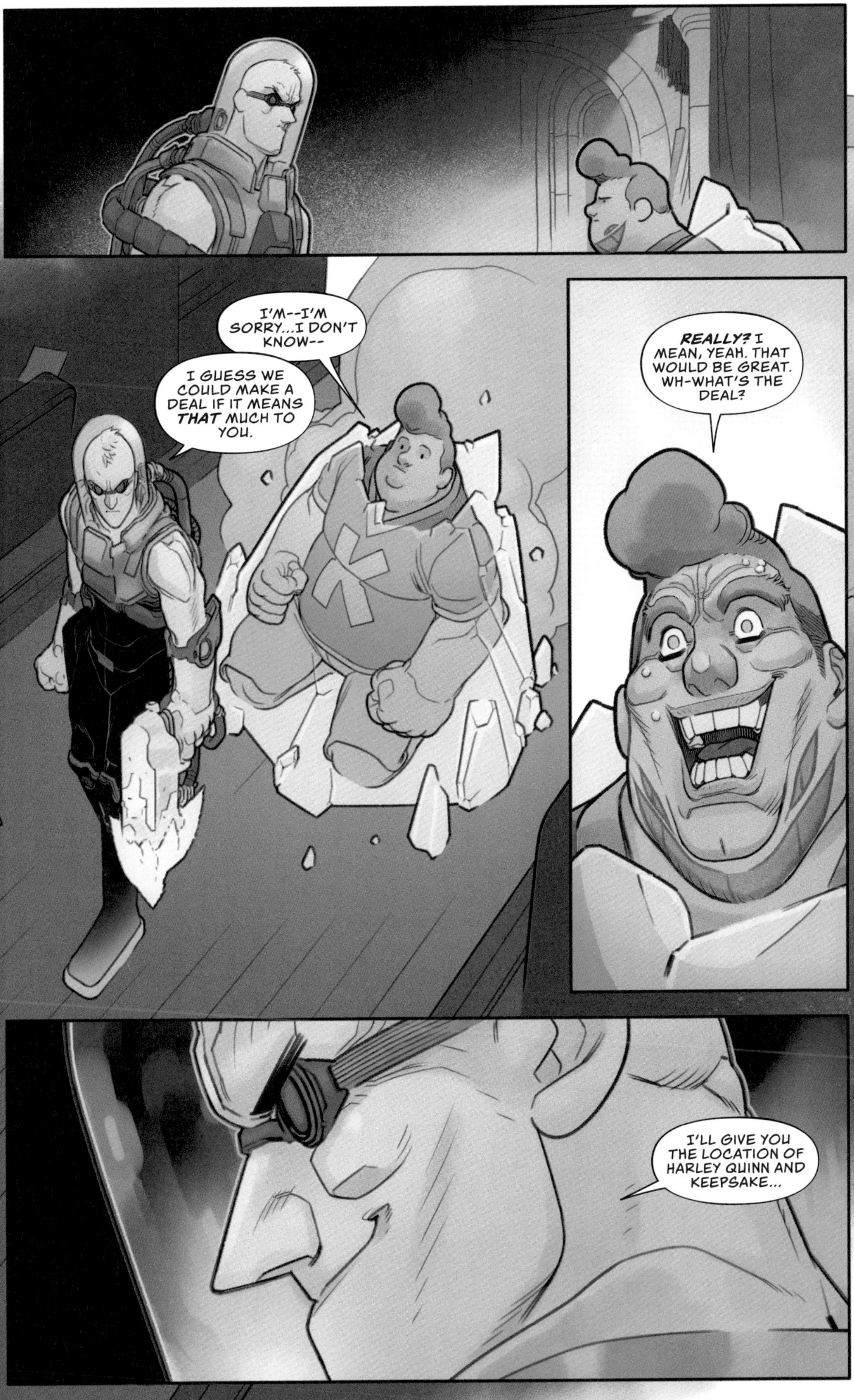
I'M--I'M SORRY...I DON'T KNOW--
I GUESS WE COULD MAKE A DEAL IF IT MEANS THAT MUCH TO YOU.
REALLY? I MEAN, YEAH. THAT WOULD BE GREAT. WH-WHAT'S THE DEAL?
I'LL GIVE YOU THE LOCATION OF HARLEY QUINN AND KEEPSAKE...

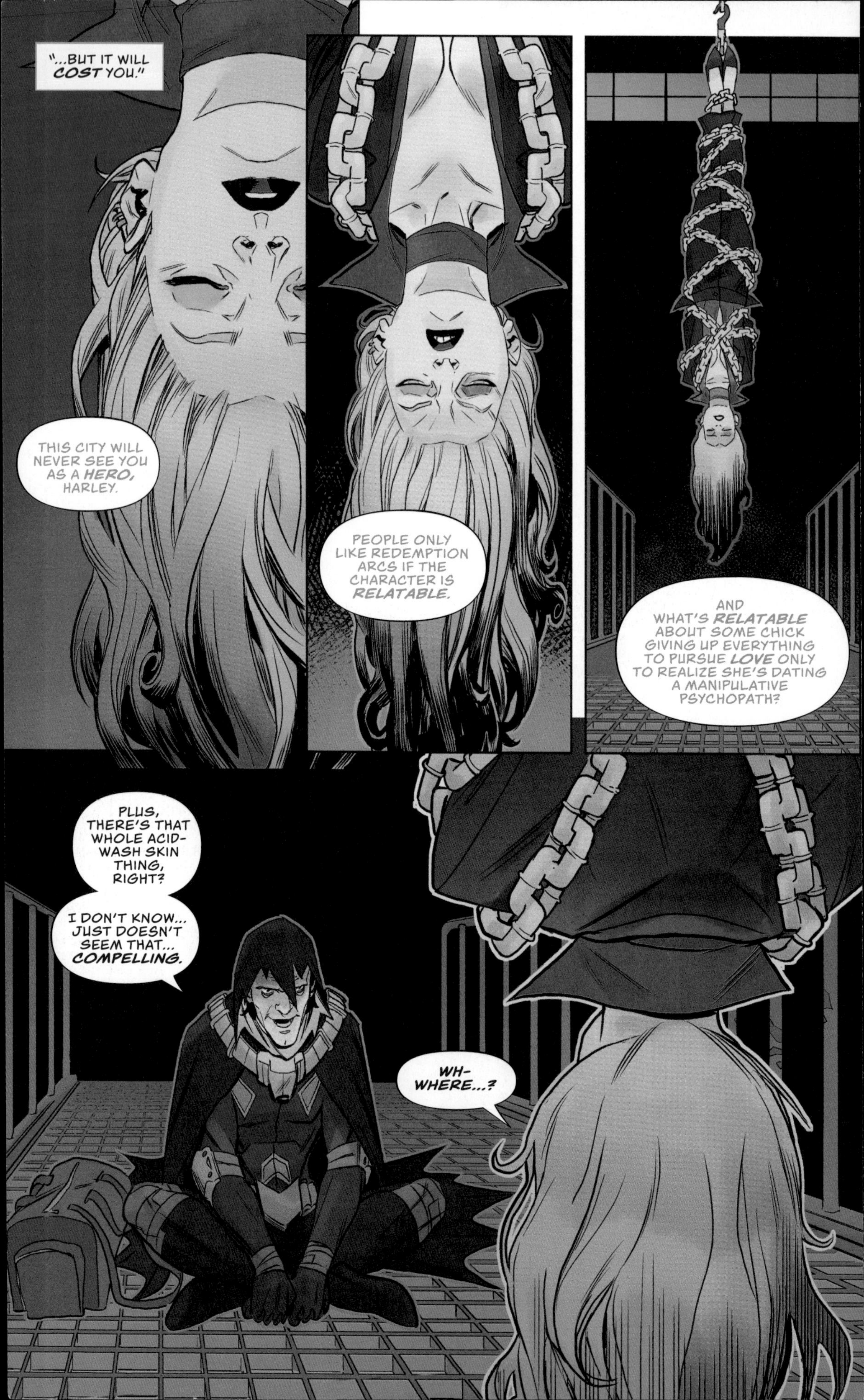

"...BUT IT WILL COST YOU."
THIS CITY WILL NEVER SEE YOU AS A HERO, HARLEY.
PEOPLE ONLY LIKE REDEMPTION ARCS IF THE CHARACTER IS RELATABLE.
AND WHAT'S RELATABLE ABOUT SOME CHICK GIVING UP EVERYTHING TO PURSUE LOVE ONLY TO REALIZE SHE'S DATING A MANIPULATIVE PSYCHOPATH?
PLUS, THERE'S THAT WHOLE ACID-WASH SKIN THING, RIGHT?
I DON'T KNOW... JUST DOESN'T SEEM THAT... COMPELLING.
WH-WHERE...?

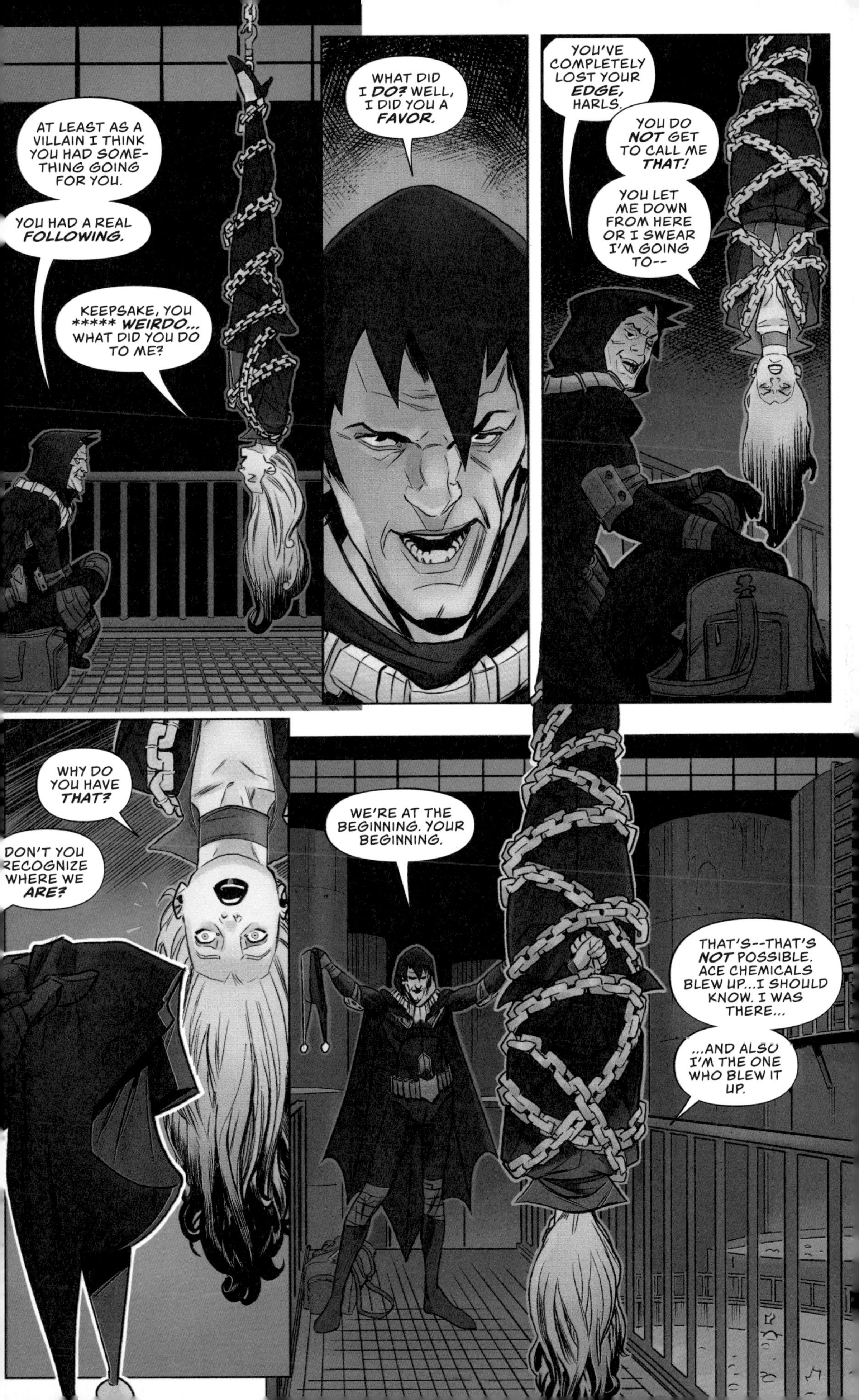
AT LEAST AS A VILLAIN I THINK YOU HAD SOME-THING GOING FOR YOU.
YOU HAD A REAL FOLLOWING.
KEEPSAKE, YOU ***** WEIRDO... WHAT DID YOU DO TO ME?
WHAT DID I DO? WELL, I DID YOU A FAVOR.
YOU'VE COMPLETELY LOST YOUR EDGE, HARLS.
YOU DO NOT GET TO CALL ME THAT!
YOU LET ME DOWN FROM HERE OR I SWEAR I'M GOING TO--
WHY DO YOU HAVE THAT?
DON'T YOU RECOGNIZE WHERE WE ARE?
WE'RE AT THE BEGINNING. YOUR BEGINNING.
THAT'S--THAT'S NOT POSSIBLE. ACE CHEMICALS BLEW UP...I SHOULD KNOW. I WAS THERE...
...AND ALSO I'M THE ONE WHO BLEW IT UP.

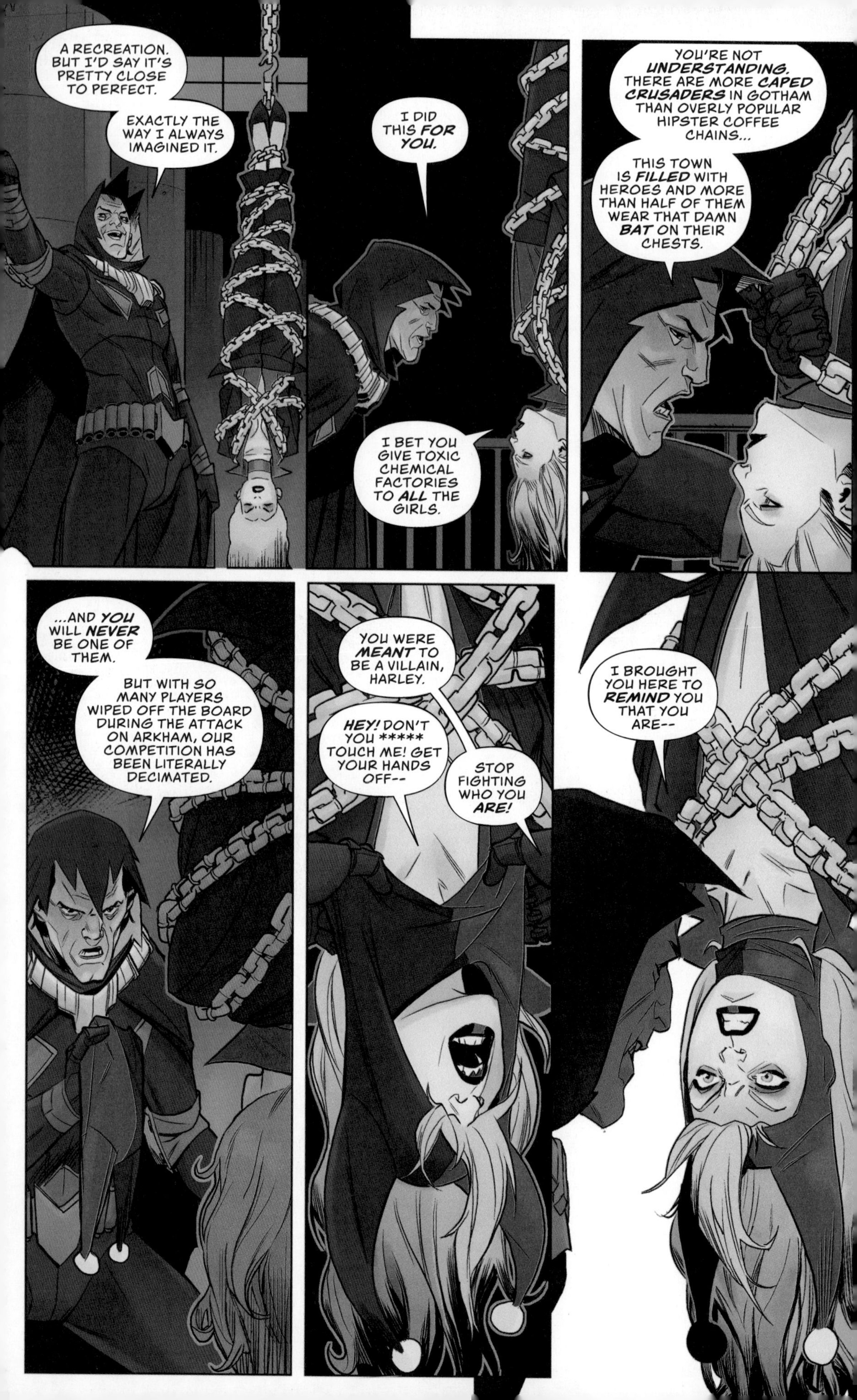

A RECREATION. BUT I'D SAY IT'S PRETTY CLOSE TO PERFECT.
EXACTLY THE WAY I ALWAYS IMAGINED IT.
I DID THIS FOR YOU.
I BET YOU GIVE TOXIC CHEMICAL FACTORIES TO ALL THE GIRLS.
YOU'RE NOT UNDERSTANDING. THERE ARE MORE CAPED CRUSADERS IN GOTHAM THAN OVERLY POPULAR HIPSTER COFFEE CHAINS...
THIS TOWN IS FILLED WITH HEROES AND MORE THAN HALF OF THEM WEAR THAT DAMN BAT ON THEIR CHESTS.
...AND YOU WILL NEVER BE ONE OF THEM.
BUT WITH SO MANY PLAYERS WIPED OFF THE BOARD DURING THE ATTACK ON ARKHAM, OUR COMPETITION HAS BEEN LITERALLY DECIMATED.
YOU WERE MEANT TO BE A VILLAIN, HARLEY.
HEY! DON'T YOU ***** TOUCH ME! GET YOUR HANDS OFF--
STOP FIGHTING WHO YOU ARE!
I BROUGHT YOU HERE TO REMIND YOU THAT YOU ARE--

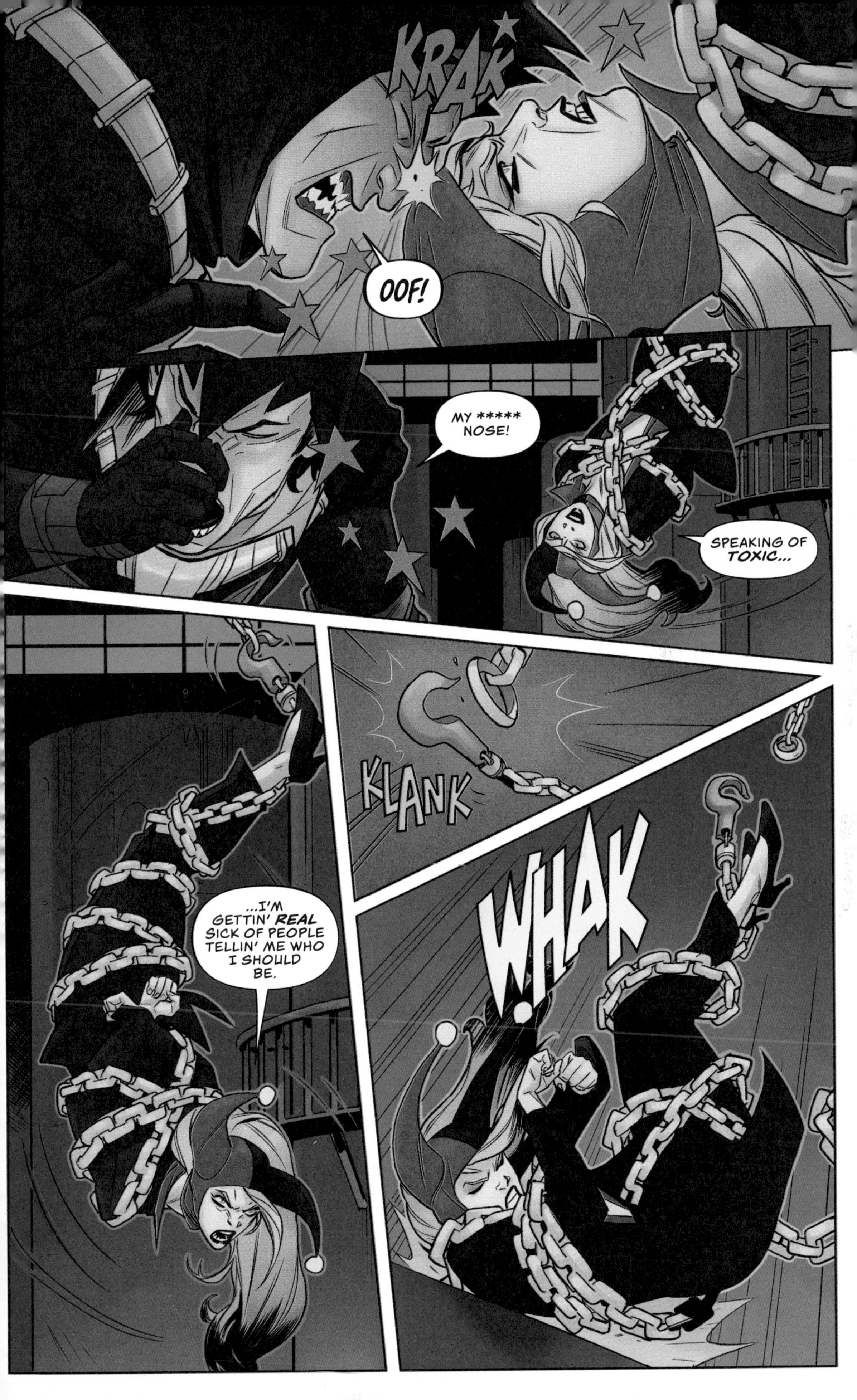
KRAK
OOF!
MY ***** NOSE!
SPEAKING OF TOXIC...
KLANK
...I'M GETTIN' REAL SICK OF PEOPLE TELLIN' ME WHO I SHOULD BE.
WHAK

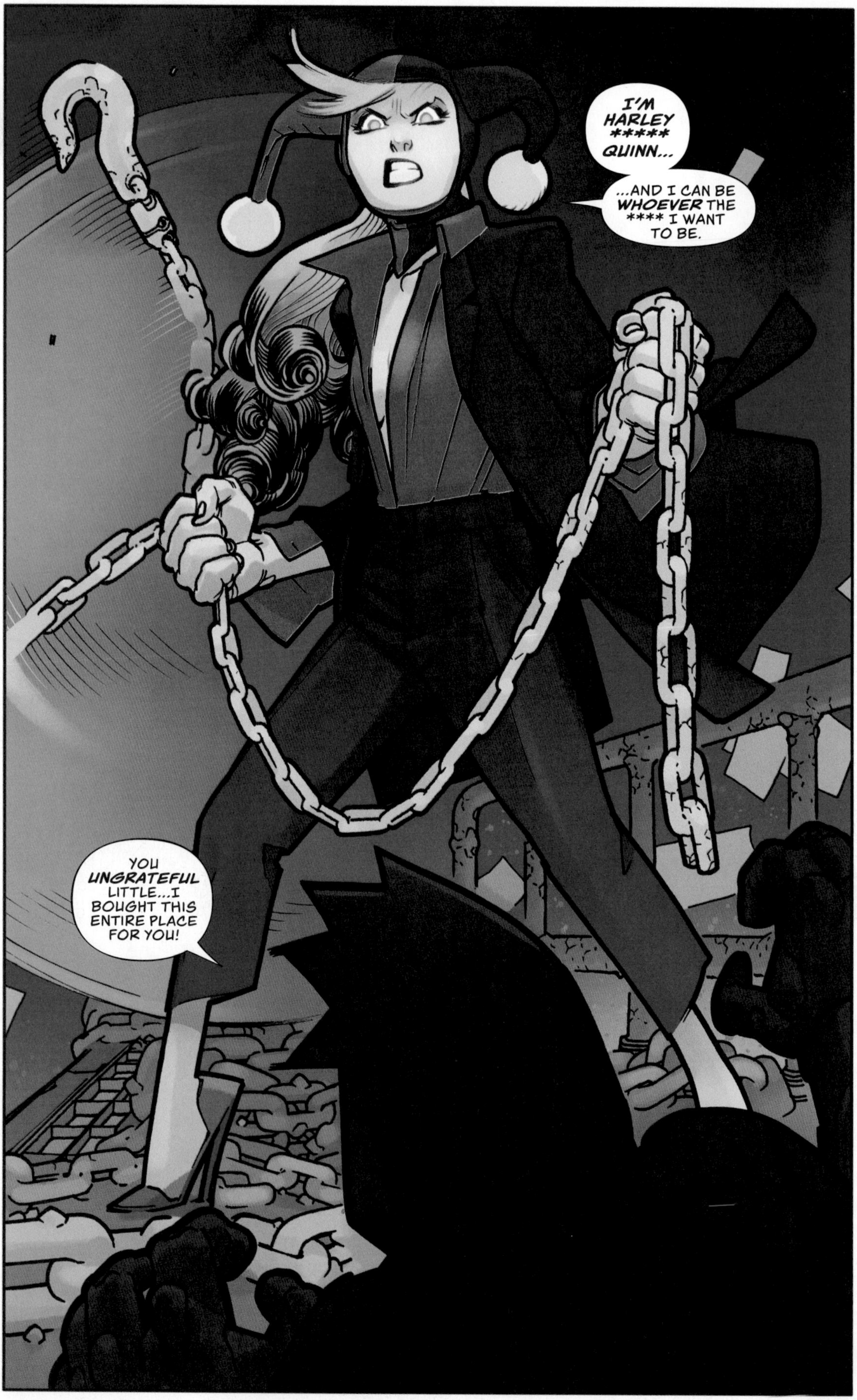
I'M HARLEY ***** QUINN...
...AND I CAN BE WHOEVER THE **** I WANT TO BE.
YOU UNGRATEFUL LITTLE...I BOUGHT THIS ENTIRE PLACE FOR YOU!

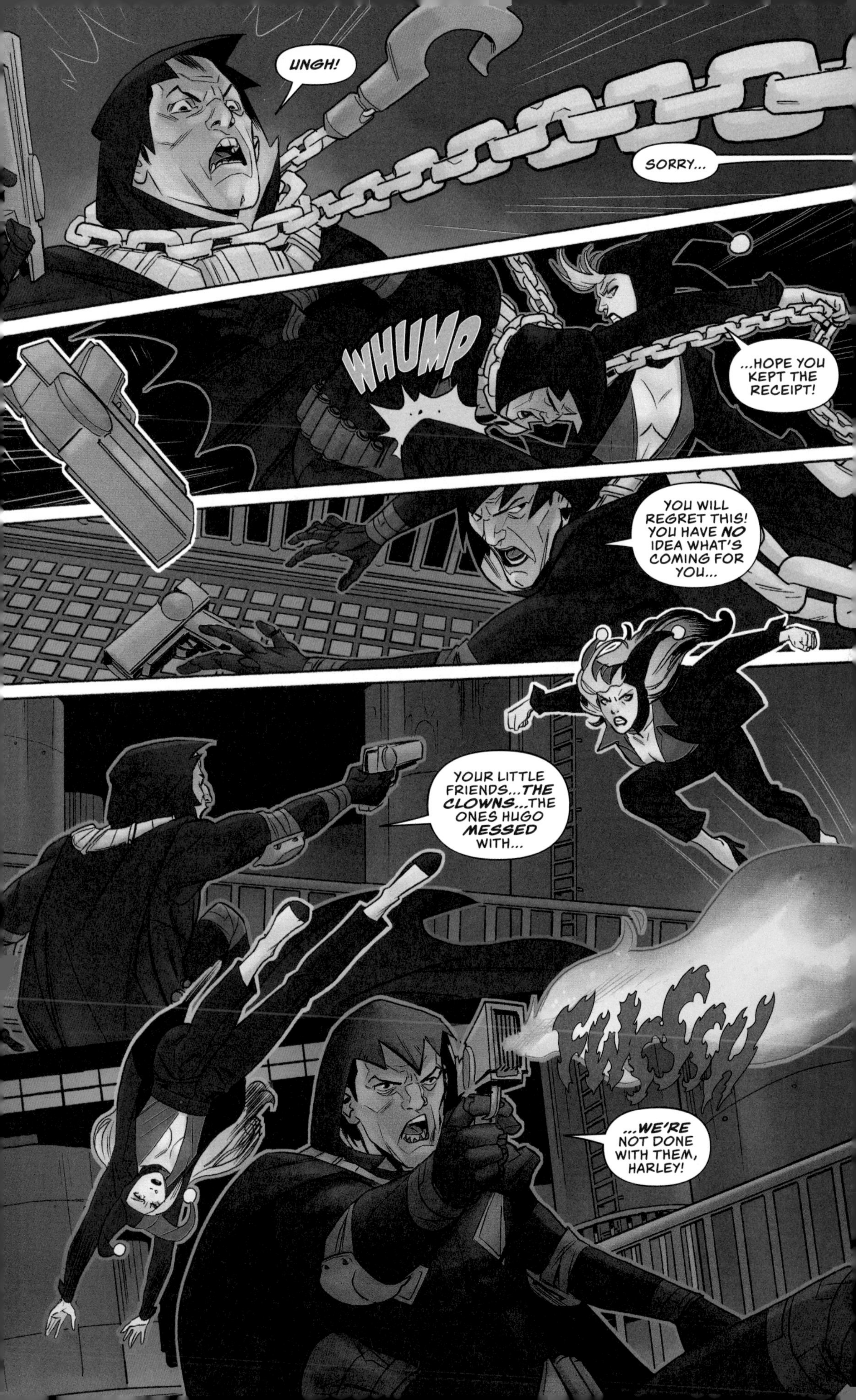
UNGH!
SORRY...
WHUMP
...HOPE YOU KEPT THE RECEIPT!
YOU WILL REGRET THIS! YOU HAVE NO IDEA WHAT'S COMING FOR YOU...
YOUR LITTLE FRIENDS...THE CLOWNS...THE ONES HUGO MESSED WITH...
...WE'RE NOT DONE WITH THEM, HARLEY!

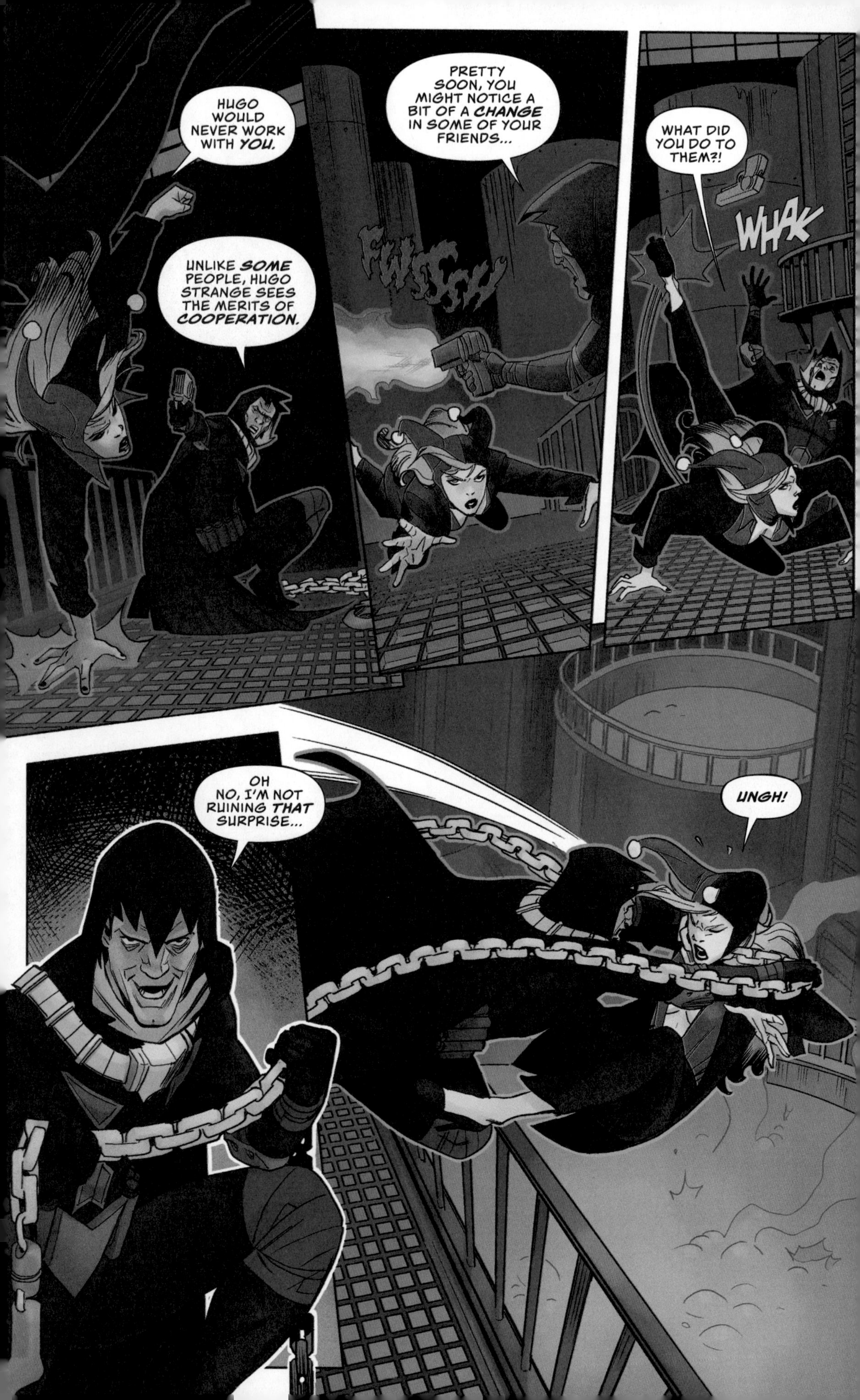
HUGO WOULD NEVER WORK WITH *YOU.*
UNLIKE *SOME* PEOPLE, HUGO STRANGE SEES THE MERITS OF *COOPERATION.*
PRETTY SOON, YOU MIGHT NOTICE A BIT OF A *CHANGE* IN SOME OF YOUR FRIENDS...
FWSSH
WHAT DID YOU DO TO THEM?!
WHAK
OH NO, I'M NOT RUINING *THAT* SURPRISE...
UNGH!

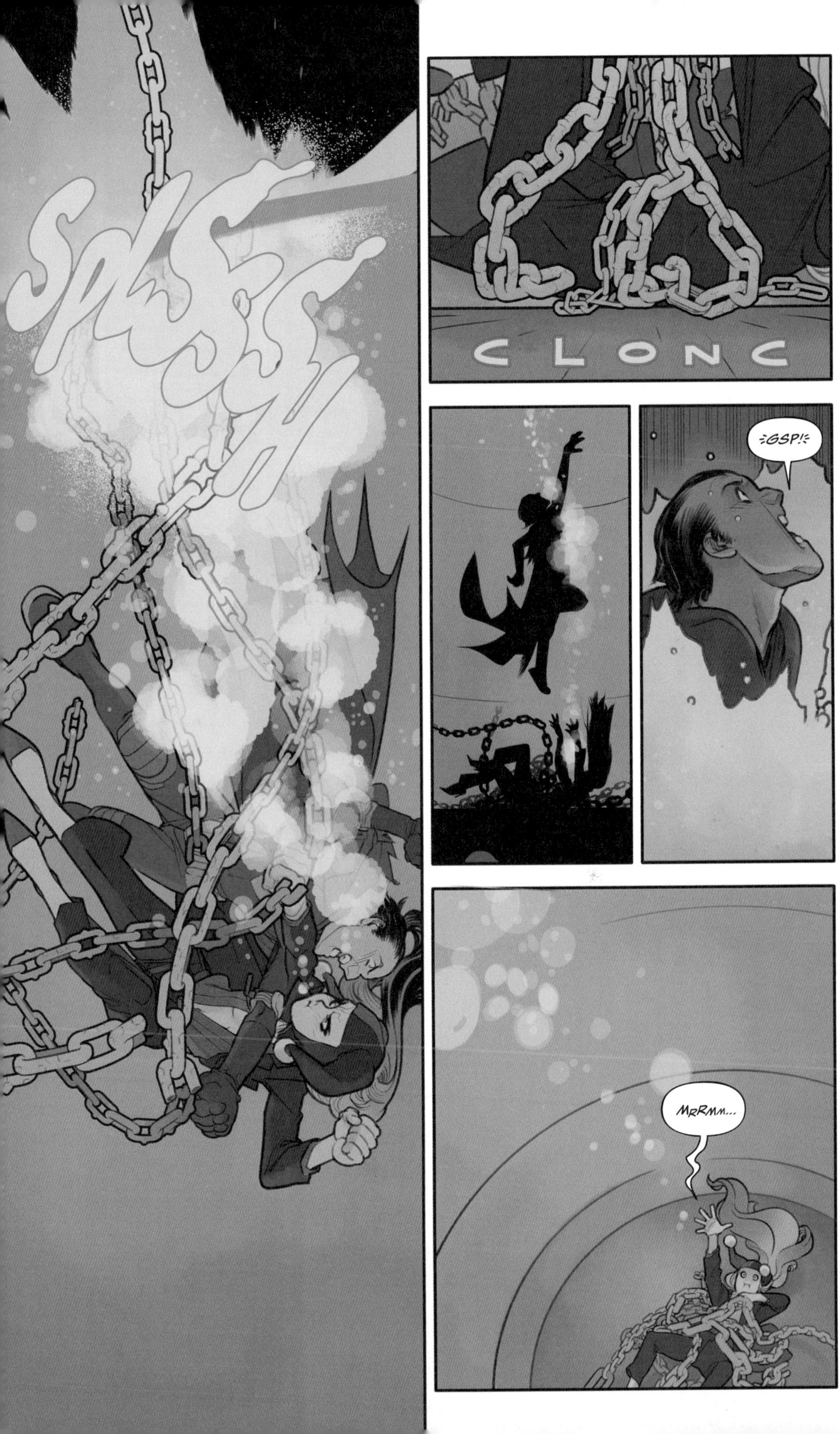
SPLOOSH
CLONC
GSP!
MRRMM...

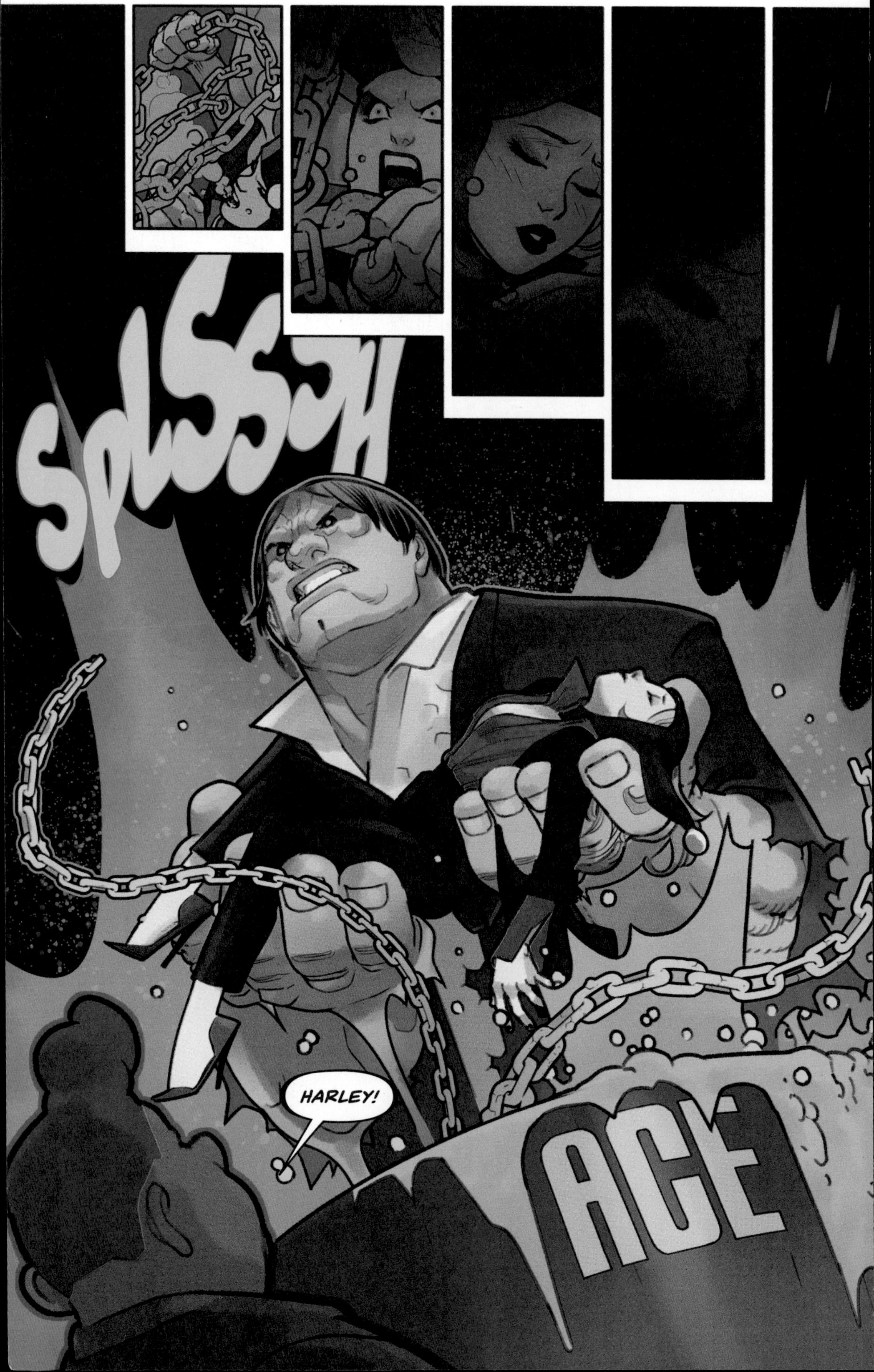
SPLSSCH
HARLEY!
ACE

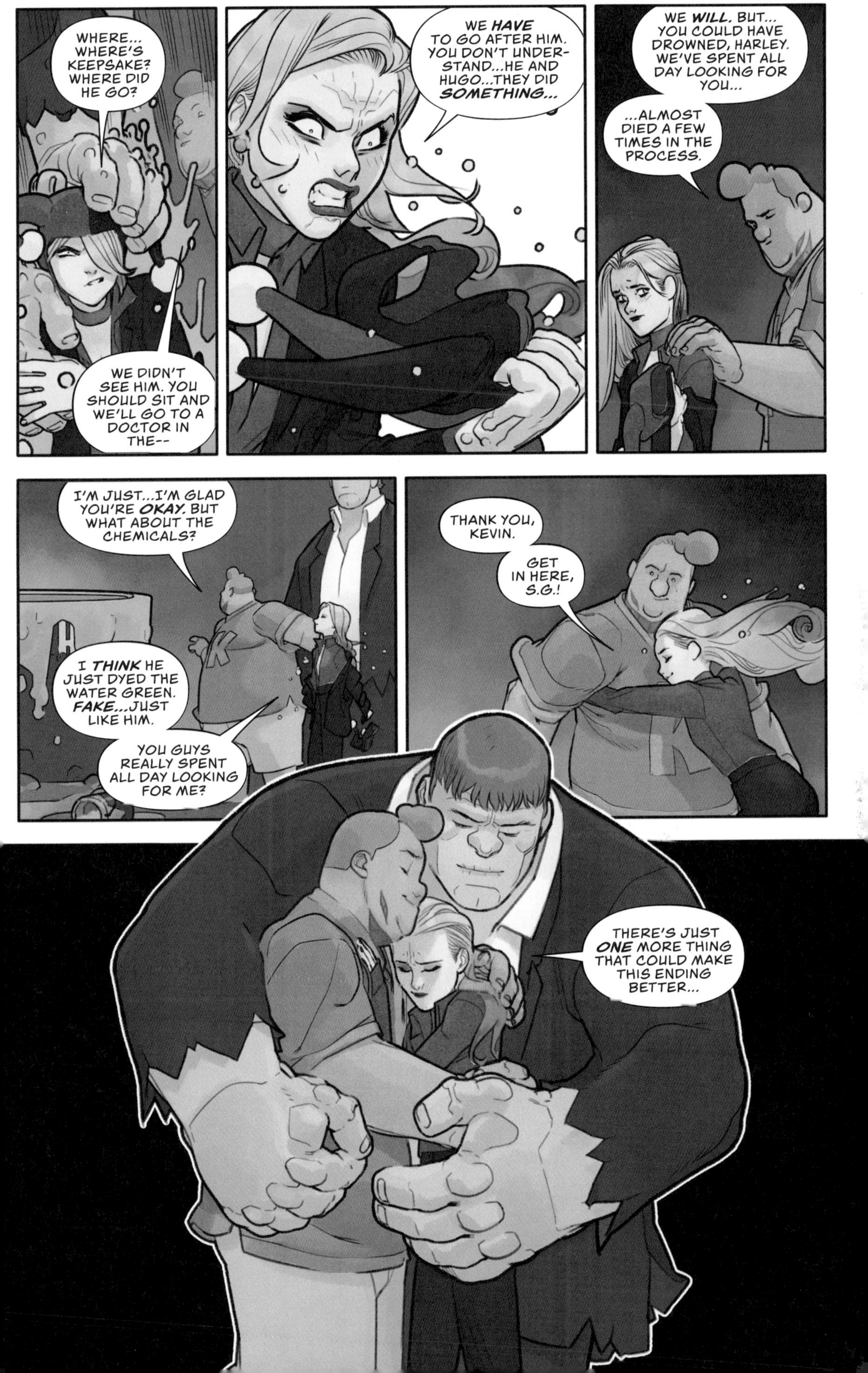
WHERE... WHERE'S KEEPSAKE? WHERE DID HE GO?
WE DIDN'T SEE HIM. YOU SHOULD SIT AND WE'LL GO TO A DOCTOR IN THE--
WE HAVE TO GO AFTER HIM. YOU DON'T UNDERSTAND...HE AND HUGO...THEY DID SOMETHING...
WE WILL. BUT... YOU COULD HAVE DROWNED, HARLEY. WE'VE SPENT ALL DAY LOOKING FOR YOU...
...ALMOST DIED A FEW TIMES IN THE PROCESS.
I'M JUST...I'M GLAD YOU'RE OKAY. BUT WHAT ABOUT THE CHEMICALS?
I THINK HE JUST DYED THE WATER GREEN. FAKE...JUST LIKE HIM.
YOU GUYS REALLY SPENT ALL DAY LOOKING FOR ME?
THANK YOU, KEVIN.
GET IN HERE, S.G.!
THERE'S JUST ONE MORE THING THAT COULD MAKE THIS ENDING BETTER...

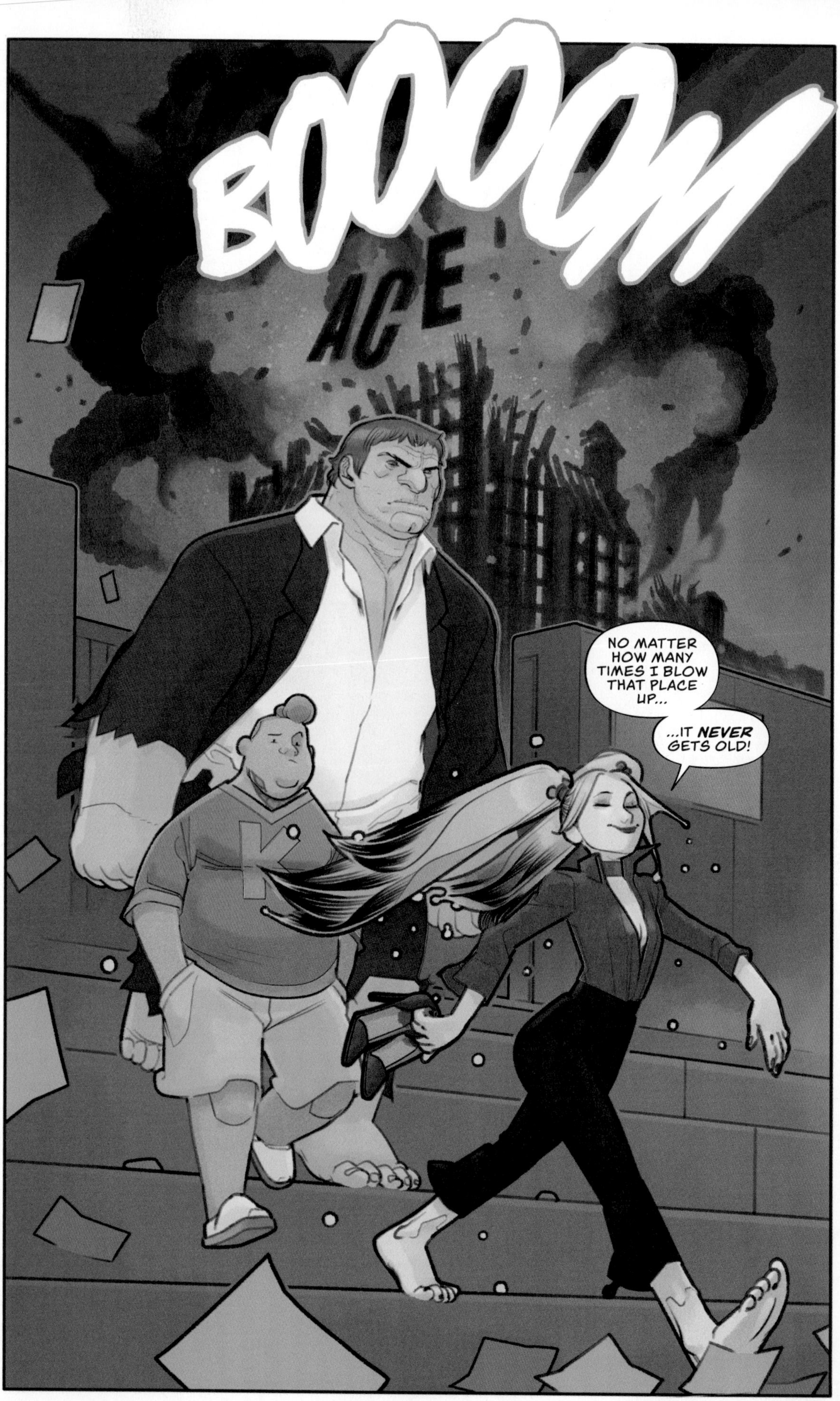
BOOOOM
ACE
NO MATTER HOW MANY TIMES I BLOW THAT PLACE UP...
...IT **NEVER** GETS OLD!

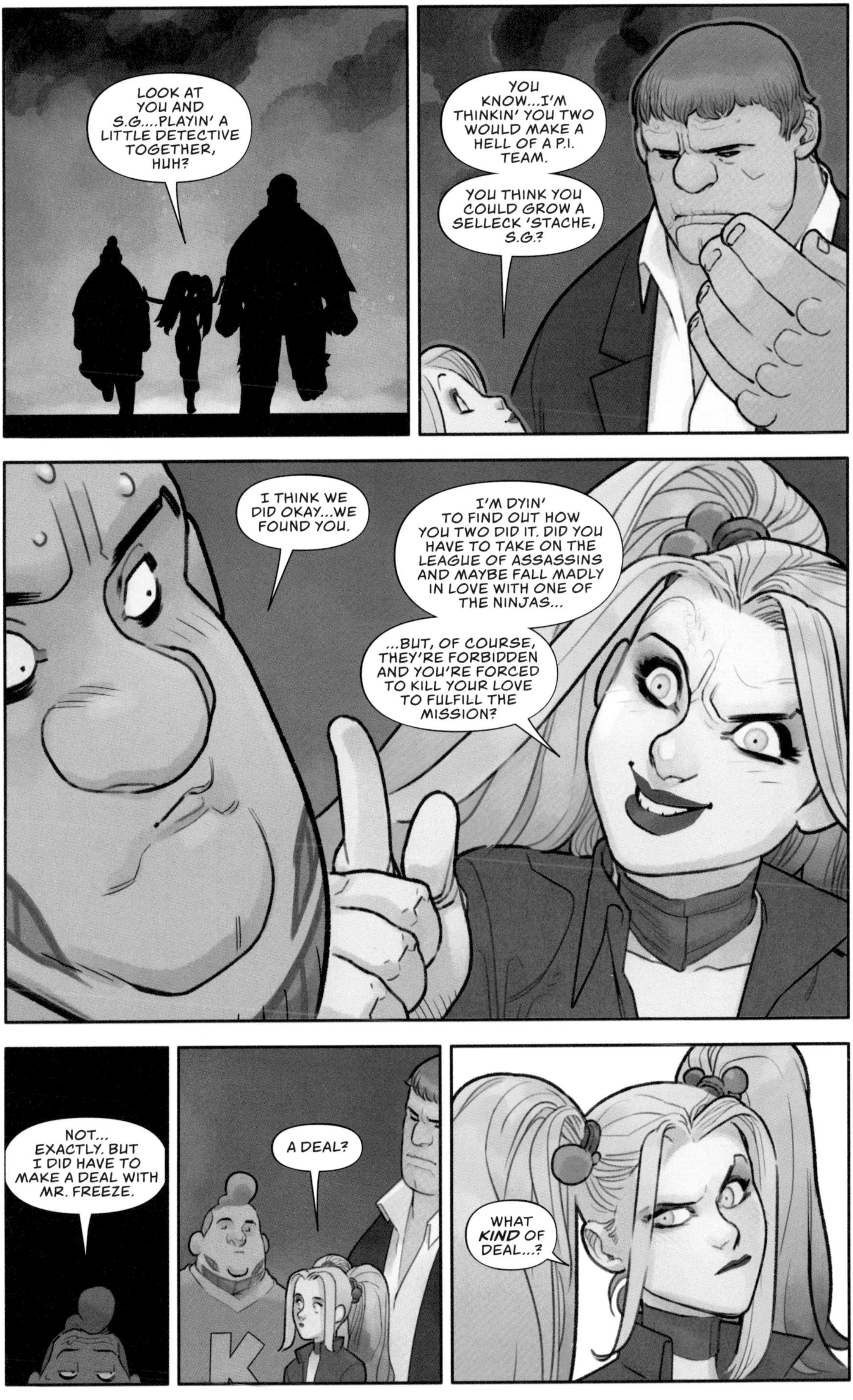
LOOK AT YOU AND S.G....PLAYIN' A LITTLE DETECTIVE TOGETHER, HUH?
YOU KNOW...I'M THINKIN' YOU TWO WOULD MAKE A HELL OF A P.I. TEAM.
YOU THINK YOU COULD GROW A SELLECK 'STACHE, S.G.?
I THINK WE DID OKAY...WE FOUND YOU.
I'M DYIN' TO FIND OUT HOW YOU TWO DID IT. DID YOU HAVE TO TAKE ON THE LEAGUE OF ASSASSINS AND MAYBE FALL MADLY IN LOVE WITH ONE OF THE NINJAS...
...BUT, OF COURSE, THEY'RE FORBIDDEN AND YOU'RE FORCED TO KILL YOUR LOVE TO FULFILL THE MISSION?
NOT... EXACTLY. BUT I DID HAVE TO MAKE A DEAL WITH MR. FREEZE.
A DEAL?
WHAT KIND OF DEAL...?

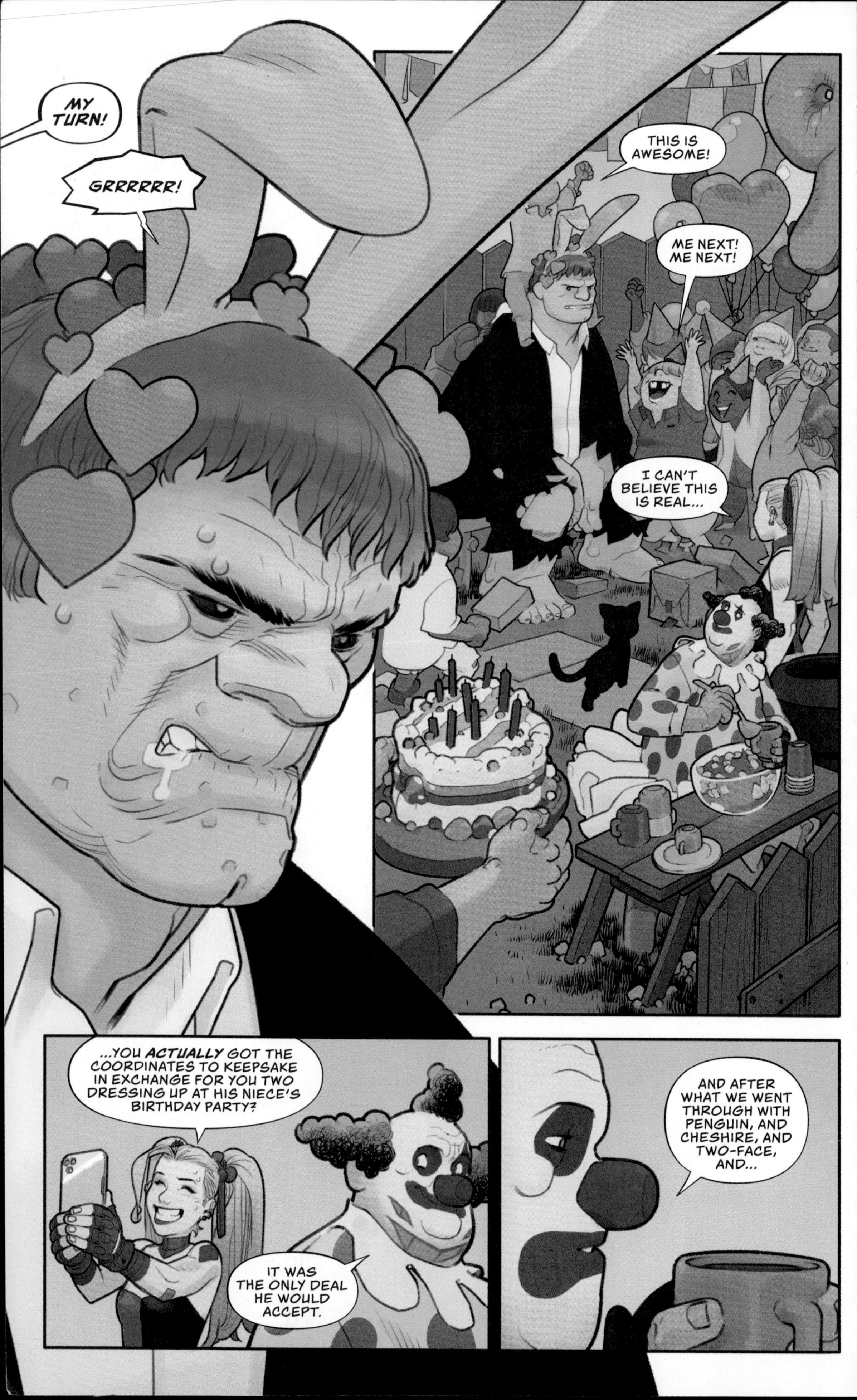
MY TURN!
GRRRRRR!
THIS IS AWESOME!
ME NEXT! ME NEXT!
I CAN'T BELIEVE THIS IS REAL...
...YOU *ACTUALLY* GOT THE COORDINATES TO KEEPSAKE IN EXCHANGE FOR YOU TWO DRESSING UP AT HIS NIECE'S BIRTHDAY PARTY?
IT WAS THE ONLY DEAL HE WOULD ACCEPT.
AND AFTER WHAT WE WENT THROUGH WITH PENGUIN, AND CHESHIRE, AND TWO-FACE, AND...

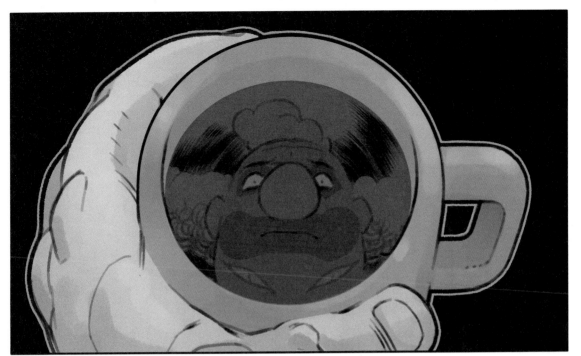

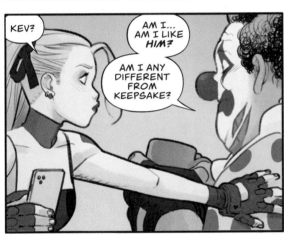

KEV?

AM I... AM I LIKE *HIM*?

AM I ANY DIFFERENT FROM KEEPSAKE?

SERIOUSLY? IT'S NOT EVEN CLOSE, KEVIN. SURE, YOU BOTH WORKED FOR THE JOKER.

BUT I ONCE WENT ICE SKATING AND THAT DOESN'T MAKE ME MICHELLE PFEIFFER.

DON'T YOU MEAN MICHELLE KWAN...?

I DUNNO...MAYBE...*POINT IS,* YOU TRY EVERY SINGLE DAY TO BE BETTER THAN YOU WERE YESTERDAY. NOT THAT *I'M* A GREAT ROLE MODEL...BUT I THINK THAT'S WHAT IT'S ALL ABOUT.

WE ***** UP. WE KNOW THAT. WE CAN'T UNDO IT. BUT, YOU AND I...

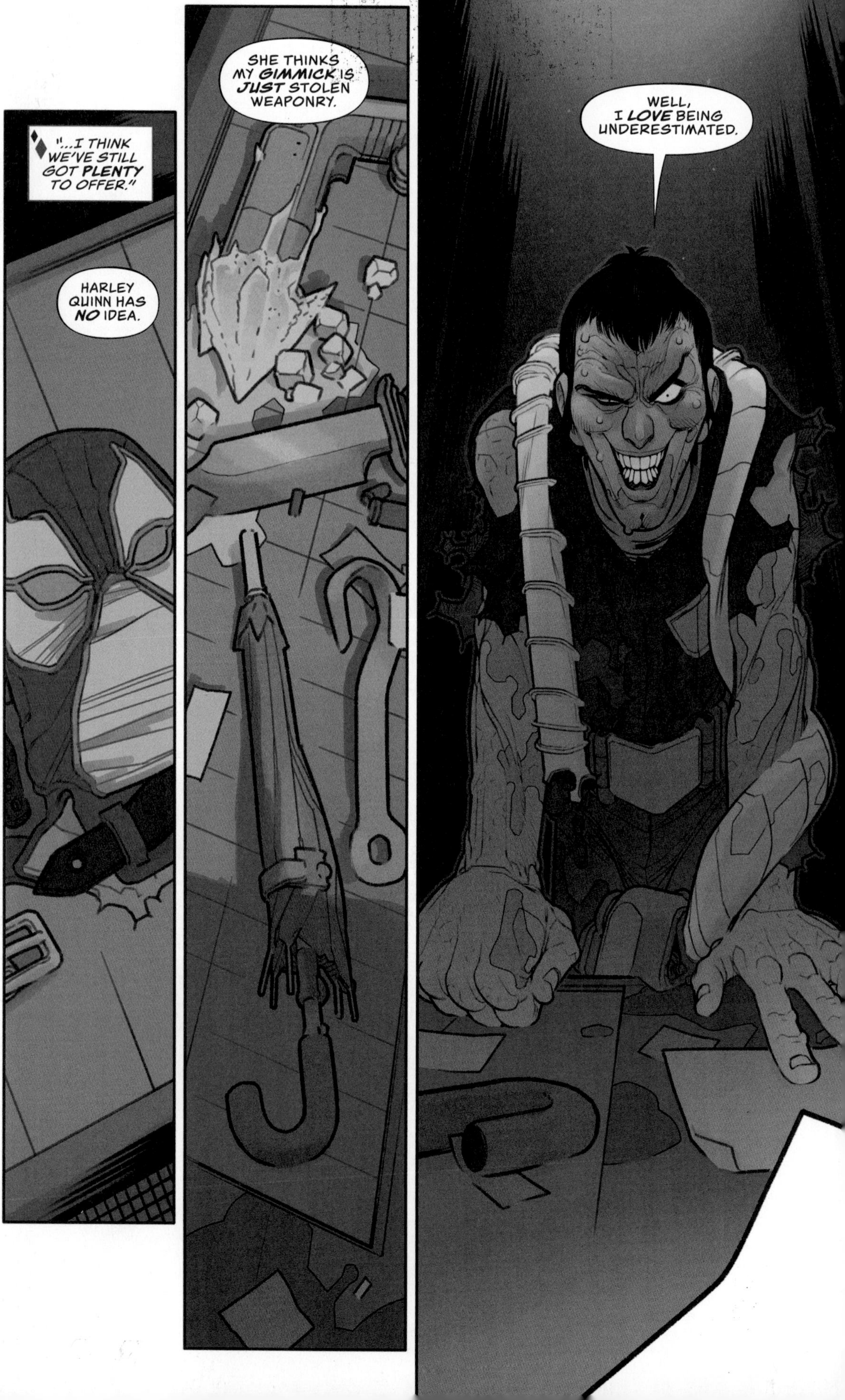
"...I THINK WE'VE STILL GOT PLENTY TO OFFER."
HARLEY QUINN HAS NO IDEA.
SHE THINKS MY GIMMICK IS JUST STOLEN WEAPONRY.
WELL, I LOVE BEING UNDERESTIMATED.